INTERACTING AND ORGANIZING

Analyses of a Management Meeting

LEA'S COMMUNICATION SERIES
Jennings Bryant/Dolf Zillmann, General Editors

Selected titles include:

Cooren/Taylor/Van Every • *Communication as Organizing: Empirical and Theoretical Explorations in the Dynamic of Text and Conversation*

Ellis • *From Language to Communication, Second Edition*

Fitch/Sanders • *Handbook of Language and Social Interaction*

Glenn/LeBaron/Mandelbaum • *Studies in Language and Social Interaction: In Honor of Robert Hopper*

Harris • *Applied Organizational Communication: Principles and Pragmatics for Future Practice, Second Edition*

Kramer • *Managing Uncertainty in Organizational Communication*

Parker • *Race, Gender, and Leadership: Re-Envisioning Organizational Leadership From the Perspectives of African American Women Executives*

Taylor/Van Every • *The Emergent Organization: Communication as Its Site and Surface*

Tracy • *Understanding Face-to-Face Interactions*

INTERACTING AND ORGANIZING

Analyses of a Management Meeting

Edited by
François Cooren
Université de Montréal, Canada

Routledge
Taylor & Francis Group
NEW YORK AND LONDON

Cover image © National Film Board of Canada.

First published 2007 by Lawrence Erlbaum Associates, Inc.

This edition published 2014 by Routledge
711 Third Avenue, New York, NY 10017, USA
2 Park Square, Milton Park, Abingdon, Oxon, OX14 4RN

Routledge is an imprint of the Taylor & Francis Group, an informa business

Copyright © 2007 by Lawrence Erlbaum Associates, Inc.

Cover image derived from *Corporation: After Mr. Sam.*
© National Film Board of Canada.

Cover design by Kathryn Houghtaling Lacey

Library of Congress Cataloging-in-Publication Data

Interacting and organizing : analyses of a management
    meeting / edited by François Cooren.
        p. cm.
    Includes bibliographical references and index.
    ISBN 978-0-8058-4855-7 — 0-8058-4855-X (cloth)
    ISBN 978-0-8058-4856-4 — 0-8058-4856-8 (pbk.)
    ISBN 978-1-4106-1892-4 — 1-4106-1892-7 (e book)
    1. Communication in management. 2. Communication in
    organizations. 3. Business meetings. I. Cooren, François.
    HD30.3.I54   2006
    658.4'56—dc22   2005051016
                                                        CIP

To *Jim* and *Elizabeth*

Contents

Preface

In many respects, this book is one of a kind in its form and content. Although in most edited books, contributions are focused on a common theme or problematic, this one proposes to bring together contrasting analyses of a singular event: a series of management meetings that took place in 1969 around the question of the succession of Sam Steinberg, one of the most important entrepreneurial figures of Quebec, Canada, at that time. The idea behind this book originally stemmed from a preconference organized on May 24, 2001, in Washington, DC, by the Language and Social Interaction (LSI) division of the International Communication Association (ICA), in collaboration with the Organizational Communication (OC) division of this same association. For that preconference, 12 guest speakers—6 representing the LSI division and 6 representing the OC division—had then been asked to compare their respective analyses of these meetings, through excerpts that had originally been shot and edited by the Canadian film director, Arthur Hammond, in his documentary film titled *Corporation: After Mr. Sam.*

Despite its own limitations, this film, produced in 1974 by the National Film Board of Canada, had been selected because it allowed us to analyze something that tends to be quite difficult to access, especially when videorecording is involved, namely management meetings. For obvious reasons of confidentiality, these types of organizational events have the reputation of being very difficult to approach. This often means that scholars who do end up accessing them can, most of the time, rely only on field notes and, exceptionally, audiotapes to complete their research. With this documentary, we had the relatively unique opportunity to deal with a videorecording that was available to the public, which meant that no issues of confidentiality were a priori involved. Furthermore, this film had the advantage of dealing with a rather important moment in the history of Canadian entrepreneurship, that is, the retirement and succession of Sam Steinberg, a key turning point in the development of the retailing empire he had founded some 30 years earlier.

Given the quality of the presentations that took place during this pre-conference, it became rapidly obvious that we had the potential to produce a book that would showcase the different analyses that had been presented at the time. The general structure of this volume thus parallels in many ways the organization of the 2001 event. It is organized in four main parts, each of them regrouping three contributions that address a similar problematic. In each part of the book, the first two chapters are authored by scholars respectively representing the LSI and OC divisions, whereas the third chapter, written by an OC or LSI scholar, aims at comparing and reflecting on the previous paired analyses. One of the objectives of the book is indeed to give the opportunity for the two ICA divisions to dialogue with each other, an objective that I think was, in many respects, fulfilled. Because of its original structure and object of analysis, this book thus contributes, in its own way, to a relatively new research agenda, which consists of focusing on organizational interactions to better understand how organizations work.

Although the organizational communication field has historically been (and still is, in many respects) associated with quantitative analyses relying on questionnaires and interviews, there is today a growing body of research that tends to seek access more directly to what actually happens in organizations. Following the interpretive turn of the 1980s (Burrell & Morgan, 1979; Putnam & Pacanowsky, 1983; Weick, 1979) and the discursive turn of the 1990s (Alvesson & Karreman, 2000; Fairhurst & Putnam, 2004; Grant, Hardy, Oswick, Phillips, & Putnam, 2004; Grant, Keenoy, & Oswick, 1998; Keenoy, Oswick, & Grant, 1997; Oswick, Keenoy, Grant, & Marshak, 2000; Putnam & Fairhurst, 2001), we could say that most of the scholars contributing to this book thus participate, in their own way, in the development of what could be called an *interactional turn*, that is, an analytical turn that consists of highlighting the details of interactions to better understand the functioning of the organizational world. To my knowledge, this is the first time ever that a volume has been entirely devoted to the systematic analysis of naturally occurring interactions taking place in an organizational setting. It is my hope that such a book will pave the way for similar studies that will truly do justice to the complexity of the phenomena they attempt to analyze.

ACKNOWLEDGMENTS

The writing of this book, based on an ICA preconference organized in May 2001 in Washington, DC, has required the help and support of many colleagues, students, friends, and relatives. First, I wish to thank Linda L. Putnam, for she was the first to encourage me to work on this book project. It was a big premiere for me as an editor and a wonderful learning experience. My deep gratitude also goes to the Department of Communication at the University at Albany, where I was working when this whole project started. I especially want to thank Shifay Cheung, who was then my research assistant and had the difficult and daunting task of completing the whole transcript of Arthur Hammond's documentary, on which this book is based. As you will notice, the result is, I think, excellent and most of the praise should go to her. I also want to especially thank my colleagues and friends at Albany, Anita Pomerantz and Robert E. Sanders, for their invaluable help during this period, both in terms of expertise and moral support. I also owe a great deal to the Département de Communication at the Université de Montréal, a wonderful place to work and study, where I always received encouragement, especially from my colleagues and friends, Chantal Benoit-Barné, Boris Brummans, Daniel Robichaud, James R. Taylor, and Elizabeth Van Every. Special thanks go to Lyne Charland, Stephanie Fox, and Consuelo Vasquez for reviewing some of the sections in this book. I also have to express my deep gratitude to Lawrence Erlbaum Associates, especially Linda Bathgate, Barbara Wieghaus, and Karin Wittig Bates, and the National Film Board of Canada, especially James Roberts, for agreeing to apply their forces and expertise to producing this whole project, which is, in many respects, quite unique in the publishing world. Finally, I owe a great deal to Nancy, my wife, and our two children, Nina and Émile, who are so good at making life such a wonderful journey.

—*François Cooren*

REFERENCES

Alvesson, M., & Karreman, D. (2000). Varieties of discourse: On the study of organizations through discourse analysis. *Human Relations, 53,* 1125–1149.

Burrell, G., & Morgan, G. (1979). *Sociological paradigms and organisational analysis: Elements of the sociology of corporate life.* London: Heinemann.

Fairhurst, G. T., & Putnam, L. L. (2004). Organizations as discursive constructions. *Communication Theory, 14,* 5–26.

Grant, D., Hardy, C., Oswick, C., Phillips, N., & Putnam, L. L. (Eds.). (2004). *Handbook of organizational discourse.* London: Sage.

Grant, D., Keenoy, T., & Oswick, C. (Eds.). (1998). *Discourse and organization.* London: Sage.

Hammond, A. (Producer/Director/Writer). (1974). *Corporation: After Mr. Sam* [Film]. Montreal: National Film Board of Canada.

Keenoy, T., Oswick, C., & Grant, D. (1997). Organizational discourses: Texts and context. *Organization, 4*(2), 147–157.

Oswick, C., Keenoy, T., Grant, D., & Marshak, B. (2000). Discourse, organization, and epistemology. *Organization, 7*(3), 511–512.

Putnam, L. L., & Fairhurst, G. T. (2001). Discourse analysis in organizations: Issues and concerns. In F. M. Jablin & L. L. Putnam (Eds.), *The new handbook of organizational communication* (pp. 78–136). Thousand Oaks, CA: Sage.

Putnam, L. L., & Pacanowsky, M. E. (Eds.). (1983). *Communication and organizations. An interpretive approach.* Newbury Park, CA: Sage.

Weick, K. E. (1979). *The social psychology of organizing.* New York: Random House.

Contributors

Steven R. Corman, *Arizona State University*
Stanley Deetz, *University of Colorado, Boulder*
Paul Denvir, *University at Albany, SUNY*
Gail T. Fairhurst, *University of Cincinnati*
Kristine L. Fitch, *University of Iowa*
Megan Foley, *University of Iowa*
Renee Heath, *University of Colorado, Boulder*
Joel Iverson, *Texas A&M University*
James Leighter, *University of Washington*
Jessica MacDonald, *University of Colorado, Boulder*
Heidi Mau, *University of Oklahoma*
Robert D. McPhee, *Arizona State University*
Cheryl Nicholas, *University of Oklahoma*
Cliff Oswick, *Leicester University, UK*
Anita Pomerantz, *University at Albany, SUNY*
Gerry Philipsen, *University of Washington*
Linda L. Putnam, *Texas A&M University*
Daniel Robichaud, *Université de Montréal, Canada*
Robert E. Sanders, *University at Albany, SUNY*
Cynthia Stohl, *University of California, Santa Barbara*
James R. Taylor, *Université de Montréal, Canada*
Karen Tracy, *University of Colorado, Boulder*
D. Lawrence Wieder, *University of Oklahoma*

Introduction

François Cooren
Université de Montréal, Canada

The fact that this book lies at the intersection of two subfields of the communication discipline—Organization Communication (OC) and Language and Social Interaction (LSI)—can be considered significant to the extent that it illustrates how these two perspectives can benefit from, and contribute to, one another. On the one hand, OC scholars tend to criticize their LSI counterparts for their lack of concern for the organization per se. In other words, they acknowledge most of the time the quality of the analyses done by their LSI colleagues in organizational or institutional settings (like the ones that can be found, i.e., in Boden, 1994, or Drew & Heritage, 1992), but deplore the absence of reflection on the organizational context. "Where is the organization in these analyses?" typically is the kind of question that will be raised by OC scholars after reading such studies. On the other hand, LSI scholars often criticize their OC colleagues for their lack of concern for the details of interactions. Most of the time, OC students are accused of adopting an airplane sightseeing perspective, which, for their LSI colleagues, does not do justice to the complexity of the organizational world, especially its interactive component. "Where are the interactions in these analyses?" would typically be their reaction after reading an OC analysis.

Although this book cannot claim to constitute the definitive answer to this clash of perspectives, I think we can reasonably say that it shows what the beginning of a middle-range approach could look like. Between what could be called LSI scholars' myopia and OC scholars' presbyopia, there should be room for an approach that is able to scale up and down the perspectives, whenever necessary (see Taylor & Van Every, 2000, for what I consider to be the best attempt so far in this regard). Borrowing a metaphor used by Latour (2005), an answer might thus be found in a perspective that does not hesitate to sometimes move like an ant and sometimes fly like an eagle, that is, an approach that would do justice to the details of naturally occurring interactions while acknowledging effects of spacing and timing, which transcend and dislocalize the here and now of the interactions (Cooren & Fairhurst, 2004).

Certainly, this book, like any scientific project, has its own limitations. First, it relies on shots taken from a documentary, which means that the data we have access to are far from being *pure data*, if this concept makes any sense. As most of the contributors to this book have observed in their analyses, it is sometimes difficult to decipher what results from the editing done by Arthur Hammond, the director of *Corporation: After Mr. Sam*, and what can be attributed to what truly happened during this series of management meetings he recorded. As Wieder, Mau, and Nicholas show very nicely in chapter 12, we have to be extremely careful not to assume that "what is seen on the screen unproblematically presents what went on in the meetings in just the fashion that an ideal data tape of interaction does" (p. 245). I think it can reasonably be said, however, that all the analysts who accepted to "play the game" for this book were aware of these constraints—most of them actually address this very issue in their own contributions—but it seems important to reiterate this point. I might not go so far as to say that "Documentaries Are Not Data" as Wieder, Mau, and Nicholas claim in the title of their chapter, but we should at least be aware that they are far from being ideal data, given the reorganization that inevitably takes place during the editing. Several passages were recorded but finally eliminated in the final state of the production of this documentary. In a way, this is the "analytical price" we had to pay to make this book project possible. Some people might say that this price is way too high, but there are times when the price is worth paying!

A second limitation concerns, of course, the date this film was shot, given that this series of meetings took place in 1969, while the release of the documentary per se is dated 1974. One question that might then be raised could be "What can truly be learned from management meetings that took place some 35 years ago?" To this, it could be answered that the problems addressed during these recorded discussions, as well as the way they are addressed by the interactants, are still quite contemporary. In terms of content, one could note that succession, objectives versus structure, nepotism, rights and responsibilities, favoritism, and so forth are, in many ways, "eternal problems" that most contemporary organizations still have to face today. Although it is true that this film is and looks dated—we just have to count how many women were present in these board meetings (the response is, of course, none!) or highlight the number of people who are smoking pipes or cigarettes during the discussions (many!)—it still constitutes a fantastic account of a series of events that have both historical and social significance. In the great tradition of the *Direct Cinéma* that was then cultivated in the National Film Board of Canada (see again, in this regard, the excellent account by Wieder, Mau, & Nicholas in chap. 12), Arthur Hammond was, in many respects, able to "let the actors speak," while highlighting very interesting episodes in their discussion. This is also why, beyond their "old-fashioned" character, these recorded meetings still represent, in terms of form, a great opportunity to highlight and analyze the tensions, power games, and strategic moves inherent in these ritual events.

A third limitation could be related, of course, to the lack of access to contextual cues. Almost none of the contributors knew of Sam Steinberg's retailing empire and success story before being invited to the ICA 2001 preconference in Washington, which explains why very few references tend to be made to the context of the management meetings during their analyses. But again, it could reasonably be argued that such a limitation does not necessarily mean that the project be considered doomed from the start. Although it is true that context adds information that can sometimes be crucial to the analysis of an event, it is also true that, in many respects, the context is in the text itself. As Heritage (1984) insightfully points out, "we can begin to think of 'context' as something endogenously generated within the talk of the participants and, indeed, as something created in and through that talk" (p. 283). In other words, it could be argued, as Heritage later says, that "it is through the specific, detailed and local design of turns and sequences that 'institutional' contexts are observably and reportably—i.e., accountably—brought into being" (p. 290), which leads him finally to claim "it is within these local sequence of talk, and only there, that these institutions are ultimately and accountably talked into being" (p. 290).

Following Heritage's (1984) points, we could then claim that these board meetings certainly do not exhaust the complexity of Steinberg Limited as it existed in 1969, but that they, in many respects, talk this organization into being. Although the contributors to this book had very little access to contextual cues like the personal story of each participant, the type of relationships they had and kept with each other, or even the financial and organizational situation of the company at that time, they were, I think, in many respects able to reconstruct some interesting information about the company just from the interactions they analyzed. In this regard, I invite the readers to look at Cynthia Stohl's (chap. 9) insightful analysis of the saliency of Jewishness in the talk and how this Jewish identity can be said to have played an important role in what and how problems were discussed during the meetings (see also Fitch & Foley, chap. 6, as well as Deetz, Heath, & MacDonald, chap. 11).

GENERAL ORGANIZATION OF THE BOOK

As mentioned previously, this book is divided into four parts; each contains three chapters. While the first two chapters are respectively written by OC and LSI scholars, the last chapter of each section is meant to be a discussion, written by an OC or LSI scholar, reflecting on the two previous analyses offered. Each section also contains an introduction that highlights and contextualizes the analyses and discussion presented. An Afterword, written by Cliff Oswick is proposed in chapter 13 to reflect on the whole project and present some possible directions for future analyses. A transcript of the whole documentary also appears in Appendix A. In order to be as faithful as possible to the original recording, we used the transcribing convention system that has been developed over the years by Gail Jefferson (1984). Whenever references are made to specific excerpts within the analyses, it is this transcript that is used. For the readers who might not be familiar with these transcribing conventions, they are invited to refer to Appendix B where these conventions are explained. Finally, Appendix C contains a brief history of Steinberg Limited, from the little store that Ida Steinberg, Sam Steinberg's mother, opened in 1917 in Montreal through its golden age from the 1950s to 1970s to the dismantling of the Steinberg Empire in 1992. A number of references are included at the end of Appendix C if readers are interested in knowing more of the Steinberg Saga.

Arthur Hammond's documentary, from which this whole project stems, is now available on a DVD produced by the National Film Board of Canada. Although this product is sold separately from the book, the reader is strongly encouraged to obtain it, because it adds precious visual and paralinguistic information that can sometimes be very hard to reproduce in a transcript, complete as it may be.

REFERENCES

Boden, D. (1994). *The business of talk. Organizations in action*. Cambridge, England: Polity Press.

Cooren, F., & Fairhurst, G. T. (2004). Speech timing and spacing: The phenomenon of organizational closure. *Organization, 11*(6), 793–824.

Drew, P., & Heritage, J. (1992). *Talk at work: Interaction in institutional settings*. Cambridge, England: Cambridge University Press.

Hammond, A. (Producer/Director/Writer). (1974). *Corporation: After Mr. Sam* [Film]. Montreal: National Film Board of Canada.

Heritage, J. (1984). *Garfinkel and ethnomethodology*. Cambridge, England: Polity Press.

Jefferson, G. (1984). On stepwise transition from talk about a trouble to inappropriately next-positioned matters. In J. M. Atkinson & J. Heritage (Eds.), *Structures of social action: Studies of conversation analysis* (pp. 191–222). Cambridge, England: Cambridge University Press.

Latour, B. (2005). *Reassembling the social: An introduction to actor-network theory*. London: Oxford University Press.

Taylor, J. R., & Van Every, E. J. (2000). *The emergent organization: Communication as site and surface*. Mahwah, NJ: Lawrence Erlbaum Associates.

I

Leadership and Speakership: Which Voice Matters?

Part I addresses, in many respects, the analytical gap that has often been identified between the LSI and OC perspectives. As mentioned in the main introduction, LSI scholars tend to be accused by their OC counterparts of focusing too much on the details of interaction while neglecting the organizational context in which these interactions occur. In other words, OC scholars accuse their LSI colleagues of studying interaction and not organizations (Fairhurst & Cooren, 2004; Putnam & Fairhurst, 2001; Fairhurst & Putnam, 2004). Alternatively, OC scholars are often accused by their LSI counterparts of neglecting the details of interaction to the benefit of large-scale organizational analyses that do not really do justice to what Boden (1994) called, in the subtitle of her groundbreaking volume, "Organizations in Action." In other words, LSI scholars accuse their OC colleagues of studying organizations and not interaction.

This tension between the two perspectives is I think best summarized by Boden (1994), whose objective precisely was to address this issue. Speaking of ethnomethodologists, as representing an LSI perspective, she wrote,

> They are not interested in organizations, but in organization, which is to say that they are animated by a curiosity for the *organization of experience* and the "extraordinary organization of the ordinary" ... Activities in organizational and work settings are, for ethnomethodologists, simply a marvelous way of unraveling the fine detail of social interaction. That organization may, indeed, be more or less hierarchically structured, resulting in more or less complexity of staffing, spatial divisions of labor,

1

line of communication, and so forth, but *how* these are achieved and occasionally subverted becomes the research question. (p. 31, italics in original)

The challenge would thus consist of *scaling up*, as Taylor and Van Every (2000) put it, from the organization of experience to the organization per se, that is, to show that it is possible to study the organization of interactions while always keeping in mind questions related to the mode of being of organizations.

In a way, this is precisely what James R. Taylor and Daniel Robichaud do in the first chapter of this section. Since his 1993 book, titled *Rethinking the Theory of Organizational Communication: How to Read an Organization*, Taylor's research agenda can be said to have been devoted to this one question: Can we identify a genuine theory of organizational communication, that is, a theory that would both enable us to scale up from communication to organization and scale down from organization to communication? This question has recently been addressed through what Taylor and Robichaud call here and elsewhere (Robichaud, Giroux, & Taylor, 2004) the phenomenon of *metaconversation*. Starting from the recursive property of language, they show that one of the ways to scale up from communication to organization is to show how in conversations, certain organizational members, especially managers, address other conversations, an activity that enables them to give a unified voice to their organization.

It is through this specific type of conversation that, according to Taylor and Robichaud, we can see the organization in the communication of managers (see also Taylor & Robichaud, 2004). In their daily conversations, managers set themselves up, among other things, as speaking on behalf of past and remote conversations and it is through this activity, typical of spokespersons, that a certain unity of the organization can be reaffirmed and reproduced. Managers constantly attempt to (re)define the identity of the organization by interactively searching for what Taylor and Robichaud call *closure*, that is, an agreement on what constitutes the organization.

Because Anita Pomerantz and Paul Denvir's chapter 2 remains, in many respects, very faithful to the LSI tradition—and more precisely to its conversation analytic branch, a branch of which Pomerantz certainly is one of the most renowned representatives (see especially, Pomerantz, 1984, 1988; Pomerantz & Fehr, 1997; Sanders, Fitch, & Pomerantz, 2000)—it constitutes, in several ways, a very nice point of comparison with Taylor and Robichaud's contribution. In their chapter, Pomerantz and Denvir analyze what they identify as the phenomenon of role enactment during organizational meetings, and more precisely how one of the participants, Harry Suffrin, enacted his function of chairperson throughout the management meetings. Through the detailed analysis of his performances, Pomerantz and Denvir are, in particular, able to show what sort of premises seem to guide this chairperson's activities and how these premises were directly or indirectly the object of active negotiations by the participants.

Although the question of organizational closure is not problematized per se by Pomerantz and Denvir, we can note that it is at least implicit in their analyses, to the extent that the negotiation about what it means to be a chairman presupposes a search for closure regarding this question. What constitutes the role of chairman appears to be negotiated through participants who explicitly or implicitly set themselves up as speaking on behalf of what should be the proper role enactment of a chairman. Beyond the quality of their very fine and detailed analyses, Pomerantz and Denvir thus invite us to look for other types of metaconversation in which organizational members explicitly or implicitly problematize, negotiate, and, in many respects, realize or incarnate the rights and responsibilities mobilized in their ongoing discussion. In keeping with Boden's (1994) point, the organization can be said to be relatively absent from their analysis, but their conversational analytic approach, coupled with Taylor and Robichaud's chapter, illustrates how fruitful a dialogue between OC and LSI scholars can and could be if these respective viewpoints are taken seriously.

If there is one OC scholar person who can be said to have engaged in such a dialogue in her past and ongoing work, it is precisely Gail Fairhurst (1993; Fairhurst & Cooren, 2004; Fairhurst & Putnam, 2004; Fairhurst & Sarr, 1996; Putnam & Fairhurst, 2001), whose contribution (chap. 3) closes this part. In her response, Fairhurst proposes to address and compare the two previous chapters in order to renew the reflection on leadership. Although the focus of mainstream research in this domain tends to be mostly restricted to the individual and psychological characteristics of leaders, Fairhurst shows in what respects Taylor and Robichaud's as well as Pomerantz and Denvir's constructivist approaches could participate in liberating leadership studies.

Instead of essentializing good or bad leaders' characteristics, these two chapters help us see, according to Fairhurst, what good or bad leadership in action looks like. In other words, she convincingly shows to what extent the detailed analysis of managerial interaction, as realized in these two chapters, could liberate leadership study by problematizing this phenomenon as an interactive organizing process. Even if some limitations are recognized—in particular, the absence of reflection on the participants' general dispositions vis-à-vis leadership, an absence mostly due to methodological constraints—Fairhurst argues persuasively here and elsewhere (Fairhurst, in press) for more constructive approaches that study leadership as it occurs in interaction.

REFERENCES

Boden, D. (1994). *The business of talk. Organizations in action.* Cambridge, England: Polity Press.

Fairhurst, G. T. (1993). The leader–member exchange patterns of women leaders in industry: A discourse analysis. *Communication Monographs, 60,* 321–351.

Fairhurst, G. T. (in press). *Discursive approaches to leadership.* Thousand Oaks, CA: Sage.

Fairhurst, G. T., & Cooren, F. (2004). Organizational language in use: Interaction analysis, conversation analysis, and speech act schematics. In D. Grant, C. Hardy, C. Oswick, N. Phillips, & L. Putnam (Eds.), *Handbook of organizational discourse* (pp. 131–152). London: Sage.

Fairhurst, G. T., & Putnam, L. L. (2004). Organizations as discursive constructions. *Communication Theory, 14*(1), 5–26.

Fairhurst, G. T., & Sarr, R. A. (1996). *The art of framing. Managing the language of leadership.* San Francisco, CA: Jossey-Bass.

Pomerantz, A. (1984) Agreeing and disagreeing with assessments: Some features of preferred/dispreferred turn shapes. In J. M. Atkinson & J. C. Heritage (Eds.), *Structures of social action* (pp. 57–101). Cambridge, England: Cambridge University Press.

Pomerantz, A. (1988). Offering a candidate answer: An information seeking strategy. *Communication Monographs, 55,* 360–373.

Pomerantz, A., & Fehr, B. J. (1997). Conversation analysis: An approach to the study of social action as sense making practices. In T. A. V. Dijk (Ed.), *Discourse as social interaction* (pp. 64–91). London: Sage.

Putnam, L. L., & Fairhurst, G. T. (2001). Discourse analysis in organizations: Issues and concerns. In F. M. Jablin & L. L. Putnam (Eds.), *The new handbook of organizational communication* (pp. 78–136). Thousand Oaks, CA: Sage.

Robichaud, D., Giroux, H., & Taylor, J. R. (2004). The meta-conversation: The recursive property of language as the key to organizing. *Academy of Management Review, 29,* 617–634.

Sanders, R. E., Fitch, K. L., & Pomerantz, A. (2000). Core research traditions within language and social interaction. *Communication Yearbook, 24.* Thousand Oaks, CA: Sage.

Taylor, J. R. (1993). *Rethinking the theory of organizational communication: How to read an organization.* Norwood, NJ: Ablex.

Taylor, J. R., & Robichaud, D. (2004). Finding the organization in the communication: Discourse as action and sensemaking. *Organization, 11*(3), 395–413.

Taylor, J. R., & Van Every, E. J. (2000). *The emergent organization. Communication as its site and surface.* Mahwah, NJ: Lawrence Erlbaum Associates.

Chapter 1

Management as Metaconversation: The Search for Closure

James R. Taylor
Daniel Robichaud
Université de Montréal, Canada

The analysis we present in this chapter is predicated on the assumption that management is accomplished as an ongoing conversation. It is, however, a conversation of a special kind, because the people who participate in it are corporate spokespersons, each of whom is the voice, in management councils, for the many absent conversations that compose the organization as a whole (Boden, 1994), and where its actual work gets done. We term this domain of managerial talk a *metaconversation*, because it is a conversation (that of management) that generates accounts about other conversations (those of the multiple communities of practice that make up the organization), all now being given a voice (however authentic the translation is) by their representatives in the managerial metaconversation. The ultimate corporate spokesperson, namely the individual who is authorized to speak for the entire organizational community as a single entity, is the president, or chief executive officer. Mr. Sam is the one individual in the filmed discussion at Palomino Lodge who is authorized to speak as the official voice of the organization as a whole. He thus stands in a special relationship with all the other conversations, including that of management, because he is the titular head of the company. He is thus the person who is entitled to speak for the organization in conversations extending beyond its boundaries, with banks, governments and the like.

Organization is thus conceived of as a many-layered embedding of conversational domains, each concentrated on its own object or objects, and each generating accounts that reflect its particular preoccupations. There are translations at more than one level, as one conversation is reproduced *in absentia* in another through the mediation of spokespersons. There are, in this sense, many levels of metaconversation that go to make up the domain of management. It is a senior executive managerial metaconversation that we analyze, however, whose object is the leadership succession, after Mr. Sam retires, and the repercussions that event will have for the company. But all the organizational conversations are interrelated, and the repercussions of the metaconversation we are considering, leading up to Mr. Sam's retirement, will be felt at every level of the company.

Our analysis of the managerial conversation portrayed in *Corporation: After Mr. Sam* explores five related hypotheses:

1. Underpinning the interactive talk of the participants—as in any organizational conversation—there exists what might be called a "constitution," which those present assume to be the basis of their relationships to each other as members of a collective community (Sacks, 1992). This constitution is both tacitly reflected, and recursively reconstructs itself, in their talk.[1] It is thus an exemplar of what Giddens (1984) called *structuration*.

2. The sensemaking exemplified in the discussion has its basis in narrative, and is typically focused on what is wrong, and needs to be corrected, for the constitution to be respected. People's interventions in the conversation we are analyzing are in some sense commentaries, framed in narrative terms, about what they perceive to be breaches of the constitution.[2] This narratively based sensemaking serves to define collaborative and competitive relationships among members of the management group and the communities they represent, as these are perceived by each narrator.

3. Understanding of what the hypothesized constitution says, however, is not uniformly shared. There are, in fact, different, and competing, versions of the constitution to which people relate. What we listen to in *Corporation: After Mr. Sam* is thus both a conversation in the usual sense, but also a metaconversation, or conversation about conversations, within which we may detect the presence of several interpretations of the constitution.

4. Although those who participate in the metaconversation do so as spokespersons for a community of work that they represent—domains of activity-oriented conversation where they hold the status of chief—they are also individuals, with, as Jack Levine puts it at one point, "their own personal goals." Their interventions may thus be read as occurring simultaneously in at least two registers, first, as that of a normal conversation and its constraints; and second, as con-

tributing to a justification of the policies of the organization as a whole: A metaconversation, with its different, and more institutionally based, constraints. Each person's talk accordingly reflects their particular community of interest, but it also reflects their own personality and interests.

5. The discussion is about arriving at closure, which is to say an agreement on the terms of the constitution, and the policy of the organization. By doing so, the metaconversation might reassert, in principle, the corporate identity of not only the company to which the managers give their loyalty, but also that of the managerial group itself. Closure is thus the ostensible object of the conversation, but this, of course, does not guarantee its attainment.

AN ORGANIZATIONAL "CONSTITUTION"?

A number of analysts have argued for a distinction between surface-level instances of talk and an underlying institutional framework. Sanders (1995), for example, conceived social interaction, not merely as a product of individual performance, but as equally "the enactment of institutional role-identities" (p. 67). As he puts it, "Having claim to a role-identity binds a person sociologically to others who have claims to reciprocal—complementary or competing—role-identities (as salespersons are bound to customers and vice versa, or family members are bound to each other)" (p. 67). Sanders thinks of the "interactive connection between one's own conduct and others' treatment of one" as "fundamentally communicative" (p. 67).

In earlier work on the analysis of conversation, Labov and Fanshel (1977) similarly argued for a distinction between "surface utterances" and "deeper actions" (p. 37). In their analysis of a mother–daughter relationship (the daughter, an anorexic, is in therapy), they observe that the position of the daughter with respect to her mother is ambiguous (at least in the daughter's view) because it is an unstable mix of dependence and independence. It is because of the dependence of the daughter on her mother, however, that issues of rights and obligations arise, because there are actions affecting the daughter's welfare that only the mother can take care of. The respective statuses of head of household (i.e., mother) and adult member of the household (i.e., daughter) each "carries with it a set of role obligations and criteria for satisfactory role performance" (p. 55). To assert that the mother occupies the status of head of the household is to simultaneously claim that she is competent to perform the obligations of that status. Challenges to the performance of the status, such as those characteristic of the daughter's talk in therapy sessions, thus amount to claiming that the individual (i.e., her mother) has not adequately carried out her responsibility as mother—that she has been, in effect, incompetent. The daughter's discourse connotes a perceived incongruity between role expectation and performance.

Reading and interpreting her discourse, however, implies decoding as acts a surface level of statement with its often veiled meaning. "The crucial actions in establishing coherence of sequencing in conversation," Labov and Fanshel (1977) observed, "are not such speech acts as requests and assertions, but rather challenges, defenses, and retreats, which have to do with the status of the participants, their rights and obligations, and their changing relationships in terms of social organization" (pp. 58–59).

Labov and Fanshel (1977) thought of these implicit assumptions as to the relationship of head to dependent, and the rights and responsibilities of each, as "propositions" (p. 55). In practice, however, given considerations of face (Goffman, 1959), these constitutional underpinnings of relationship are seldom referred to in so many words: "Participants in therapy and in conversation normally do not argue the propositions directly, but argue whether or not the events being talked about are instances of these general propositions" (Labov & Fanshel, 1977, p. 53). It is, they say, "rarely possible to 'say what you mean'" (p. 53). Challenges to competence, thus, usually do not deny that a person holds a certain status, but rather that their performance has not lived up to expectations.

Consider the following sequence in the film, which illustrates what we mean by an assumed constitution that specifies rights and obligations, although the reference to such a constitution linking president to other members of management is, as Labov and Fanshel (1977) predicted, oblique. Observe how challenges are issued, and counterattacked.

64	SAM S:	This is exactly how I feel (0.5). Now listen to what I'm telling,
65		each and every one of you. (0.5) Evidently over the past four o'
66		five weeks, (0.5) a hundred or two hundred items (0.5) have to
67		be increased in price
68	JACK L:	<Seventy-two items> =
69	SAM S:	= Alright, well, I'm telling you what I heard. [so- .
70	JACK L:	[(accumulated) on
71		four weeks, seventy-two items =
72	SAM S:	= Okay. Let's (0.2) let's say it's seventy-two items. (1.0) So
73		here's what happens. I meet one of our managers having lunch
74		upstairs who's the manager of St-Lawrence and Cremazie. I
75		walked over an' say "Hello, how are you?" and everything else,
76		"How is it going?" He says "Very fine, sales are up thirteen or
77		(0.2) fourteen percent" but he says he's terribly dis<u>turbed</u>. (0.5)
78		They got in a wh:ole list of items that they have to increase the
79		prices on (0.5) and he's disturbed because now they'll be going
80		back to what they did in the past, erasing prices an' (.) putting

81		on higher prices an 'everything else.
82	JACK L:	Mr. President =
83	( ):	=[hhuhh
84	( ):	[Could I ... Could I=
85	JACK L:	=No, [just a minute
86	( ):	[Could I ... could I..could I get =
87	JACK L:	=Will you wait a minute? Mr. President look, this is what-
88		this's <u>why</u> I want to talk about structure first. (1.0) It happens
89		that I and you communicate. (0.5) > Twice a day three time a
90		day four times a day- no matter what time of day it is eh? <
91	SAM S:	Ri[ght.
92	JACK L:	[We communicate, I communicate to you, you com'nicate to
93		me. And I brought up to you (1.0) this perplex thing. 'Cause I
94		have to have somebody to speak to too (.) outside of my peers
95		who we speak to, eh? So I communicate with this. ((*Spoken*
96		*with intensity and pointing finger*)) Have you got the same
97		problem in Toronto?
98		(1.0)
99	JACK L:	Do you know what's happening at Toron[to?
100	SAM S:	[No, (I don't).
101	JACK L:	((*Spoken with intensity and pointing finger.*)) Are you running
102		one company or two companies? Is the <u>struc</u>ture that's wrong?
103		Is it professional management's wrong? Is it a (box) wrong?
104		<u>How</u> do you communicate? <u>They</u> communicate an' listen to this
105		an' an' I this is why I say structure (.) is so important an' how
106		we're gonna do it an' feedback an' control. .hh <u>Th:ey</u> been
107		raising prices from the first week. We kept prices back four
108		weeks, we did- though we got a co-co<u>st</u> increases, four (0.2)
109		three four weeks 'go three weeks 'go, so forth, we kept back
110		four weeks. They've been e- every week, putting in the price
111		changes though they come in- the same problem with- They
112		discuss it with you?
113		(.)
114	SAM S:	No =
115	JACK L:	= Have they communicated with you? =
116	SAM S:	= No.
117	JACK L:	((*Spoken with intensity and pointing finger.*)) = Have they
118		communicated with anybody here? (0.5) How many companies
119		are you running? (0.5) <u>What</u> philosophy do you want? That's
120		why my <u>first</u> thing on page <u>six</u> (0.2) page <u>six</u> and I want you to
121		go back and read it. This is exactly- I I am <u>very</u> glad you
122		brought it up. Because page six I say, for God sake, "the
123		<u>objec</u>tives and goals and corporate philosophy, the objectives
124		and goals must be spelled out." ↑<u>What</u> is your goals for Tor- ?
125		Are you running one business? Are you still running an- an
126		Ontario business? You wanna be the general manager here? Or
127		do you want to act as the President? Do you wanna act as a
128		corporate- as a corporate President for everybody or for one?

This segment of interaction exemplifies two "challenges," each taking its force from the usually unspoken understanding that both Jack L. and Sam S. are linked to each other by complementary responsibilities that define part of a tacit managerial constitution. The first challenge is initiated by Mr. Sam himself. He complains that someone (not directly identified) has been raising prices. To understand the basis of this complaint, some historical context is needed. Sam Steinberg adopted a philosophy early in his career that today is more commonly associated with retailers like WalMart and Costco: no sales, but prices uniformly low enough to beat the competitors' best price. At the time the film was made, it was well understood that this was the reason for the company's phenomenal growth and total dominance in its own market. Mr. Sam is complaining that someone is breaking the rule.

To make his complaint he tells a story. Jack Levine responds with his own challenge, and in effect initiates a different story—that of a careless company head. Both draw on narrative as the means to make their point, as Labov and Fanshel (1977) also found (Labov was, of course, one of the innovators in using recordings of narrative talk in naturalistic settings as the basis of his research).

NARRATIVE AS THE BASIS OF SENSEMAKING

To voice a challenge, as we see illustrated here, conversationalists typically resort to a narrative mode of argument; they tell stories that illustrate what they mean by an inadequate performance on the part of the delinquent partner (Labov & Fanshel, 1977). The general theory of narrativity, as enunciated by authors as widely divergent in their approaches as Bruner (1991) and Greimas (1987), confirms Labov and Fanshel's (1977) idea of an interconnection between "surface utterance" and "deeper action."

Bruner (1990), for example, remarked "stories have to do with how protagonists interpret things, what things mean to them. This is built into the circumstance of story—that it involves both a cultural convention and a deviation from it" (p. 51). Bruner (1991) observed that although narrative is a relation of specific events with specific actors in specific circumstances, yet the essence of narrativity is generic. Although individual actors, on one hand, are identifiable as real people, in a material world, the meaning of their actions, on the other hand, is always set against a culturally based model of role assumptions.

Greimas (1987) expressed this same idea somewhat differently. He makes a distinction between "actors" and "actants" (p. 106). An *actor* is a recognizable person, with a name and a unique history. An *actant* is the realization of an actantial role that is determined by the structure of narrative: victim, hero, antihero, benefactor, ally, and so on. Labov and Fanshel's (1977) "head" is an actantial role; so is their "dependent." The mother and the daughter, however, are actors.

Greimas (1987) also supported Labov and Fanshel's contention that the "challenges" the latter analyze in their research derive from an embedded cultural assumption about the rights and obligations of partners whose relationship to each other is asymmetric, or complementary (Watzlawick, Beavin, & Jackson, 1967). A complementary relationship, in which one person is acting as an agent for the other in the performance of some task or "doing" (Greimas, 1987) is called by him a "communication schema" or "structure of exchange" (p. 77). He assumes it to be the basis on which all communication rests. (Greimas, 1993, uses the term *contractual structure* to refer to the agency relationship).

Narratives, it has been argued, are motivated by the perception of a breakdown of some sort, or a deviation from what was generally expected to happen. Bruner (1991) remarked, for example, that "[f]or it to be worth telling, a tale must be about how an implicit canonical script has been breached, violated, or deviated from in a manner to do violence to what Hayden White terms the 'legitimacy' of the canonical script. This usually involves what Labov calls a 'precipitating event'" (p. 11). The breach, or threat to the underlying social order, is commonly attributable to the failure on someone's part to respect the terms of a contract (Greimas, 1983, 1987).

Now let us see how these features of narrative serve to clarify what is going on in the managerial conversation. Mr. Sam is particularly skilled in using narrative to make his point. He develops a homely little story:

```
72   SAM S:                                              So
73          here's what happens. I meet one of our managers having lunch
74          upstairs who's the manager of St-Lawrence and Cremazie. I
75          walked over an' say "Hello, how are you?" and everything else,
76          "How is it going?" He says "Very fine, sales are up thirteen or
77          (0.2) fourteen percent"
```

So far so good. Then Mr. Sam discovers to his apparent displeasure, a state of mind he clearly intimates to his listeners, that his interlocutor at St. Lawrence and Cremazie is not a happy camper: "But he says he's terribly disturbed." (77). The problem, it turns out, is that

```
78   SAM S:   They got in a wh:ole list of items that they have to increase the
79            prices on (0.5) and he's disturbed because now they'll be going
80            back to what they did in the past, erasing prices an' (.) putting
81            on higher prices an 'everything else.
```

Notice how many actants Mr. Sam has managed to work into his discourse: a "disturbed" store manager, himself not just as story-teller but as participant in a dialogue with the manager, an unnamed but clearly irresponsible "they," himself the narrator as patriarch (in effect delivering a "tut tut" to his subordinates), and, by implication, a company policy. Cooren (2001; Cooren & Taylor, 2000) saw this narrative strategy as *association*: a rhetorical device to marshal a coalition of discursive allies whose links must be dismantled one by one by the targeted interlocutor if the latter is to defend himself. Jack L., for example, has been in effect sandwiched between his superior, Mr. Sam, and his own subordinate, the store manager, while being reduced to an anonymous and inferentially guilty "they" who is "going back to what they did in the past." No wonder he reacts vigorously! What else could he do?

Interestingly enough, after sputtering for a while, trying vainly to undo the knot of associations Mr. Sam has tied together, he finds an out; an ideal strategy, one is tempted to say. He resorts to what might be called, colloquially, a "meta." Rather than refute the accusation, he reframes it to make it no longer a reproach for a breach of company policy, but as itself an instance of breach: a failure to play the presidential role. Now he has initiated a new narrative line in which the hero of the first story, Mr. Sam, is transformed into a delinquent in the second. It is the president himself who is guilty of not treating his subordinates equitably. (Interestingly enough, Mr. Sam reacts rather passively to the accusation, leading the analyst to wonder whether he may not have been quite satisfied with the result he has produced, whatever his motive. After all, Jack L. and Sam S. knew each other so well, and interacted so often, that they probably had little chance of surprising one another.)

Now let us take a look at a second excerpt that illustrates both how narrative is used to construct an argument to make a point, and again how the story turns on the device of a breach. This time it is Mr. Sam's nephew who initiates the story. Note that once more, the issue of constitution is implied by the construction of the intervention as a complaint.

622 ARNOLD S: I think (.) there's been a number of very m:ajor decisions which
623   have been taken (.) uh (.) there seems to be an assumption (.)
624   that there's a-an eternal t:ap? that we turn on and the cash just
625   flows out. And frankly uh unfortunately we're at the stage
626   where just the reverse happens to be true where there is no more
627   cash. And unless we we follow these events very closely we
628   could find ourselves in serious trouble. Let me give you
629   another example: we at the present time (0.2) have four million
630   dollars invested in the restaurant business (.) four million
631   ↓dollars (.) There was never a decision made to invest anything
632   like that kind of money (0.5) by any one individual= I doubt
633   frankly that anyone in this room even ↑knew we have four

634   million dollars (.) invested in the restaurant business and that
635   doesn't include the buildings. This is I'm talking just about the
636   leasehold improvements and the equipment and the inventories,
637   four million dollars. Now that was no <u>planned</u> decision (0.5)
638   and yet it someh:ow with the loose kind of organization we
639   have, we find ourselves at the beginning of nineteen sixty-nine
640   with a four million dollars investment and we will lose this year
641   something like four hundred thousand dollars in that business.
642 JAMES D: Well Arnold, that particular type you've been
643   [giving an example
644 ARNOLD S: [I've been giving an <u>example</u> of the barriers.
645 JAMES D: You have given an example of what I was going to cite myself
646   as a combination of a) one-to-one decision-making and b) and f)
647   family organization. 'Cos if ever there was an example of the
648   <u>family</u> (0.5) and one-to-one decision-making (.) getting us in a
649   spot (.) that is it. (1.0) As every- uh certainly Bill knows this (.)
650   and I'm I'm sure uh Bill did it (.) and I did it (0.2) we were
651   against this whole thing. (1.0) We (.) vr' - I was most
652   vociferously against it (0.5) uh in principle > right from the
653   start=I said "If we're going to go into this kind of an outside
654   venture< (.) let us go out and get the best possible people we
655   <u>can</u> (0.8) <u>and</u> (1.0) let's not settle for any second best (.) let's not
656   go into the basis of (.) buying a company that is <u>already</u> (0.8)
657   not making money (0.2) but losing money." (0.8) That there's a
658   a specific (.) eviden- example of two barriers (.) where the one-
659   to-one decision-making is made (.) and at the same time (.) it's
660   the family organization=when I say organization (.) the family
661   (.) if you like (.) pulling rank (.) on the rest of the non-family
662   executives in the corporation an' saying "Well that's the way it's
663   goin' to be."
664   (2.0)
665 JAMES D: An' an' an' in effect (.) the non-family part of the business had
666   absolutely nothing to say about that and what they did say (.)
667   was absolutely ignored.

Arnold S. is also telling a story: the tale of how someone (unnamed) rashly spent $4 million of the company's money to buy into a money-losing business. Again this is clearly a "breach" (although it is referred to in the mitigated terms of managerial discourse as *barriers, deficiencies,* or *shortcomings*). Note, however, how much ambiguity remains. According to Arnold, there was never any one individual who took the decision ("there was never a decision made"). No single person is on the hook, unlike in the case of the previous excerpt we analyzed. The investment in the restaurant business was, he asserts, never planned at all. The "villain" in the story, in other words, is not an individual, but "the loose kind of organization we have." Losing $4 million in an unprofitable venture is certainly a breach of policy for a company such as Steinberg's. But Arnold is even more careful than his boss had been earlier (with his reference to an anonymous "they") not to pinpoint the individual or individuals who are responsible (other than, of course, by inference on the part of his listeners). He stays away, in other words, from the issue of guilt for the breach of the constitution, other than by implication.

However, this sequence illustrates another principle of conversational storytelling: that the narrative develops its own internal dynamic as others, in this case, James D., add their own embellishments. James Doyle, however, is considerably more explicit. He points out the moral of the story as he interprets it: family interference in the affairs of the business, on one hand, and "one-to-one decision-making" on the other hand.

The "one-to-one decision-making" complaint echoes the reproach formulated by Jack Levine earlier: an instance of favoritism and thus deviating from what might be considered the appropriate relationship of head to dependents. Although we might speculate as to who the other "one" in James Doyle's "one-to-one" is, no one could possibly doubt that one of the ones is Mr. Sam himself. Nobody in a company like Steinberg's gets to spend that kind of money (this is 1969, when $4 million was still a sizable sum) without at least the tacit approval of the head of the company.

Dealing one-on-one with people was Mr. Sam's way. It always had been. This was not a man much attracted to abstractions. He reacted to Jack Levine's later elaborate proposed reorganization of the senior management structure with evident skepticism: "I am still confused" (288), he said, "You can't all call yourselves vice-presidents but one vice-president is different from the other vice-presidents" (313–314). It is not that he really doesn't understand ("I'm fully aware of what's happening" [329–330]); it is just that this is not, to him, how to run a company, even though his most trusted lieutenants disagree with him. The personal style of Mr. Sam is at odds with what a significant number of the senior executives think of as correct behavior for a chief executive officer: how a president should govern, and be governed. He, on the other hand, is an old-fashioned pragmatist. They are seeing the constitution through a different, and more modern, lens.

Which brings us to the third of our hypotheses: that understanding what the constitution actually says varies, depending on who is interpreting it, and from what perspective they do so.

COMPETING CONCEPTUALIZATIONS: WHY IT IS A "META" CONVERSATION

James Doyle's reshaping of Arnold Steinberg's restaurant complaint is not only, it will be recalled, a critique of Mr. Sam's one-on-one manner of managing the company (the point that is implicit in Arnold's interpretation). It goes further to raise the issue of family interference; a theme that runs through much of the Palomino discussion. Steinberg's is characterized by a schism: family versus nonfamily, old-fashioned patriarchal leadership versus "modern" professional management, nepotism versus system. Once again the issue is introduced by Arnold Steinberg:

```
766  ARNOLD S:  Harry, I would like to deal with a barrier that has been talked
767             about and uh by many people. One which (.) I am, I guess
768             particularly sensitive to, that has to do with number f) family
769             organization.
770  (    ):    (xxxx)
771  ARNOLD S:  Uh uh I think there's implied in many if not (0.5) most of the
772             submissions that deal with professional management leadership,
773             > I think all of them pretty much do < (.) the idea that most or
774             a:ll of the members of the family (.) would prefer working in an
775             organization (.) where professional management takes a
776             secondary role (.) to nepotism or or or fam- or family
777             preference. (0.5) An' in this area I I can obviously only speak
778             for myself (1.0) but I think I'm speaking for for most if not a:ll
779             of the second generation (.) family members when when I state
780             that that nep- that n-nepotism (0.2) generates sa-satisfaction to
781             any (.) particular individual for a very short period of time. (0.8)
782             And that in the long run uh career satisfaction of an individual
783             (0.2) uh let me put it differently (.) that that when (.) nep-
784             nepotism plays an important role (.) in the choice (0.2) of an
785             individual for management (.) the satisfaction that comes from
786             that is very short lived to any particular individual (.) who
787             thinks of himself (.) in a management capacity (.) and I think as
788             I said I speak well I know I only speak for for myself (.) in fact I
789             suspect that I'm voicing the opinion (.) of all if not most of the
790             members of the family.
```

Once introduced, the issue quickly takes on a life of its own.

```
824  IRVING L:  Well I tell you, I just wanna comment a little on this because uh
825             (0.2) I've had a lot of uh people uh come to me and talk to me
826             about this bec- may be because:e you know I'm a little younger
827             and only joined the company .hh uh some eleven years ago and
828             uh went through all this and in my case obviously it was no
829             great deterrent for me. .hh but uh let me just say this, that uh
830             there is an awareness (0.5) in the co- in many of the people in
831             the company that uh there is such a thing as an informal
832             organization at Steinberg's (0.8) which is directly linked to the
833             family (.) and there's an informal organization perhaps in every
```

834		company but this one happens to be directly linked to the family
835		.hh to the point wh:ere (.) there uh there (.) if you're sitting
836		among a group of <u>peers</u> (0.5) that the fact th', and I'm gonna
837		level here and tell you that the standard joke is (.) that the <u>key</u>
838		decisions are <u>not</u> made at the management committee (.) or with
839		the President (.) but at Friday night supper (1.0) and this in itself
840		is very indicative because I'm sure you've all heard the same e-
841		expressions used (0.2) and it's very indicative (.) as to how
842		people see the organization an' how they read it. They don't see
843		(.) <u>equ:ality</u>; if one fella happens to be Vice-President of this
844		and another fella Vice-President of that and they're both putting
845		forth their opinions, if one happens to be <u>related</u> (.) the feeling
846		is (.) that he's got an awful lot more to say (.) a) because he is
847		much closer, b) it's sort of his money involved and, c:) it's
848		because (.) he goes to the Friday night supper as opposed to the
849		other party (.) and I think that this (.) is the feeling among a lot
850		of the people (.) in the organization. They feel it definitely
851		has hampered in the past (.) and I might add (.) that uh perhaps
852		from my own point of view anyways is probably is <u>less</u> so <u>now</u>
853		than it has been (0.5) and it's been very severe in the past (.) in
854		my opinion.
855		(2.0)
856	IRVING L:	And I can tell you there's a lot of people they spend a lot of
857		time talking about this stuff (0.2) a lot of ↓time. And so I think
858		we have to recognize it and be aware of it.
859		(4.0)
860	SAM S:	I just wanna make (.) I just wanna ask you one question=Is it
861		your charm or ability got you where you are now? That's all I
862		want to know. *((laughing.))* =
863		˙ *((People speaking at once.))*
864	( ):	=Good looks …
865		*((Laughter.))*
866	MEL D:	No, he attended the Friday night dinner.
867		*((Everybody laughing.))*
868	JAMES D:	No yeah but to to support everything that Irving is saying uh
869		there is also and I think Irving could, might call in on this (.)
870		there's a sort of uh (0.5) another:r feeling around (0.5) that (0.5)
871		a a certain amount of this has (.) definitely been taken care of in
872		a much better way in recent years with the appointment of other
873		non-family people to very senior positions. But running along
874		with that wh-whether we like to admit it or not there's a there's
875		one school of thought going around which sort of looks as us a
876		little bit like the Negroes in a cabinet (0.5) you know (.) that
877		really we're we're there more for show *((starting to laugh))* than
878		for performance. And that the real decisions are still made as
879		Irving says in the in the Friday night eh meetings whether that's
880		(0.5) has validity or not, that's what they believe=
881	SAM S:	=(xxxx) I don't think I need to answer that but certain you were

```
882              never put on for show.
883              (1.2)
884  MORRIS S:   Nepotism can actually exist (.) not only in family but when a:
885              General Manager in his own division can have nepotism in his
886              ((one person speaking at the same time)) own family. So
887              nepotism does not only exist in a in a uh family.
888              (0.5)
889  ARNOLD S:   The whole question of nepotism (.) in my opinion is not really
890              (.) coming out on the table. (0.5) In this sense from what I
891              gather and and it's may be not right for me to to bring it up uh
892              (.) uh but (.) throughout the reports (0.8) throughout the reports
893              (0.2) there is (0.2) if not (0.2) written certainly between the
894              lines (1.0) there is the the the uh obvious statement (.) that this
895              company h:as been ruled (.) and is suffering (0.8) badly (.) as a
896              result of nepotism. And frankly I have a feeling that if a vote
897              was taken (1.0) by the people here more people would vote in-
898              in to the correctness of that statement than to the wrongness of
899              that statement.
```

The competing claims of corporation and family as the basis of authority of the president are the single most persistent theme in the Palomino meeting. The issue is simply whether the head of the corporation should be governed by the same constitution as the head of the household (to use Labov & Fanshel's, 1977, formulation). Even though most of Mr. Sam's managers think otherwise, it would seem, from this distance, that Mr. Sam did not perceive any great discontinuity between the two roles he was playing. A head's a head, isn't he? (he must have thought to himself). As he says at one point, he has always thought of his closest business associates as "members of the family" (not to mention that two of his brothers are vice presidents and his nephew, Arnold, is an influential voice within management).

The issue of family was not, however, the only division of interest and point of view to come up for discussion. Managers who participate in the metaconversation of the organization confront two kinds of exigency: sorting out their relationship with their superior (an example of which we have just been commenting on) and negotiating relationships with their peers. Because the peers within the metaconversation represent different agencies within the organization, and because those agencies are typically in competition for the resources of the company, part of the metaconversation is taken up with what might be called "turf" issues. Once again, the managerial discussion in *Corporation: After Mr. Sam* illustrates what we mean.

```
669  JACK L:   I want to keep [on this (xxxx)=
670  JAMES D:               [Certainly.
671  JACK L:   =only because I think we're getting some feelings out. For
```

672		three, four, five years, Mel and I have been saying very clearly,
673		yearly, we used to do it yearly, that the organization being (.)
674		built at corporate was much too heavy for our retail k:ind of
675		operation that we're into. .hh and we just talked against the
676		wind. As we talked it grew bigger and as we talked it grew
677		bigger .hh and (.) it- this costs us time and money and
678		competitiveness because of this one kind of act=and we couldn't
679		make any change. We had no power=I had no power making
680		change, .hh M:el (.) didn't have the power because I know Mel
681		yelled as much I did, no power. Now where is there an
682		organization ↑responsibility? (0.5) and a function of a
683		management (.) in order to take this kind of v-view into fact and
684		see if we can afford what we're building. (0.5) Never was? Is
685		that, is that making manag- professional management as a
686		professional management exercising (.) decision-making? I
687		think we, we've failed=
688	ARNOLD S:	=I'm (not sure) about that Jack. Which what you're saying
689		impl:ies (.) that there was duplication (.) that was unnecessary
690		building. [Isn't that what you're implying?
691	JACK L:	[Mmh, yes, absolutely.
692	ARNOLD S:	But surely the corollary to that (.) is that the duplication existed
693		at the corp- at the divisional level. You're saying that the
694		divisional level had to have what the corporate didn't. Wo' but
695		surely (.) in in a discussion (0.2) which is now coming out in
696		the in in work that Bill's group is doing (.) they're discovering
697		that the duplication is in fact taking place at the division (.) and
698		the real need is at -corporate? I mean all I'm saying Jack is that
699		in fact I agree that duplication exists.
700	JACK L:	But Arnold=
701	ARNOLD S:	=But you're assuming that duplication is at the corporate an' not
702		at the division
703	JACK L:	((Shouting.)) But (.) corporate started to build up (immaterial)
704		that was at the division. Now where should it be?=
705	ARNOLD S:	=Maybe [xxx corporate who say the division grew up not=
706	JACK L:	[xxx at corporate?
707	ARNOLD S:	=even though it was at the corporate. (xxxx) Jack, I am agreeing
708		that some[one should have sat down.
709	JACK L:	[Okay (0.5) Right! That's all what I am saying.

Jack and Arnold find themselves, somewhat uncomfortably, at an intersection of two relational frameworks, one of which is horizontal and differentiates their interest, and the other which is vertical, and unites them in their common relationship to their superior. They sort it out as best they can, to give a sense of solidarity, but naturally, traces of contentiousness remain; there is no real closure. Tensions between the different roles that individuals embody in their person, and that surface in conversation when they must simultaneously realize more than one of those roles, are described by Engeström (1990) as "latent tensions" (p. 84). They are, he believes, an intrinsic property of any complex system of activities. We conceptualize these discontinuities differently, as *registers*.

REGISTERS

Our curiosity about the phenomenon of register was piqued by a shift of form of address that occurs early in *Corporation: After Mr. Sam*. Jack Levine, a vice president, but also one of the founder's oldest and closest associates, interjects, in trying to interrupt his boss, "But Mr. Sam …" (44). Shortly afterward, again in response to an intervention by Mr. Sam, Levine changes to "Mr. President" (82). And then, almost immediately, he reiterates: "=Will you wait a minute? Mr. President look …" (87) and he continues with the rest of his remarks.[3] Why the shift from "Mr. Sam" to "Mr. President," we asked ourselves? And what does this shift tell us about the organizing dynamic of the managerial conversation? It seems obvious that the exchange between Jack Levine and Mr. Sam occurs on at least two planes, that we term registers: that of a well-established interpersonal relationship of long standing, and that of a vice president addressing the president.

Conversation analysis, of the kind illustrated by the work of Schegloff, Heritage, Jefferson, Pomerantz, and others, emphasizes the conventions that are in play in the maintenance of coherent interaction in talk. *Corporation: After Mr. Sam* illustrates at every point the characteristics of the usual to-and-fro of talk—the conversational dynamic. But the logic of a metaconversation is slightly different. In the meta-conversation, whole communities of activity are interacting through their spokespersons. What Levine and Arnold Steinberg are saying to each other, in the excerpt we have already cited, is done so, as they make clear, in their respective identities of "divisional" and "corporate." Levine alleges that corporate is top-heavy; Arnold Steinberg counters that there has been unwarranted duplication at the divisional level. Each, in other words, prepares to build a story about what they take to be a breach of the implicit constitution underpinning the corporate-divisional relationship, seen from opposing perspectives. Confronted with the prospect of a serious division among allies, who in other respects are in agreement, they quickly find an alternative source of the problem, and associated culprit: "someone," who "should have sat down" (708) to resolve the duplication. (Notice again the ambiguity: Perhaps everyone in the room can guess who the "someone who should have sat down" is but they haven't named him in so many words.) However, as the announcer who voices the narrative of the film documentary points out, these two men are prime candidates to replace Mr. Sam when he leaves. Again, their interaction needs to be read as occurring simultaneously in more than one register.

There had been discussions leading up to the meeting in the Palomino Lodge, and people came prepared with documented position papers that presumably were meant to express the points of view of the different communities making up the firm, and not just the personal opinions of the individual participants. The participants, or at least several of them, are thus performing a role of collective agent, representing their community's interests. But they are at the same time caught up in conversation, and adjusting to its exigencies as it unfolds, with the result that what they are saying can be read as taking place in two registers: that of the conversation, and that of the metaconversation, or negotiation of relationships between different communities, and not just between individuals.

The word "register" means, among other things, a "range of possibilities" (The Concise Oxford Dictionary, 1976). It is used, for example, to refer to the range of a given voice (soprano vs. alto, tenor vs. bass). It also refers to a device in an organ by means of which a particular set of pipes is controlled. It can also mean "a form of language customarily used in particular circumstances" (The Concise Oxford Dictionary, 1976). We borrow the word here to capture the idea that different levels of the communicative convention of the organization may be simultaneously operative in a conversation. Sometimes, as we have seen in the Jack Levine–Mr. Sam episode we cited earlier, the levels are reflected in the forms of language that people use: "Mr. Sam" versus "Mr. President."[4]

The interaction between Jack L. and Arnold S. similarly illustrates both the register of a metaconversation and that of a conversation. The interaction is at one and the same time a negotiation involving differing communities and an interpersonal relation, grounded in an association of two individuals, with the multiple unspoken assumptions that such a relationship connotes.

The concept of *register* is, however, not limited to the distinction between interpersonal and interstatus. There is also another register to be taken account of in this film: that of the family. The family's constitution, like that of the company, transcends that of an interpersonal relationship because it specifies an interrelation of roles, and rules of association that a given society takes to be appropriate for the different statuses that define the family. As Steinberg (cited earlier) observes, he is "particularly sensitive" (768) to the issue of family because, although he clearly identifies with his kin, his reading of what that closeness means is different from that of the previous generation: less patriarchal, one supposes. As he says, "I can obviously only speak for myself (1.0) but I think I'm speaking for for most if not a:ll of the second generation (.) family members." (777–779). He is all too aware that whenever he enters into conversation, there may be a reasonable doubt as to whom he speaks for: himself, his branch of the company, or his family. Others such as Mr. Sam's son-in-law, Mel Dobrin, are in the same boat.

THE SEARCH FOR CLOSURE

Greimas (1993) pointed out that sensemaking, which is grounded in narrative, has what he calls "a certain economic organization" (p. 22). As he puts it, "the undermining of the social order is followed by a return to a state of order, and the alienation is repaired by the rediscovery of the lost values. It is as if the narrative organization obeyed a principle of equilibrium which transcends and governs human actions accomplished by subjects" (p. 22; a free translation from the original French).[5] The imminent departure of the man who had for so long incarnated Steinberg's in his own person, and guided its development with authority (in both senses of that word, confidently and bossily), constituted for his company "an undermining" of its "social order." The linchpin was being pulled, and the company risked losing its sense of direction (which, in fact, is what eventually transpired following his retirement). And there is a clear desire to "return to a state of order" although not that which had previously reigned; given the departure of Mr. Sam, there was no way to return to the status quo ante. It is this search for a new social constitution that we mean by *closure*.

Closure means not just repairing the lost world of the company under Mr. Sam, but of finding a new identity, and a new way to bridge the multiple identities of the organization by building a consensual corporate identity. In such a reconstruction of its identity, Steinberg's, many in the group felt, would also have to shed its close ties to the family.

But that was not going to happen, and, in this frustration of the purposes of many of the managers, the dominant figure, as always, would be Mr. Sam himself. Every time the issue of nepotism, and family interference in the affairs of the company, came up, Mr. Sam reacted. For example, here is how he responded to Arnold's intervention, cited earlier:

```
792  SAM S:   .hh now uh (0.8) uh the only comment I would like to make at
793           this mom- this moment was that I read a Harvard report (0.5)
794           where it deals with families in organizations=
795  (    ):  =We all read it. ((People interrupting and agreeing.))
796  SAM S:   Alright! So it tells you that after a period of twenty years there
797           is more family than ever before=and that hasn't affected the the
798           performances as I read it in these companies. (1.0) On the >
799           other hand < (0.5) I think that when we look around the table
800           over here, we talk about family, (1.0) well (.) I looked upon
```

```
801              Jack as a member of the family=I look up:on (.) Oscar as a
802              member of the family (.) I've looked upon Jack Ginser always
803              as a member of the family (.) and I think that they look upon
804              ↑themselves as a member of family.
805              ((Four or five people talking at the same time.))
806 (    ):     That's not a very good example.
807 (    ):     Your definition of family and everyone else's xxx
```

And again here is how Mr. Sam countered Irving Ludmer's statement on
the issue of family influence, using another favorite tactic, teasing:

```
860 SAM S:   I just wanna make (.) I just wanna ask you one question=Is it
861          your charm or ability got you where you are now? That's all I
862          want to know. ((laughing.))=
```

A further instance is the following, in which Mr. Sam exploits his own
variant of the Socratic method: pinning down his opponents by pointing up through focused questions the absurdity of the conclusions their
position would lead to.

```
907 SAM S:    You're talkin' about how would you say eh (3.0) I had the word
908           on the tip of my tongues when you say franchise but this (1.0)
909           u:h (.) I'll say is this=I'll put it simpler "Does this rule out (0.5)
910           ((pointing to Arnold)) Arnold because he's a member of the
911           [family?"
912 (    ):   [No ((several people speaking)) no, no.
913 SAM S:    Well, of course I've got to make sure that I understand that
914           clearly, he's a member of the [family.
915 (    ):                                  [We're coming to that (xxxx)
916           We're coming to that.
917           ((People still talking at the same time.))
918 JACK L:   What are you asking? Come on. What is he asking?
919 (    ):   I'm not sure.
920 JACK L:   I don't know what he is asking?
921 (    ):   Are you are you doing something underhand?
922 (    ):   Our boss is doing something (xxxx)
923 (    ):   I don't know, I mean.
924 SAM S:    Let me finish please (0.5) let me finish.
925 HARRY S:  Satisfied?=
926 SAM S:    =Now if the man can't be considered for the job because he's a
927           member of the family we better know the ground rules right at
928           the beginning.
929           ((People talking, some laughing.))
```

In the end, Mr. Sam wins, however, not because there is support for a
continuation of family dominance, but because almost no one wants to
look outside the company for a successor. Only John Paré supports the

idea of going outside. The search for closure means more than simply finding a resolution to its state of uncertainty in the wake of the retirement: the term *closure* also points to a continuing, hermetically sealed culture. But perhaps the greatest impediment to closure is Mr. Sam himself. On one hand, he seems to encourage a great freedom of expression, and an opening up of the dialogue to new ideas:

```
752  SAM S:      When I started out the meeting I said each one of you in your report
753             there must be something that you feel and we recognize that and
754             this is one of the reasons we're here. So if there are in those (.) those
755             items that you (.) consider uppermost that you reduce to writing and
756             felt free to say so (.) what is uppermost in your minds that you feel
757             has some restraining influence I think it should like Jack said
758             (0.5) uh (0.7) brought out?
759  *JACK L:    °Absolutely°
760  SAM S:      Fr:eely spoken.
761             (0.5)
762  (    ):      [Well I I
763  SAM S:      [To the extent that we think it's pretty well covered by what's
764             already been said then we move ↓forward.
```

This is Mr. Sam, the savvy psychologist, the man who knows how to take the measure of the individuals who surround him. Several times we have alluded to the ambiguity of people's interventions—oblique references to unnamed individuals. Mr. Sam himself is a master of ambiguity, and seems to thrive in an atmosphere of equivocal allusions to this or that breach of the constitution. But perhaps there is a reason for his affability and his tolerance of ambiguity: It forestalls closure on the part of his associates. And it leaves ample room to maneuver for the other Mr. Sam, the autocratic patriarch, who, in the end, will impose his own will on his subordinates.

```
989  SAM S:      I don't even need to have a family get-together.
990             (1.0)
991  (    ):      This is true.
992  SAM S:      One man (1.0) my own person have a hundred percent control
993             of this company. I don't have to ask anybody so it's no use even
994             talkin' about a discussion the the there's no need for a
995             discussion. (1.0) Uh (1.0) I don't need anybody's approval=
```

Closure? Not any time soon, it would seem.

```
1490 HARRY S:    Are we going to talk about time dimension here? (0.2) no?
1491 (    ):      Yeah I=
1492 (    ):      =I think we should=
```

```
1493 (    ):    =Absolutely.
1494            ((A few people talking at once.))
1495 (    ):    Would you expand that, John?
1496 SAM S:     I think that this this decision will be taken (.) in a period, may
1497            be three to six months
1498            (0.5)
1499 SAM S:     Not sooner.
1500            (1.0)
1501 (    ):    Three to six months?=
1502 SAM S:     =That's right.
1503            (1.0)
1504 ARNOLD S:  You're saying it will be at the earliest three months at at the
1505            latest six months, or at at the earliest three to six months?
1506            (0.5)
1507 SAM S:     You put it well, at the earliest three months at the latest six.
1508            (4.5)
1509 JACK L:    In my opinion that's too long. But uh (.) I think that uh (0.5) the
1510            organization as a whole is waiting (0.5) And I think three to six
1511            months is uh a long time for uh after going through what we've
1512            done (.) now I was thinking about I would have had hoped (.)
1513            that the final decision will be within three months, not three to
1514            six months.
1515 SAM S:     Well you don't happen to be the- (0.5) in my position, sitting in
1516            my seat, so
```

CONCLUSION

We have approached the analysis of *Corporation: After Mr. Sam* from the perspective of researchers who study organization using the window on it provided by talk and text, not as specialists in the analysis of discourse. We are, in other words, interested above all in the dynamic of organizing as it is mediated by dialogue, whether materialized in spoken or written form. The result is quite deliberately a broad-brush interpretation of the episodes the filmmaker chose to include in the documentary: All that remains, in the end, of that now long-ago discussion taking place at the Palomino Lodge, in the Laurentians. There is, however, more than enough redundancy in this kind of managerial interaction to justify, we believe, the kind of interpretation we have developed, however incomplete and selective the film as a record of what was said may be.

We have tried to read the sequence as a whole, to discover who the parties to the discussion were, and how their evolving co-orientation to each other as they dialogued with each other serves to illustrate the principles of analysis we have privileged. We thus think of the film less as data for a detailed analysis than as an illustration of what we believe to be general principles of analysis. What we perceive, taking such an overview, is in certain respects, much as Goffman (1969) encouraged us to do, a kind of human chessboard, except that the "pieces" on it move themselves, rather than wait for external players to impose a strategy; they are both the players and the played. Board configurations become visible as the pieces interact, and then are transformed as moves are made. A kind of game is played. What emerges is, however, something like a stalemate; neither side is clearly victorious. Closure is imposed, not reached. It is Mr. Sam himself who, in the end, "metas" the metaconversation—walks away from the game before it has ended, you might say.

Obviously, *Corporation: After Mr. Sam* can claim no more than to have been a partial (in both senses of the word) account of what occurred in one managerial discussion. What we postulated by our hypotheses, however, is that an equivalent managerial game is common to every such managerial metaconversation. They all tend, in our experience, to line up, black against white—family orientation versus professional management orientation being but one such possible configuration—depending on the context and history of the organization and the ideology of its component members. It may be that organizing exhibits a form that is not just an effect of filmmaking: less structure, in the traditional sense, than a self-generated patterning of its interactive organizing. Perhaps the real task of the organizational communication analyst is to strip away the surface characteristics of the conversation to reveal its underlying form, much as Bakhtin (1981, 1986) suggested is the specificity of the novel—like a large organization, the quintessential expression of modernity, both in its diversity of voices and in its search for a unifying meaning (see Taylor, 2004).

The perspective we develop is in marked contrast to the commonly held view of management. Nonaka and Takeuchi (1995), for example, spoke of an organizational "intention" that is formulated by the president, and becomes the standard against which any proposed innovation is measured. Hammer and Champy (1993) described a leader who "creates a new vision" and who "creates an environment" (p. 104) conducive to change. Our conception of the *dynamic of management* is quite different: closer to a view of a political process in which the various embedded-in-practice interests of the many communities of the organization strive to establish an organizational "intention" that corresponds to their own philosophy. Rather than uniquely focus on the person of the president or chief executive officer (CEO) who imposes a view, we perceive normal management to be closer to what Giroux and Taylor (2002) described as an ongoing and highly interactive justification of belief. This is not to deny the importance of the role of the head of the organization—far from it. But it is to admit that, as Latour (1986) pointed out, no leader's power remains effective in the absence of followers. Pity the company head or department chief who fails to develop a supportive managerial cadre. Even dictators need allies if they are to remain in power.

We believe that such a perspective on management provides a productive springboard for research. To take but one example, consider the role of the head of the organization and his or her special place within the metaconversation. We touch here, in other words, the topic of leadership. In the usual course of events, the head of the organization, Mr. Sam, for example, is embedded in a managerial conversation; the people who compose senior management are those within the organization with whom he or she most frequently interacts. They are supposed to represent to him or her the interests of the communities of practice for which they speak. But, as we believe *Corporation: After Mr. Sam* illustrates, the managerial metaconversation tends to develop its own dynamic, and what occurs there reflects as much or more its own communicational properties as the reality of what is occurring elsewhere in the organization. The chief executive thereby risks becoming isolated from the day-to-day realities of his or her own organization. It follows that the selection of those who will participate in senior management and the dynamic of the resulting metaconversation that unfolds are of crucial importance to the coherence of management. How the metaconversation unfolds, of course, also hinges on the personality and expectations of the chief.[6]

Mr. Sam makes an interesting case study in this respect. For example, he exhibits a considerable tolerance for ambiguity. He appears to encourage expression of views that are not always very flattering to himself. "What is uppermost in your minds" (756–757), he says, should be "brought out" (758), "[f]reely spoken" (760). He himself, however, is often oblique in communicating his meaning. He makes little attempt to direct the progress of the meeting; he is not chairing it so he seems reactive rather than proactive but he is visibly the center of attention. He listens tolerantly to Jack Levine's tirades but he doesn't buy the argument. He responds with moderation to the accusation of nepotism. It is true that his brothers hold sinecures rather than carry key managerial responsibility but he also avoids the impression that he wants a management committee that is nothing but a rubber stamp. When both Irving Ludmer and James Doyle, in quite different ways, indicate that they think of themselves as not part of the inner circle, he is quick to counter their positions. "Is it your charm or ability got you to where you are now?" (860–861) he responds to one, and "you were never put on for show" (881–882) to the other. And he makes sure that everyone knows that he makes it his business to circulate regularly among the members of the organization who are not part of the metaconversation.[7] But in the end it is he who makes the decisions.

It is one way of being head of an organization. And it is also one way of relating to the metaconversation in doing so. There are obviously others. What we need to better understand are the effects of different patterns of interaction at the level of the metaconversation. Imagine, for example, another kind of leader who structures a clear agenda, sets a decisive tone with well-defined objectives, and who believes that everyone should be "reading from the same page of the book." In such an organization investing in a chain of restaurants would have had to be, as Nonaka and Takeuchi (1995) might put it, shown to be in conformity with the overall organizational intention.

It sounds more businesslike and professional, but is it really a better administrative philosophy? Weick (1979, 1995; Weick & Sutcliffe, 2001) has over the years reminded us that organizations confront an equivocal environment where what is happening may be evident, but what it means is not evident. He argues that often what appears superficially to be a messy organizational process, without a tightly controlled central control, may in fact generate the necessary variety to deal effectively with changing and unpredictable circumstances. Perhaps losing $4 million is not so dumb, after all? Was perhaps "the loose kind of organization we have" (638–639), as his Harvard MBA nephew, Arnold, puts it, Mr. Sam's way of responding to the vicissitudes of an unpredictable marketplace? We have no idea, but it does suggest that these and other similar issues of leadership appear in a different light when we relate them to an ongoing metaconversation. Perhaps a measure of political savvy is as important to the chief executive as decisiveness, direction, analytical skill, and personality.

TOWARD A PHILOSOPHY OF RESEARCH

In this chapter, we emphasized the role of narrative in organizational sense-making. The student of organizational communication is also a sense-maker: also someone who, in conducting the kind of analysis we have been making, is narrativizing what has already been narrativized by the filmmaker who made *Corporation: After Mr. Sam.* Can we claim this kind of analysis to be in any respect "scientific"? And what role does narrative play in communication research, where the object is an organization?

The answer one gives to these questions depends on what one thinks science is. Maturana (1991, 1997) provided an answer with which we are comfortable (for greater elaboration, see Taylor & Van Every, 2000). The scientific activity is a communal activity. Those who belong to the community are those who have learned to formulate explanations, grounded in empirical inquiry, that satisfy the exigencies imposed by the community on its members. What counts as truth is dependent on its conformity to the "criterion of explanation" (Maturana, 1991, p. 44) that the community has adopted. What makes an explanation "scientific" is its subjection to the standards of the scientific community. The community is, in turn, defined by its practices in observing and explaining in a way that allows others to know how they made their observation, how it conforms to the criteria of exposition acceptable within the community, and is subsequently subjected to peer review.

It is our belief that the natural way of making sense of the communicational experience out of which organization emerges is narrative. What makes it scientific is not denarrativizing explanations, but, as this book itself very well illustrates, in presenting a variety of strategies of narrativizing: to encourage the reader to develop his or her own standards of sensemaking—and to be self-critical, once these standards are developed. It is in this kind of sharing of sense-making strategies that we perceive the future of the organizational communication community of scholars to lie. We too are part of a metaconversation.

ENDNOTES

1. Harris and Cronen (1979) employ the expression "master contract," with somewhat similar intention: They see an organization's culture as related to an acceptance of a rule-based constitution.
2. It is of course possible that the degree to which the conversation is focused on differences of interpretation of the constitution is an effect of editing. Filmmakers tend, for obvious reasons, to privilege sequences that are characterized by tension and difference; it makes for better television.
3. Note, incidentally, Jack Levine's use of the word *we*. He speaks in his own name, but it is also evident that he speaks for his division.
4. The most overt illustration of register occurs in an exchange between Harry Suffrin and Jack Levine, where the former is scolding his colleagues for not respecting meeting protocol (one intervention at a time, no interruptions, etc.), only to become himself a target for Levine's passionate plea to be passionate: "get out feelings on the table," "I want some heat to come out," and so forth (to which Mr. Sam responds positively, it might be noted). Suffrin perceives the occasion to be a semiformal meeting, and plays his role accordingly; Levine seems to come closer to a T-group view of the encounter (T-groups were still in vogue at the time).
5. Actually Greimas (1993) employed the term *destruction* that we have translated as "undermining." The term destruction seems more appropriate to an encounter between James Bond and Dr. No, or Goldfinger, than to a management meeting of senior executives in a retailing operation, and we have preferred the softer term, *undermining*, as an appropriate translation in this context.
6. The senior author of this chapter recalls an instance of this phenomenon. Called in to advise on the communication problems of a government agency, following serious personnel disturbances, he found a senior management team so isolated from the rest of the organization and so preoccupied by its own inter-

nal games that there was very serious alienation at the working level, and severe problems of morale. The head of the organization, a man of decided opinions and dominating personality, had come up through the ranks. The author recalls a long conversation with him in which, at one point, he said: "You know, Jim, I worked with these people. I know most of them by name. I can't understand what they are thinking about. They've changed!"

7. Sam Steinberg's style of leadership, throughout his career, was highly personal. He knew literally scores of employees, throughout the firm, by their first names. He was there to give them sympathy when there was a tragedy in their family. He had an eye for detail. He would prowl around his stores, looking at how products were being merchandized, checking prices, chatting with employees. In a way, he invented "managing by walking around" before it had been invented.

REFERENCES

Bakhtin, M. M. (1981). *The dialogic imagination* (M. Holquist, Ed.; C. Emerson & M. Holquist, Trans.). Austin: University of Texas Press.

Bakhtin, M. M. (1986). *Speech genres and other late essays* (V. W. McGee, Trans.). Austin: University of Texas Press.

Boden, D. (1994). *The business of talk: Organizations in action.* Cambridge, England: Polity Press.

Bruner, J. S. (1990). *Acts of meaning.* Cambridge, MA: Harvard University Press.

Bruner, J. S. (1991, Autumn). The narrative construction of reality. *Critical Inquiry*, 1–21.

Concise Oxford dictionary. (1976). Oxford: Clarendon Press.

Cooren, F. (2001). Translation and organization in the organization of coalitions: The Great Whale case. *Communication Theory, 11*, 178–200.

Cooren, F., & Taylor, J. R. (2000). Association and disassociation in an ecological controversy: The Great Whale case. In N. W. Coppola & B. Karis (Eds.), *Technical communication, deliberative rhetoric, and environmental discourse: Connections and directions* (Vol. 11, pp. 171–190). Stamford, CT: Ablex.

Engeström, Y. (1990). *Learning, working, and imagining: Twelve studies in activity theory.* Helsinki, Finland: Orienta-Konsultit.

Giddens, A. (1984). *The constitution of society.* Cambridge, England: Polity Press.

Giroux, H., & Taylor, J. R. (2002). The justification of knowledge: Tracking the translations of quality. *Management Learning, 33*(4), 497–517.

Goffman, E. (1959). *The presentation of self in everyday life.* New York: Doubleday Anchor.

Goffman, E. (1969). *Strategic interaction.* Philadelphia: University of Pennsylvania Press.

Greimas, A. J. (1983). *Structural semantics: An attempt at a method.* Lincoln: University of Nebraska Press.

Greimas, A. J. (1987). *On meaning: Selected writings in semiotic theory.* Minneapolis: University of Minnesota Press.

Greimas, A. J. (1993). *Les acquis et les projets* [What we know and what remains to be done]. In J. Courtès (Ed.), *Sémiotique narrative et discursive* (pp. 5–25). Paris: Hachette.

Hammer, M., & Champy, J. (1993). *Reengineering the corporation: A manifesto for business revolution.* New York: HarperCollins.

Harris, L., & Cronen, V. E. (1979, Winter). A rule-based model for the analysis and evaluation of organizational communication. *Communication Quarterly,* 12–27.

Labov, W., & Fanshel, D. (1977). *Therapeutic discourse: Psychotherapy as conversation.* New York: Academic.

Latour, B. (1986). The powers of association. In J. Law (Ed.), *Power, action and belief: A new sociology of knowledge.* London: Routledge & Kegan Paul.

Maturana, H. (1991). Science in daily life: The ontology of scientific explanations. In F. Steier (Ed.), *Research and reflexivity: Self-reflexivity as social process* (pp. 30–52). Newbury Park, CA: Sage.

Maturana, H. (1997). *La objetividad, un argumento para obligar* [Objectivity: A compelling argument]. Santiago, Chile: Dolmen.

Nonaka, I., & Takeuchi, H. (1995). *The knowledge-creating company: How Japanese companies create the dynamics of innovation.* New York: Oxford University Press.

Sacks, H. (1992). *Lectures on conversation* (Vols. 1 & 2). (G. Jefferson, Ed.). Oxford: Blackwell.

Sanders, R. E. (1995). A neo-rhetorical perspective: The enactment of role-identities as interactive and strategic. In S. J. Sigman (Ed.), *The consequentiality of communication.* Hillsdale, NJ: Lawrence Erlbaum Associates.

Taylor, J. R. (2004). Dialogue as the search for sustainable organizational coorientation. In R. Anderson, L. A. Baxter, & K. N. Cissna (Eds.), *Dialogue: Theorizing difference in communication studies* (pp. 125–140). Thousand Oaks, CA: Sage.

Taylor, J. R., & Van Every, E. J. (2000). *The emergent organization: Communication as its site and surface.* Mahwah, NJ: Lawrence Erlbaum Associates.

Watzlawick, P., Beavin, J. H., & Jackson, D. (1967). *Pragmatics of human communication: A study of interactional patterns, pathologies, and paradoxes.* New York: W.W. Norton.

Weick, K. E. (1979). *The social psychology of organizing.* New York: Random House.

Weick, K. E. (1995). *Sensemaking in organizations.* Thousand Oaks, CA: Sage.

Weick, K. E., & Sutcliffe, K. M. (2001). *Managing the unexpected: Assuring high performance in an age of complexity.* San Francisco: Jossey Bass.

Chapter 2

Enacting the Institutional Role of Chairperson in Upper Management Meetings: The Interactional Realization of Provisional Authority

Anita Pomerantz
Paul Denvir
University at Albany, SUNY

The aim of this chapter is to explain and illustrate a conversation-ana-lytic approach to understanding role enactments during organizational meetings. In this chapter, we limit our discussion to the enactment of one role: chairperson of upper management meetings. When an upper management meeting is conducted within an organization, it is a common practice for a single participant to act as the chairperson. Although the CEO of a corporation often chairs upper management meetings, there are occasions in which this is not the case.

The role of chairperson is institutionally recognizable in terms of the rights and responsibilities afforded to the person who is an incumbent in this role. All participants in such a meeting, including the participant who occupies the role of chairperson, bring to the meeting certain culturally and organizationally informed understandings about the kinds of activities that are anticipated from the chairperson and the kinds of activities to which the chairperson may be uniquely entitled. These understandings may not match perfectly among all participants and may, in fact, be negotiated throughout the meeting. Still, the expectation for participants is that a certain set of communicative activities will be communally understood as associated primarily with the role of chairperson. Some of the more commonly recognized activities may include (a) opening and closing the meeting, (b) introducing items or topics designated on the agenda, (c) facilitating the closing down of talk on one agenda item and the introduction of talk on a next agenda item, (d) allocating turns-at-talk by formally granting participants the right to be next speakers, and (e) sanctioning inappropriate meeting conduct. When persons perform such activities, they can be understood as enacting the chairperson role with which those activities are associated.

Although persons perform these activities in the capacity of chairperson, they do not necessarily perform them in the exact same ways. Various matters shape how they enact the role. They may operate with one or another premise regarding the proper functioning of the chairperson in the particular meeting. For example, a chairperson may assume that exercising leadership, allowing the participants to voice their views, or efficiently arriving at decisions has top priority for the meeting in question. A chairperson presumably operates with premises that are appropriate for the purpose of the meeting, the number of participants, the institutionally recognized statuses of the other participants, and the customary working methods in the group, among other factors. Additionally, what happens during the meeting may be crucially important for the way the chairperson enacts his or her role, particularly as other participants respond to the chairperson's attempts to carry out the chairing activities. When the participants ratify, or challenge, the chairperson's right to move through agenda items, add new agenda items, sanction inappropriate conduct, and allocate turns, the chairperson reacts to their actions and reactions, and those negotiations shape what turns out to be the enactment of the role. Our interest in this chapter is to describe and illustrate a way of studying role enactment; we do so by examining the ways in which a particular chairperson carried out his chairing activities during upper management meetings of a corporation in transition.

The data for our analysis consisted of a film, *Corporation: After Mr. Sam*, which represented portions of meetings of the upper management personnel of a corporation in transition. The primary purpose for the meetings was to discuss the succession of the current president and founder of the company, Sam Steinberg, who was planning on stepping down from president of the corporation to chairman of the board. In the planning meeting, the participants worked on an agenda for meetings that would occur during a several-day retreat at Palomino. In the Palomino meetings, there were four items on the agenda: decision-making, professional management, succession, and structure. In both the planning meeting and the Palomino meetings, Harry, the director of organizational development, served as chairperson. We assume that the role had been formally granted to him; it appears that all the participants understood Harry's role as chairperson and that no one contested it.

The goal of this analysis is to show that the ways in which Harry carried out a number of his chairing activities were consistent with two interrelated premises that seem to have shaped or guided the participants' conduct.[1] The first premise was that the wishes of the participants should be taken into account when performing such activities. When Harry performed certain actions on behalf of the group, he often did so in ways that explicitly displayed his orientation to those actions as requiring input and/or ratification from other meeting participants. In this sense, Harry might have considered his role one of facilitating group participation and participatory decision making. Even in performing actions that could rightly be considered the prerogative of the chairperson, Harry showed himself to be attentive to the needs and preferences of the other meeting participants.

The second premise was that the wishes of the other participants, rather than the wishes of the chairperson, should carry more weight in determining how the meeting is run. In effect this meant that Harry deferred to other participants' voices on issues of procedures. Harry often treated his services as chairperson as contingent upon the emergent preferences of the group. Harry made judgments about when to exercise his prerogative to intervene as chairperson but was also quick to withdraw or abandon actions that were met with resistance from the group. Although Harry operated with a sense of procedural propriety, he did not push the group to operate accordingly if they displayed an unwillingness to do so. In accordance with this premise, when Harry performed chairing activities, these activities were shaped by the actions and reactions of other participants, particularly Mr. Sam.[2]

METHODS

Our analysis of the chairperson's conduct was developed using conversation analytic methods. Conversation analysts describe the practices through which members of a culture conduct and understand social interaction, including how participants coordinate social activities, accomplish conversational actions, and negotiate taking turns. For a more complete discussion of the assumptive base of conversation analysis, see Garfinkel and Sacks (1970), Heritage (1984), Atkinson and Heritage (1984), Maynard and Clayman (1991), Schegloff (1992), and Pomerantz and Fehr (1997).

Our analysis of the enactment of the chairperson's role is an application of a conversation analytic approach to studying relationship and role enactments. Pomerantz and Mandelbaum (2005) clarified and further developed a framework for studying how persons rely on assumptions and understandings regarding incumbents of particular role and relationship categories when they interact. Pomerantz and

Mandelbaum showed how people in interaction use their knowledge of the activities, motives, rights, responsibilities, and competencies that they regard as appropriate for incumbents of a role category when they interact, both in enacting particular roles and in explicitly invoking those roles.

The film, *Corporation: After Mr. Sam*, was far from ideal data for this conversation-analytic project. First, the film record of the conduct during the meetings omitted an unknown number of segments, which meant that we had little confidence that the sequence of events presented in the film represented the actual sequence of activities. Even more problematic for our purpose, usually only the current speaker and sometimes the intended recipient of the talk were visually presented on the film. The conduct of other participants was unavailable to us. We abandoned several projects when it became clear that the data necessary to confirm or disconfirm our claims were unavailable.

Once we decided to focus our study on the enactment of the chairperson's role, we watched the videotape for all instances in which the chairperson engaged in verbal and/or nonverbal conduct. We then identified the activities and actions performed in each instance and formed collections (e.g., dealing with agenda items, sanctioning conduct, summarizing and interpreting participants' contributions, and allocating turns). We analyzed each instance in each collection and looked for similarities and differences in the collections.

ANALYSIS

In the first section of the analysis, we discuss three instances in which Harry performed chairing activities in ways that encouraged contributions from other participants and worked to ensure that decisions were made with consent from other group members. In the second section, we examine three instances in which Harry performed chairing activities in ways that displayed his orientation to the chairperson role for these meetings as deferential, merely serving the will of the group. In each of these three instances, Harry's attempts to perform chairing activities were met with resistance or opposition, and Harry deferred to the views of the other participants and/or abandoned his attempts.

Part I—Facilitative Chairing

Example 1 of Facilitative Chairing.   One of the four topics for discussion at the Palomino meetings was structure, whether and how the corporation should be restructured. When Harry introduced the topic and led up to initiating discussion, he did so in a way that invited the participants' input on the procedure for the discussion.

226 HARRY S: ... structure should look like. The most important point (.) is that
227   everyone recognizes a need for a new look into this (.) structure.
228   (2.0) ((*Rustle of pages being turned.*)) Your task gentlemen
229   (0.8) based upon your reading of the organizational reports
230   submitted to the President, the pre-reading provided for you,
231   and the discussion outline, determine the senior management
232   structure of Steinberg's Limited, taking into consideration the
233   decision-making process, the implementation of the decision,
234   the relationship of senior management to the rest of the
235   organization, the integration of divisional organizations, and the
236   functioning of the corporation. (3.0) ((*Rustle of pages being*
237   *turned.*)) Now how do you wish to proceed. A suggestion was
238   made to me during the ... ((*Talk covered over by the voiceover*)).

In (237), Harry indicated that he was seeking the participants' views on the procedure they should follow in discussing advocated senior management structures ("Now how do you wish to proceed."). However, rather than ending at that point and waiting for their suggestions, he continued on to offer a suggestion. Yet, in offering it, he did not claim authorship but rather credited another participant, unnamed, with the suggestion ("A suggestion was made to me during the ..." [237–238]).

In opening the discussion, Harry employed several practices that displayed a view of the role of the chairperson as a facilitator. Rather than asserting how they would proceed in the discussion, Harry treated the procedure as a decision for the group to make. He framed the procedure for the discussion as a group decision in three ways: (a) by prefacing his offering of a proposed procedure with a request for the participants' input ("how do you wish to proceed"); (b) by formulating the proposed procedure as a "suggestion," which set up the relevance of the participants' accepting or rejecting the suggestion; and (c) by crediting the authorship of the "suggestion" to another participant, thereby reinforcing the legitimacy of other meeting participants' making procedural suggestions.

Example 2 of Facilitative Chairing.   During the Palomino meetings, Harry, as chairperson, structured the discussion around the topics that the group had previously decided would be on the Palomino agenda. Although the group had been discussing the issue of professional management, a topic on the agenda, Irving proposed an activity that had not been agreed upon in advance, namely that each group member share what he saw as barriers to professional management. As chairperson, Harry might have unilaterally adopted or rejected the suggested activity; instead, he treated the suggestion as a matter about which the group should decide.

```
597  IRVING L:   =and I will (.) Alright so I say, to start it off, why don't we give,
598              why don't we take the barriers .hh as Oscar just suggested and
599              say we have a whole bunch of stuff listed that-these are the
600              reasons w:hy we're not a professional (.) uh company eh? We
601              don't run a professional managerial style. hh so let's take these
602              things and let's put 'em on the table=I would like to suggest that
603              we do this .h and let's hear w:hy people have suggested them
604              and why they feel or what things they're referring to and I don't
605              think we should defend any of these things, > I don't think the
606              objective is to come and say "Well you know why we did this
607              was because we had that." I think we should just bring out and
608              let the people say w:hy they feel these things were suggested (.)
609              and I think we're gonna learn more (.) about what's wrong (.)
610              than we would in any other manner. <
611              ((Several people talking at once.))
612  (    ):    (I think that was) a good suggestion (.) actually?
613  (    ):    The that we look at barriers to [xxx
614  HARRY S:                                  [How do you feel about barriers?
615              You wanta go into barriers?=
616  (    ):    =Yes I would=
617  (    ):    =I think it's a good suggestion.
618  (    ):    (xxxx)
619  (    ):    Absolutely.
620  HARRY S:   (xxxx) We're on barriers now.
```

After Irving made his suggestion, the speaker of (612) responded positively and the speaker of (613) may have been positive as well. Having heard Irving's suggestion and at least one endorsement, Harry turned to the group to ask if they would like to discuss barriers, ostensibly attempting to determine whether or not there was sufficient support for the proposed activity (614–615). In response, three unidentified speakers indicated support for discussing barriers (616, 617, and 619). It was only after soliciting the group's sentiment and seeing a show of support for the proposed activity that Harry announced engagement in that activity ("We're on barriers now." [620]).

To reiterate, Harry enacted his role of chairperson by facilitating the realization of another participant's suggestion regarding the next appropriate activity for the group. He did this through a combination of polling the group for support or opposition (614–615) and then explicitly "announcing" the group's decision (620). With the announcement, he marked the transition from discussing professional management in general to discussing barriers to professional management, a transition that thereby was framed as made in the service of the participants' preferences.

Example 3 of Facilitative Chairing.　There are a number of ways in which a chairperson can bring a meeting to a close. Chairpersons may unilaterally announce that it is time to adjourn the meeting, they may ask for a motion to adjourn the meeting, they may suggest ending the meeting and solicit reaction, to name but a few possibilities. The practices that a chairperson uses to close a meeting are part of how he or she enacts the role of chairperson.

Near the end of one of the days at the Palomino meetings, Harry used one set of practices to close the meeting that was consistent with the role of facilitative chairing. He initiated an adjournment sequence, displaying an orientation to the potential offense of delaying an issue that was just raised by one of the participants. James had just made an appeal to Mr. Sam that, just as he would likely discuss succession with his family, so too should he discuss it with his senior executives. Mr. Sam responded, indicating that he was doing just that with these meetings. At that point, with no gap, Harry addressed James and initiated an adjournment sequence (1015).

1008	JAMES D:	But the fact is, if you're
1009		willing to accord then (.) because of the (.) family ties, the
1010		matter of discussion on a rational basis (.) with the family (.) we
1011		think that it should be done (.) on a rational basis also with your
1012		senior executives.
1013		(0.2)
1014	SAM S:	That's why you're here tonight=
1015	HARRY S:	=Well eh Jim that's in view of the eh (0.5) we agree to adjourn
1016		at ↑nine > I don't think there's much sense in starting the next
1017		item on the agenda, which is succession < (.) With a your
1018		agreement, I suggest we adjourn (.) here and ↑now gives us a
1019		good night's ↑rest.
1020	( ):	(xxxx) finish it off in ten minutes.
1021		((Laughter and people talking.))
1022	HARRY S:	Huh?
1023	( ):	I think we'll all sleep on it.
1024	HARRY S:	Alright, we'll all sleep on it. (0.5) ((Somebody starts to speak.))
1025		(1.0)
1026	HARRY S:	Alright the (.) meeting is adjourned 'til tomorrow morning at (.)
1027		nine o'clock when we'll discuss succession.

In negotiating the adjournment, Harry showed himself to be attentive to the fact that James had just broached a legitimate agenda item and treated this item as worthy of eventual discussion. The warrant Harry provided for shelving the succession discussion at that time was that the group had made a prior agreement to meet until 9 p.m. In his language choices, specifically "With a your agreement" (1017–1018), he displayed his orientation to decision making in the group as a matter of consensus. Instead of performing the adjournment either by declaring the meeting adjourned or by requesting a motion to adjourn, he opened the adjournment sequence with a mitigated recommendation or suggestion ("… I don't think there's much sense in starting the next item on the agenda, which is succession<(.) With a your agreement, I suggest we adjourn" (1016–1018)). This allowed an opportunity space for other participants to comment on the move to adjourn before it was actualized. After one intendedly humorous counterargument to delaying the topic of succession until the next day (1020), another speaker supported delaying the succession discussion until the next day (1023). Harry accepted and echoed this position (1024). Having provided the opportunity for the participants to react to the adjournment suggestion and having received support for the idea, Harry then declared the meeting adjourned (1027–1028).

Part II—Deferential Chairing

In two instances, Harry attempted to sanction what he considered to be inappropriate meeting conduct. In both cases, Harry's attempts were met with opposition. In the face of opposition, particularly from Mr. Sam, Harry deferred.

Example 1 of Deferential Chairing.   During the planning meeting, Mr. Sam and Jack had a fairly long confrontational exchange. Jack was clearly loud and forceful in his speech. After one emotional speech, several participants started to respond to Jack's point. In this context, Harry attempted to exercise some control over the direction and/or manner of the discussion (134, 136).

```
125  JACK L:    Are you running one business? Are you still running an- an
126             Ontario business? You wanna be the general manager here? Or
127             do you want to act as the President? Do you wanna act as a
128             corporate- as a corporate President for everybody or for one?
129             (1.0)
130  (    ):    [Jack
131  JACK L:    [That's a very, exactly the same [as I'm bringing out.
132  (    ):                                      [Jim (xxxx)
133  (    ):    [I just want to make sure we get, Mr. President
134  HARRY S:   [Um Uh … uh … C'd I- C'd I [bring this back (0.5)
135  (    ):                               [I just want to raise =
136  HARRY S:   = C'd I bring this back on course (1.0) th[at uh
137  SAM S:                                               [You're bringing it
138             back on course
139  HARRY S:   I'm bringing it [right back on course] and say let's get right=
140  SAM S:                     [(We're on course)   ]
141  HARRY S:   =back to the problem of making maximum use (0.5) best use of
```

```
142              our time (0.8) and I don't think that this kind of interchange
143              (0.5) has contri[buted anything
144 ARNOLD S:              [Well, I think Jack has raised a good
145              ex[ample ((several voices speaking at once.))
146 (   ):      [a ve[ry good example
147 ARNOLD S:         [a good [example
148 (   ):      ((Yelling.))      [The whole purpose of all our exercise is if
149              we're not going to run our business right.
150 ARNOLD S: I think Jack has given an excellent ((voices speaking at once))
151              example of the shortcomings =
152 (   ):      =Yes.
153 ARNOLD S: in the struc[ture
154 HARRY S:              [Alright. [Alright.
155 ARNOLD S:                      [toward (xxxx) control
156 JACK L:    That's right!
157 (   ):      It's all how you interpret it. I thought Jack gave an excellent
158              example=
159 (   ):      =Excellent=
160 (   ):      =of the shortcomings of not having clear un-
161              [clear understanding of the business.
162 (   ):      [Right. That's the way I interpreted it.
163 JACK L:    ((Yelling.)) Yeah! That's right. But you first have to have
164              struc[ture to, in order to do it.
165 HARRY S:         [Alright
166 HARRY S:   Alright, Mel Mel has the floor.
167 MEL D:     Obviously (.) gentlemen ...
```

In (134), Harry made his first attempt to control or redirect the discussion in overlap ("Um Uh ... uh ... C'd I- C'd I bring this back"). He made a second attempt in (136), this time speaking in the clear ("C'd I bring this back on course (1.0) that uh"). In and through these attempts at intervention, Harry displayed that he was monitoring the participants' conduct so as to determine the appropriateness or inappropriateness of it at that point in the meeting, and he treated himself as entitled to sanction inappropriate meeting conduct. The inappropriateness of the conduct, as Harry formulated it, involved deviating from the meeting's business. That is exactly the type of monitoring that a chairperson would be expected to do. When Harry attempted to "bring this back on course," the implicit message was that, in his judgment, either the topic of the discussion or their manner of speaking had gotten "off course." In the capacity of chairperson, Harry treated himself as entitled to judge particular conduct as inappropriate for accomplishing the meeting's business and consequentially as entitled to attempt to alter it.

Although he treated himself as entitled to alter the participants' conduct during the meeting, his practices for intervening were consistent with those of a chairperson who used facilitative practices. Rather than asserting that Jack (and perhaps others) were engaging in inappropriate conduct, he tempered the criticism and the forcefulness of the action by employing an interrogative formulation, "C'd I bring this back on course." Although he was sanctioning proposedly inappropriate conduct, he used a formulation, "C'd I," that seemed to ask the participants for their willingness to comply.

Mr. Sam took issue with Jack's intervention, implying that any corrective action was unwarranted ("We're <u>on</u> course" [140]). Mr. Sam's counter occurred in overlap with Harry's speech so it is not clear whether Harry heard it. Harry continued with his critique of the participants' conduct, claiming that the interchange between Mr. Sam and Jack had not made the best use of the meeting time. Harry's critique was strongly formulated: "I don't think that this kind of interchange (0.5) has contributed anything" (142–143). Although Harry might have been seen to be criticizing both Mr. Sam's and Jack's conduct when he characterized the problematic discussion as an interchange, in actuality Jack had been the more vocal participant in the preceding exchange and the other participants treated Harry's criticism as directed at Jack's talk.

Arnold likewise took issue with Harry's criticism, defending the usefulness of what Jack had said ("Well, I think Jack has raised a good example" (144–145)). At that point, several speakers echoed the sentiment that they valued Jack's talk and/or that they viewed the preceding interchange as legitimate. In this interactional environment, support for Jack's comments and/or for the utility of the interchange were offered as a disagreement with, or rejection of, Harry's attempted sanctioning of their conduct. In light of the responses that his criticism received, Harry yielded ("Alright Alright" [154]) and abandoned his attempt to further redirect the discussion. Although explicitly acceding was a way of ending the sequence that he started, Harry definitively closed the sequence by granting Mel the right to be next speaker (166).

To summarize, Harry's criticism of the participants' conduct during discussion was formatted in a way that might have invited responses. The responses of the other participants could be seen as a fairly pronounced "backlash" in the wake of Harry's attempt to regulate a heated interchange between Jack and Mr. Sam and to sanction Jack. After provoking strong resistance toward, and disagreement with, his criticism, particularly from Mr. Sam, Harry acquiesced, deferring to the views of the other participants. His selecting next speaker opened up the possibility of shifting the talk away from the participants' opposition to his attempt at controlling their conduct.

Example 2 of Deferential Chairing. Prior to the segment to be presented, Irving proposed an exercise in which the participants articulated the specific barriers that they believed were preventing the full development of a professional managerial style. Several participants shared what they believed were such barriers. Jack, building on a point that James had made, argued that the structure at the corporate level was too heavy for their retail operation and suggested that more decision-making authority should rest at the divisional level. Arnold expressed some opposition toward this argument and then further developed his perspective on the problem, arguing that the duplication of organizational duties did not exist at the corporate level but at the divisional level. What was emerging was a clear disagreement about whether the duplication was at the corporate or divisional level.

```
692  ARNOLD S:  But surely the corollary to that (.) is that the duplication existed
693             at the corp- at the divisional level. You're saying that the
694             divisional level had to have what the corporate didn't. Wo' but
695             surely (.) in in a discussion (0.2) which is now coming out in
696             the in in work that Bill's group is doing (.) they're discovering
697             that the duplication is in fact taking place at the division (.) and
698             the real need is at ↑corporate? I mean all I'm saying Jack is that
699             in fact I agree that duplication exists.
700  JACK L:    But Arnold=
701  ARNOLD S:  =But you're assuming that duplication is at the corporate an' not
702             at the division
703  JACK L:    ((Shouting.)) But (.) corporate started to build up (immaterial)
704             that was at the division. Now where should it be?=
705  ARNOLD S:  =Maybe [xxx corporate who say the division grew up not=
706  JACK L:           [xxx at corporate?
707  ARNOLD S:  =even though it was at the corporate. (xxxx) Jack, I am agreeing
708             that some[one should have sat down.
709  JACK L:            [Okay (0.5) Right! That's all what I am saying.
710             ((Everybody talking at the same time.))
711  HARRY S:   Would you please speak (.) one at a time and I think
712             professionalism can start right here the way we conduct the
713             meeting. Too many meetings in the past have been
714             unprofessional in that (.) problems in an unorganized manner
715             have been tossed on the table. Philosophies are spewed out.
716             (0.5) So professional at the meeting means (.) identifying the
717             problem? (0.5) moving from there to different means of solving
718             them (.) a:nd this is where we fall flat on our (.) backs again and
719             again (.) is not nailing down ((hand taps table)) who's to do
720             what and when ((hand taps table)) and how ((hand taps table)).
721             (0.5) If you want to turn this thing into (.) a >fish market
722             gentlemen<, it's your meeting but=
723             ((Harry's gaze during above comment was directed to the entire
724             table, moving from person to person))
725  JACK L:    =Look Harry, uh I I wanna stop (.) and critique what you're
```

```
726                saying with your=
727  HARRY S:     =Go ahead=
728  JACK L:      =I am saying that at least if you don't get out feelings ((hand
729                tap)) on this ((tap)) table ((tap)) today ((tap)) and Monday
730                ((tap)) and Tuesday ((tap)), we'll all go ((tap)) back and say
731                "We're-we should have said and we didn't say" ((tap)) and it's
732                the feelings ((tap)) that count ((tap)). It's the commitment
733                ((tap)) one feels inside (.) that counts, it's not words (.) and it's
734                not it's the deeds and the feelings and the commitment we have
735                (.) to this organization to be better tomorrow and today. And I
736                for one am objecting to your system of method and monitoring
737                because I am not doing this for a mental exercises, I am doing
738                this much more, there's much more at stake than a mental
739                exercise (.) and I don't want that kind of monitoring from you=
740  HARRY S:     =But m:y [my commitment
741  JACK L:               [I want some heat to come out (.) ((repeated finger-
742                pointing shake probably toward Harry)) I want some feeling to
743                come out and I want this thing to come out so that when you go
744                away we know we've done the job (.) thoroughly and we
745                understand our job to do so we all go back and do the job
746                together (.) not disjointedly (.) and not feeling that we haven't
747                been heard and seen and felt'n put the things we feel on the
748                table
749                ((People talking at once.))
750                ((Jack's gaze during the above comment was directed solely
751                toward Harry))
752  SAM S:       When I started out the meeting I said each one of you in your
753                report there must be something that you feel and we recognize
754                that and this is one of the reasons we're here. So if there are in
755                tho:se those items that you (.) consider uppermost that you
756                reduce to writing and felt free to say so (.) what is uppermost in
757                your minds that you feel has some restraining influence I think
758                it should like Jack said (0.5) uh (0.7) brought out?
759  JACK L:      °Absolutely°
760  SAM S:       Fr:eely spoken.
761                (0.5)
762  (    ):       [Well I I
763  SAM S:       [To the extent that we think it's pretty well covered by what's
764                already been said then we move ↓forward.
765                (1.0)
766  ARNOLD S:    Harry, I would like to deal with a barrier that has been talked
```

As can be seen from the beginning of this segment, Jack and Arnold were continuing their oppositional exchange. The manner in which they discussed the issue involved considerable competition for speaking turns and they spoke using comparatively loud and forceful intonational contours. In (710), multiple participants began to speak at the same time. There was clear competition for the speaking floor just after this contentious exchange between Arnold and Jack.

In (711–722), Harry provided a heavy critique of the manner in which the participants had been conducting the discussion. Several aspects of this critique are noteworthy. Harry directed the participants to speak one at a time. Although it was grammatically formulated as a request ("Would you please speak one at a time" [711]), it was produced intonationally as a directive. In directing the participants to speak one at a time, Harry was enacting a responsibility associated with chairing: sanctioning conduct during the meeting that proposedly is inappropriate or counterproductive for accomplishing the meeting's goals. Given that multiple participants had just been speaking simultaneously, Harry's directive also functioned to sanction their conduct. Thus, Harry treated himself as entitled not only to issue directives about appropriate conduct during meetings but also to issue sanctions when actual conduct fell short of these standards.

Part of what gave Harry's turn the flavor of a heavy critique were the words he chose to describe the interactional conduct of participants. In (714–715) Harry claimed that problems are "tossed on the table" in an unorganized manner, in (715) he argued that philosophies are "spewed out," and in (721–722) he used the powerful metaphor of a "fish market" to frame the participants' conduct as consonant with a radically different interactional setting than what is ostensibly called for in a professional management meeting. With these language choices, he cast the participants' communicative behavior as undisciplined or unfocused gushing. This comparatively strong and critical language added to the impression that he was engaged in a strong critique.

Interestingly, in (721–722), Harry appeared to take the position that his attempts to monitor and regulate speakership issues were contingent upon the wishes of the group. In saying, "If you want to turn this thing into (.) a >fish market gentlemen<, it's your meeting but" Harry treated his services as chair as optional, contingent upon the wishes of the other meeting participants, although he also implicitly proposed that these services were part of what prevented the meeting from simply dissolving into a contest of who could be the most aggressive in their turn-taking behavior.

Jack jumped in to announce that he wanted to critique Harry's activity (725–726). In keeping with his participatory style, Harry ratified Jack's right to critique his chairing activity ("Go ahead" [727]). At this point, Jack launched into an extended argument about the necessity for participants to openly express their feelings about the organization and explicitly criticized Harry's system of monitoring, essentially claiming that it prevented the full expression of their feelings.

Following Jack's strong objection to Harry's monitoring and controlling the participants' conduct, Mr. Sam supported Jack's argument about the need for feelings to come out in the open. Insofar as there was a dispute about communication style on the floor between Harry and Jack, Mr. Sam took Jack's side in the dispute. Harry did not attempt to further his argument once Mr. Sam articulated his position.

Example 3 of Deferential Chairing.   Although most of the participants' turns were initiated with no intervention from the chairperson, there are a number of instances in which participants sought the right to be next speaker from the chairperson and in which the chairperson granted that right to a participant.[3] In almost all cases in which the chairperson granted a participant the right to be next speaker, the designated person took the floor and the other participants refrained from starting to speak. On one occasion, however, the chairperson's attempt to grant a participant the right to be next speaker failed; it was not ratified and was in fact disregarded by the other participants.

In the interaction leading up to the segment to be presented, Jack described his vision for a potential restructuring of the company. After Jack introduced the details of his plan, several contentious exchanges emerged among some of the participants. Mr. Sam expressed some confusion and/or skepticism about this restructuring plan; Jack and other participants responded with attempts to clarify the details of Jack's proposal. Oscar criticized Jack's plan, arguing that it would not substantively alter the current working methods. Mr. Sam asked Oscar if he would accept the plan, setting aside the issue of job titles; Oscar replied that he would not because it imposed a structure on the incoming president that he may not want. Oscar also criticized the plan for putting too many people in a position to be reporting to the president. Mr. Sam disagreed with that claim, arguing that there would actually be fewer people reporting to the president. While Oscar and Mr. Sam continued to debate about what the reporting relationships would look like, Irving attempted to gain the floor and Harry attempted to grant Irving the right to be the next speaker (379–390).

```
369  SAM S:     [There will be fewer people, there will be fewer people if you
370             have group Vice-Presidents.
371  OSCAR P:   No we'll gonna have uh … [(xxxx)
372  SAM S:                               [Fewer people than he would now
373             ↑ha:ve, then the man couldn't be in charge of a group of areas =
374  OSCAR P:   =I'm talking about the people answering to the President.
375  (     ):    Eleven now.
376             (2.0)
377  SAM S:     There'd be fewer people.
```

378   ((*Five or six people talking at the same time.*))
379 IRVING L: You know something (0.2) Can I say something (1.0)
380 HARRY S: Irving.
381 IRVING L: Could I say something? (1.5) Could I say something?
382 ARNOLD S: All the areas now report to all the people in this ↑room, =
383 IRVING L: =Look=
384 (HARRY S): =Irving=
385 IRVING L: =Look, let me let me just add this =
386 ARNOLD S: =How can you. How can you talk about the President, a man a
387   man who doesn't exist at the present time ... =
388 (   ):   =Talking about yourself.
389 ARNOLD S: Uh ... but now you're gonna start talking about yourself =
390 IRVING L: =You know, right now, =
391 JAMES D: =All our previous discussions, and we had some before we
392   came up here to Palomino, we thought ...

As Oscar and Mr. Sam continued to argue about the ramifications of Jack's plan for restructuring, several participants made simultaneous bids for the floor, perhaps to break the apparent deadlock (378). This was clearly developing into a highly competitive interactional environment, one that was itself built out of the larger debate about the proper kind of restructuring that should be undertaken.

In (379), Irving attempted to secure a turn-at-talk in this competitive environment ("You know something [0.2] Can I say something"). Whereas other speakers had simply self-selected and began to make their points, Irving self-selected and provided only a bid to secure a subsequent slot for himself to speak in the clear. Harry clearly oriented to Irving's bid when he said "Irving" (380). Like many of the other occasions in which Harry granted a participant the right to be the next speaker, Harry performed this granting simply by saying the participant's name. Unlike the other occasions in which Harry allocated a next turn to a participant at the completion of a sequence of actions, on this occasion Harry granted Irving right to next turn while other participants were still vying for the floor. Neither Irving's turn nor Harry's turn were fully in the clear. Although he had been recognized to speak by the chairperson, Irving did not take the turn that he had projected he would take.

Notice that Harry granted Irving the right to be next speaker even though multiple speakers had laid claim to the floor. Harry recognized Irving to the exclusion of other potential speakers. One explanation for Harry's selecting Irving over the other participants is that Irving's talk was built to secure permission to speak whereas other participants simply began speaking. It is not clear whether Irving was speaking principally to Harry when he said, "You know something (0.2) Can I say something" (379); regardless, it may be just the kind of formulation

that the chairperson will treat as an opportunity to exercise his prerogative to allocate turns.

When Arnold spoke next (386–387), he oriented to the debate between Oscar and Mr. Sam regarding the reporting relationships rather
than to Irving's turn bids (379, 381, 383) or Harry's turn-granting
(384). Irving again attempted to speak, this time employing a turn-
initial "look," which, in this context, appeared to be an attempt to
bring other participants into alignment as recipients. This was a comparatively more assertive interactional method for securing a turn-at-
talk than the prior attempt in that it did not request subsequent access
to the speaking floor but instead provided an explicitly other-directed
bid for the other participants' attention. Harry again recognized Irving
to speak, again using his first name to grant the right to the next turn
(384). Clearly, Harry was tracking who in the meeting wanted to
speak. By twice recognizing Irving to speak in such close proximity, it
is likely that Harry also was orienting to the difficulty that Irving was
having in securing a turn. Irving attempted to speak (385, 390) but
then abandoned the attempts possibly because other participants either were speaking or simply not displaying recipiency. Harry did not
attempt to recognize Irving after these attempts.

For Harry, one aspect of enacting the role of chairperson was calling
on other participants to speak. One of the main reasons for assuming
that responsibility is to ensure that all participants who desire to speak
are given an opportunity. This process worked well in almost all instances in the meetings; when Harry recognized someone as the legitimate next speaker, that person took the next turn with no other
participants competing for the floor. When turn-taking happened in
that fashion, it represented tacit ratification of Harry's right to allocate turns. In this case, however, that ratification was absent. Instead,
participants failed to orient to Harry's recognition of the next speaker
and, in so doing, denied his authority to allocate turns. Thus, it appears that Harry's authority to allocate turns was context-sensitive.
Ratification of his right in one instance did not necessarily imply stable
or absolute entitlement in all circumstances. The failure of the participants to ratify Harry's claimed authority to allocate the next turn
probably was due to the very contentious and competitive interactional environment in which the attempts were made. In this environment, Mr. Sam and Oscar had previously expressed absolutely
polarized versions of the ramifications of Jack's proposed restructuring and the other participants showed heavy investment in weighing
in on Jack's proposal. One possibility is that in such an environment,
Harry's entitlement to formally recognize next speakers was a rather
low priority. Perhaps their own commitment to weigh in on the con-

troversial plan overshadowed their respecting Harry's chairing activity of allocating turns.

DISCUSSION

We have shown that the enactment of the chairperson role in organizational meetings is an interactional matter, involving not just the participants' existing understandings of chairpersons' customary role-based rights and responsibilities, but also the contingent realization of those rights and responsibilities through the communicative behavior of all meeting participants. We have further shown that role enactment is not achieved unilaterally by the incumbent in a given role, but rather that this achievement is a product of the complex interactional dynamics between role incumbent and other meeting participants. Role incumbents may speak in ways that propose their entitlement to perform certain actions associated with their role, though such proposals are subject to implicit or explicit ratification or opposition from others.

We have argued that Harry enacted the role of chairperson in the planning meeting and in the Palomino meetings in ways that displayed his orientation to that role as involving: (a) facilitation of group participation and participatory decision making, and (b) deference to other participants regarding the need for the chairperson's services on a case-by-case basis. Importantly, this orientation is an alternative to other styles of chairing meetings, although we have not examined enough data from meetings to offer a description of those other styles. Numerous factors may shape the particular style with which chairpersons enact their role, including their analysis of the organizational setting and their analysis of the emergent interactional demands of the meeting. Harry's style of enacting the chairperson role in these meetings appeared to be tailored to both the organizational setting and to the interactional issues that emerged in the meeting.

With respect to the organizational setting, we would argue that Harry's facilitative, participatory style of chairing the meetings was especially well-suited to the setting. The meetings consisted of high-ranking management personnel, including Mr. Sam, the president of the organization. The very future of the corporation—its leadership, its organizational structure, its working methods—was arguably at stake in these meetings and the decisions made would likely affect all meeting participants. Given their organizational positions and the task before them, the participants in these meetings may have assumed that they were entitled, even obligated, to fully voice their perspectives and persuade other participants of their views. In such a setting, it might have been especially difficult or problematic for Harry to enact the chairperson role in more authoritative ways, by restricting opportunities for others to contribute or by unilaterally transitioning through the agenda items. This likely presented a significant challenge for Harry, who had to find ways to balance the potentially competing goals of ensuring productive dialogue in a timely manner (ostensibly the task with which he had been charged) and respecting the contributions of important organizational members. More data would be needed to determine whether Harry generally enacted facilitative and/or deferential chairing or if he varied his chairing practices according to the context.

With respect to the emergent interactional demands of the meeting, we have shown that Harry performed chairing activities in ways that displayed his awareness and analysis of the ongoing sequences of actions and activities. When James introduced the issue of succession near the scheduled time to conclude the meeting (Excerpt 3) and when Irving attempted to secure a turn-at-talk (Excerpt 6), Harry performed subsequent actions in ways that demonstrably took the current activities and interests of these meeting participants into consideration. Thus, Harry's enactment of chairing involved not just his abstract awareness of what might be generally expected from the chairperson in such a setting but also a practical analysis of how to perform his duties as chairperson in ways that would show himself to be oriented to the activities and interests of other meeting participants.

We conclude with some comments on a kind of contribution that conversation analysts can make with respect to studying role enactments in organizational contexts that was not discussed thus far. The six excerpts discussed in this chapter contained instances of activities commonly performed by chairpersons: introducing and framing issues for discussion that were on the agenda (Excerpt 1), dealing with participants' suggestions to address particular issues as the next order of business (Excerpt 2), adjourning the meeting (Excerpt 3), sanctioning proposedly inappropriate meeting conduct (Excerpt 4 and Excerpt 5), and managing the participants' taking of turns (Excerpt 6).[4] In each of the instances discussed in the chapter, the activity in question was the official interactional business being addressed.

In addition to studying blatant or explicit instances of activities, conversation analysts study the ways in which people perform activities off the record, embedded in other activities. For example, Jefferson (1987) studied ways in which persons may correct other persons without correction being the official interaction business. They do this by embedding the correction in talk that is occupied with other official interactional business. Lerner (2003) showed how speakers may select persons to be a next speaker not with any apparent or obvious next speaker selection technique (e.g., by gaze or name) but by, for example, seeking information about a matter about which only some participants have knowledge.

In this chapter, we discussed two instances in which Harry's attempts to sanction meeting conduct were met with resistance from other group members. In both instances, Harry backed down from his critique. Thus, it appears that Harry's willingness to sanction inappropriate meeting conduct was contingent upon the ratification or rejection from other group members. Two features of the sanctioning attempts should be highlighted. The first is that in both instances the primary thrust of Harry's talk was to sanction inappropriate behavior. It was the official interactional business being conducted. The second feature was that Harry's sanctions were formulated in ways that projected ratification or resistance as relevant next actions. In Excerpt 4, Harry's interrogative formulation ("C'd I bring this back on course") framed the action of "bringing this back on course" as contingent upon the group's willingness to allow it. In Excerpt 5, Harry's extended turn began with "Would you please speak one at a time." Although he spoke through the projected slot for others to actually register acceptance or rejection, the action itself was formulated as a request, not a directive. In sum, in both instances Harry performed explicit sanctions and the sanctions were formulated in ways that provide for the relevance of ratification or resistance as relevant next actions.

In addition to the explicit, on-the-record attempts to sanction inappropriate meeting conduct, Harry performed embedded sanctions of inappropriate meeting conduct. In two instances, the on-the-record action or official interactional business was selecting a next speaker, an action that Harry and others treated throughout the meetings as provisionally within the rights of the chairperson. In the process of selecting a next speaker, Harry was able to perform an off-the-record sanction. We did not, in the first instance, notice these interactional events as possible sanctions, that is, until we applied the techniques of conversation analysts, specifically close examination of the details of interaction.

In our attempt to study the practices used for granting and taking turns, we identified all the instances in which Harry attempted to grant a participant the right to be next speaker. In examining the ways in which he called on participants, we noticed that most of the time, a simple name sufficed. On two occasions, he used more interesting and complicated formulations to call on a next speaker.

On one occasion during the Palomino meetings, there were several instances of overlapping speech and overtly competitive simultaneous speech among an unknown number of participants. In close proximity to this competitive interactional environment, Harry selected Arnold as next speaker ("Arnold you're speaking. I recognize you" [440]). In contrast to the usual way that Harry selected next speakers (saying first name only), here he provided an additional explicit authorization to speak, one that was comparatively formal and conventionally procedural ("I recognize you"). In this interactional environment, Harry's selection of a displayedly formal procedure for allocating a speaking turn may have functioned as a "reminder" of the proposed need for orderly and equitable turn-taking procedures and, through this, as an implicit critique of the proposedly less orderly quality of the turn-taking behavior in the preceding interactional environment.

The second occasion also involved a point at which multiple parties were competing for the speaking floor. Within this sequence, Harry interjected a story and then called on Guy to speak. Following Guy's turn, there was appreciative applause and then Harry called on Jack to speak by saying "Jack, you have the legitimate floor" (476). Similar to the first occasion, Harry first named the selected next speaker and then supplemented it with an explicit authorization to speak. Harry's framing of Jack's claim to the floor as "legitimate" can be heard as a subtle implication that some claim to the floor had been illegitimate. This implication is available in large part because of the details of the preceding interactional environment, which included multiple instances of overlapping speech and competition for the speaking floor, both of which may be, at least for Harry, illegitimate forms of participation.

Because the off-the-record sanctions were embedded within the action of selecting a next speaker, the next relevant responses would be to ratify or not ratify Harry's selection of next speaker, not to ratify or reject the sanction. In these instances, the tacit ratifications of Harry's selections of next speaker became the interactional business at hand. The end result was that Harry used a method for implicitly critiquing meeting conduct, a method that was not subject to the conditional relevance of ratification or rejection. At this point, we do not know whether or not participants change their sanctioned meeting conduct in response to embedded sanctions and, if they do, in what circumstances they do so. But without careful observational studies of the actual conduct of participants during a meeting, there is a danger of missing the subtle, implicit, and embedded ways that participants attempt to negotiate and carry out the responsibilities associated with their roles.

ENDNOTES

1. The notion of premises or cultural premises is being borrowed from Fitch (1998), who examined relationship conduct in terms of the cultural premises, which both informed actors' choices of the conduct and provided a framework for actors to understand the conduct.
2. The facilitative and deferential practices employed by Harry in the planning and the Palomino meetings seemed appropriate to the setting. The meetings consisted of high-ranking management personnel, including Mr. Sam, the president of the organization. It might have been especially difficult or inap-

propriate for Harry to enact the chairperson role with more authority and/or attempt to perform actions unilaterally in such a setting. More data would be needed to determine whether Harry generally enacted facilitative and/or deferential chairing or if he varied his chairing practices according to the context.

3. Very little work has been done on the types of occasions in which both unmoderated turn organization and moderated turn organization operate. We do not know whether one type is the default and the other type is used for "special circumstances," whether particular participants stick to using one type over the other, or whether the different types are employed for different meeting activities. To answer these questions, we would need to systematically investigate the local circumstances in which instances of each type of turn organization are employed.

4. In the first three instances, we showed that the chairperson performed these activities in ways that were consistent with a commitment to participatory decision making; in the last three instances, we demonstrated that the enactments of the chairing activities were joint production of the participants.

REFERENCES

Atkinson, J. M., & Heritage, J. C. (Eds.). (1984). *Structures of social action: Studies in conversation analysis.* Cambridge, England: Cambridge University Press.

Fitch, K. L. (1998). *Speaking relationally: Culture, communication, and interpersonal connection.* New York: Guilford.

Garfinkel, H., & Sacks, H. (1970). On formal structures of practical actions. In J. C. McKinney & E. A. Tiryakian (Eds.), *Theoretical sociology: Perspectives and developments* (pp. 337–366). New York: Appleton-Century-Crofts.

Heritage, J. (1984). *Garfinkel and ethnomethodology.* Oxford: Polity Press.

Jefferson, G. (1987). On exposed and embedded correction in conversation. In G. Button & J. R. E Lee (Eds.), *Talk and social organization* (pp. 86–100). Clevedon, England: Multilingual Matters Ltd.

Lerner, G. H. (2003). Selecting next speaker: The context-sensitive operation of a context-free organization. *Language in Society, 32,* 177–201.

Maynard, D., & Clayman, S. E. (1991). The diversity of ethnomethodology. *Annual Review of Sociology, 17,* 385–418.

Pomerantz, A., & Fehr, B. J. (1997). Conversation analysis: An approach to the study of social action as sense making practices. In T. A. van Dijk (Ed.), *Discourse: A multidisciplinary introduction* (pp. 64–92). London: Sage.

Pomerantz, A., & Mandelbaum, J. (2005). Conversation analytic approaches to the relevance and uses of relationship categories in interaction. In K. Fitch & R. E. Sanders (Eds.), *Handbook of language and social interaction* (pp. 149–171). Mahwah, NJ: Lawrence Erlbaum Associates.

Schegloff, E. A. (1992). Introduction to volume 1. In G. Jefferson (Ed.), *Lectures on conversation* (Vols. 1 & 2, pp. ix–lxiii). Oxford: Blackwell.

Chapter 3

Liberating Leadership in *Corporation: After Mr. Sam:* A Response

Gail T. Fairhurst
University of Cincinnati

Chapter 1 by Taylor and Robichaud and chapter 2 by Pomerantz and Denvir are thought provoking, not just in terms of what we learn about the organizing properties of interaction in *Corporation: After Mr. Sam*, but also in terms of what we learn about leadership. Interestingly, neither chapter sets out to study leadership per se, nor do the authors spend much time on theories-in-use about leadership (although Taylor and Robichaud come closest in this regard). In that sense, these chapters are quite reflective of the growing literature on leadership discourse.

What is so unusual about this stance? A comparison of these chapters with more mainstream leadership research reveals less emphasis on the individual and psychological and more emphasis on the social and cultural. Mainstream leadership research is often leader centric (Gronn, 2002). Like other psychological research on cognitive, affective, and conative variables that purportedly capture experience, it reduces behavior to statements of intention while losing all sense of coordinated action (Cronen, 1995). As Hosking and Morley (1991) observed, when leadership is viewed as resulting from variables "inside" or "outside" the person, the only interaction that is studied is a statistical one.

There is yet another, perhaps less obvious difference between the approaches of these two chapters with mainstream leadership research over essentializing theory. An *essence* suggests that things are what they are because that is their nature or true form despite all appearances. They are "given" objects in the world whose underlying essence must be grasped or discovered. Mainstream leadership research draws from trait, situational, and contingency theories, which suggests that there is an essence to either the leader, context, or both (Grint, 2000). For example, the trait approach emphasizes the essence of individual leaders, qualities that make them leaders regardless of the context or circumstances in which they may find themselves. Situational approaches like the Ohio State Leadership Studies emphasize the essence of particular contexts, the effective handling of which requires one leadership style over possible others. Finally, contingency approaches emphasize the essence of individual and context, where individuals must gauge their alignment with the context and respond accordingly (e.g., when a strong leader and a crisis coincide). (Although not addressed by Grint, 2000, the currently popular neocharismatic models of leadership appear to straddle essentializing leaders and leader-context combinations.)

To reject the notion of essences is to embrace a constructionist view of leadership (Grint, 2000). Without diminishing the differences between the foregoing chapters' theoretical stances, both meet the conditions of a constructionist stance as outlined by Hacking (1999). To paraphrase him, leadership "need not have existed, or need not be at all as it is." Leadership "is not determined by the nature of things; it is not inevitable" (p. 6). Hacking argues that essentialism is but the strongest form of inevitability, and abandoning it can be liberating—or can it? It is the question of just what is liberating for leadership study in the chapters by Taylor and Robichaud (chap. 1) and Pomerantz and Denvir (chap. 2) that guides this response. However, before proceeding on to this task, the terms *discourse* and *leadership* must first be unpacked.

DEFINING TERMS

It is helpful to position the two chapters in terms of the discursive analyses that they undertake. Alvesson and Kärreman (2000) generally distinguish discourse as language in use and interaction process from *Discourses*, which are constellations of talk patterns, ideas, and assumptions à la Foucauldian discursive formations. However, a closer reading of their work reveals four versions of discourse analysis that are useful to distinguish:

1. A *microdiscourse approach* focuses on social texts and the detailed study of language in use in a specific microcontext.
2. A *mesodiscourse approach* is relatively sensitive to language in use, but is interested in broader patterns and going beyond the text in order to generalize to similar local contexts.
3. A *grand discourse approach* is an assembly of discourses, ordered and presented as an integrated framework that may refer to and/or constitute organizational reality.

4. A *megadiscourse approach* suggests a more or less universal connection of discourse material, suggesting standardized ways of referring to and/or constituting certain phenomena (Alvesson & Kärreman, 2000, p. 1134).

Pomerantz and Denvir's (chap. 2) conversation analysis is clearly a microdiscourse approach, although their ethnomethodological ties would no doubt lead them to reject any micro–macro distinction. The LSI connection may also suggest a more micro approach, but it would be quite incorrect to infer that a micro approach is necessarily more interpersonal and less organizationally relevant as Boden (1994) so aptly demonstrated. By contrast, Taylor and Robichaud's (chap. 1) analysis is located at the meso level, although their discussion sometimes veers toward the grand discourse level as they talk of the clash of ideologies (e.g., family vs. managerialist).

Moreover, Taylor would prefer the term *communication* over discourse. For him, communication is interactive speech mediated by text or communication is an intertext mediated by interactive speech (Taylor & Van Every, 2000). Studying communication one way suggests conversation, whereas studying it another way suggests text. He avoids using the term *discourse* because he believes it obscures rather than clarifies the duality of this relationship (J. R. Taylor, personal communication, 2002). By contrast, many conversation analysts resist using the term *communication* because it suggests an emphasis on speaker intentions and communication as an act of transmission (Edwards, 1997). Qualifications notwithstanding, I neither embrace a narrow reading of the term *communication*, nor do I find the term *discourse* objectionable so long as the proper distinctions are made such as between language in use and systems of thought. For my purposes, leadership is an activity performed in communication and through discourse.

Unfortunately, *leadership* is no less loaded a term. Although past definitions have focused on individual traits, behaviors, influence, interaction patterns, role relationships, outcomes, and the occupation of an administrative position (Rost, 1991), I prefer Robinson's (2001) more task-focused definition: "Leadership is exercised when ideas expressed in talk or action are recognized by others as capable of progressing tasks or problems which are important to them" (p. 93). Robinson's definition addresses three key points. First, leadership is not leader communication; it is a process of influence among actors. Second, leadership is also not necessarily performed by one individual. Gronn (2000) argued that an individualistic view of leadership results in a rather unsophisticated leader–follower dualism in which "leaders are superior to followers, followers depend on leaders and leadership consists in doing something to, for, and on behalf of others" (p. 319). According to Gronn, this results in an exaggerated sense of agency because of an undertheorized view of task performance and accomplishment. With a view toward the division of labor, leadership may be distributed and shifted among several organizational members. Third, Robinson's definition is clearly task focused, a subject to which i will return.

Given the definitions and qualifications of the terms *discourse* and *leadership*, I argue that both chapters liberate leadership study and practice because their respective discursive analyses reveal the articulation points of action, its turning points in advancing the task, and how the constructed world could have been otherwise. The rejection of essentialism makes this possible.

THE ESSENTIALIST DEBATE AND LEADERSHIP DISCOURSE

In critiquing conversation analysis and other discourse analyses, Hammersley (2003) noted that both are marked by a "refusal to attribute to particular categories of actor distinctive, substantive psychosocial features—ones that are relatively stable across time and/or social context—as a basis for explaining their behavior" (p. 750). In other words, discourse analysts (broadly defined) eschew essentialism by their unwillingness to view actors as controlled by distinctive and stable individual characteristics such as attitudes, personalities, strategic orientations, and so forth, or contextual features such as organizational norms, values, rules, and so forth. Instead, these analysts hold that actors regularly deploy a set of culturally and organizationally informed resources—potentially available to all members—in some occasioned fashion. According to Hammersley (2003), it is what any "member" could or would do, not what is distinctive about actor or context.

For example, Pomerantz and Denvir's (chap. 2) conversation analysis with its ties to ethnomethodology never treats leadership as a given object whose essence must be gleaned or apprehended, nor is it embodied within persons, traits, styles, or individual role behaviors. This is not to deny that leadership exists, only that it is realized through the methods by which organizational life is reflexively and continuously constituted. The availability of shared methods for sensemaking allows actors in a leadership relationship to discover meanings in the midst of producing them, account for their facticity, and coordinate their actions. Molotch and Boden (1985) argued that if there is hierarchical domination by a person with authority, it is first and foremost an interactional accomplishment created by the asymmetries of access to the procedures of talk and usage of such procedures.

But are Pomerantz and Denvir (chap. 2) actually studying leadership or even hierarchy? After all, they focus almost exclusively on Harry Suffrin's role enactment of chairperson or procedural leader, and their position on leadership is one that I extrapolate from their analysis and the literature. However, I will show that it is precisely because Pomerantz and Denvir focus on the ratification of Harry Suffrin's chairing activities that they offer a unique perspective from which to view leadership, given Robinson's (2001) more task-focused definition.

Moreover, despite Pomerantz and Denvir's unexplicated views on leadership, Boden's (1994) argument regarding the concept *organization* and the attendant view of structure as organized from within (Garfinkel, 1967) is useful here. The organization is not a particular kind of object arising from actions that build toward a larger entity, but emerges in a laminated accounting process in which the global, enduring, and structural collapse into immediate action in a self-organizing system of relevancies. Just as organizations are realized in the continuous flow of conduct, we can infer that leadership also emerges in a laminated accounting process as actors "make reasonable" their behavior to one another in their occasioned, methodical selections of linguistic resources. In their accounts, actors may objectify leadership by retrospectively assessing the asymmetric or distributed use of such resources within the flow of conduct and attributing leadership to one or more actors who further the task at hand. However, the facticity of account making is always "in flight," historical and locally attuned, yet provisional and subject to constant clarification and revision (Boden, 1994; Garfinkel, 1967). Importantly, an attributive or discursively created object in flight is not the same thing as a given object in the world whose essence must be gleaned.

Taylor and Robichaud (chap. 1) waste no time in declaring in their first sentence that "management is accomplished as an ongoing conversation" (p. 5). Their chapter parallels Pomerantz and Denvir in at least five ways. First, leadership assumes a "self-generated patterning of interactive organizing," thus embedding leadership in social practices and breaking with the leader centrism of mainstream research (p. 25). Second, reminiscent of Boden's (1994) lamination, organizations are conceived of as a many layered embedding of conversational domains. Third, both chapters focus on role identities vis-à-vis interlocking role enactments by others, never individual performances. Fourth, although there is no language that refers to "members' methods," they focus on common methods by which meaning is intersubjectively managed such as linguistic ambiguity and narrative. Fifth, Taylor and Robichaud focus on actors' sensemaking through account giving. Unlike Pomerantz and Denvir (chap. 2), the accounts assume a narrative form whose function is to represent or translate the interests of various organizational communities. Also differing from Pomerantz and Denvir, Taylor and Robichaud regard as ideal stripping away "the surface characteristics of the conversation to reveal its underlying form"

(p. 25). They term this underlying form a *constitution*, which, in the case of *Corporation: After Mr. Sam*, is characterized by a plurality of voices, contestation, and yet a search for a unifying meaning and identity. They ground leadership in a political process in which the "embedded-in-practice interests" of the many communities of the organization compete to establish an organizational intention close to their own interests and concerns (p. 25).

Taylor and Robichaud (chap. 1) also argue that conversations go "meta" whenever managers represent their communities of practice to others within management. These conversations and, by implication, leadership resist essentializing because they produce a self-generated pattern of interactive organizing. In other words, managerial conversations assume a dynamic unique unto participants in a given social setting at some historical moment. This is due in no small measure to the communication taking place in and out of multiple registers (e.g., individual, organization, family) and sets of competing interests that are likely to produce contested interpretations of the constitution. Reminiscent of Watzlawick, Beavin, and Jackson (1967), the managerial conversation is reflective of multiple realities whose patterns resist essentializing because they must always be codefined.

As already mentioned, essentialism is but the strongest form of inevitability and abandoning it can be liberating. For leadership study, this occurs when leadership is grounded in social process and made central to organizing.

LEADERSHIP IS CENTRAL TO ORGANIZING

At first glance, this heading seems almost banal. Yet, in the same way that container views of the organization rendered communication as epiphenomena, so too was leadership disadvantaged by such a view. Assuming that the organization is an entity can lead one away from questioning how the organization got to be an entity in the first place and/or how it maintains itself as an entity (Fairhurst & Putnam, 2004; Hawes, 1974). When researchers ignore the processes of organizing, there is "a sharp divide between person and organization such that the agent, responsible for the latter, is left untheorized as an agent" (Hosking, 1988, pp. 149–150). It is no wonder that scholars have commented on the disconnect between leadership research and the rest of the field (Bryman, 1996; Robinson, 2001). When researchers embrace the processes of organizing, leadership becomes intrinsic to organizing because the skills of leadership are the skills of organizing (Hosking, 1988).

What are the skills of organizing? Each chapter focuses on a variety including (in no particular order) linguistic ambiguity, problem setting, sense making, direction giving, inquiry, sanctioning, and the like. However, it would not be surprising if those familiar with the leadership literature, yet unfamiliar with discursive study, would react to this statement with a metaphorical yawn: "And the insight here would be what exactly?"

Edwards (1997) argued that although many discursive concepts are rather easily understood, even mundane, it is only when these concepts come to life as actors use them in the context of some unfolding scene of action that they develop interest and import. In Staw's (1985) words, we become more problem driven and less literature driven than mainstream leadership research, whose debates are about gaps in the literature, challenges to conventional wisdom, fresh perspectives, and so forth. To become problem driven is to focus on the task at hand. Indeed, both chapters study interlocking role enactments as they are embedded in the task discussions of organizational structure and succession. Especially in chapter 2 by Pomerantz and Denvir, the study of leadership does not float ethereally above task accomplishment as some metalevel commentary as it does in mainstream leadership research (Robinson, 2001).

From these chapters we also learn that an organizing skill can neither be studied apart from its enactment nor the enactment of other skills. For example, several scholars have written about the strategic virtues of linguistic ambiguity because it can minimize face threat, promote creativity, forestall closure, and permit deniability (Eisenberg, 1984; Pascale & Athos, 1981; Weick, 1979). A second often underrated skill is problem setting, in which actors name and formulate problems to be attended to and solved (Schön, 1983; Weick, 1995). Finally, narrative can be a sensemaking tool utilized for the logic that a sequential order imposes and common script elements with attributable heroes, villains, and organizational life lessons (Bruner, 1986, 1990; Cooren, 2001; Taylor & Van Every, 2000; Weick, 1995). However, knowing that these are the possible functions of such skills is not the same as realizing how conversations turn on their combined use.

For example, Taylor and Robichaud (chap. 1) begin their analysis of *Corporation: After Mr. Sam* by observing Mr. Sam's identification of a problem, which he perceives to be a violation of his lowest cost philosophy (64–81). To set the problem, he uses a narrative, one that describes his disturbing conversation with the manager of St-Lawrence and Cremazie. As the narrative unfolds, a strategically ambiguous "they" emerges as the instigator of the price increases (78–80). Ordinarily, by not naming names, an anonymous they can remain anonymous and discussion can proceed unchallenged.

However, Mr. Sam's linguistic ambiguity fails in the ensuing discussion as Jack Levine assumes that he is the object of the criticism. He never refutes it (indeed, earlier he offers the correct numbers on the items whose price increased [68–71]), but resets the problem by assigning blame to Mr. Sam for failing to act presidential. While Taylor and Robichaud (chap. 1) prefer to speak in terms of narrative (87–97), a key focus emerges in the way Levine formulates the problem vis-à-vis two contextually opposing membership categories: general manager and president ("You wanna be the general manager here? Or do you want to act as the President?" [126–127]). The former is restrictive to Ontario and suffers by comparison to leading the corporate community of the whole. Such contrasts are usually resolved through assigning categorical precedence (Jayyusi, 1984), but in this instance, Mr. Sam is obviously already president. Thus, the choice put before Mr. Sam is really no choice at all; it is an indictment. Moreover, Levine's switch of registers, to borrow from Taylor and Robichaud, from "Mr. Sam" (44) as a form of address to the role category "Mr. President" (82, 87, 133) now appears to serve as strategically ambiguous (and plausibly deniable) reminders of the expectable duties and obligations of categorical incumbency much more than a polite, deferential form of address. It bookends the president–general manager contrast where Mr. Sam is given a choice between being "Mr. President" and "Mr. President-*not*," depending on whether or not he disagrees with Jack Levine (and can withstand the latter's formidable attack mode with his finger pointing "you," rapid-fire delivery, argumentative tone, forward posture, etc.). Thus, I agree with Taylor and Robichaud's conclusion, but would highlight Levine's strategic use of membership categories more than they do.

Enter Harry Suffrin, who sanctions Jack Levine with a metacommentary that seeks to bring the discussion "back on course" (136) because it is not the "best use of our time" (141–142) and "this kind of interchange" has not contributed to the task at hand (142). Pomerantz and Denvir's (chap. 2) analysis focuses on Harry Suffrin's role enactment as chairperson, which includes the responsibility to sanction conduct during the meeting that is purportedly inappropriate or counterproductive for accomplishing the meeting's goals. Because their analysis puts the emphasis squarely on the ratification of Harry's conduct, it also offers a referendum on leadership in this episode in a rather unexpected way. Recall Robinson's (2001) earlier definition: "Leadership is exercised when ideas expressed in talk or action are recognized by others as capable of progressing tasks or problems which are important to them" (p. 93). Using this definition, consider how Harry's critique of Jack Levine draws a sharp rebuke from Arnold Steinberg (144–145), as several other participants appear to simultaneously affirm the value and/or legitimacy of Jack's contribution to the advancement of the task (146–153). Although Pomerantz and Denvir prefer to cast this as an instance of deferential chairing, their very focus on the ratification of Harry's role enactment reveals an emerging consensus over Jack

Levine's advancing-the task-leadership on this matter, Harry's views notwithstanding.

However, Pomerantz and Denvir (chap. 2) focus on yet a second instance of deferential chairing by Harry in which the same kind of referendum on leadership is offered. After a competitive interchange between Jack and Arnold (671–710), Harry sanctions the pair for speaking simultaneously (711–713) and unproductively (713–722). With respect to the latter problem setting, Harry formulates a membership category when he says, "professional at the meeting <u>means</u>" (716) after which he recommends a problem-solving sequence by way of remedy (716–722). As Pomerantz and Denvir observe, what gives Harry's turn the strong sense of an indictment is his language. He refers to problems as "tossed out on the table" in an unorganized manner (715), philosophies that are "spewed out" (715), and speakers' undisciplined behavior that was not unlike a "fish market" (721), clearly a radical counterpoint to this professional setting.

Yet again, Harry's problem setting is rejected. Jack criticizes Harry's stance ("I don't <u>want</u> that kind of monitoring from you" (739)) and offers an alternative ("I want some heat to come out" [741]). Amid several participants talking at once, Mr. Sam intervenes, sides completely with Jack Levine (757–758), draws his affirmation (760), and formulates a rule ("To the extent that we think it's pretty well <u>covered</u> by what's already been said then we move ↓forward." (763–764)). Although it is not altogether clear whether the other voices heard were in agreement with Jack Levine's critique of Harry, it is clear from Mr. Sam's view that Jack and the category of contributions for which he is arguing advances the task. Harry subsequently defers to this de facto ruling.

Three observations must be made at this point. First, although Pomerantz and Denvir (chap. 2) identify the aforementioned sequences of deferential chairing by Harry as member-affirmed tests of whether or not the task is being advanced, it is not likely they would see these actions as a referendum on leadership per se unless and until participants specifically make this known to one another (Pomerantz & Fehr, 1997). Second, notice how these two excerpts offer a referendum on Jack Levine's leadership, not Mr. Sam's. At the very least, when leadership is viewed as advancing the task at hand, it becomes possible to see it as a much more distributed phenomena than the mainstream literature reflects to this point (Gronn, 2002; Robinson, 2001). Third, because Jack Levine's contribution remains contested when Harry's position is considered, there is no right and final rendering of leadership if it remains an attributional phenomenon (Calder, 1977; Meindl, 1995).

However, the sense that we get from Taylor and Robichaud is that Mr. Sam's behavior trumps all. How might this be true if we continue to use Robinson's advancing-the-task view of leadership? Taylor and

Robichaud spend a lot of time in chapter 1 on the concept of *closure*. As is Taylor's fashion, the concept is itself linguistically ambiguous, involving the search for a new constitution, a new consensual corporate identity, and/or a continuing hermetically sealed culture. In general terms, closure for Taylor and Robichaud comes off as issue resolution. However, if we examine Mr. Sam's behavior vis-à-vis episodic closure, akin to Cooren and Fairhurst's (2004) notion of spatiotemporal closures, Mr. Sam trumps all with the last or near-to-last words in several episodes.[1]

In the first segment, a chicken and egg argument erupts over objectives versus structure, the resolution of which occurs when Mr. Sam reads a statement of company philosophy (as told by the voiceover). The segment ends with Mr. Sam having the last word over a discussion of structure, although the camera cuts away to the next scene so it is difficult to determine the precise ending of this episode. However, two interesting disagreements characterize the second segment. The first involves the aforementioned conflict between Harry Suffrin and Jack Levine over how many personal feelings should be shared in the midst of problem solving. Mr. Sam's response and rule formulation (763–764) clearly decided that conflict as Arnold Steinberg quickly moves on to set a new problem (766–770). The second conflict occurred over the role of the family in the business and what role they can and should play in succession. Mr. Sam effectively closes this discussion by asserting his authority ("I don't need to have a family get-together ... One man (1.0) my own person have a hundred percent control of this company ... I don't need anybody's approval" [989–995]). James Doyle affirms this authority (997–1005) as he makes one last point (1006–1012) before Harry Suffrin's decision to adjourn, which is ratified by all (1015–1027). Finally, Taylor and Robichaud focus on the third segment in which Mr. Sam again effectively closes a discussion of succession time frame when he announces that his decision will be forthcoming in 3 to 6 months (1496–1497). Jack Levine objects (1509–1514), Mr. Sam holds firm (1515–1516), and James Doyle immediately sets a new problem concerning the rumor mill that is swiftly resolved (1518–1550) before this meeting is adjourned. Although Taylor and Robichaud argue that Mr. Sam forestalls closure vis-à-vis constitutional concerns, he nonetheless appears to trigger several episodic closures with authority displays. Although the effects of editing clearly cannot be discounted, neither can the swift topics shifts of Arnold Steinberg and James Doyle in at least two of the instances, which implicitly acknowledge the authority-based resolution of the prior issue.

What is the significance of Mr. Sam's authority displays vis-à-vis task accomplishment? As Taylor and Robichaud (chap. 1) rightly note, Mr. Sam also encourages freedom of expression, withstands criticism, and uses linguistic ambiguity to great effect. However, what they fail to observe is the likely sequencing effect of these more moderating influences relative to the authority displays that come at or near the end of often arduous discussion.[2] Extrapolating from Robinson's definition, these displays effectively stop the competitive debate and advance the task by moving to a solution—Mr. Sam's, of course, not the consensus solution of democratic decision making.

Whether it is direction giving, linguistic ambiguity, sanctioning, or narrative sense making, the skills of leadership are the skills of organizing given the ways in which the trajectory of the discussion and player positioning was altered when the combined use of these skills are considered. Moreover, when we consider the referendum on Jack Levine's contributions taken by the chairperson, Harry Suffrin, or Mr. Sam's authority displays that effectively close the discussion, individuals' use of these skills also passes the litmus test for leadership because of the ways in which participants view them as advancing the task. The foregoing analysis thus "liberates" leadership study because it reclaims leadership as an interactive organizing process and avoids the mainstream literature's individualism with its reifying, retrospective gloss of behavior captured in summary judgments and 7-point scales. Instead the focus is on the articulation points of action, its turning points in advancing the task, and the ways in which leadership becomes central to organizing whoever happens to fill that role episodically. To paraphrase Deidre Boden (1990), it is leadership as it happens.

LIBERATING OR NOT?

Are there ways in which the discursive analyses reflected in Taylor and Robichaud (chap. 1) and Pomerantz and Denvir (chap. 2) do not liberate leadership study? To answer this question, it is important to recall Hammersley's (2003) criticism of conversation and discourse analysis as failing to focus on the dispositional, which results in a rather "thin" model of the human actor. Because discourse analysts are concerned with the orderliness of social life, they are disinclined to view behavior as controlled by stable individual characteristics such as attitudes, personalities, strategic orientations, and so forth, or contextual features such as organizational norms, values, rules, and so forth. Clearly, Pomerantz and Denvir's conversation analysis focuses on the culturally and organizationally informed resources that any member could employ, not what is distinctive about actor or context. Taylor and Robichaud likewise appear to view leadership as a discursive product of social actors in communication, built through a kind of textualized speech agency (Taylor & Van Every, 2000). Both chapters focus mainly on social coordination, not individual predilections.

Hammersley's criticism of discursive approaches is particularly salient for leadership study, whose mainstay from the beginning has been what Gronn (2000) characterized as "belief in the power of one" (p. 319). Whether the search for leadership is in leaders' traits (e.g., intelligence, achievement motivation, physical energy, or self-confidence), situations requiring particular styles (e.g., consideration and initiation structure, or autocratic, participative, *laissez faire* decision-making styles), leader and situation combinations (e.g., strong leadership and crisis conditions, or leader style and maturity of followers), or leader behaviors (e.g., strategic visioning, charisma, or ability to inspire), the emphasis is on stable and distinctive leader dispositions and/or contextual features (Bass, 1981; House & Aditya, 1997; Yukl, 2002). Only recently has the bias toward individualism and psychological reductionism been questioned in the literature, although quite separate from discursive approaches (Gronn, 2000, 2002; Yukl, 1999).

The emergence of discursive approaches to leadership throws into relief the kinds of questions that individual and/or psychological approaches are best suited for and the kinds of questions for which they are not suited. Specifically, if one is interested in the individual experience of leadership or studying leadership trends out of context vis-à-vis the cognitive or motivational tendencies of leaders as a group, common functions of leadership, comparison of leader practices aimed at effectiveness, or leader behavior frequencies, then the discursive analyses in these two chapters are hardly liberating. An individual and/or psychological focus is needed to reclaim the experience of leadership in which the actors' interpretations or summary judgments elicited in surveys or interviews are central. Additionally, when studying leadership out of context, one must minimize contextual concerns in order to understand convergences, divergences, and frequencies across contexts. Clearly, many important questions fall within these domains.

However, whether actors' views are elicited in scaled judgments or interview questions that prompt meaning assignments and sensemaking and regardless of how these measurements may or may not be summarized across contexts, let us not pretend that an individual and/or psychological focus is tantamount to studying interaction process. Clearly, *Corporation: After Mr. Sam* makes apparent a number of distinct individual perspectives on organizational structure and succession that are, at best, cognitive and/or linguistic resources from which individuals draw to discuss and debate the path forward. To study social interaction is to focus on how actors reveal their sensemaking to one another as they coordinate their behavior turn by turn and form patterns of interlocking role enactments over time.

Unfortunately, the psychological reductionism of leadership study is so profound that participants' individual meanings and summary judgments consistently take precedence over interaction process. Too often, the former are used as questionable proxies for interaction process, the net effect of which is to privilege individualism and give too little attention to the processes of organizing in leadership study (Bryman, 1996; Gronn, 2000, 2002; Hosking, 1988). It also promotes a "one size fits all" paradigmatic approach to leadership study overly enamored with cause–effect "why" questions that require a variable analytic focus not well suited to the "How is leadership brought off?" questions that capture the contextual, contingent, and contested nature of social interaction as it unfolds. But why should an individualistic and/or psychological focus consistently prevail over a social interaction focus (or vice versa)? At what point is the context allowed back into the analysis in order to study the coordination of behavior of actors in communication, phenomena that cannot be reduced to one actor's view of the world? At what point do we recognize that socially coordinated behavior is always contestable because it is reflective of multiple realities whose patterns must always be codefined?

As exemplified in the foregoing chapters, to study leadership in context requires a discursive orientation for which most individual and/or psychological approaches are ill suited. It requires, according to Potter (2003), "a certain kind of thinness" in the actor that is best characterized as lacking "a predefined model of the human actor" (pp. 790–791) in order to focus upon social practices, the constitutive role of language, and the contributions of the cultural. It also requires a multilayered view of the context that has both communicative and organizational underpinnings.

Part of the difficulty also lies in how agency is conceptualized in the leadership and discourse literatures, the implications of which problematize what Hammersley (2003) referred to as "thin" versus "thick" model of the actor. With respect to the leadership literature, recall Hosking's (1988) argument that leadership research is divorced from the rest of the organizational sciences because of an undertheorized view of agency. Too often the organization is conceived of as an entity, the origins and maintenance of which are rarely problematized. If they were, the agency status of the actors in a leadership relationship would have to be recognized because the focus shifts to organizing activity, the redundancies of which make reification possible. However, remember that Gronn (2000) made the case for exaggerated agency, especially in neocharismatic approaches to leadership, because of an undertheorized view of task performance and accomplishment and too much focus on the leader. If the division of labor were truly examined, leadership would surface as a more distributed phenomenon.

Can Gronn (2000) and Hosking (1988) start from the same individualistic model and arrive at two different senses of agency? Yes, and both have a point. Gronn (2000) was correct in noting the strong individualism and the overstatement associated with the heroic capabilities of charismatic leaders, which would lead to his attribution of exaggerated agency. Yet, Hosking (1988) was also correct because across this genre of theories (and most others), agency is never explicitly theorized, the organization ontological status is assumed, and the disconnect between leader and organization perpetuates itself with inattention to the processes of organizing. Leadership is still a phenomenon embodied in persons with finely tuned inner motors, not as organizing process.

From a discursive perspective, agency can be conceptualized in both an internal and external sense. An *externalist* conception occurs when agency becomes an enactment that depends on a connection in a network/system of relations (McPhee, 2001). Thus, several discursive approaches ascribe constrained choice to actors, but deemphasize their active, interpretive role in making these choices largely because they remain true to only what the text reveals (vs. treating the individual as a source of information about the text; Fairhurst, 2004). They adopt a thin model of the actor in Hammersley's sense. Conversely, when agency moves beyond agents' activities and relationships to include connections between meaning, sensemaking, and action, such as in beliefs about cause and effect, values and interests, and how they are reflected in action (Hosking, 1988), a more internalized conception of agency follows. Yet methodology also enters in because, as Potter (2003) observed, "Particular models of the person may be dependent on certain assumptions wired into method" (p. 791). Clearly, this book is testimony to this observation as the chapters here are premised solely upon the videotape and transcript made available to all of us. Agency, if conceptualized, is necessarily external or thin because of lack of access to actors' perspectives and meaning assignments except as they make them known to one another.

To close the discussion of how discursive approaches may or may not be liberating of leadership, one can certainly assert that the individual and the social are two very different kinds of questions about leadership (Fairhurst, 2001). Mutually exclusive in data and interest in many ways, both are critical to understanding leadership because they remain quite complementary. However, resolution of this issue seems less about asking, "Why can't we all just get along?" and more about, "When the individual and/or psychological is the focus, what can be said about social interaction?" and "When social interaction is the focus, what can be said about the dispositional tendencies of actors or the stable characteristics of context?" These are the kinds of questions where survey researchers, interviewers, and discourse analysts gather at the crossroads to venture into each other's territory less with caution and more with a little "poaching" in mind.

Regarding the first question and what can be said about interaction process when the focus is on the individual and/or psychological, one person's view of the world is just that, nothing more and nothing less. As Taylor and Robichaud's (chap. 1) analyses so aptly reveal, the interaction process is characterized by actors' contested views of the world. It is impossible to say who has the correct view because the world is pluralistic with some views more privileged than others. Likewise, Pomerantz and Denvir's (chap. 2) analysis of the ratification of Harry Suffrin's chairing activities remind us that interaction patterns are always codefined. Assertions of control by Harry Suffrin mean little without knowing of the backlash to his actions in two separate episodes, first by the group and then by Mr. Sam. The discussion would have looked far different had Jack Levine been silenced in the ways in which Harry had urged.

Regarding the second question's focus on what can be said about the dispositional tendencies of actors when studying social interaction, the issues are twofold: what is analytically usable information vis-à-vis what actors say about the social world and assessing sufficient redundancies in behavior over time. Regarding the former, Hammersley (2003) criticized conversation and discourse analyses for its refusal to treat what actors say about the social world as a source of information about it because it is "topic not resource" (p. 792). In other words, actors' accounts of themselves or interaction dynamics fall into the category of that which is to be explained, which is indeed the position assumed by Pomerantz and Denvir and Taylor and Robichaud, quite apart from the constraints of only being able to analyze the *Corporation: After Mr. Sam* tape and transcript.

Regarding assessing sufficient redundancies in behavior over time, conversation analysts rarely follow one individual throughout a period of time long enough to make dispositional attributions. It is likely the major reason why Pomerantz and Denvir refrain from making them in chapter 2.[3] However, note Taylor and Robichaud's description in chapter 1 of Mr. Sam as an "old-fashioned pragmatist" (p. 14), a "savvy psychologist, the man who knows how to take the measure of individuals who surround him" (p. 23), and an "autocratic patriarch who, in the end, will impose his own will on his subordinates" (p. 23). Aren't these dispositional attributions? They appear to be, but two points must be made here. First, going back to the distinctions made about these two chapters regarding the definition of discourse, Taylor and Robichaud adopt a mesodiscourse approach that is relatively sensitive to language in use, but is interested in broader patterns and going beyond the text in order to generalize to similar local contexts (Alvesson & Kärreman, 2000). By comparison, Pomerantz and Denvir (chap. 2) adopt a more microdiscourse approach that stays very close to the text. Taylor and

Robichaud (chap. 1) clearly make a broader sweep of the transcript than does Pomerantz and Denvir, who prefer to focus on a few segments of Harry Suffrin's chairing activities. Second, Taylor and Robichaud generally argue that there is sufficient redundancy to warrant the kind of interpretation they offer. However, although "autocratic patriarch" is easy enough to accept given Mr. Sam's repeated assertions of authority, there is a sense in which these analysts have perhaps gone well beyond the discourse when making attributions like "old-fashioned pragmatist" and "savvy psychologist, the man who knows how to take the measure of individuals who surround him" that warrant a different approach to leadership study than they offer. Thus, clearly those who would study interaction must also guard against using it as a proxy for an individualistic leadership focus.

LIBERATING FOR LEADERS?

To this point, the focus of discussion has been on liberating the study of leadership. However, it is also fair to raise the question of whether chapter 1 by Taylor and Robichaud and chapter 2 by Pomerantz and Denvir are liberating the practice of leadership. Here I would have to don my role as an executive coach by asking how the constructed interaction in *Corporation: After Mr. Sam*, as revealed through their analyses, could have gone otherwise. What might a coach say to major players like Mr. Sam, Jack Levine, James Doyle, and Harry Suffrin if they were interested in a different outcome or in improving their effectiveness? Because the chapters' analyses reveal the articulation points of action, these questions are fairly easy to address.[4] For example, both chapters call attention to Mr. Sam's authority displays and the manner in which he is able to abort discussion in rather short order. As a coach, my job would be to make him aware of the effect of the timing of these displays and the consequences of the use of authority versus that of consensus. Taylor and Robichaud make note of Mr. Sam's rather complex style; thus I would also target the manner in which he tempers his authority displays with linguistic ambiguity, humor, and acceptance of criticism. Linguistic ambiguity deserves particular attention for the ways in which it can help or hinder communication.

Taylor and Robichaud (chap. 1) also pay particular attention to Jack Levine, who forcefully challenges Mr. Sam and others in several instances throughout the videotape. Jack Levine appears quite willing to put important issues on the table, but with more fire than the finesse of James Doyle, who is equally critical of Mr. Sam. Thus, as Jack Levine's coach, I would encourage him to better understand the impact of his emotions, especially when in attack mode he employs the finger pointing "you," rapid-fire questioning, argumentative tone, forward lean, raised voice, and so forth. James Doyle appears to be a particularly effective communicator in this videotape, who skillfully puts forth his views using humor and affirmation before making his points.

In chapter 2, Pomerantz and Denvir's analysis of Harry Suffrin's chairing activities suggests that he could benefit from coaching in the differences between dialogue and problem-solving discussion (Isaacs, 1999). Harry's inclination to quash emotion and move forward with a rigid, linear problem-solving sequence reflects a lack of understanding of the need to adequately set problems in dialogue that encourages freedom of expression and empathic understanding before attempting to solve them. Moreover, Harry's mental model of linear problem solving should be surfaced and questioned for its veridicality vis-à-vis the group's discussion mode, indeed most small group interaction.

CONCLUSION

Chapter 1 by Pomerantz and chapter 2 by Denvir and Taylor and Robichaud are good examples of the ways in which discursive analyses may liberate leadership study and practice—although not all leadership study and practice. Therein lies the task of leadership researchers to understand how best to use discourse analyses as well as those focusing on the individual and/or psychological when leadership interaction is the focus. The burgeoning literature on discursive approaches holds great promise for leadership study. Although it may be seen merely as a qualitative alternative to more mainstream empiricist approaches, it is much more than that. As demonstrated in the chapters by these two sets of authors, they pose different kinds of questions about leadership. They also employ theoretical frameworks rarely seen in the leadership literature and use methodologies that depart significantly from its surveys and 7-point scales. This is in no way to discount the contributions of decades of leadership research employing a more traditional focus, only to clarify what each perspective may ultimately offer the other.

ENDNOTES

1. As Pomerantz and Denvir note, the film *Corporation: After Mr. Sam* is far from ideal data. The impact of editing is difficult to determine here and thus must be considered as a plausible alternative interpretation for the way in which each segment ends.
2. Taylor and Robichaud do make the statement "… the other Mr. Sam, the autocratic patriarch, who, in the end, will impose his own will on subordinates" (p. 23). However, consistent with their earlier views, I take this statement to refer to issue resolution, not episodic closure.
3. Indeed, Pomerantz and Denvir (chap. 2) allow that "More data would be needed to determine whether Harry generally enacted facilitative and/or

deferential chairing or if he varied his chairing practices according to context" (p. 48).

4. Although it is easy to answer this question, it is much more difficult to affect change in executive coaching when attempting to modify what may or may not be conscious behavior.

REFERENCES

Alvesson, M., & Kärreman, D. (2000). Varieties of discourse: On the study of organizations through discourse analysis. *Human Relations, 53*, 1125–1149.

Bass, B. M. (1981). *Stogdill's handbook of leadership.* New York: The Free Press.

Boden, D. (1990). The world as it happens: Ethnomethodology and conversation analysis. In G. Ritzer (Ed.), *Frontiers of social theory: The new synthesis* (pp. 185–213). New York: Columbia University Press.

Boden, D. (1994). *The business of talk: Organizations in action.* Cambridge, England: Polity Press.

Bruner, J. S. (1986). *Actual minds, possible worlds.* Cambridge, MA: Harvard University Press.

Bruner, J. S. (1990). *Acts of meaning.* Cambridge, MA: Harvard University Press.

Bryman, A. (1996). Leadership in organizations. In S. R. Clegg, C. Hardy, & W. R. Nord (Eds.), *Handbook of organization studies* (pp. 276–292). London: Sage.

Calder, B. J. (1977). An attribution theory of leadership. In B. M. Staw & G. R. Salacik (Eds.), *New directions in organizational behavior* (pp. 179–202). Chicago: St. Clair Press.

Cooren, F. (2001). *The organizing property of communication.* Philadelphia: John Benjamins.

Cooren, F., & Fairhurst, G. T. (2004). Speech timing and spacing: The phenomenon of organizational closure. *Organization, 11*, 793–824.

Cronen, V. E. (1995). Coordinated management of meaning: The consequentiality of communication and the recapturing of experience. In S. J. Sigman (Eds.), *The consequentiality of communication* (pp. 17–65). Hillsdale, NJ: Lawrence Erlbaum Associates.

Edwards, D. (1997). *Discourse and cognition.* London: Sage.

Eisenberg, E. (1984). Ambiguity as strategy in organizational communication. *Communication Monographs, 51*, 227–242.

Fairhurst, G. T. (2001). Dualisms in leadership research. In F. M. Jablin & L. L. Putnam (Eds.), *The new handbook of organizational communication: Advances in theory, research, and methods* (pp. 379–439). Thousand Oaks, CA: Sage.

Fairhurst, G. T. (2004). Textuality and agency in interaction analysis. *Organization, 11*, 335–353.

Fairhurst, G. T., & Putnam, L. L. (2004). Organizations as discursive constructions. *Communication Theory, 14*, 5–26.

Garfinkel, H. (1967). *Studies in ethnomethodology.* Englewood Cliffs, NJ: Prentice Hall.

Grint, K. (2000). *The arts of leadership.* Oxford, England: Oxford University Press.

Gronn, P. (2000). Distributed properties: A new architecture for leadership. *Educational Management and Administration, 28*, 317–338.

Gronn, P. (2002). Distributed leadership as a unit of analysis. *Leadership Quarterly, 13*, 423–451.

Hacking, I. (1999). *The social construction of what?* Cambridge, MA: Harvard University Press.

Hammersley, M. (2003). Conversation analysis and discourse analysis: Methods or paradigms. *Discourse & Society, 14*, 751–781.

Hawes, L. C. (1974). Social collectivities as communication: Perspectives on organizational behavior. *Quarterly Journal of Speech, 60*, 497–502.

Hosking, D. M. (1988). Organizing, leadership and skillful process. *Journal of Management Studies, 25*, 147–166.

Hosking, D. M., & Morley, I. E. (1991). *A social psychology of organizing: People, processes and contexts.* New York: Harvester/Wheatsheaf.

House, R. J., & Aditya, R. N. (1997). The social scientific study of leadership: Quo vadis? *Journal of Management, 23*, 409–473.

Isaacs, W. (1999). *Dialogue: And the art of thinking together.* New York: Currency.

Jayyusi, L. (1984). *Categorization and the moral order.* Boston: Routledge & Kegan Paul.

McPhee, R. D. (2001, May). *Formal structure, text, and equivalence.* Paper presented at the International Communication Association Conference, Washington, DC.

Meindl, J. R. (1995). The romance of leadership as a follower-centric theory: A social constructionist approach. *Leadership Quarterly, 6*, 329–341.

Molotch, H. L., & Boden, D. (1985). Talking social structure: Discourse, domination and the Watergate Hearings. *American Sociological Review, 50*, 273–288.

Pascale, R. T., & Athos, A. G. (1981). *The art of Japanese management.* New York: Simon & Schuster.

Pomerantz, A., & Fehr, B. J. (1997). Conversation analysis: An approach to the study of social action as sense making practices. In T. A. van Dijk (Ed.), *Discourse as social interaction* (Vol. 2, pp. 64–91). London: Sage.

Potter, J. (2003). Discursive psychology: Between method and paradigm. *Discourse & Society, 14*, 783–794.

Robinson, V. M. J. (2001). Embedding leadership in task performance. In K. Wong & C. W. Evers (Eds.), *Leadership for quality schooling* (pp. 90–102). London: Routledge/Falmer.

Rost, J. C. (1991). *Leadership for the twenty-first century.* New York: Praeger.

Schön, D. A. (1983). *The reflective practitioner: How professionals think in action.* New York: Basic Books.

Staw, B. M. (1985). Repairs on the road to relevance and rigor: Some unexplored issues in publishing organizational research. In L. L. Cummings & P. J. Frost (Eds.), *Publishing in the organizational sciences* (pp. 96–107). Homewood, IL: Irwin.

Taylor, J. R., & Van Every, E. (2000). *The emergent organization: Communication at its site and surface.* Mahwah, NJ: Lawrence Erlbaum Associates.

Watzlawick, P., Beavin, J. H., & Jackson, D. D. (1967). *Pragmatics of human communication.* New York: Norton.

Weick, K. (1979). *The social psychology of organizing* (2nd ed.). Reading, MA: Addison-Wesley.

Weick, K. (1995). *Sensemaking in organizations.* Thousand Oaks, CA: Sage.

Yukl, G. (1999). An evaluation of conceptual weaknesses in transformational and charismatic leadership theories. *Leadership Quarterly, 10*, 285–305.

Yukl, G. (2002). *Leadership in organizations* (5th ed.). Upper Saddle River, NJ: Prentice Hall.

II

Organizing and Emotional Display: Contradictions and Paradoxes

If there is one topic that tends to be relatively neglected in social sciences in general, it could arguably been claimed that it is the study of emotions. Although many interesting organizational studies on this subject have flourished since Hochschild's (1983) landmark contribution (see also Kramer & Hess, 2002; Murphy, 1998; Putnam & Mumby, 1993), the implications from the role of emotions in organizations often do not take the route of the way we conceive of interaction and organizations. This should be of no surprise if we consider that the basic anthropological hypotheses from which scholars implicitly or explicitly start from when they conduct their analyses consists of positioning the human being as the starting point of the reflection.

As we know, the 1980s' interpretive turn in organizational studies (Burrell & Morgan, 1979; Putnam & Pacanowsky, 1983; Weick, 1979) centered human interaction and interpretation at the forefront of analysis. The reasoning roughly worked (and still works, in many respects) as follows: Because the organization is a construction, we have, as analysts, to focus on the builders, that is, the members who interactively manage to produce and reproduce this form of life that we call *organization*. Interestingly enough, LSI scholars use the same starting point. For instance, Pomerantz and Fehr (1997) specified that the central defining focus in conversation analysis is: "the organization of the meaningful conduct of people in society, that is, how people in society produce their activities and make sense of the world about them. The core analytic objective is to illuminate how actions, events, objects, etc., are produced and understood ..." (p. 65). In other words, interactants are positioned at the origin of analysis, because LSI studies show how participants interactively and reflexively manage their interactions by invoking or orienting to specific norms of conduct, or positioning themselves and others as enacting specific roles or identities (Garfinkel, 1967; Heritage, 1984; Sacks, 1992).

In many respects, recovering the question of emotion within the social sciences consists not in destroying such basic anthropological foundations, but more in qualifying them by showing their limitations. Indeed, recognizing that emotions play a role in interactional and organizational phenomena illustrates that the positioning of the human being at the origin of analysis is, to say the least, problematic.

Etymologically speaking, the term *emotion* comes from the Latin word *movere*, which means "to move." In other words, experiencing or feeling an emotion consist of being moved by something or someone, a phenomenon that does not necessarily fit nicely with the anthropological preconceptions already discussed. Once we recognize that interactants can be moved, whether it is by passion, interests, or emotions, which may stem from objects, faces, situations, memories, and so forth, we also confront the realization, as Foucault (1977) did some 30 years before, that people are spoken as much as they speak, or that, like Latour's (1994, 1996, 1999, 2002) studies show today, there is no true point of origin to action.

Although the three chapters in this part do not necessarily problematize the question of emotion from the origin of action, they trigger a discussion that might foster a reconceptualization of human agency (Cooren, 2004). In chapter 4, Karen Tracy claims, for instance, that the discursive practices that convey emotion should never be separated from the more rational ones associated with organizational meetings, a claim that she identifies as the basic assumption of her chapter. Throughout her detailed analysis of what she calls a "feeling-limned interactional moment" (p. 78) during the management meeting, she convincingly shows how two participants managed to express competing moral assessments about how the meeting should be conducted by instantiating, evaluating, and accounting for specific emotional displays. In other words, Tracy shows how emotion and calculation are, to a certain extent, intertwined and contrasted in these sequences that question the way that feelings are marginalized in such meetings.

Interestingly enough, Tracy (chap. 4) also shows how these two participants enact behaviors that appear quite opposite to what they preach: The person who pleads for the right and necessity to express feelings appears to develop a very elaborate and articulate argument, whereas the person who calls for the necessity to be in control ends up using a relatively harsh vocabulary that sparks reaction and anger from his audience. This paradox could be said to illustrate basic tensions that seem to always exist between the calculable and the incalculable or between action and passion. As Tracy's chapter shows very nicely, social interaction is produced as though these poles were always present in any discussion and that participants must navigate, the best they can, between them.

The tension between talking about feelings and expressing them is also addressed by Linda Putnam in chapter 5. By focusing on how participants talk about feelings during the meeting, she shows how they implicitly address three basic dichotomies throughout the meeting: professional versus unprofessional, feeling rules versus work feelings, and open versus closed space for action. As she demonstrates, these dichotomies surface as organizational norms used to resist and comply with the exercise of control during the meeting.

What is also especially interesting in her analysis is the way she shows how this question of emotional display can be studied from multiple levels: interpersonal, meeting, organizational, and even stakeholder levels. These multiple readings thus illustrate the extent to which emotional expression becomes part of a decision-making performance in which ironically no actual choice is made. By venting their feelings or calling for suppression of them, the participants appear to be both passionate and rational; that is, they air central issues, while sustaining order and self-control, which, in the end, maintains a form of the status quo.

Finally, in chapter 6, Kristine Fitch and Megan Foley's response extends the two preceding chapters by exploring the persuasive and cultural nature of emotion displays. Although Tracy's and Putnam's analyses shows how reason and emotion are constantly intertwined in the packaging of talk, Fitch and Foley investigate the suasory power of emotion expression. Examining the same passages analyzed in the two previous chapters, they convincingly show how participants' expressions of feelings create real constraints on the way that other members can react to contradictory feelings. In other words, Fitch and Foley illustrate how emotional displays function as strategic moves to frame the discussion in a way that serve the interests of some participants over others.

Exploring the cultural nature of emotional expressions, Fitch and Foley (chap. 6) also show how these emotions function as cultural persuadables , that is, matters about which members of a given culture can be persuaded because of their shared understanding of their level of acceptability or appropriateness. The display of emotions is thus codified within specific systems of meaning, a point that allows the authors to draw some very nice hypotheses about the organizational culture of Steinberg Ltd.

REFERENCES

Burrell, G., & Morgan, G. (1979). *Sociological paradigms and organizational analysis: Elements of the sociology of corporate life*. London: Heinemann.

Cooren, F. (2006). Textual agency: How texts do things in organizational settings. *Organization, 11*(3), 373–393.

Fitch, K. L. (2003). Cultural persuadables. *Communication Theory, 13*, 100–123.

Foucault, M. (1977). *The archaeology of knowledge*. London: Tavistock.

Garfinkel, H. (1967). *Studies in ethnomethodology*. Englewood Cliffs, NJ: Prentice-Hall.

Heritage, J. (1984). *Garfinkel and ethnomethodology*. Cambridge, England: Polity Press.

Hochschild, A. R. (1983). *The managed heart*. Berkeley: University of California Press.

Kramer, M. W., & Hess, J. A. (2002). Communication rules for the display of emotions in organizational settings. *Management Communication Quarterly, 16*, 66–80.

Latour, B. (1994). On technical mediation—philosophy, sociology, genealogy. *Common Knowledge, 3*(2), 29–64.

Latour, B. (1996). On interobjectivity. *Mind, Culture, and Activity, 3*(4), 228–245.

Latour, B. (1999). *Pandora's hope : Essays on the reality of science studies*. Cambridge, MA: Harvard University Press.

Latour, B. (2002). Gabriel Tarde and the end of the social. In P. Joyce (Ed.), *The social in question. New bearings in history and the social sciences* (pp. 117–132). London: Routledge.

Murphy, A. G. (1998). Hidden transcripts of flight attendant resistance. *Management Communication Quarterly, 11*(4), 499–535.

Pomerantz, A., & Fehr, B. J. (1997). Conversation analysis: An approach to the study of social action as sense making practices. In T. A. V. Dijk (Ed.), *Discourse as social interaction* (pp. 64–91). London: Sage.

Putnam, L. L., & Mumby, D. K. (1993). Organizations, emotion and the myth of rationality. In S. Fineman (Ed.), *Emotion in organizations* (pp. 36–57). London: Sage.

Putnam, L. L., & Pacanowsky, M. E. (1983). *Communication and organizations. An interpretive approach*. Newbury Park, CA: Sage.

Sacks, H. (1992). *Lectures on conversation*. Oxford: Blackwell.

Weick, K. E. (1979). *The social psychology of organizing*. New York: Random House.

Chapter 4

Feeling-Limned Talk: Conduct Ideals in the Steinberg Succession Meeting

Karen Tracy
University of Colorado, Boulder

Emotion displays have their proper places in unfolding episodes of interpersonal reaction; they are acts embedded in patterns of acts ... that allow for assessment of the correctness or impropriety of emotions.
—Parrott and Harré (1996, p. 1)

We express anger, annoyance, exasperation, impatience, disgust, disdain, and disrespect largely through the same channels that we use to recognize those things in others.
—Haviland (1989, p. 28)

Just as overt cultures are not equally shared by all those who interact, so also knowledge of covert cultures is differentially distributed.... [The] capacity to make use of what "officially" is deemed not to exist and therefore is "officially" not available for use is one of the factors regulating relative power.
—Bailey (1983, pp. 19–20)

These three snippets are main ingredients for this chapter's meal. By the chapter's conclusion, it will be apparent that the dish being prepared is a stew. When ready for consumption, it will be difficult to tell where each unboxed ingredient—feelings, moral assessments, logical argument, and strategic displays—begins and ends; each will have coated and flavored the other. A stew, I would suggest, is the diet staple of people who spend a lot of time in meetings. And, as is typical of stews, certain ones are often among people's favorite dishes. On occasion, though, and in certain kitchens quite often, stews become unsavory disasters that no one will eat and about which everyone jokes. If organizational meetings

77

are "stews," then, as many organizational scholars (e.g., Fineman, 1993; Mangham, 1998; Putnam & Mumby, 1993) are recognizing, practices typically equated with the "rational," such as argument-making and evidence giving, neither can nor should be separated from the discursive practices that convey emotion and render moral assessment. This is the starting assumption of this chapter.

The chapter is organized into two parts. The first provides background on meetings and feeling expression; the second analyzes the Steinberg succession meeting. Following a brief history of meetings, I sort through the terminological morass about emotion. Then, I describe what recent language and social interaction research tells us about feeling expression in discourse. In the next section, I examine one particularly feeling-limned interactional moment in the Steinberg succession retreat. Focusing on two participants, I analyze how competing moral assessments about desirable meeting conduct were conveyed through the particular emotion-logic package that instantiated each man's talk. In the conclusion, I use the Steinberg case to make visible a paradox that confronted these two participants, and presumably confronts many meeting participants, as they craft their communicative contributions.

MEETINGS AND FEELING EXPRESSION

An Historical Appetizer

Modern meeting behavior, as van Vree (1999) showed in his historical account of meetings in Europe and the United States, has changed radically from what it was in the past. Until the 1400s, only monarchs had the right to call a meeting. At that time, a meeting involved the monarch's subjects seated in rows to hear their king's presumably God-inspired comments. Up until the 1600s, meetings were not places where people discussed or disagreed with each other. Because the monarchs were regarded as God's emissaries, disagreement at the meeting was a sign of ungodliness. As the balance of power among categories of people in society became less unequal, and as the bible became a competing authority to the institutional church, the notion that words could be used to negotiate, persuade, and prevail became more common. During the Protestant Reformation in the 17th century, ordinary people were learning how to solve differences through words. A typical meeting at this time would began with a reading of conduct rules in which participants would be instructed that knife pulling and glass throwing were forbidden, and that fines would be given for swearing and sleeping. With the industrialization of European societies, meetings as we now know them came into being. Meetings became places where people would talk, disagree, and negotiate, but did not pull swords, throw knives and glasses, or accuse other participants of being thieving murderers. The growth of meetings, in other words, was a force in civilizing people. As van Vree (1999) argued, modern meetings "require a relatively large, precise, constant, and flexible self regulation of expressions of affect and emotions" (p. 197). The expectation about emotional self-regulation is especially strong in North American society with regard to the feeling of anger (Stearns & Stearns, 1986).

Although expression of emotion is considerably more regulated today than it was in the past, it is by no means absent. In a study of several contemporary businesses, Boden (1994) described meetings as "ritual affairs, tribal gatherings in which the faithful affirm solidarity and warring factions engage in verbal battles" (p. 81). Meetings may fundamentally be about relationship negotiation and status struggles, yet they are routinely treated as being for decision-making and business matters. Schwartzman (1989) suggested that organizational meetings are important "because they generate the *appearance* that reason and logical processes are guiding discussion and decisions" (p. 42, italics in original). "Discussion of social relationships can always be framed as 'business'—and therefore conflict is legitimated and framed as 'business'" (p. 128). To put it all together, through the presentation of logical proposals with affect displays smuggled into their expressive form, modern meeting participants enact and negotiate relationships as they inform, plan, and make decisions.

To complicate things further, not only does meeting talk express opinions and display feelings, it also conveys moral evaluations about the reasonableness and rightness of self and other's actions (Bergmann, 1998). People are tied to their past actions, proposed future ones, and ideas they espouse. Evaluation of person-tied actions, plans, and ideas, therefore, is inherently a judgment about a person's savvy, good sense, ethical character, and so on. Most frequently, evaluation is accomplished implicitly; through the way a scene or action is described, the reasonableness or unreasonableness of the person responsible for that act or scene is constructed (Drew, 1998). At times, however, social conduct itself becomes an explicit topic for talk. It is at these moments that participant beliefs about what are right and reasonable ways to connect feelings and logic become especially clear.

The kinds of feelings that are likely to be expressed at a meeting can be expected to depend on the meeting type. Groups that have been put together to reflect the different departments and interests in an organization can be expected to have more overt feeling displays than meetings where individuals have no obvious stake in an outcome and are selected because of their presumed expert or thoughtful judgment (Bailey, 1983). Meetings in which a group's job is to give input and advice to the organizational leader, rather than make the decision itself, will need to address leader- and organizationally linked sensitivities in selecting the content and crafting the form of the advice it offers. It is rarely the case that a meeting group charged with giving its input is requested to say exactly what it thinks. Instead, groups are expected to take account of leader- and organizationally assumed constraints, as well as avoid excursions into what the powerful regard as taboo topics.

Language About Emotion: A Terminological Mess

Although people's ordinary communicative expression allows them to join feeling with reasoning in interesting and complicated packages, our theoretical metalanguage to discuss the emotional dimension of social life is both impoverished and confusing. Parkinson (1995), for instance, as is true of many psychological approaches, primarily distinguishes emotions from moods, seeing *emotions* as short-lived intentional states that are intrinsically evaluative and *moods* as more general affective states that persist for a long time. Winton (1990) saw affect as a synonym for emotion, but Ochs and Schieffelin (1989) treated it as broader than emotions, including feelings, moods, dispositions, and attitudes associated with persons and situations. Forgas (2000), like Ochs and Schieffelin, used *affect* as a term that is broader than emotion but includes only moods and emotions as the subparts. Fineman (1993) treated feelings and emotions as synonyms whereas Besnier (1990) distinguished feelings from emotions and affect, defining feelings as person-centered psychophysiological sensations in which emotions are a subset of the most visible and identifiable feelings. For Besnier, affect is the subjective state that observers ascribe to persons on the basis of their conduct.

My purpose in showing the diversity among definitions is not to argue for a best one (what is best will depend on a scholar's purpose and audience) but to alert readers to the fact that these key terms may mean different things. Given an interest in meetings, the most useful terms, I suggest, are *feeling displays* and *feelings*. Feeling displays I will define as the linguistic, vocal, and embodied actions that, as a set, are taken as cues that a person is experiencing some feeling. Feelings, then, are the internal states that participants and observers attribute to the person enacting a display. Whether, in fact, a speaker has actually experienced the attributed feeling is not particularly important. The significant fact is that members of a community will routinely assume that an identifiable display in a specific situation means that a person is feeling a particular something: amusement, irritation, pleased with self, bored, impatient, disgusted, upset, and so on.

In addition, feelings as a term directs our attention, not only to big expressions, but to the small as well. When we focus on feelings we are led to the multilayered, not-easy-to-categorize reactions and stances that are an ongoing part of working with other people. Emotion, in contrast, draws our attention primarily to big, intense feelings (e.g., happiness, anger, fear, sadness) that are infrequent in everyday life. Although naming feelings is difficult, and most certainly is a messy business, people routinely do so. Everyday talk is replete with comments where people describe their own and others' situated feelings. Sometimes these names are single-word, dictionary-type feelings (*resigned* or *exasperated*); at other times, the feelings names evoke an experience in living and its usual accompanying feeling (e.g., when a person says she feels "jazzed," or "pissed"). More pervasive than naming, though, is that through selected discursive choices (e.g., words, argumentative positions, voice, gestures) speakers create complex covert messages that cue their feelings.

Important to remember is that feeling displays are situationally and culturally shaped. Although the channels for expressing feelings may be largely the same channels that people rely on to infer feeling states, the system works best when displayers and inference makers are steeped in similar situations and cultures. For instance, consider the organizational meeting situation. Given the powerful norms that have evolved across the centuries about behavior, it is reasonable to expect relatively subtle expressions of emotion to be interpreted as more intense feelings than would have been the case in earlier times and probably would be currently the case in intimate or friendship contexts. On the cultural front we know that a communicative act such as overlapping speech may be judged to cue a negative feeling, such as impatience, or a positive one such as engaged involvement. Sacks (1992) nicely explicates the link between interruption and negative feelings, noting if

> you want to show that something that somebody is saying really angers you, then placing your utterance by starting while they're still talking seems to be more effective than waiting and placing it after they've finished.... placing it after they've finished is something we would talk about as "keeping under control," "not really being bothered that much," etc. (p. 642)

At the same time, anger is not the only meaning of interruption; interruption can indicate involvement or excitement. Which meaning is more likely will vary culturally. In a study of British and Italian business meetings, Bargiela-Chiappini and Harris (1997) found that Italians, compared to their British counterparts, used interruption more frequently and interpreted the acts more benevolently.

The Emotional Side of Talk

Language has a heart, Ochs and Schieffelin (1989) proclaimed a number of years ago. Determining what any particular speaker's heart is saying, however, is invariably an interpretive feat. The discourse features that display feelings typically do other kinds of interactional work. For instance, and most basically, we need to inhale and exhale air to speak. Yet a speaker that performs this basic function in a slightly more audible way than usual could be judged as feeling burdened, relieved, or, perhaps, expressing excitement (Bloch, 1996). Besnier (1989) saw the multifunctionality of affective devices as an interactional resource rather than a problem. Given that participants' feelings may be "officially" unsayable in a meeting, the potential multiple meanings of most discourse devices enable unofficial expression of the unsayable, as well as insuring deniability for a speaker. An offended other's reaction to what is self-expressed, especially when subtle feeling devices are used, may be cast as the other person "reading too much in" or being an overly sensitive type, rather than a self who is out of control or inappropriately emotional.

Table 4.1 and Table 4.2 identify discourse features that vary in meetings that have the potential to convey information about a participant's feelings. The tables reflect my synthesis of how various studies and reviews could be applied to the meeting context. Some of the actions are particular to meetings; others will occur in many contexts. The main sources I drew upon in constructing the tables included (Besnier, 1989; Biber & Finegan, 1989; Bloch, 1996; Buttny, 1997; Drew & Holt, 1989; Haviland, 1989; Jay, 1992; Ochs & Schieffelin, 1989; Pittam, 1994; Planalp, 1999; Sacks, 1992; Tracy, 2002). Table 4.1 focuses on the embodied aspects of talk—how a meeting participant looks and how talk sounds, whereas Table 4.2 considers a few language-linked aspects of talk. What feeling is likely to be attributed to a set of cues will depend, of course, on all kinds of things: (a) the other features co-occurring with a cue; (b) a speaker's baseline communicative style; (c) his or her usual position on certain argued-about issues and what is being said at the moment; (d) who a speaker or listener is (what organizational role, how the person is known to be positively or negatively connected to other members); (e) the time a cue is displayed in the meeting (at the end of 5 hours?); and (f) the particular topic, to identify but the most important.

Although nonverbal cues are often treated as the most feeling-informative actions, these cues are quite difficult to make sense of without a close look at the accompanying language. The situated meaning of a segment of talk will be shaped by the message content and the linguistic form of what is being said. The gist of what is being said and the particular words and phrases that are selected to make a speaker's point are crucially important in interpreting feeling displays. The kinds of language-linked features that convey a speaker's feeling about self, other, or the topic are quite extensive. Almost any way that language varies can lead to a feeling-loaded attribution (Besnier, 1990). For instance, the forms selected to address another or refer to them (e.g., first names,

TABLE 4.1

Some Embodied Feeling Cues

Gaze patterns	• Whose gaze is sought? Ignored or avoided? • Is gaze elsewhere (down at papers, out the window)? • Anybody's gaze held longer than usually expected? • Are others' facial reactions inspected surreptitiously? How often?
Face	• Does a person's face change colors (get red or turn pale)? Do color changes occur during talking or in reaction? • How frequently are there up-and-down head nods? Sideways shakes? Where are they placed? • What kinds of movements of a person's eyes, brows, and mouth occur? How pronounced are they? Are they full movements or started and suppressed?
Trunk movements	• Is a person leaning in or away from the center of the group space? Any sudden changes of posture? When do they occur? • How erect or slouched is a person's posture usually and at the moment? • Are there any "accidents" such as knocking things over or off the table? Where do they occur?
Hand movements	• Is a meeting participant writing? Does it seem connected to the focus of discussion? • How often are grooming and nervous gestures done? When do they occur? • What is the size and frequency of the hand gestures that are accompanying speech? • Are hand gestures done that seemed interpretable as a point? A trembling hand or a hand shaking at someone? A pound?
Voice quality and vocal particles	• Is a person speaking faster, louder, and/or using more varied intonation than usual? • What particular words and phrases are highly stressed or uttered very softly? • What vocal sounds are hearable (e.g., inhalations, laughs, indecipherable mutters) Where do they occur and how frequent are they? • How fluent or halting is a person's speech in general and at what conversational moments does it get less fluent?
Conversational pacing	• Where in a person's talk do pauses occur? Are there lengthy pauses after particular comments? • How much overlapping or interruptive speech happens? With whom and for how long?

no-names, nicknames, last names, titles) will be taken as cues of how a speaker feels toward the other (close, distant, friendly, hostile, comfortable, awkward). Terms used to reference categories of people (labels for

TABLE 4.2
How Language Features Convey Negative Sentiment

Person-reference Practices	Ex. 1: Referring to a known other using a more distant form than would be expected suggests some kind of negative feeling. "You know what your assistant said to me," rather than "you know what Jerry said to me."	Ex. 2: Describing a 55-year old as "The middle-aged woman in the main office broke the copy machine today," rather than "The new staff person broke the copy machine." The first formulation conveys a more negative view of the staff person's competence.
Speech act design	Ex. 1: Is a face-threatening act such as a reproach done in an aggravated or mitigated fashion? Said to a meeting leader, "Is this meeting ever going to end?" rather than " I was wondering when we'll be stopping today?"	Ex. 2: Praising a person for the way they did a job that everyone regards as easy is a way to convey superiority and a negative assessment.
Features of stories	Ex. 1: Use of reported speech in telling a story can be used to convey a speaker's negative feeling while taking minimal responsibility for being negatively evaluative. Said to a co-worker: "After he arrived half an hour late as I'm leaving 5 minutes early, which I had mentioned at the meeting's start, he says to me, 'Kathy, it's important that you keep this whole time period open when we schedule a meeting.'"	Ex. 2: Use of clichés or idioms in making a point convey a more intense negative feeling and is harder to disagree with. "Talking with her is like banging your head against a brick wall" rather than "Talking with her is difficult."

race, gender, or departmental groups; e.g., "the number crunchers"), pronoun choices such as "we" or "they") may be taken as evidence of whether a speaker feels respectful or dismissive.

Certain kinds of words are generally treated as evidence of a specific feeling. To give just a few examples: (a) interjections such as "oh no," "you're kidding," or "wow" are likely to cue surprise; (b) "sure, sure" or an elongated "an::::d?" with rising intonation may signal that a speaker feels the other has said something obvious, not in need of saying, lacking a point to the discussion; (c) "Well" and "yeah, but" signal that the person doesn't like what was just said and is going to disagree; (d) referring to what another said as "their story," "your version," or saying "quote, unquote" will convey skepticism (Pomerantz, 1989); and (e) use of profanity will often cue hostility toward the topic or other to whom it is directed (Jay, 1992).

Longer units of talk (e.g., speech acts, narratives, or arguments) also are revealing. Acts that compliment and criticize, for instance, are inherently feeling-tinged, as are apologies, jokes, and so on. Disagreements almost always have feelings lurking around their edges. Although a distinction can be made between idea-focused disagreement and person-centered attacks, in the fray of a speaking moment, they may be not that easy to tell apart (Tracy, 1997). Quite often when communicative conduct becomes a topic of talk, the original speaker will claim an idea-focused disagreement whereas the recipient of a remark will see it as personal attack. As Bailey (1983) noted, "although the distinction between debate and altercation is clear enough in principle (the former addresses the problem and the latter addresses the person), in practice it may be difficult to separate them, and the aggressor will surely claim to be a debater acting in the mode of the civic self" (p. 80). Conversely, a speaker whose position is disagreed with in a meeting, can frame what the conversational other is saying as an expression of personal hostility, undeserving of serious substantive engagement.

When stories are used to make discussion points, rather than packaging a stretch of talk in a formal argument (a claim and reasons), a speaker will be judged as more involved (Tannen, 1989). Moreover, the content of stories and arguments supplies "descriptions" of people and actions. These descriptions are rarely neutral—it takes a lot of design energy to actually accomplish neutrality (Clayman, 1992; Tracy & Spradlin, 1994)—and, instead, descriptions convey, sometimes quite subtly, the speaker's moral assessment (someone is silly/smart, glib/pretentious, serious) and acts (something is reasonable/unreasonable, doable/impractical). Moral assessments by their nature are expressions of positive or negative sentiment. Table 4.2 gives a few examples of how language features may be used to convey negative feelings.

THE STEINBERG SUCCESSION MEETING

Over several days, the 13 upper level managers and the president, Sam Steinberg, met at a retreat center to discuss the future of the Steinberg Company: Who was to succeed Sam Steinberg and how, if at all, should the company be reorganized? Throughout the multiday meetings, participants displayed a range of feelings, including interest, involvement, boredom, irritation, impatience, caution, and anger. The moment that is the focus of this analysis occurred during the second day of the retreat after the family dinner on the first night. During this segment of the retreat the group had defined their task as identifying barriers that kept the company from being adequately "professional." The group had begun to discuss an especially sensitive topic: differences between family and nonfamily personnel with regard to decision-making rights and prerogatives. Doyle, the vice president in charge of legal, had framed the issue this way: "the family(.) if you like (.) pulling rank (.) on the rest of the non-family executives in the corporation an saying 'Well that's the way it's goin' to be'" (660–663). Following his comment the discussion had became especially animated—one might say "heated"—with multiple people speaking loudly and interrupting each other (665–744). In the moment that followed, two participants made explicit arguments as to what the appropriate role for feelings should be in this meeting in which they were all involved. Consider both the argument each man put forth and the feeling-logic style he used to advance his proposal; first, a look at the meeting segment:

THE FEELING-LIMNED MOMENT

Transcript: Harry S. and Jack L.'s Ideas About Suitable Meeting Conduct (710–764)

710		*((Everybody talking at the same time.))*
711	HARRY S:	Would you <u>please</u> speak (.) one at a time and I think
712		professionalism can start right <u>here</u> the way we conduct the
713		meeting. Too many meetings in the past have been
714		unpro<u>fess</u>ional in that (.) problems in an unorganized manner
715		have been <u>tossed</u> on the table. Philosophies are spewed out.
716		(0.5) So professional at the meeting <u>means</u> (.) identifying the
717		problem? (0.5) moving from there to different means of solving
718		them (.) a:nd this is where we fall flat on our (.) backs <u>again</u> and
719		<u>again</u> (.) is <u>not</u> <u>nail</u>ing down *((hand taps table))* who's to do
720		what and when *((hand taps table))* and how *((hand taps table))*.
721		(0.5) If you want to turn this thing into (.) a >fish market
722		gentlemen<, it's your meeting but=
723		*((Harry's gaze during above comment was directed to the entire*
724		*table, moving from person to person))*
725	JACK L:	=Look Harry, uh I I wanna <u>stop</u> (.) and critique what you're
726		<u>say</u>ing with your=
727	HARRY S:	=Go ahead=
728	JACK L:	=I am saying that at least if you don't get out <u>feel</u>ings ((hand
729		tap)) on this *((tap))* table *((tap))* today *((tap))* and Monday
730		*((tap))* and Tuesday *((tap))*, we'll all go *((tap))* <u>back</u> and say
731		"We're- we should have said <u>and</u> we didn't say" *((tap))* and it's
732		the <u>feel</u>ings *((tap))* that <u>count</u> *((tap))*. It's the com<u>mit</u>ment

733		((tap)) one feels in<u>side</u> (.) that counts, it's not words (.) and it's
734		not it's the <u>deeds</u> and the feelings and the commitment we have
735		(.) to this organization to be <u>bet</u>ter tomorrow and today. And <u>I</u>
736		for one am ob<u>jec</u>ting to your system of method and <u>mon</u>itoring
737		because I am not doing this for a <u>mental</u> exercises, I am doing
738		this much <u>more,</u> there's much more at stake than a mental
739		exercise (.) and <u>I</u> <u>don't</u> <u>want</u> that kind of monitoring from you=
740	HARRY S:	=But m:y [my commitment
741	JACK L:	[I want <u>some</u> heat to come out (.) ((repeated finger-
742		pointing shake probably toward Harry)) I want some <u>feeling</u> to
743		come out and I want this thing to come out so that when you go
744		away we know we've done the job (.) <u>tho</u>roughly and we
745		under<u>stand</u> our job to do so we all go back and do the job
746		together (.) <u>not</u> disjointedly (.) and <u>not</u> feeling that we haven't
747		been heard and seen and felt'n put the things we feel on the
748		table
749		((People talking at once.))
750		((Jack's gaze during the above comment was directed solely
751		toward Harry))
752	SAM S:	When I started out the meeting I said each one of you in your
753		report there must be <u>something</u> that you <u>feel</u> and we recognize
754		that and this is one of the reasons we're here. So if there are in
755		tho:se those items that you (.) consider uppermost that you
756		reduce to writing and felt free to say so (.) what is uppermost in
757		your minds that you feel has some restraining influence I think
758		it should like Jack said (0.5) uh (0.7) <u>brought</u> <u>out?</u>
759	JACK L:	°Absolutely°
760	SAM S:	Fr:ee<u>ly</u> spoken.
761		(0.5)
762	( ):	[Well I I
763	SAM S:	[To the extent that we think it's pretty well <u>cov</u>ered by what's
764		already been said then we move ↓forward.

The Espoused Argument and Enacted Stance
Regarding Feeling Expression

In this interactional moment, Harry and Jack verbally stake out different positions regarding the appropriate expression of feeling and logic in meetings. Of note, this disagreement is not an abstracted argument about good conduct in the world in general; it is one about the group's here-and-now conduct in the current meeting. How should the men themselves and the other meeting participants be speaking to and with each other? The first standpoint on the issue is offered by Harry (711–722). When we reconstruct his position to give it the most coherent shape possible, as argument scholars suggest be done (e.g., van Eemeren, Grootendorst, Jackson, & Jacobs,

1993; Walton, 1992), Harry's argument can be stated as "meeting members need to be professional."

Being professional, as Harry develops it, involves two related practices. First, the group's verbal expression should be controlled. People should not interrupt each other but should "speak one at a time" (711). In addition, being controlled means avoiding a "fish market" style of talking (721). Harry's metaphor creates an evocative vivid image. In using this description, participants are being reprimanded for engaging in a loud, hawking, squabbling kind of interaction, a style that may be acceptable among uneducated, working class fish sellers but not one suitable for the current group. In relating the group's current behavior to an identity clearly at odds with how meeting participants could be expected to identify, Harry is using a strong persuasive appeal to get people to change what they are doing.

The second leg of being professional, according to Harry, is that the group needs to follow an orderly process. But rather than describing what people ought to be doing, Harry advances his argument by identifying what needs to be avoided. People should avoid tossing problems on the table (714–715) and spewing out philosophies (715). He concludes by saying that the group needs to avoid "not nailing down who is to do what and when, and how" (719–720); of note, he frames this activity as one the group has repeatedly failed to do ("this is where we fall flat on our backs again and again" [718–719]). In sum, we could say that Harry argues for a rational stance toward meetings and organizational life, one that minimizes emotion as much as possible. In making this argument, Harry is espousing what many see as the official and dominant ideology of organizational life (Fineman, 1993; Putnam & Mumby, 1993).

In contrast, Jack develops a quite different standpoint. In this meeting about the company's future leadership, Jack argues, authentic expression is needed. Authentic expression requires that there be some "heat" (741) and that people need to get feelings out (728, 742–743). He provides an elaborated argument as to why this is the best way for participants to act. His argument (728–748) links five smaller claims: (1) feelings count, (2) feelings reveal commitments, (3) commitments tie to deeds, (4) deeds are crucial for building a better organization, and (5) feeling expression enables doing the job "thoroughly" (744), not "disjointedly" (746). Besides making the case for the advantage of feelings being expressed in the meeting, Jack directly argues against Harry's proposal. Where Harry equated controlled and orderly expression with being professional, Jack treats such conduct, at least given the occasion, as a sign of inauthentic expression. But in contrast to Harry's use of a vivid metaphor (fish market) to convey what he is against, Jack offers an extended argument. Harry's espoused mode of conduct, according to

Jack, is not professional, the frame Harry is seeking to impose, but it is a "method of monitoring" (739), a way of expressing self that goes with "mental exercises" (737) rather that how people act when there is something "at stake" (738). Furthermore, Jack argues, for the group to proceed collectively on such an important matter as the direction of the company's future requires that everyone feels they've been seen, heard, and had a chance to "put the things we feel on the table" (747–748). In sum, then, Jack's argument about how participants ought to be talking in their meeting gives feelings a central and positive role, and he makes the case using a detailed verbal argument.

In the next turn at talk (752–758), President Sam Steinberg enters the conversation. Although not explicitly positioning himself as the arbiter of this disagreement, his institutional status gives his words this weight. His comment is not neutral; he sides with Jack. He, too, expected participants' reports to convey, "something that you feel" (753). Quite directly, Sam aligns with Jack, commenting that his own position is, "like Jack said" (758). In this moment of conflict, then, Jack's argument about appropriate feeling expression would seem to be the official victor. But the actual picture is more complicated. For not only is each man making an explicit verbal argument about how one should or should not express feelings but each person is also enacting a stance through his talk.

Harry and Jack's remarks, by virtue of what talk always does, are packaging feelings with their message's verbal content. Through the language devices, vocal features, and embodied actions that each man selects to make his explicit argument, a claim about the suitable link between feelings and logical argument is being enacted as well as stated. That is, through the way a speaker talks his or her stance toward an issue—in this case, how feelings and logic should be linked—may be inferred (Ochs, 1993; Tracy, 2002). At the enacted level a different, much more confusing picture emerges. Consider what we see.

Both men express feelings, but the kind (and intensity) each one expresses is different. Jack's feeling stance could be described as "intense but measured," "feeling strongly about the issue (feeling-logic links) but expressing it in a controlled fashion." Feeling intensity is conveyed through voice; Jack systematically and methodically stresses key words in the argument he is building. In addition, his taps on the table, also rhythmic and measured and clearly not "pounding," occur at the end of verbal clauses, therein contributing to an impression of controlled intensity. Moreover, rather than directing his comment to the entire group, his comment is addressed to Harry. Beginning with the announcement that he wants to "critique what you're saying" (725–726), Jack seems to looks directly at Harry through the entirety of his comment. His unwavering gaze toward Harry communicates a focused involvement with Harry, a sense that he is not attending to other participants in the group much. Including all members of a group in one's gaze as a person talks conveys that everyone in the group is a recipient of one's comments. It is generally a desirable communicative practice, but it is effortful. Such group monitoring is especially likely to drop out when a speaker gets involved with a particular other or when a person is developing a cognitively complex message. Both attributions seem plausible in Jack's case.

Although Jack is displaying feelings, they are the kind of feelings most likely to be seen as reasonable and "rational" in organizational meetings. His intensity conveys a caring about the issue under discussion and a willingness to disagree with a fellow participant. There is little sense that he is being hostile or inappropriately personal. His intensity is paired with an elaborate verbal argument rather than, say, a story, and the language he selects is not particularly vivid or metaphorical. Jack's conversational style could be described as impassioned rationality, surely what Bailey (1983) had in mind when he argued for the tactical advantage of passion in meetings.

The linguistic clothing of Harry's markedly shorter comment is decidedly less rational. Although we can reconstruct what he said as an argument—"this group should act professionally and here are my reasons for that position"—this was not the structure of the comment. Harry's turn begins with a statement that it is virtually impossible to hear as other than a reprimand ("Would you please speak (.) one at a time and I think professionalism can start right here the way we conduct the meeting" [711–713]). Given that the topic of the meeting is "barriers to professionalism," his comment that the group is being unprofessional is a pointed criticism. In addition, because his comment lacks the indirection usually exhibited in meetings when people criticize each other, it conveys a sense that he is speaking without thought, offering an unedited, albeit mild expression of hostility. Compare this opening to one in which a group leader said, "Let me the stop the discussion for a sec and ask us to reflect on how we're talking. I think that we need to ..."). Furthermore, Harry's remark treats what he is saying as a straightforward description; he includes none of the verbal devices (e.g., "I'd like to interject my opinion about what's going on here") that mark what he is saying as an interpretation of what is going on, a characterization with which others might disagree. Finally, his absence of "we" language conveys the sense that it is only others who are transgressing; his criticism does not include himself.

The end of his turn, "if you want to turn this into a fish market gentlemen, it's your meeting but" is a particularly interesting discourse move. Because being like a fish market is an unimaginable goal for a business group, the remark comes across as sarcastic. Utterances that offer others a "description" of another's action that invoke a vivid negative scene that the person could be expected to deny wanting, are a powerful indirect strategy to legislate another's behavior. This kind of speech act, I would suggest, occurs when a speaker is irritated and exasperated. Its presence, thereby, conveys those feelings. Consider how common it is to hear a parent say to a misbehaving child, "Do you want to go to bed right now? Then just keep doing what you're doing." In addition Harry's speech is peppered with idioms ("not nailing down" [719], "falling flat on our backs" [718]) and intense language ("spew[ing]" [715] philosophies and "toss[ing]" [715] problems) that advance his position while seeking to frame all other positions as unreasonable and nonarguable.

Harry's vocal and embodied actions include many of the same features as Jack's; he uses his voice to stress key points and he taps the table several times. Through these actions, Harry conveys that he feels intensely about what he is saying. At the same time, Harry's intensity is accompanied by a not-so-subtle display of irritation (a feeling presumed to be fleeting) directed at people. In addition, because Harry's initiating speech act is a metatalk reproach directed to all in the group (see his gaze), it has more of an outburst quality than if his remark had engaging with a particular other's assertion. Thus, Harry's argument about the inappropriateness of feeling expression in their meeting is enacted in a style that contradicts what he is saying. His remark is limned with negative feeling. *Limning*, as Mangham (1998) unpacks, is the process of illuminating a manuscript's letters with gold or other distinctive features. Both speakers' comments are limned with feeling; Harry's, though, are limned with those feelings organizational members are likely to identify as undesirable, not fully in control (impatience and irritation) and, generally, deserving repression.

THE UPSHOT: THE STEINBERG MEETING AND MEETINGS IN GENERAL

What is the role for feeling expression in meeting talk? How should people conduct themselves? What ought to be the ideal for work meeting conduct? The interactional moment analyzed in this chapter is, admittedly, a small slice of the kinds of feelings that are routinely felt and expressed in meetings. Noticeably absent from the Steinberg meeting excerpt were: (a) expressions of amusement, warmth, and connection that a spate of teasing and laughter might make apparent; (b) expressions of pride and self-confidence, or nervous insecurity that might be conveyed in giving a report; and (c) expressions of disinterest and boredom, the feelings that meetings are ever so frequently accused of engendering (Seibold & Krikorian, 1997). Recognizing this limitation, nevertheless, let us consider what a close look at this one meeting moment suggests.

First, Jack's argument about feeling expression suggests one particularly important situational feature that needs to be considered: the issue (topic) of a meeting and how consequential it is in the organization's life. Jack's argument about feeling expression highlighted that what was being discussed in the Steinberg meeting was not run-of-the mill; it was a direction-setting, unusually important topic. An implication of his argument, then, is that what is appropriate conduct will depend on what is being discussed: Organizationally important issues both engender and deserve more intense feeling expression. Thus, how much organizational members should "get [their] feelings [out] on [the] table" (728–729) will depend on the issue. It is reasonable and right, I would argue, to have an expectation that organizational members will both express and repress feelings. Not being willing to express feelings at some meeting moments is as inappropriate conduct as is a failure to adequately dampen negative feelings at others. It is probably desirable for workplace meetings to allow for greater feeling expression than they normally do. At the same time, it is a good thing that people no longer throw glasses or knives at each other, or call each other "thieving murderers."

Second, "feelings" and "logic" refer to many aspects of demeanor that are different from each other and are cued by distinct packages of interactional particulars. In the Steinberg meeting, for instance, that speakers felt strongly about a topic (intensely) seemed most directly tied to a speaker's vocal quality (loudness, speaking rate, use of vocal stress), embodied actions (gestures and gaze), and features of the group's conversational pace (absence of pauses, frequency of overlap). In contrast, irritation with others, as was seen with Harry's comment, was made visible primarily through selected speech acts, the content of what was said, and particular words and phrases. Being "in control of one's feelings," what most often is referenced as "being rational," would seem linked to the elaborateness of verbal argument whereas venting or being emotional would seem to go with nonelaborate argument, idioms, and intense language in a context where verbal argument is frequent and expected.

Third, analysis of this moment showed that contradictions between espoused ideals of meeting conduct and what is enacted is not unusual, even in moments where a person is directly stating an ideal. Both Jack and Harry enacted stances toward the role of feeling expression that were contradictory, at least partly, with what each verbally said. Jack developed an extended argument (i.e., selected a highly rational and not very emotional form) to argue for the need for feelings whereas Harry commented emotionally on the importance of restrained feelings and meeting orderliness. In addition, neither Harry nor Jack seemed aware that their communicative actions could be regarded as somewhat at odds with what they were saying. Billig (1987) argued that reasonable conduct in social life requires the use of contrary principles. As he puts it, "Because every absolute principle has the character of overstepping the bounds of reality, each principle needs to be held in check by the countervailing force of contrary principle" (p. 211). If Harry and Jack are typical meeting participants, it would appear that principle checking goes on even within individual speakers' utterances within a single moment of expression.

Feelings and thoughts need each other and can be expected to come out together. The practical issue in reflecting about how to act in meetings is which specific feelings and thoughts are to be expressed (or repressed) and exactly how to package them. For individuals' sense of their own efficacy, for the good of the group, and for the success of an organization, it is important to get the packaging right. At the same time, situated judgments as to whether an individual, a group, or organization, in fact, did get it right, are themselves likely to be contested and become especially feeling-limned controversies. For how else can it be? Moments where one participant argues explicitly how self and other ought to be behaving—almost always at times where the speaker sees the other already doing wrong—are emotion-generating, morally consequential moments. It would be undesirable for it to be otherwise.

REFERENCES

Bailey, F. G. (1983). *The tactical uses of passion*. Ithaca, NY: Cornell University Press.

Bargiela-Chiappini, F., & Harris, S. J. (1997). *Managing language: The discourse of corporate meetings*. Amsterdam: John Benjamins.

Bergmann, J. R. (1998). Introduction: Morality in discourse. *Research on Language and Social Interaction, 31*, 279–294.

Besnier, N. (1989). Literacy and feeling: The encoding of affect in Nukulaelae letters. *Text, 9*, 69–91.

Besnier, N. (1990). Language and affect. *Annual Review of Anthropology, 19*, 419–451.

Biber, D., & Finegan, E. (1989). Styles of stance in English: Lexical and grammatical marking of evidentiality and affect. *Text, 9*, 93–124.

Billig, M. (1887). *Arguing and thinking*. Cambridge: Cambridge University Press.

Bloch, C. (1996). Emotions and discourse. *Text, 16*, 323–341.

Boden, D. (1994). *The business of talk: Organization in action*. Cambridge, England: Polity Press.

Buttny, R. (1997). Reported speech in talking race on campus. *Human Communication Research, 23*, 477–506.

Clayman, S. E. (1992). Footing in the achievement of neutrality: The case of news interview discourse. In P. Drew & J. Heritage (Eds.), *Talk at work: Interaction in institutional settings* (pp. 163–198).

Drew, P. (1998). Complaints about transgressions and misconduct. *Research on Language and Social Interaction, 31*, 295–325.

Drew, P., & Holt, E. (1989). Complainable matters: The use of idiomatic expressions in making complaints. *Social Problems, 35,* 398–417.

Fineman, S. (1993). Introduction. In S. Fineman (Ed.), *Emotion in organizations* (pp. 1–8). London: Sage.

Forgas, J. P. (2000). The role of affect in social cognition. In J. P. Forgas (Ed.), *Feeling and thinking: The role of affect in social cognition* (pp. 1–28). Cambridge, England: Cambridge University Press.

Haviland, J. B. (1989). 'Sure, sure': Evidence and affect. *Text, 9,* 27–68.

Jay, T. (1992). *Cursing in America.* Philadelphia: John Benjamins.

Mangham, I. L. (1998). Emotional discourse in organizations. In D. Grant, T. Keenoy, & C. Oswick (Eds.), *Discourse and organization* (pp. 51–64). London: Sage.

Ochs, E. (1993). Constructing social identity: A language socialization perspective. *Research on Language and Social Interaction, 26,* 287–306.

Ochs, E., & Schieffelin, B. (1989). Language has a heart. *Text, 9,* 7–25.

Parkinson, B. (1995). Emotion and motivation. In B. Parkinson & A. M. Colman (Eds.), *Emotion and motivation* (pp. 1–21). Essex, England: Longman.

Parrott, W. G., & Harré, R. (1996). Overview. In R. Harré & W. G. Parrott (Eds.), *The emotions: Social, cultural and biological dimensions* (pp. 1–24). London: Sage.

Pittam, J. (1994). *Voice in social interaction.* Thousand Oaks, CA: Sage.

Planalp, S. (1999). *Communicating emotion: Social, moral and cultural processes.* Cambridge, England: Cambridge University Press.

Pomerantz, A. (1989). Constructing skepticism: Four devices used to engender the audience's skepticism. *Research on Language and Social Interaction, 22,* 293–313.

Putnam, L. L., & Mumby, D. K. (1993). Organizations, emotion and the myth of rationality. In S. Fineman (Ed.), *Emotion in organizations* (pp. 36–57). London: Sage.

Sacks, H. (1992). *Lectures on conversation.* Cambridge, MA: Blackwell.

Schwartzman, H. B. (1989). *The meeting: Gatherings in organizations and communities.* New York: Plenum Press.

Seibold, D. R., & Krikorian, D. H. (1997). Planning and facilitating group meetings. In L. Frey & K. Barge (Eds.), *Managing group life* (pp. 270–305). Boston: Houghton Mifflin.

Stearns, C. W., & Stearns, P. (1986). *Anger: The struggle for emotional control in America's history.* Chicago: University of Chicago Press.

Tannen, D. (1989). *Talking voices: Repetition, dialogue, and imagery in conversational discourse.* New York: Cambridge University Press.

Tracy, K. (1997). *Colloquium: Dilemmas of academic discourse.* Norwood, NJ: Ablex.

Tracy, K. (2002). *Everyday talk: Building and reflecting identities.* New York: Guilford.

Tracy, K., & Spradlin, A. (1994). Talking like a mediator: Conversational moves of experienced divorce mediators. In J. Folger & T. Jones (Eds.), *New directions in mediation* (pp. 110–132). Thousand Oaks, CA: Sage.

Van Eemeren, F. H., Grootendorst, R., Jackson, S., & Jacobs, S. (1993). *Reconstructing argumentative discourse.* Tuscaloosa: University of Alabama Press.

Van Vree, W. (1999). *Meetings, manners and civilization: The development of modern meeting behaviour.* London: Leicester University Press.

Walton, D. N. (1992). *Plausible argument in everyday conversation.* Albany: State University of New York Press.

Winton, W. M. (1990). Language and emotion. In H. Giles & P. W. Robinson (Eds.), *Handbook of language and social psychology* (pp. 33–49). Chichester, England: John Wiley.

Chapter 5

Contradictions in the Metatalk About Feelings in *Corporation: After Mr. Sam*

Linda L. Putnam
Texas A&M University

The study of emotions has not typically held center stage in the literature on organizational decision making. Our rational models of group decision processes lead us to treat individuals as problem solvers rather than as political and personal beings. Previous research on emotions at work focuses on emotional labor, display rules for emotional expression, and positive and negative emotions (Rafaeli & Sutton, 1987; Waldron, 1994). But emotions are also discursive acts that demonstrate how members regulate, control, and resist organizational actions (Fineman, 1993).

This chapter examines metatalk about feelings in the transcription and videotape of *Corporation: After Mr. Sam*. In particular, it highlights how metatalk functions to express and suppress feelings, open and close spaces for action, and resist and comply with power relationships. Using an approach aimed at deciphering dualities in talk, it centers on the tensions implicit in this meeting and an analysis of the multimeanings surrounding these tensions. It sets forth three major dichotomies in which tensions about emotional display surface. The first dichotomy, professional versus unprofessional, refers to the orderly procedures, professional controls, and task-oriented leadership. Issues of professionalism, tensions between mind and feelings, and concerns for commitment fall into this larger duality of professionalism. The second major dichotomy, feeling rules versus work feelings, arises from the way that appeals for expressing feelings aims to resist managerial goals and prerogatives while complying with norms for conducting meetings. The third major dichotomy, open versus closed, focuses on the ways that monitoring work process governs patterns of organizing. Issues of diplomacy and tact arise within the rules for handling confrontation in meetings. Dualities also exist in the ways metatalk functions through asserting and retracting, displaying and masking, and resisting and complying with power. On another level, the metatalk about feelings also functions as a text within a text for an audience that is not present at this meeting—the employees of the organization and the general public. Hence, the latter part of this chapter introduces an intertextual reading of the role of emotions in this meeting.

Overall, these contradictions reveal ironies that surface in the weekend retreat; that is, emotional expression leads to suppression, resistance reaffirms power, and ambiguity about a successor generates clarity of choice. Thus, the metatalk about feelings and the management of dualities reconstitutes Mr. Sam's domination of the organizational process, his control in the choice of a successor, the normative family traditions in which the company has operated for years, and more importantly, his company's domination in the industry.

This chapter parallels and yet departs from Tracy's (chap. 4) analysis of the ways that participants negotiate the conduct of organizational meetings. Similar to Tracy, this chapter examines the discursive positions that key players take and the way that discourse accomplishes meetings. However, it departs from Tracy's study in focusing on contradictions that both produce and resist organizational constraints, particularly in terms of norms of expression, references to hidden agendas, and negotiation of power relationships.

This chapter begins with a review of the literature on emotion and emotional labor and then it explores the role of dualities in the discourse about feelings. After a brief discussion of assumptions, the chapter presents an analysis of the three major dichotomies in metatalk about feelings, focusing primarily on lines (711–764) of the full transcript and videotape of *Corporation: After Mr. Sam.*

EMOTIONS AND EMOTIONAL WORK

The study of emotions and emotional labor in organizations has gained increasing popularity in the past decade (Fineman, 1993, 1996, 2000; Morris & Feldman, 1996; Waldron, 1994). Emotional displays, typically defined as the expression of affected states, such as joy, love, fear, and anger, differ from feelings, which is the subjective experience of emotions (Fineman, 1996). Emotions typically entail three components—cognitive appraisals, expressions, and action tendencies (Jones, 2001; Lazarus, 1994)—whereas feelings do not necessarily involve cognitive components (Damasio, 1994). Emotions and feelings do not always coincide; hence, a person can show happiness without feeling happy.

Moreover, emotional expressions are socially shared scripts that are culturally determined (Abu-Lughod & Lutz, 1990); thus, organizational cultures shape not only the language and nonverbal signs linked to emotions but also the appropriateness of emotional displays.

Several principles underlie this analysis of emotions in organizations. First, emotional displays are socially constructed; that is, social settings and norms influence both the interpretation and expression of feelings (Jones, 2001). Secondly, evaluations or interpretations of events elicit emotions. For example, when a plan or goal is interrupted, individuals respond with frustration or disappointment. Thus, a thwarted or blocked goal or an unexpected outcome can trigger an emotional reaction (Batson, Shaw, & Oleson, 1992). Third, emotional displays are constituted through discourse or communication (Planalp, 1999; Rosenberg, 1990). Discourse, here, includes linguistic as well as symbolic and rhetorical forms such as rituals, narratives, and nonverbal behaviors. At the linguistic level, the very structure of the text, significant pauses and intonations, the inclusion of negative and positive statements, and the use of contradictions—all convey emotional expressions (Perinbanayagam, 1991). Even the choice of words or semantics of language reflects types and degrees of emotions. For example, the use of the term *embarrassment* suggests a milder feeling than does the term *shame*. Nonverbal cues such as eye gaze, hand movements, and body position reinforce or often contradict verbal expressions.

The fourth principle is that emotion displays are rule-governed in that families, society, and organizations enact implicit and explicit feeling rules to govern how individuals "ought" to feel in particular settings. These feeling rules act as organizational norms for expected behavior. Just as language is rule-governed, Averill (1994) noted that feeling rules are constitutive, regulatory, and procedural. *Constitutive rules* refer to how an emotion is defined and *regulatory rules* prescribe how it should be socially enacted. *Procedural rules*, in turn, refer to the strategic expression of emotion, or the way emotional displays are used procedurally to enact a particular strategic message (e.g., displays of anger used strategically to evoke a reaction from the other person). Thus, feeling rules exist on three different levels, even though most studies focus only on the constitutive and the regulatory levels.

Feeling rules are closely linked to emotional work in that individuals consciously suppress private feelings in order to display expected or appropriate emotions. When this occurs as part of one's employment, it is often referred to as *emotional labor*, the requirement to adopt specific feeling rules as part of one's job, for example, to be compassionate, to be cheerful, or to show firmness to accomplish one's tasks (Hochschild, 1983). The problem with emotional labor is that managers and bureaucracies, with their productivity concerns, dictate the terms of appropriate emotional displays (Wharton, 1993, 1999). Moreover, the control of emotional displays in the service of bureaucratic ends treats personal feelings as a commodity that serves managerial goals rather than individual and relational aims (Mumby & Putnam, 1992). Feeling rules in organizations, then, are linked to power in that the norms for appropriate emotional displays often serve the ends of the more powerful members. Less powerful organizational members engage in self-surveillance, compliance, or resistance of emotional control.

The study of emotional labor, mostly in the service industries, has centered primarily on the discrepancy between felt and displayed emotion through either surface or deep acting (Ashforth & Humphrey, 1993). Research addresses the role of emotional labor in the fast food industry (Leidner, 1993), with flight attendants (Hochschild, 1983; Murphy, 1998; Wouters, 1989), with supermarket cashiers (Rafaeli, 1989; Rafaeli & Sutton, 1987, 1989), with insurance agents (Leidner, 1991), bill collectors (Sutton, 1991), and cruise coordinators (Tracy, 2000). Most of the employees in these industries undergo explicit training on appropriate emotional displays. Moreover, newcomers are socialized through employee manuals and corporate mission statements that embody display rules for emotional expression. Performance in accordance with prescribed feeling rules is monitored and explicitly tied to rewards (Steinberg, 1999; Steinberg & Figart, 1999).

The problem with this approach is that employees also monitor their emotions spontaneously and genuinely to adjust to and promote effective interpersonal interactions (Ashforth & Humphrey, 1995; Planalp, 1999). Professional employees, such as doctors, nurses, pastors, and counselors rarely have explicit instructions on feeling rules appropriate for their professional tasks, yet their jobs require emotional management to foster effective client relationships (Miller, 2002). Emotional labor and the feeling rules linked to it, then, need to be broadened to include professional roles and assessment of relationships as well as individual behaviors (Fineman, 1996).

In studies of how employees learn the rules for emotional display, professionalism surfaces as the major explanatory factor (Kramer & Hess, 2002). Understanding professionalism typically requires tacit knowledge acquired through training, socialization, and observation rather than through employee handbooks. Irrespective of training, maintaining professionalism is central to effective emotional management for both positive and negative emotions. Inappropriate display of positive emotions at work includes poor timing of positive comments, misdirected praise, or showing too much personal affection at work. In contrast, appropriate display of negative emotions at work usually requires masking one's feelings. Hence, people tone down their anger or hold back feelings of disappointment. One overall conclusion of Kramer and Hess's (2002) study is that appropriate communication of emotion focuses on others rather than on oneself. In effect, consideration of other's feelings overrides explicit and direct expression of emotions in the workplace, especially if it would hurt work relationships. Overall, more research is needed on work feelings that emerge from spontaneous interactions, relational messages, and the enacted meanings within a particular setting rather than from emotional labor required to accomplish managerial goals (Mumby & Putnam, 1992; Putnam & Mumby, 1993).

DUALITIES IN METATALK ABOUT FEELINGS

One area that has received limited attention is the metatalk about feelings. Perhaps because metatalk, also known as "communication about communication," is so uncommon in work settings, researchers rarely focus on how employees talk about the way they interact, what their messages mean, or how they feel in a situation. Metatalk embodies certain dualities in communication in that it is simultaneously conscious and unconscious and invokes present, past, and future interactions (Watzlawick, Beavin, & Jackson, 1967). At one level, individuals know that they are talking about the ways they interact and yet at another level, they are not always conscious about how they are conducting their metatalk. Metatalk also exists in the present and yet it pulls from the past to anchor relationships for the future.

Metatalk is also tied to the report and command aspects of language in that each message contains information or content as well as command or relational cues as to how the message should be interpreted. A person can give the same content message by saying "Why don't we all stand up?" and "All rise." The difference in these two messages resides in the way discourse conveys command or relational cues as to how the message should be interpreted. In the first example, the syntax of the request indicates equality in asking the other person to stand, while the imperative order in the second example suggests inequality, if not superiority. Hence, metatalk can be implicit in the way that discourse signals how messages should be interpreted and how actors should relate to each other.

Just as metatalk signals both content and relational meanings, dichotomies arise from metatalk itself. These dichotomies evolve from recognizing and yet denying the metatalk, asserting and retracting initiatives, and opening and closing interaction. In a postmodern perspective, metatalk functions to introduce multiple meanings that create ambiguity, open space for resistance, and introduce diversity. Thus, dichotomies that arise from the metatalk create space for resistance and for shifting organizational power relationships (Putnam & Fairhurst, 2001).

Metatalk about feelings is a particular type of communication that lives out the relationship between emotion and rationality. Although existing in tension with each other, emotions and rationality can be viewed as intertwined (Fineman, 1996; Miller, 2002; Mumby & Putnam, 1992). Emotions inform rationality through the way decision-making functions as intuition, hunches, and personal calls. That is, hunches and intuitive insights are often driven initially through emotional or "gut feelings" rather than logical analysis. Gaining a rational view of feelings is vital for developing perceptual awareness and for understanding diversity in the workplace (Vaughan, 1989). Rationality, then, is a social phenomenon in which emotions play an integral part. In like manner, the management of emotions incorporates intelligence through rational processes (Barrett & Gross, 2001). Emotional intelligence becomes a way of understanding others and knowing how to act in particular situations. Because the two can be intertwined, the way organizational members process both emotionality and rationality is a key to opening spaces for action and to altering power relationships.

METATALK AND THE DISCOURSE OF FEELINGS IN *CORPORATION: AFTER MR. SAM*

This study examines the dualities in the metatalk about feelings in the videotape *Corporation: After Mr. Sam*. The first stage centers on discourse in the text of the transcript of this company retreat. Thus, it treats the transcript of *Corporation: After Mr. Sam* as the action text of the meeting without attending to why it was taped, who taped it, and how it was edited. The second stage of analysis shifts to a larger audience in which the very act of videotaping this retreat has the potential to be shown to others, revisited, and reviewed. This intertextual reading takes into account that this meeting has a public presence and an audience outside the seclusion of its participants. From an intertextual analysis, the discourse in this meeting has layers of complexity as participants enact performances for multiple audiences, not just individuals in the room. First, however, this chapter focuses on an analysis of a segment of interaction during the meeting. It draws from three major dichotomies—professional and unprofessional, feeling rules and work feelings, and open and closed systems—to interpret how these dualities play out in the deliberation about whom will be Mr. Sam's successor.

Professional and Unprofessional

The tensions between rationality and emotion begin with a discussion of professionalism and unprofessional behavior (711–748). After a discus-

sion about the company being built at corporate, Harry S., the facilitator, comments:

```
711  HARRY S:  Would you please speak (.) one at a time and I think
712            professionalism can start right here the way we conduct the
713            meeting. Too many meetings in the past have been
714            unprofessional in that (.) problems in an unorganized manner
715            have been tossed on the table. Philosophies are spewed out.
716            (0.5) So professional at the meeting means (.) identifying the
717            problem? (0.5) moving from there to different means of solving
718            them (.) a:nd this is where we fall flat on our (.) backs again and
719            again (.) is not nailing down ((hand taps table)) who's to do
720            what and when ((hand taps table)) and how ((hand taps table)).
721            (0.5) If you want to turn this thing into (.) a >fish market
722            gentlemen<, it's your meeting but=
```

In this example, Harry raises the issue of *professionalism* as a norm
that must be upheld at the meeting. *Professional* in this passage is
equated with rational practices such as identifying the problem and
moving to solve the problem. *Unprofessional*, in Harry's view, refers to
an unorganized manner, tossing things on the table, and turning the
meeting into a fish market. Tossing things on the table juxtaposes professionalism with irrationality and with the norms characteristic of a
fish market in which people talk loudly, all at once, grabble and barter
for merchandise, as Tracy notes in chapter 4. Harry does not want to
see this meeting turn into a session in which group members grabble
and barter for ideas. The issue of professionalism sets up other dualities in the discourse through the relationship between feeling rules and
emotional expression.

Other dualisms occur in the following passage in which Jack L.
comments:

```
725  JACK L:   =Look Harry, uh I I wanna stop (.) and critique what you're
726            saying with your=
727  HARRY S:  =Go ahead=
728  JACK L:   =I am saying that at least if you don't get out feelings ((hand
729            tap)) on this ((tap)) table ((tap)) today ((tap)) and Monday
730            ((tap)) and Tuesday ((tap)), we'll all go ((tap)) back and say
731            "We're-we should have said and we didn't say" ((tap)) and it's
732            the feelings ((tap)) that count ((tap)). It's the commitment
733            ((tap)) one feels inside (.) that counts, it's not words (.) and it's
734            not it's the deeds and the feelings and the commitment we have
735            (.) to this organization to be better tomorrow and today. And I
736            for one am objecting to your system of method and monitoring
737            because I am not doing this for a mental exercises, I am doing
```

738   this much <u>more</u>, there's much more at stake than a mental
739   exercise (.) and <u>I</u> <u>don't</u> <u>want</u> that kind of monitoring from you=
740 HARRY S: =But m:y [my commitment
741 JACK L: [I want <u>some</u> heat to come out (.) *((repeated finger-*
742   *pointing shake probably toward Harry))* I want some <u>feeling</u> to
743   come out and I want this thing to come out so that when you go
744   away we know we've done the job (.) <u>thoroughly</u> and we
745   under<u>stand</u> our job to do so we all go back and do the job
746   together (.) <u>not</u> disjointedly (.) and <u>not</u> feeling that we haven't
747   been heard and seen and felt'n put the things we feel on the
748   table
749   *((People talking at once.))*
750   *((Jack's gaze during the above comment was directed solely*
751   *toward* Harry))

In (728), Jack opposes and even challenges Harry's dichotomy of professional and unprofessional with an appeal for the discussion of feelings and explicit metatalk about feelings. Feelings then become linked to a mental exercise (738–739), "there's much more at stake than a mental exercise." Jack, then, separates himself from the norm of professionalism, as defined by Harry. In Jack's view, professional is not simply orderly conduct of a meeting, rather it entails commitments tied to deeds. Professionalism is not just a mental exercise.

Jack then introduces the dichotomy of feelings and mind (mental exercises) and the duality of what really counts in an organization—commitments versus your system of monitoring (734, 736). As Jack notes, "it's not words (.) and it's not the <u>deeds</u> and the feelings" (733–734) NOT "your system of method and monitoring" (736). Thus, Jack equates monitoring as a mental exercise that stands in opposition to expression of feelings. He contends that it is not the rational system that is the driver, rather it is the "commitment we have (.) to this organization to be <u>better</u> tomorrow and today" (734–735). This sentence suggests that Jack's appeal is to Sam, the company CEO, particularly in the statement (739), "And I <u>don't</u> <u>want</u> that kind of monitoring from you." In doing so, Jack engages in a discursive struggle to object to Harry's brand of professionalism, to introduce feelings as juxtaposed to mind, and to align feelings with commitments; thus resisting Harry's brand of rationality.

Sam responds to these dualisms by realigning feelings with rationality as he comments:

752 SAM S: When I started out the meeting I said each one of you in your
753   report there must be <u>something</u> that you <u>feel</u> and we recognize
754   that and this is one of the reasons we're here. So if there are in
755   tho:se those items that you (.) consider uppermost that you

756		reduce to writing and felt free to say so (.) what is uppermost in
757		your minds that you feel has some restraining influence I think
758		it should like Jack said (0.5) uh (0.7) <u>brought out</u>?
759	JACK L:	°Absolutely°
760	SAM S:	Fr:ee<u>ly</u> spoken.
761		(0.5)
762	( ):	[Well I I
763	SAM S:	[To the extent that we think it's pretty well <u>covered</u> by what's
764		already been said then we move ↓forward.

In this passage, Sam locates emotions as reasons linked to the mind. In (753–754), Sam acknowledges something you feel as the <u>reasons</u> why we are here and he urges the participants to say what is uppermost in their "<u>minds</u> that you feel" (757). Thus, Sam picks up on the dichotomy and reclaims feelings as an expression of the mind and as subsumed under the goals and reasons that senior executives are gathered at the retreat. Drawing upon his power, he also links talk about feelings to his authority, "When I started out this meeting" (752) and what "you [have] reduce[d] to writing" (755–756), thus reclaiming feelings as part of professionalism and rationality.

This passage from Mr. Sam, then, illustrates how different speakers vie for their definitions of social reality through negotiating the relationship between professional and unprofessional. Harry defines these constructs through aligning professionalism with rationality. Jack then challenges Harry's definitions and aligns feelings, not with disorderly rationality, but with commitment to the organization and with doing the job thoroughly. Drawing from and discrediting Harry's notion of rationality, Jack contends he does not want to adhere to the norm of professionalism for some "mental exercise" (738–739). Feelings, instead, are genuine forms of commitment. Sam responds to Jack by reclaiming the link between feelings and rationality, making feelings part of the reasons for the gathering and for what resides "uppermost in [their] minds" (756–757). Thus, the discourse moves back to professionalism through appropriating feelings to reasons and minds.

Feeling Rules and Work Feelings

Most studies of feeling rules link this concept to emotional labor or to the use of emotional displays to perform one's role or particular job, such as a bill collector, an airline steward, or a counselor. In this analysis of Mr. Sam, the concept of *feeling rules* refers to the implicit norms that govern how emotional displays should be handled in meetings, especially those practices linked to professional decorum. *Work feelings*, in contrast, are those expressions that emerge from spontaneous interactions and are linked to the relational messages and enacted meanings in the setting. Analysis of the transcript suggests that work feelings come into contention with the feeling rules that govern the norms for professionalism. These tensions introduce modes of resistance to organizational rationality and power relationships.

Linguistic indicators of appropriate displays of feelings surface in Harry's comments (711–722). Both constitutive and regulatory rules call for an orderly, task related session—to aid in "nailing down who is to do what and when" (719–720) and to avoid "toss[ing problems] on the table" (715) and "turn[ing] this thing into (.) a >fish market." (721–722). Expressing feelings would need to conform to Harry's view of an orderly, rational process. As a hired facilitator, Harry's job as a professional is to keep the group on task, translating feelings into organizational goals and channeling issues to Sam, the president. Ironically, Harry's statements (711–722) are highly expressive, even irritated, as seen in the use of such vivid language as "toss[ing problems]" (714–715), "spew[ing philosophies]" (715), and "turn[ing the meeting] into (.) a *fish >market*" (721). Hence, in many ways, Harry displays his feelings through invoking his appeal for professionalism and by expressing his irritation verbally through his linguistic choices rather than through his nonverbal cues.

Jack's concerns (725–748) aim to balance his work feelings with the feeling rules that govern task-related interaction. He displays frustration and anxiety about the unspeakable issues, namely, nepotism and family governance, as evident in his use of demands, such as "I *want* some feeling to come out" (742–743) and "I *don't want* that kind of monitoring from you" (739), and vocal intonation and strong emphasis on such words as "feelings" (742) and "mental exercises" (737). Lines (734–738) contain another speech act that points to strong emotion, a warning:

```
728  JACK L:    =I am saying that at least if you don't get out feelings ((hand
729                tap)) on this ((tap)) table ((tap)) today ((tap)) and Monday
730                ((tap)) and Tuesday ((tap)), we'll all go ((tap)) back and say
731                "We're-we should have said and we didn't say" ((tap)) and it's
732                the feelings ((tap)) that count ((tap)).
```

Moreover, his nonverbal behaviors of tapping on the table increase in intensity to a level of pounding by (732). These nonverbal expressions suggest that Jack is more frustrated than his words suggest. Hence, he appears to be masking his feelings while he simultaneously discusses the need to express them. These displays of frustration may stem from Jack's belief that the goal of the meeting has been thwarted. Lines (741–748) suggest that Jack's concern about whether "we've done the job (.) thorou<u>gh</u>ly and we unders<u>tand</u> our job" (744–745) implies that he does not think they are working effectively in the meeting. These linguistic markers reaffirm that Jack is trying to open up discussion of the unspeakable in a cautious and guarded way.

Several features in the text affect the tensions between feeling rules and work feelings. First, procedural rules in this instance appear to supersede regulatory rules. Procedural rules refer to the meanings aligned with strategic expression of emotion or the use of emotion for strategic ends. Throughout this retreat, Jack has raised issues about the structure of the company, the number of stores, and the nature of the food business. His contributions to the ongoing interaction in light of his plea to "get out feelings on [the] table" (728–729) occur within the context of selecting a successor to the company president; he and others around the table are potential candidates. Thus, his expression of emotion in this context fits into his strategic ends of having a voice in the selection of a successor. This context, in turn, serves as a backdrop for procedural rules linked to concealing his feelings while revealing the need to discuss them. His emotions become intertwined with his strategic aims to make covert statements about the way the company is being run and to exert voice in the selection of a successor.

A second factor that reflects the tensions between feeling rules and work feelings is the professional norm for conducting the meeting. These norms point to the timing of emotional displays and the use of tact and diplomacy. For example, the timing of Jack's appeal to "want[ing] <u>some</u> heat to come out" (741) and his objection to the system of monitoring comes after considerable discussion of the structure and nature of the company. The timing of emotional expression and the absence of personal attack seem appropriate and "professional" in this setting (Kramer & Hess, 2002). Had Jack introduced his plea for "heat to come out" (741) early in the meeting, the issues of company structure, the changing marketplace, and options for CEO leadership would not be on the table. Making his plea amid these rather underdeveloped issues is appropriate given a need to unpack them and "get out feelings" (728) about these concerns.

Moreover, the norms of tact and diplomacy also govern emotional expression. Tact conveys a regard for standpoints and statuses of others so that the ongoing activity will not dissolve or degenerate into conflict (Powell, 1988). In tactful discourse, expressions of high regard are integrated with subtle forms of altercating. Specifically, Jack casts his objections to Sam's control in diplomatic terms of "a system of method and monitoring" (736). Rather than chastise the team for going in circles, he appeals to them to do their "job (.) thoroughly" (744) or "to do the job together (.) <u>not</u> disjointedly" (745–746). The discourse of tact then is directly tied to professional decorum that constrains while it reveals through metatalk about feelings. In effect, emotional expression in this text vacillates between feeling rules and work feelings, aligning with diverse and competing norms of professionalism while appealing for openness in the discussion through masking feelings.

Open and Closed

The dualities of open and closed also surface in the metatalk about feelings. Metaphorically, Jack raises objections to Harry's closed organizational system as a "system of method and monitoring" (736) that constrains his feelings as well as the hidden agendas in the room. His use of words such as "get out" (728), "come out" (741, 743) and his reference to phrases such as "we should have said and we didn't say" (731) and "haven't been heard and seen and felt" (746–747) support Jack's plea for having an open discussion about hidden agendas.

Sam responds to this discursive move by appropriating openness to a closed system as stated in (759–760): "that you feel has some restraining influence" (757). In this way Sam links openness to limiting emotional expression and closing off discussion (760, 763–764), "Fr:eely spoken" "to the extent that we think it's pretty well covered by what's already been said then we move ↓forward." These sentences suggest that openness has a restraining influence and to the degree that it has already been said, it is unnecessary. In effect, open and closed become intertwined through juxtaposing "get[ting] out feelings" (728) with "restraining influences" (757) that have "already been said" (764).

Open and closed also function in the metatalk about feelings through simultaneously asserting and retracting, displaying and masking, and resisting and complying. While Jack asserts the need "to put the things we feel on the table" (747–748), ironically, he retracts it by not disclosing what kind of heat should come out. He calls for "get[ting] out feelings" (728), yet he never shares his subjective experiences with the team. He displays his emotions of frustration and anxiety by masking his feelings about specific issues through strategic ambiguity. He never directly states what feelings should come out, which feelings count, or what feelings are negative or positive. In the next segment of this meeting, Arnold Steinberg, who is a family member, introduces the topic of the family-run business, nepotism, and the Friday night meetings. Sam again appropriates these issues to organizational norms by retorting that all senior executives are company family members and that blood relatives, who gather on Friday nights, do not make the company decisions. Even though Jack opens up this hidden agenda, he remains silent throughout much of this discussion.

In effect, at the report level of metatalk, Jack asserts the need to "get out feelings" (728), but at the command level, he does not label his feelings directly. Although he is explicit about his concerns, he does not speak about his own feelings. Instead, he displays his frustrations through vocal overtones, nonverbal behaviors, and choice of words, thus masking his exact feelings through strategic ambiguity. Jack resists Harry's ideal of professionalism characterized by orderliness, identifying the problem, and moving to solve it but he adheres to rationality by masking his objections to nepotism and family rule and complying with Sam's view of restraining influences. In this sense, Jack's metatalk about feelings invokes rational norms for emotional expression, that is, disguise the nature of your feelings while calling for others to get their emotions "on the table" (748).

This analysis of the metatalk about feelings demonstrates how emotionality and rationality function together in this setting and how power operates in tandem with resistance. In this text, emotionality and rationality function as a vicious cycle. Harry's emotional proclamation for a rational, orderly process triggers Jack's very rational plea for getting feelings out on the table. Jack's call for feelings elicit Sam's rational feeling rules indicating when and how to express appropriate emotions. In the end, tensions between emotionality and rationality failed to open space for alternative deliberations and participants could not simultaneously embrace both poles. Thus, the group opts for rationality as the dominant modality of organizing.

Rationality and feeling rules are closely tied to power and resistance. Throughout the text, both expression and suppression of feelings become a way to achieve managerial goals, control agendas, and make emotions consistent with instrumental needs. Rituals for conducting the meetings such as the use of a facilitator, frequent topic changes, and Sam's redefinition of volatile issues reinforce a strong organizational culture that relies on family rule. Responses to statements and issues raised as modes of resistance reaffirm the status quo and the power relationships between Sam and his senior executives. The meeting concludes with a list of the qualities that a successor should possess, a discussion of inside versus outside candidates, agreement that the job should go to the most qualified person, and ways to communicate with the rank and file. The spaces for resistance introduced through the simultaneous tensions of rationality and emotionality close up as the discussion evolves in line with one end of this continuum.

The management of the dualities suggests another irony. Discussion of the president's succession in the midst of potential successors overrides the expression of feelings. Could any senior executive talk openly about the comment that "this company h:as been <u>ruled</u> (.) and is suffering (0.8) <u>badly</u> (.) as a result of nepotism" (894–896) or that decisions get made in a family "Friday night supper" (839, 848)? Thus, being a successor suppresses talk about succession.

AN INTERTEXTUAL READING
OF THE METATALK ABOUT FEELINGS

An alternative reading of this text moves beyond the transcript of this meeting to audiences outside of this retreat. Interactions about consequential company decisions, such as the selection of a successor, are rarely videotaped for prosperity. The fact that this retreat was recorded and likely edited indicates that multiple audiences exist for its viewing. Those audiences include employees of the company, employees at different locations throughout Canada, customers of the grocery chain, and industry leaders. Viewing this meeting from the angle of multiple texts leads to alternative interpretations, particularly that emotional work and metatalk about feelings may not be aimed solely at the senior executives in this room.

In this broader context, the purpose of this meeting, allegedly the selection of a successor to Mr. Sam, may really be nondecision, aimed at reassuring the larger community of employees, customers, and industry leaders that *Corporation: After Mr. Sam* will continue as it has in the past. In this reading, deliberations about company structures and policies are enacted paradoxically to convince the larger audience that the succession of Mr. Sam will not change the company's dominance in the industry. Discourse during the meeting, then, functions reflexively to produce inaction or nondecision.

Although not scripted or staged, emotional expression becomes part of a decision-making performance. In a performance, the metatalk about feelings signals to the larger audience that participants have aired the important issues. Emotional displays, countered with rational positioning, demonstrate vigilance in the decision process. Jack, as the apparent challenger during the meeting, emerges as the most compliant executive by staging the performance and helping Sam reaffirm that nothing will really change. In this way, Mr. Sam's surveillance extends beyond the participants in the room to a larger audience thereby reproducing his industry control.

CONCLUSION AND IMPLICATIONS

The corporate control of emotion is seductive. It is a feature of routine, taken-for-granted interactions in which parties express and suppress organizational control and resistance. This analysis of the transcript of Mr. Sam serves as a text for multiple readings across levels of analysis. One such analysis emanates from the role of emotional work and metatalk about feelings in the meeting per se. This reading reveals that emotional work is not just relegated to the expression of feelings for organizational ends. Rather emotion work also entails compliance with or resistance to organizational norms. Moreover, metatalk about feelings draws from past practices to either challenge or comply with organizational power relationships. Thus, discourse not only serves to accomplish a meeting per se, but to alter or reaffirm the very nature of an organization. At the context level, the interactions during this meeting are not just about professional decorum, but rather aim to appease anxious employees, retain customers, and sustain industry control. Discourse, then, functions intertextually to interact with immediate and remote audiences.

This chapter also demonstrates how discourse contributes to meso-analysis across multiple levels of the organization. Namely, dualities function differently within and across organizational levels, leading to different insights about the role of contradictions in organizations. At the interpersonal level, Harry's emotional appeal for a rational orderly process and Jack's rational discussion of "getting feelings out on the table" illustrate how emotionality and rationality work in tandem to simultaneously open up and close off discussion. At the meeting level, tensions between professional and unprofessional, feeling rules and work feelings, and open and closed interactions function to express and suppress organizational norms and to resist and comply with Mr. Sam's control over the meeting. At the organizational level, the tensions between emotional and rational in the metatalk about feelings enact both resistance and organizational control, without engaging in direct confrontation over the issues or the definition of the situation. Finally, at the stakeholder level, the performance of this meeting sets up contradictions between action and inaction, deciding and not deciding, being vigilant and derelict, and changing the organization or staying the same. In many ways this meeting can be viewed as a pseudodecision process or a collective effort to not decide. Thus inaction, under the appearance of vigilance, serves to embrace change while keeping the organization the same.

Overall, dualities produced through the discourse of organizing provide important insights as to how metatalk about feelings expresses and suppresses controversies in organizational life. A discursive approach to understanding these contradictions and how they function at multiple levels aids in unpacking the layers of the process of organizing.

REFERENCES

Abu-Lughod, L., & Lutz, C. A. (1990). Introduction: Emotion, discourse, and the politics of everyday life. In C. A. Lutz & L. Abu-Lughod (Eds.), *Language and the politics of emotion* (pp. 1–23). New York: Cambridge University Press.

Ashforth, B. E., & Humphrey, R. H. (1993). Emotional labor in service roles: The influence of identity. *Academy of Management Review, 18,* 88–115.

Ashforth, B. E., & Humphrey, R. H. (1995). Emotion in the workplace: A reappraisal. *Human Relations, 48,* 97–125.

Averill, J. (1994). Emotions becoming and unbecoming. In P. Ekman & R. J. Davidson (Eds.), *The nature of emotion: Fundamental questions* (pp. 265–269). New York: Oxford University Press.

Barrett, L. F., & Gross, J. J. (2001). Emotional intelligence: A process model of emotion representation and regulation. In T. J. Mayne & G. A. Bonanno (Eds.), *Emotions: Current issues and future directions* (pp. 286–310). New York: Guilford.

Batson, C. D., Shaw, L. L., & Oleson, K. C. (1992). Differentiating affect, mood, and emotion: Toward a functionally based conceptual distinction. In M. S. Clark (Ed.), *Emotion* (pp. 294–326). Newbury Park, CA: Sage.

Damasio, A. R. (1994). *Descartes' error: Emotion, reason and the human brain.* New York: G. P. Putnam.

Fineman, S. (1993). Organizations as emotional arenas. In S. Fineman (Ed.), *Emotions in organizations* (pp. 9–35). London: Sage.

Fineman, S. (1996). Emotion and organizing. In S. R. Clegg, C. Hardy, & W. R. Nord (Eds.), *Handbook of organizational studies* (pp. 543–564). London: Sage.

Fineman, S. (Ed.). (2000). *Emotions in organizations* (2nd ed.). London: Sage.

Hochschild, A. R. (1983). *The managed heart.* Berkeley: University of California Press.

Jones, T. S. (2001). Emotional communication in conflict: Essence and impact. In W. F. Eadie & P. E. Nelson (Eds.), *The language of conflict and resolution* (pp. 81–104). Thousand Oaks, CA: Sage.

Kramer, M. W., & Hess, J. A. (2002). Communication rules for the display of emotions in organizational settings. *Management Communication Quarterly, 16*, 66–80.

Lazarus, R. (1994). Meaning and emotional development. In P. Ekman & R. J. Davidson (Eds.), *The nature of emotion: Fundamental questions* (pp. 362–366). New York: Oxford University Press.

Leidner, R. (1991). Serving hamburgers and selling insurance: Gender, work, and identity in interactive service jobs. *Gender and Society, 5*, 154–177.

Leidner, R. (1993). *Fast food, fast talk: Service work and the routinization of everyday life.* Berkeley: University of California Press.

Miller, K. (2002). The experience of emotion in the workplace. *Management Communication Quarterly, 15*, 571–600.

Morris, J. A., & Feldman, D. C. (1996). The dimensions, antecedents, and consequences of emotional labor. *Academy of Management Review, 21*, 986–1010.

Mumby, D. K., & Putnam, L. L. (1992). The politics of emotion: A feminist reading of bounded rationality. *Academy of Management Review, 17*, 465–486.

Murphy, A. G. (1998). Hidden transcripts of flight attendant resistance. *Management Communication Quarterly, 11*, 499–535.

Perinbanayagam, R. S. (1991). *Discursive acts.* New York: Aldine de Gruyter.

Planalp, S. (1999). *Communicating emotion: Social, moral, and cultural processes.* Cambridge, England: Cambridge University Press.

Powell, J. O. (1988). Diplomatic discourse and the process of negotiation. In D. R. Maines & C. J. Couch (Eds.), *Communication and social structure* (pp. 285–299). Springfield, IL: Charles C. Thomas.

Putnam, L. L., & Fairhurst, G. T. (2001). Language and discourse in organizations. In F. M. Jablin & L. L. Putnam (Eds.), *The new handbook of organizational communication* (pp. 78–136). Newbury Park, CA: Sage.

Putnam, L. L., & Mumby, D. K. (1993). Organizations, emotion and the myth of rationality. In S. Fineman (Ed.), *Emotion in organizations* (pp. 36–57). Newbury Park, CA: Sage.

Rafaeli, A. (1989). When clerks meet customers: A test of variables related to emotional expressions on the job. *Journal of Applied Psychology, 74,* 385–393.

Rafaeli, A., & Sutton, R. I. (1987). Expression of emotion as part of the work role. *Academy of Management Review, 12,* 23–37.

Rafaeli, A., & Sutton, R. I. (1989). The expression of emotion in organizational life. *Research in Organizational Behavior, 11,* 1–42.

Rosenberg, M. (1990). Reflexivity and emotions. *Social Psychology Quarterly, 53,* 3–12.

Steinberg, R. J. (1999). Emotional labor in job evaluation: Redesigning compensation packages. *Annals of the American Academy of Political and Social Sciences, 561,* 143–157.

Steinberg, R. J., & Figart, D. M. (1999). Emotional labor since *The managed heart. Annals of the American Academy of Political and Social Sciences, 561,* 8–26.

Sutton, R. I. (1991). Maintaining norms about expressed emotions: The case of bill collectors. *Administrative Science Quarterly, 36,* 245–268.

Tracy, S. J. (2000). Becoming a character for commerce: Emotional labor, self-subordination, and discursive construction of identity in a total institution. *Management Communication Quarterly, 14,* 90–128.

Vaughan, F. E. (1989). Varieties of intuitive experience. In W. H. Agor (Ed.), *Intuition in organizations* (pp. 40–61). Newbury Park, CA: Sage.

Waldron, V. R. (1994). Once more, with feeling: Reconsidering the role of emotion in work. In S. A. Deetz (Ed.), *Communication yearbook* (Vol. 17, pp. 287–365). Thousand Oaks, CA: Sage.

Watzlawick, P., Beavin, J. H., & Jackson, D. D. (1967). *Pragmatics of human communication.* New York: W. W. Norton.

Wharton, A. S. (1993). The affective consequences of service work: Managing emotions on the job. *Work and Occupations, 20,* 205–232.

Wharton, A. S. (1999). The psychosocial consequences of emotional labor. *Annals of the American Academy of Political and Social Science, 561,* 158–176.

Wouters, C. (1989). The sociology of emotions and flight attendants: Hochschild's "managed heart." *Theory, Culture, and Society, 6,* 95–123.

Chapter 6

The Persuasive Nature of Emotion and the Cultural Nature of Feelings in Organizations

Kristine L. Fitch
Megan Foley
University of Iowa

Tracy (chap. 4) and Putnam's (chap. 5) focus on expression of feelings as a part of organizational decision making opens fertile ground for exploring the role of emotion in organizational communication, and in social interaction more generally. Their chapters present a convincing case that the issue of emotion has been neglected and even seen as antithetical to the communication characteristic of organizational life. In this essay we extend their argument in two directions, the persuasive and the cultural. We first build on the observation of both Putnam and Tracy that the separation between "irrational" emotion and reasoned argument constitutes a false dichotomy, by further exploring the suasory power of expressions of emotion in *Corporation: After Mr. Sam.* We then expand on this observation by exploring the culturally situated nature of both organizations and emotion itself. We conclude by proposing that expressions of feelings are persuadable, as well as persuasive; they are constrained by, and interpreted within, norms and premises for communication in particular groups of people, in this case an organization deliberating its future within a particular historical and social context.

THE PERSUASIVE NATURE OF FEELING-LIMNED TALK

The essays in this section demonstrate, in different ways, that expressing feelings should be heard as part of reasoned argument, rather than its opposite. One extension of this useful insight is to examine other

113

ways in which talk that expresses emotion is persuasive, first in a theoretical sense, and then in two other moments of the meeting in *Corporation: After Mr. Sam.*

Kenneth Burke's (1950) view of persuasion as a process of identification is a useful starting point for examining the suasory power of expressions of feeling. Becoming "substantially one" (p. 21) with others requires inferring and, to some extent, adopting common sensations, concepts, and attitudes. Identification is not becoming identical; it is joining an individual locus of motives to a common enterprise or shared principle. To make Person A consubstantial with Person B is a persuasive act: The enterprise must be seen as worthy, the principle must be claimed as one they share. It is reasonable to infer that part of identification involves the internalization of social feeling rules that Hochschild (1979, 1983) described as the first stage of emotion management. Hochschild (1979) noted that this internalization is "a clue to the depth of social convention, to one final reach of social control" (1979, p. 564). Internalization of feeling rules is one form of a social actor's identification with others. Perhaps more importantly, because emotion management is substantially a process of self-control, successfully enacting or displaying identification with others requires self-persuasion. For the self-concept to be experienced as coherent, any conflict between avowed social feeling rules and the personal experience of emotion—the duality Putnam describes between *feeling rules at work* and *work feelings*—must be reconciled. That reconciliation, we propose, is a persuasive process: Either the inner experience (the work feelings) must change to something more in line with the outer world (the feeling rules at work), or, less plausibly, the feeling rules at work must be challenged to be closer to the actual work feelings. Either of those requires social influence, directed at the self or at others in the work environment. That social influence, we suspect, is generally quite subtle and indirect, making indispensable the fine-grained analysis of transcripts such as the one that is the focus of this volume.

Specifically, for feeling-limned talk to emerge at the succession meeting, there must be identification of the men involved in the discussion, with each other and with the organization. That identification is in part internalizing the feeling rules of the organization, and in part understanding and enacting the interactional rules for expressing those feelings.

A further consideration of the suasory nature of emotion may be drawn from Aristotle's assertion, perhaps as widely utilized as identification, that persuasion happens only in the realm of the contingent. If organizational life were either truly devoid of emotion, or completely off limits for the expression of emotion in favor of rational argument, there would be no room for identification in the sense just sketched. The dispute over what kind and what magnitude of emotion may be appropriately expressed in a situation where "rational" decision-making is required is made explicit in the fragment analyzed by Tracy (chap. 4) and Putnam (chap. 5), marking the role of feelings within organizational life as contingent in this interaction. Feelings, about the company and about roles of the individuals gathered at the table to decide its future, are raised as relevant at other moments in the discussion that illustrate the issues of identification and contingency. We turn now to examine two such moments.

Fragment 1

```
467  HARRY S:  Alright. Guy
468  GUY N:    Yah. (1.0) As far as I'm concern I must say (0.5) that (.) there is
469            a time to disagree (0.5) and this is what we're doing (.) the
470            present time .hh but I must say though that (0.2) as s:oon as a
471            decision is made .hh which is considered to be in the best
472            interest of the company hh Guy Normandin won't resent (.)
473            being (.) demoted if this is called demotion (.) and he will be
474            prepared to pull 'n the same direction as other people.
475            ((Two applause.))
476  HARRY S:  Alright. Jack, you have the legitimate floor.
477  JACK L:   I (.) kn:ew we would get at some point (.) of this kind of
478            contention (0.5) and uh uh (.) I was willing, myself, to take that
479            risk and stand ab't to the job that I will be allocated to, to my
480            ability, based on the evaluation of my present superior, which
481            happens to be Sam Steinberg. (1.0) I think that if we don't look
482            at the barriers and put [ourselves
483  SAM S:                          [You'd be up in Siberia if it was up to
484            me.
485            ((Laughter.))
486  JACK L:   Then I'll [go.
487  (    ):             [That's where you'll put 'em.
488  JACK L:   When I put these things out I feel deeply about the organization
489            and where it's going and where it should go. An' I'm willing to
490            (.) subject my own personal goals at this point- though I 'ave
491            personal goals- to the good or welfare of the organization. So
492            I'm not looking at j:obs or job descriptions or job titles hh what
493            will be best for the company I'm prepared to do.
494            (1.5)
495  SAM S:    That was always understood.
```

Both Guy and Jack set up a distinction here between their personal goals and the organizational goals. Guy distinguishes (a) a "time to disagree" (469) where individuals may air individual concerns in an emotionally laden way from (b) a time after a decision has been made when he will (and implicitly argues, others should) accept "the best interest of the company" (471–472). Presumably, "the best interest of the company" is something members of the organization should have some degree of positive feeling about, even if their personal feelings about the position to which they are ultimately assigned might be disappointment, even bitterness. Guy publicly declares his willingness to conform to organizational feeling rules, regardless of his personal emotional reaction. Positioning the terms in this way not only signals Guy's willingness to take on the emotional stance of the organization over his own; it instructs the other people around the table to do the same.

Jack links his emotions even more specifically to the good of the organization (488): "I feel deeply about this organization." When he moves on to second Guy's position (489–491) that he is willing to subject his own goals "to the good or welfare of the organization," he first makes explicit that he does have personal goals of his own. This acknowledgment suggests the contingent nature of his position: A reasonable person (one could say in this instance, without much fear of correction, particularly a reasonable *man*) could as easily pursue his own career goals whether or not they coincided with the best interest of the company. He will not do so, however, and by making that explicit Jack engages in a persuasive attempt directed at both his colleagues ("so all you guys better do the same, or risk looking self-centered") and, in the self-presentation sense, at Mr. Sam ("See? I am someone who cares more deeply—whose emotional attachment is stronger—to the company than to my own ambitions.") Mr. Sam offers acceptance of this expression of feeling (495): "That was always understood." One hearing of that utterance, and other formulations of it (most notably, "That goes without saying,") raises a Grice's Maxims (Grice, 1975) question: If someone says something that everyone (or at least the relevant hearers in the group) already knows, what does it mean for them to have said it? In this case, what it means to express out loud the feeling of commitment to the company's goals over one's own seems to be that a persuasive attempt is underway: Guy and Jack want to subtly suggest that the other men in the group should feel this way, and they want to convince Mr. Sam of their own loyalty and willingness to sacrifice. A second fragment in which identification and contingency are hearable in talk is the following.

Fragment 2

```
391  JAMES D:  =All our previous discussions, and we had some before we
392            came up here to Palomino, we thought (.) uh it was impressed
393            on us and many individuals raised the point that we should be
394            try:ing (0.2) > difficult as it is for all of us< to be objective
```

```
395                about what we said in these reports (.) and to th:ink of the
396                organization (.) not in terms of the incumbency in any one
397                position but as to h:ow the organization itself (.) should be (.)
398                best structured from the point of view, and w:orry about the
399                b:odies to fill the positions afterwards. And that is what, if
400                we're going to be objective, we should be doing here (0.2) and
401                we're d:odging the issue because we're saying "Ah (0.5) it might
402                possibly point the finger at any one of us, and that's a- too
403                delicate area for us to discuss" =
404  (    )        = (x[xx)
405  JACK L:            [You know what I think? I think- I think we're getting
406                chicken!
407  JAMES D:  Yeah!=
408  JACK L:   =We all ought to have enough nerve, gumption, look at the
409                company hh and say to our present President (.) in writing
410                "Look Mr President, you have to reorganize (0.2) because we
411                have certain weaknesses that if we don't do this, the company is
412                not gonna move." (0.2) Along with somebody else, everybody
413                in this room was willing to do it. When it comes to
414                individually, you wanna chicken out because you may have
415                [to give, you may have to take.
416  JAMES D:  [Exactly.
417                ((Two or three people talking at the same time.))
418  ARNOLD S:  It just seems to me th't, th't while there may be some benefits (.)
419                from the exercise (0.2) I really see that (.) for the most part we
420                will go through the exerc', it will take several hours (0.5) maybe
421                several days (.) we will have a very heated discussion, it's
422                inconceivable to me that it can be resolved without a heated
423                discussion, and then (.) the wh:ole thing could be a complete
424                waste of time because (.) of the of the the relationship between
425                the Chairman and the President and how they see the job.
426  JACK L:   I disagree.
```

This exchange captures another moment of dispute over the role of emotion for the organizational task at hand. James first positions "objectivity" as desirable (394, 400) and as opposed to feelings that could get in the way of "being objective" ("worry about the bodies to fill the positions." [398–399]). Such worry over "bodies" creates the risk of "dodging the issue" (401) and making objectivity, and successful completion of the task, impossible. Jack puts a strongly undesirable label on the potential feeling of "worry over bodies": This would amount to being "chicken." He puts forth the negative state as one in which he himself may be implicated, and as something currently in progress (405–406): "I think we're getting chicken!" James concurs emphatically with this interpretation (407), and a feeling rule is ratified: Objectivity is good, worry over bodies is not objective and is bad.

Arnold, however, raises a different view of what emotion might be at stake: Although it is inevitable that the current discussion, "objective" or not, will be "heated" ([421–422], suggesting that the feelings involved would be as much anger as "worry"), that emotion and time spent in discussion could all be for naught:

```
423  ARNOLD S:                    (.) the wh:ole thing could be a complete
424          waste of time because (.) of the of the the relationship between
425          the Chairman and the President and how they see the job.
```

In other words, if the matter at hand is not truly contingent—if the question of making decisions about organizational structure and succession of Mr. Sam is not really going to occur through discussion by this group but instead has already been decided, neither anger nor worry is a reasonable feeling to have. Arnold's observation also is a direct challenge to the identification of members of the group with each other as a body entrusted with resolving the issue of succession: To the extent that Mr. Sam and Jack have a "relationship" that precludes consideration of other possibilities, none of the other potential successors to Mr. Sam can truly be consubstantial in the same way or to the same degree.

Our point in this section has been that feelings, both those that might exist and thus could be expressed and those that are actually expressed, are potentially as persuasive as any reasoned argument. In *Corporation: After Mr. Sam*, the men gathered to discuss pressing decisions facing the company show their identification with the organization by making explicit their commitment to the company's best interest. That move has clear implications for the impression they present to the group and Mr. Sam. It also constrains expression of other, contradictory feelings by the other men present. That constraint leads to our next observation of emotion as persuasion: the culturally situated nature of both emotion and feelings, and the distinctive illumination that situatedness gives to what we understand persuasion to be.

THE CULTURAL NATURE OF EMOTION, FEELINGS, AND PERSUASION

Part of Hochschild's (1979, 1983) well-known position on emotion management is the notion that people are taught how to feel and how to put a particular name on a feeling, as well as what counts as appropriate expression of their feelings. Hochschild postulates a three-step process that individuals use to make sense of raw emotion: attention, codification, and management. People attend to feelings by selecting them out of visceral experience and according importance to them. To this view, Heelas (1996) added that emotions that members of a group talk about a great deal are then emotions that they think about a great deal—a distinction known in anthropology as *hypercognized emotion*. Levy (1984) noted, as cited in Planalp (1999), that hypercognition "involves a kind of shaping, simplifying, selecting, and standardizing" (p. 222) of emotions through talk. In Hochschild's terms, emotion is encoded into compositions, or sets of indicators that define particular feelings. Thus, the meaning of emotion depends on the codes used to interpret it. An individual's experience of anxiety, for example, is the composition of visceral reactions, such as, perhaps, an upset stomach and a sensation of pressure, that the individual labels "nervousness." In this way, visceral physical reactions are rendered meaningful within particular codes or systems of meaning. Like other aspects of human experience of emotion, the codification of visceral responses is partly universal and, to a noticeable extent, culturally situated. The process of emotion management, in which individuals are persuaded to change their raw emotions to conform to social feeling rules, is as much a part of enculturation as the codification of feelings into nameable, thinkable entities.

This cultural nature of emotion and feelings suggests another direction from which emotion is linked to persuasion, in a way that can shed a different light on this aspect of the interaction in *Corporation: After Mr. Sam*, and on organizational interaction more generally. In any culture, some communicative acts can be rendered sensible on the basis of available resources for constructing meaning—shared experience, norms for behavior, premises that underlie those norms, symbolic forms, and so forth—while others cannot. *Cultural persuadables* (Fitch, 2003) is a term intended to capture those issues about which members of a culture can be persuaded based on their shared understandings. The realm of the persuadable lies between *coercion*, in which people are overtly forced to behave in certain ways, and *socialization*, in which certain behaviors appear natural and not open to persuasion. At both the coercion and socialization ends of the spectrum, there appears to be no reasonable choice of action or belief; thus, the persuadable is, once again, that which is understood to be contingent.

The feeling-limned talk in *Corporation: After Mr. Sam* thus reflects the emotions that are persuadable within the cultural context of the interaction. Commitment to the company is as reasonable as is each man's commitment to his own individual career, such that the feeling that must be persuaded is the former over the latter. Worrying about the "bodies," that is, the individual sacrifices the men at the table might have to make to support an objectively derived organizational structure, is a comprehensible feeling and thus, must be persuaded against. (Alternatively, potential guilt over structuring the company in such a way that particular individuals see themselves as demoted is a more specific interpretation of the utterance "worry about the bodies" [398–399]).

Just as important are the feelings that are not the subject for persuasion in this group, on this occasion. Although "heated discussion" (421–423) is to be expected and, for at least some members of the group, is a desirable aspect of a decision-making process for which the stakes are very high, neither anger nor resentment is hearable, in this transcript, as persuadable (i.e., reasonable or comprehensible) sources of such heat. Yet the nonverbal signs of heated discussion could readily be seen and heard, on the videotape, as anger. Voices are raised, the table is tapped, according to Tracy (chap. 4; or pounded, according to Putnam, chap. 5), speakers take on accusatory tones to deliver what could be heard as insulting—or at least uncomplimentary—characterizations of others' behavior:

```
721  HARRY S:   (0.5) If you want to turn this thing into (.) a >fish market
722             gentlemen<, it's your meeting but=
```

Putnam's interpretation of the feeling expressed in this instance is frustration, and the various reasonable alternatives to that interpretation underscore the issue of how emotion becomes codified within particular groups of people. Are anger and resentment irrelevant to the matter at hand? Are they out of place in a work group, among colleagues entrusted with the future of a large and successful corporation? Are those emotions outside the range of what members of the group can be persuaded to feel, or are they simply labels that are too extreme to be allowed near the visceral reactions evident on the faces, and in the voices, of the participants? From Hochschild's positing of management of emotion to Putnam's expansion on it in this volume, we might draw the conclusion that such questions can only be answered from within the group itself. Even then, if such emotions are outside the realm of the speakable, group members may not be able to articulate them—or even, to take Hochschild to a logical extension, to feel them.

The group-specific nature of emotion work and expression of feelings, however, raises one more aspect of culture in relation to emotion, feelings, and persuasion that is worth a close look. Having noted that emotions and their expressions are codified within specific systems of meaning, we turn now to explore the nature of these codes.

ORGANIZATIONS AS CULTURES, AND AS CULTURALLY SITUATED

Culture has been a rich metaphor for the study of meaning in organizations for some time, and as such has had a profound impact on both the study of organizations and on the practices of organizational life (Tretheway, 1997). Rather than describe the various theoretical approaches to organizational culture or recap debates over different ways to understand organizations as cultures, we begin by pointing out that every organization has a particular history and identity. From those emerge some degree of shared understanding among the members of the organization about symbolic communication practices, although different perspectives and sometimes competing aims and motives within organizations mean that culture is never complete consensus.

In terms of emotion work, then, the opposing views of appropriate talk at the meeting—objective and rational decision making, or necessarily heated and disputatious discussion—illustrates the pulls and tugs within this particular organizational culture with regard to the place of feelings at work. Its identity as a company owned and operated by Sam Steinberg's family members is, in fact, both a central aspect of its organizational culture (Irving L. comments [831–834], "there is such a thing as an informal organization at Steinberg's (0.8) which is directly linked to the family (.) and there's an informal organization perhaps in every company but this one happens to be directly linked to the family") and one of the central controversies in the meeting. Perhaps not surprisingly, it is precisely when the issue of what "family" means with regard to this organization that feelings are most directly described and addressed:

Fragment 3

```
660   JAMES D:                      =when I say organization (.) the family
661                  (.) if you like (.) pulling rank (.) on the rest of the non-family
662                  executives in the corporation an' saying "Well that's the way it's
663                  goin' to be."
664                  (2.0)
665   JAMES D:  An' an' an' in effect (.) the non-family part of the business had
666                  absolutely nothing to say about that and what they did say (.)
667                  was absolutely ignored.
668                  1.0)
669   JACK L:   I want to keep [on this (xxxx)=
670   JAMES D:                 [Certainly.
671   JACK L:   =only because I think we're getting some feelings out. For
672                  three, four, five years, Mel and I have been saying very clearly,
673                  yearly, we used to do it yearly, that the organization being (.)
674                  built at corporate was much too heavy for our retail k:ind of
675                  operation that we're into.
```

James' claim that family members pull rank over nonfamily members is the sharpest criticism so far in the meeting (661). Besides Mr. Sam, who up to this point in the film has been spoken of and to in reverential terms, three other family members are present. After an explicit ratification of the expression of feelings as an appropriate and necessary part of the decision making (671), Jack adds other evidence to the argument by way of specific details of efforts he and Mel have made to suggest necessary changes to organizational structure. Those efforts were unsuccessful, which he attributes—without saying so directly—to the fact that he was not part of the family. After some elaboration of this point and the exchange examined closely by Tracy (chap. 4) and Putnam (chap. 5), the issue of family is raised again, more pointedly. Although lengthy, this part of the transcript merits close attention because of the clarity with which opposing meanings of "family," and conflicting evaluations of those meanings, are voiced:

Fragment 4

```
777  ARNOLD S:                        I can obviously only speak
778            for myself (1.0) but I think I'm speaking for for most if not a:ll
779            of the second generation (.) family members when when I state
780            that that nep- that n-nepotism (0.2) generates sa-satisfaction to
781            any (.) particular individual for a very short period of time. (0.8)
782            And that in the long run uh career satisfaction of an individual
783            (0.2) uh let me put it differently (.) that that when (.) nep-
784            nepotism plays an important role (.) in the choice (0.2) of an
785            individual for management (.) the satisfaction that comes from
786            that is very short lived to any particular individual (.) who
787            thinks of himself (.) in a management capacity (.) and I think as
788            I said I speak well I know I only speak for for myself (.) in fact I
789            suspect that I'm voicing the opinion (.) of all if not most of the
790            members of the family.
791            (1.0)
792  SAM S:   .hh now uh (0.8) uh the only comment I would like to make at
793            this mom- this moment was that I read a Harvard report (0.5)
794            where it deals with families in organizations=
795  (    ):   =We all read it. ((People interrupting and agreeing.))
796  SAM S:   Alright! So it tells you that after a period of twenty years there
797            is more family than ever before=and that hasn't affected the the
798            performances as I read it in these companies. (1.0) On the >
799            other hand < (0.5) I think that when we look around the table
800            over here, we talk about family, (1.0) well (.) I looked upon
801            Jack as a member of the family=I look up:on (.) Oscar as a
802            member of the family (.) I've looked upon Jack Ginser always
803            as a member of the family (.) and I think that they look upon
804            ↑themselves as a member of family.
805            ((Four or five people talking at the same time.))
806  (    ):   That's not a very good example.
807  (    ):   Your definition of family and everyone else's xxx
```

Arnold brings the issue of whether family members exercise undue influence in the company quite concretely into the discussion by speaking as a member of the family. His many restarts suggest that the issue is sensitive, perhaps painful. He contradicts himself twice in stating the position from which he speaks: He "speaks only for (him)self" (777–778) but "for most if not a:ll of the second generation family members" in the very next two lines, an ambiguity he restates just as emphatically at the end of his utterance (788–790). He offers a candid statement of the truth as he understands it: *Nepotism* is at best a temporary satisfaction for members of the family. Mr. Sam's counterargument takes two intriguingly distinct forms. First he refers to an article out of Harvard that states (though he is reminded that everyone has read it, he reiterates his understanding of its main points) that family members working within the same organization are a more frequent occurrence than ever before, and that the performance of companies in which that happens has not been affected—"as (he) read it" (798). Having presented one piece of presumably objective evidence, his second argument is, tellingly, based on emotion: He looks upon some members of the organization as family, and believes they view themselves in the same way (798–804). This move is quickly rejected by two speakers whose identities are unclear:

806 (   ):   That's not a very good example.
807 (   ):   Your definition of family and everyone else's xx

Mr. Sam goes on to talk in terms of "blood relations" (814) as the category of family relevant to the negative associations of influence and advancement encompassed in the term nepotism. Simply feeling close enough to someone to "look upon them as family" does not constitute their BEING family. In this organizational culture, the presence of family members related by blood and marriage highlights the symbolic nature of the term when applied to other men who have been around since "the very beginning" (809). The implications of this symbolic/literal split are made starkly clear: The blood relatives in the organization exert influence above and beyond that due to their position and expertise, enough for nonblood relatives to see themselves as less able to be persuasive, even if they are among those who are "looked upon" as family.

Shortly thereafter, Irving L. brings up another concrete instance of a symbolic event perceived to be definitive within the organizational culture: Friday night suppers, where the real decisions are made: ([1837–1839], "the key decisions are not made at the management committee (.) or with the President (.) but at Friday night supper ...") Irving goes on to make explicit that Friday night suppers involve the Steinberg blood family, not the perceived family:

Fragment 5

```
843  IRVING L:              if one fella happens to be Vice-President of this
844             and another fella Vice-President of that and they're both putting
845             forth their opinions, if one happens to be related (.) the feeling
846             is (.) that he's got an awful lot more to say (.) a) because he is
847             much closer, b) it's sort of his money involved and, c:) it's
848             because (.) he goes to the Friday night supper as opposed to the
849             other party (.)
```

In this fragment, an aspect of the Steinberg company's organizational culture can be heard to intersect with culture in a broader sense. Family-owned companies that stay within the family, although not unique to Jewish culture, are a recognizable tradition within it. "Friday night suppers" (848) are more identifiably associated with celebration of the Jewish Sabbath than with important business decisions being made, yet the perception that "the key decisions" (837–838) take place on those occasions is openly articulated and goes unchallenged. No one asks what Irving is referring to, because all are assumed to understand: There is an unstated premise about the nature and significance of Friday night suppers to Jewish families in general and the Steinbergs in particular. That premise makes Irving's reference to them intelligible as part of a larger argument about the weight of literal family, as opposed to symbolic family, in this organization.

After a playful exchange in which Mr. Sam asks Irving whether it was his charm or his ability that got him where he is now ([860–862], to which Mel retorts "No, he attended the Friday night dinner" [866], which is greeted by widespread laughter) ethnicity is invoked in a meta-phorical sense which may, ironically, make the practical side of the Friday night suppers more explicitly relevant:

Fragment 6

```
874  JAMES D:                                            there's
875             one school of thought going around which sort of looks as us a
876             little bit like the Negroes in a cabinet (0.5) you know (.) that
877             really we're we're there more for show ((starting to laugh)) than
878             for performance. And that the real decisions are still made as
879             Irving says in the in the Friday night eh meetings whether that's
880             (0.5) has validity or not, that's what they believe=
```

The phrase "Negroes in a cabinet ... there more for show ... than for performance" is difficult to imagine in a business meeting filmed for national broadcast within the last 20 years. Like the Friday night suppers—which James refers to, with the briefest of hesitations, as "eh meetings"—no one challenges or disputes either the term or the association, though Mr. Sam immediately responds, "I don't think I need to answer that but certain you were never put on for show." By raising the possibility that nonfamily members might be there "for show," James emphasizes the persuasive disadvantage of family membership in the symbolic sense. By invoking "Negroes in a cabinet" as the comparison point, he makes possible the interpretation that not being Jewish (and thus less likely to be included in the Friday night suppers, and if included, as a guest rather than a member of the group), has also worked to their disadvantage.

There are other clear signs of the time frame in which this meeting took place: All of the participants, representing the top management of the company, are White men. Several of them smoke cigarettes while sitting around the conference table and after dinner (described in the voice-over as *"Dinner was a family affair"*—there's that word "family" again!—*"with Mrs. Sam Steinberg supervising the cooking and waiting on table."*) All of these details from the video show an interaction firmly situated within a time and social context quite far removed from the ones we as viewers and analysts experience. Perhaps for that reason, the cultural distinctiveness of the organizational moment was particularly noticeable. It seems plausible that the expressions of feelings that played such a noticeable and prominent part of the discourse of this succession meeting were as much a product of the post-1960s ethos of emotional openness as anything specific to this organization or to the construction of logical arguments within social interaction more generally. We doubt that middle-aged White businessmen talked so openly, and frequently, about their feelings as they made corporate decisions in the 1950s; and wonder whether they were still doing so in the harsher business climate of the 1980s. Those unknowables aside, the larger issue is how the specifics of this organization, its people and its meeting, connect to social interaction in organizations more generally. We take up this issue by way of conclusion.

IMPLICATIONS OF A CULTURAL VIEW

In this chapter, we have extended the discussion of how expressions of feelings enter into organizational discourse into consideration of the culturally situated nature of both emotion and such expressions of feelings. This analysis suggests that the persuasive potential of expressions of feelings varies both by organizational culture and by cultural context in the larger sense of time, space, and ethnicity. What transcends those particulars, however, is the persuasive nature of cultural feeling rules, approached here as feeling rules particular to work and organizational settings. To the extent that people identify with a group, they are faced with a choice to either shape their emotions into the categories expected and recognized by the group, or live with contradictions between their inner states (and more importantly, their expressions of those states in social interaction) and the feelings acceptable to the group. We suspect that individuals largely navigate between those positions, sensing at times that they are going through the motions of expected feeling expressions or having to actively suppress their true feelings in the interest of conforming to expectations. The most fruitful aspect of the chapters in this section seems to us to be that such navigation usually goes completely unnoticed, particularly in the workplace where, as noted, emotion and feelings of any kind can readily be deemed irrelevant to the organizational task at hand. By excavating the complicated influences of this judgment of irrelevance (or inappropriateness) of emotion to interaction within organizations, Tracy (chap. 4) and Putnam (chap. 5) have clearly opened an important avenue for further exploration.

REFERENCES

Burke, K. (1950). A rhetoric of motives. Berkeley: University of California Press.
Fitch, K. L. (2003). Cultural persuadables. Communication Theory, 13, 100–123.
Grice, H. P. (1975). Logic in conversation. In P. Cole & J. L. Morgan (Eds.), Syntax and semantics: Vol III. Speech acts (pp. 41–58). New York: Academic.
Heelas, P. (1996). Emotion talk across cultures. In R. Harré & W. G. Parrott (Eds.), The emotions: Social, cultural, and biological dimensions (pp. 171–199). London: Sage.
Hochschild, A. R. (1979). Emotion work, feeling rules, and social structure. American Journal of Sociology, 85, 551–575.
Hochschild, A. R. (1983). The managed heart: Communication of human feeling. Berkeley: University of California Press.
Levy, R. I. (1984). Emotion, knowing, and culture. In R. A. Schweder & R. A. LeVine (Eds.), Culture theory: Essays on mind, self, and emotion (pp. 214–237). New York: Cambridge University Press.
Planalp, S. (1999). Communicating emotion: Social, moral, and cultural processes. New York: Cambridge University Press.
Tretheway, A. (1997). Organizational culture. In P. Y. Byers (Ed.), Organizational communication: Theory and behavior (pp. 203–234). Boston: Allyn & Bacon.

III

Strategies of Decision Making: Competencies and Coherences

How decisions get made is, to put it mildly, a traditional topic in organizational studies. From Dewey's (1910) classic model of the group decision-making process to more contemporary models like the ones proposed, for instance, by March (1988) and his colleagues, scholars have for decades tried to grasp the logic by which people manage to arrive at a decision in an organizational setting (or indeed elsewhere). Even if human beings' rationality is said to be bounded and the decision they make merely satisficing (Simon, 1955), a fascination with the process stems from our desire to better comprehend what factors appear to make a difference. Although the focus was initially on the presumably rational character of decisions, some analysts have since shown that this type of activity appears, in fact, highly contextual, that is, largely driven by contextual factors, which have often very little to do with the topic on which the decision is supposed to be made (Cohen, March, & Olsen, 1972; March, 1988; Reed, 1991; Weick, 1993).

This has led some scholars, like Klein, Orasanu, Calderwood, and Zsambok (1993), to argue for the necessity to study what they call *decisions in action*, that is, observing how decisions actually get made in natural settings, instead of laboratory experiments. Although the field of decision-making processes tends to be predominated by economical, algorithmic, and mathematical models, inviting March (1988) to call it "the established church of social sciences" (p. 2), now might actually be time for heresy, heterodoxy, not to say schism! If we are indeed interested in the process of decision making, why don't we spend more time, as analysts, observing how people actually make decisions, something that LSI and organizational communication scholars should be very well equipped to do.

A more inductive approach might enable us to identify key phenomena that have so far been neglected by more traditional approaches based on hypothetical–deductive models with fixed parameters. For instance, we could follow Weick's (1993, 1995) counsel, inviting us to make a shift of focus from decision making to sensemaking. As Weick (1993) noted, "reality is an ongoing accomplishment that emerges from efforts to create order and make retrospective sense of what occurs ... Sensemaking emphasizes that people try to make things rationally accountable to themselves and others" (p. 634). In other words, by concentrating on sensemaking processes, which is, according to Pomerantz and Fehr (1997), the central and defining focus of conversation analysis,[1] one could end up showing that how decisions are made mostly depends on how problems and situations are set, something that Schön (1983) argued more than 20 years ago, but that still needs to be illustrated empirically.

As Weick (1995) noted again,

> When we set the problem, we select what we will treat as the "things" of the situation, we set the boundaries of our attention to it, and we impose upon it a *coherence* which allows us to say what is wrong and in what directions the situation needs to be changed. Problem setting is the process in which, interactively, we name the things to which we will attend and frame the context in which we will attend to them. (p. 9, italics added)

Although decisions can be crucial moments in organizations—Sam Steinberg's succession certainly being one of them—this shift of focus to sense making and problem setting might show that it is in the way reality is interactionally constructed that we can hope to find how we actually make decisions. In other words, once participants in a discussion are able to negotiate a coherent version of reality, decisions can then appear almost nonproblematical to them (which, of course, does not mean that the decisions they make are the "right" decisions).

Interestingly enough, this, in certain respects, parallels Derrida's (1992) reflection on decision making. As he noted, if a decision appears decidable because the way the problem is set leads logically and reasonably to a specific conclusion, then we cannot, according to him, really speak about a decision that was made. What decision makers did was just follow algorithmically the rational conclusions they were led to because of the way they coherently described the situation. Following Kierkegaard (1983), Derrida (1995) pointed out that a true decision must experience what could be compared to a leap of faith, that is, it must experience undecidability and uncalculability. That is, it is only when the situation appears to be undecidable that a decision takes on its full meaning (Cooren, 2004). This idea is perhaps better conveyed in French, because people often use the verb *trancher,* meaning literally "to slice, to cut through," in order to express the idea, "to come to a decision."

This might explain why the focus on sense making and problem setting could be more productive than the one on decision making per se. Because Derrida's reflection shows us that no model will ever be able to exhaust the incalculable (i.e., the irrational, in the etymological sense of the term) character of a true decision, one might be better served by focusing on the way people manage to create a coherent picture of reality. In other words, by focusing on problem setting and collective sense-making, we end up focusing on what will allow participants to not really decide. This, in fact, is what the next three chapters address, each in their own way.

Using a discourse analytic method called Centering Resonance Analysis (CRA), developed by Corman and his associates (Corman, Kuhn, McPhee, & Dooley, 2002), Robert D. McPhee, Steven R. Corman, and Joel Iverson (chap. 7) draw on Structuration Theory (Giddens, 1984) to illustrate to what extent the communication processes enacted during the management meeting contribute to the structural reproduction of Steinberg Limited. In other words, their quantitative and qualitative analyses convincingly show how recurring links among terms or themes evoked during the management meeting develop and create a form of coherence that ends up reaffirming what they call the constitution of Steinberg Limited, that is, what appears to constitute this organization.

Although the management meeting was supposed—at least for some of the vice presidents present—to bring about some changes in the way the organization was designed and structured, McPhee, Corman, and Iverson's (chap. 7) analysis shows how the rules and resources organization members invoke or mobilize during their discussion lead them not to make any consequential decisions, that is, decisions that would modify the very structure of the organization. Although tensions and contradictions are identified (e.g., what they characterize as the opposition between professionalist and personalist positions), no transformation really occurs and the self-structuring process inherent in this meeting appears to invariably lead to the same coherent picture of what Steinberg is and ought to be.

Although Robert Sanders' (chap. 8) analysis stems from a very different perspective, it is noteworthy that his study confirms, in many respects, McPhee, Corman, and Iverson's conclusions regarding discursive coherence. Since his landmark 1987 book, *Cognitive Foundations of Calculated Speech*, Sanders has investigated through numerous empirical studies how participants in interactions appear invariably constrained by what has been said previously in the discussion and what could be relevantly said next. What Sanders' (1987, 1995a, 1995b, 1997; Sanders & Fitch, 2001; Sanders & Freeman, 1997) studies tend to demonstrate is that people involved in conversations are far from being free to say whatever they want and are sometimes even trapped in interactional situations where they end up being unable to defend their own interests or positions because of the way these latter could be interpreted or evaluated.

It is specifically these types of constraints that Sanders investigates in the Steinberg management meeting through his neorhetorical perspective. As he elegantly shows in his analyses, some participants to this meeting are often caught in situations where they appear to be literally constrained to say things that obviously go against their interests because saying something else would appear irrelevant or incoherent vis-à-vis what has been said thus far. In other words, Sanders' analyses help us see to what extent talk in interaction has to function as a coherent whole to which people constantly orient, whether strategically or not, and that it is this principle of coherence that in many respects dictates what is being said. Ultimately, Sanders' analysis shows how interactional competencies can be quite consequential vis-à-vis the ways problems are set and decisions made, which is another way to argue for the necessity to study "decisions in action."

Finally, in her response to these two chapters, Cynthia Stohl (chap. 9) illustrates to what extent what happens during the management meeting interactions ("what is there") is influenced by what may remain invisible to analysts unfamiliar with the context of the discussion ("what is not there"). Stohl builds on her bona fide group perspective (Putnam & Stohl, 1990, 1996; Stohl & Putnam, 1994) to show how the participants appear to constantly manage what she perceives as a tension between the topic of discussion and the social and cultural context in which these discussions take place. By focusing on the Jewish identity of many participants in the meeting and what she identifies as the pivotal role of Irving Ludmer, Stohl nicely demonstrates how this identity appears to make a crucial difference in the way the meeting evolves at certain moments.

More specifically, Stohl shows how Irving Ludmer's position in the organization—he is Jewish, but he is not a member of the Steinberg family—seems to allow him to side with the status quo while introducing delicate topics in the discussion, like the one related to the importance of blood ties. As Stohl insightfully illustrates, everything happens as though his insider/outsider status enabled him to challenge the system while reproducing it. In other words, it ends up providing coherence to the discourse by resolving the tensions and contradictions that pervade the meeting. It is precisely this effect of coherence that McPhee, Corman, and Iverson as well as Sanders had perfectly noted and that Stohl brilliantly illuminates.

ENDNOTE

1. As Pomerantz and Fehr (1997) wrote, "The organization of talk or conversation (whether 'informal' or 'formal') was never the central, defining focus in CA [conversation analysis]. Rather it is the organization of the meaningful conduct of people in society, that is, how people in society produce their activities and make sense of the world about them" (p. 65).

REFERENCES

Cohen, M. D., March, J. G., & Olsen, J. P. (1972). A garbage can model of organizational choice. *Administrative Science Quarterly, 17*(1–25).

Corman, S. R., Kuhn, T. R., McPhee, R. D., & Dooley, K. J. (2002). Studying complex discursive systems: Centering resonance analysis of communication. *Human Communication Research, 28,* 157–206.

Cooren, F. (2004). The communicative achievement of collective minding: Analysis of board meetings excerpts. *Management Communication Quarterly, 17*(4), 517–551.

Derrida, J. (1992). Force of law. In D. Cornell, M. Rosenfeld, & D. C. Carlson (Eds.), *Deconstruction and the possibility of justice* (pp. 3–67). London: Routledge.

Derrida, J. (1995) *The gift of death.* Chicago: Chicago University Press.

Dewey, J. (1910). *How we think.* Boston: Heath.

Giddens, A. (1984). *The constitution of society.* Cambridge, England: Polity Press.

Kierkegaard, S. (1983). *Fear and trembling, and repetition.* Princeton, NJ: Princeton University Press.

Klein, G. A., Orasanu, J., Calderwood, R., & Zsambok, C. E. (1993). *Decision making in action: Models and methods.* Norwood. NJ: Ablex.

March, J. G. (1988). *Decisions and organizations.* New York: Blackwell.

Pomerantz, A., & Fehr, B. J. (1997). Conversation analysis: An approach to the study of social action as sense making practices. In T. A. Van Dijk (Ed.), *Discourse as social interaction* (pp. 64–91). London: Sage.

Putnam, L., & Stohl, C. (1990). Bona fide groups: A reconceptualization of groups in context. *Communication Studies, 41,* 248–265.

Putnam, L., & Stohl, C. (1996). Bona fide groups: An alternative perspective for communication and small group decision making. In R. Hirokawa & M. Poole (Eds.), *Communication and group decision making* (pp. 147–178). Thousand Oaks, CA: Sage.

Reed, M. (1991). Organizations and rationality: The odd couple. *Journal of Management Studies, 28,* 559–567.

Sanders, R. E. (1987). *Cognitive foundations of calculated speech: Controlling understandings in conversation and persuasion.* Albany: State University of New York Press.

Sanders, R. E. (1995a). A neo-rhetorical perspective: The enactment of role-identities as interactive and strategic. In S. J. Sigman (Ed.), *The consequentiality of communication* (pp. 67–120). Hillsdale, NJ: Lawrence Erlbaum Associates.

Sanders, R. E. (1995b). The sequential inferential theories of Sanders and Gottman. In D. P. Cushman & B. Kovacic (Eds.), *Watershed research traditions in human communication theory*. Albany: State University of New York Press.

Sanders, R. E. (1997). The production of symbolic objects as components of larger wholes. In J. O. Greene (Ed.), *Message production: Advances in communication theory* (pp. 245–277). Mahwah, NJ: Lawrence Erlbaum Associates.

Sanders, R. E., & Fitch, K. L. (2001). The actual practice of compliance-seeking. *Communication Theory, 11*, 263–289.

Sanders, R. E., & Freeman, K. E. (1997). Children's neo-rhetorical participation in peer interactions. In I. Hutchby & J. Moran-Ellis (Eds.), *Children and social competence: Arenas of action* (pp. 87–114). London: Falmer.

Schön, D. (1983). *The reflective practitioner: How professionals think in action.* London: Maurice Temple Smith.

Simon, H. A. (1955). A behavioral model of rational choice. *Quarterly Journal of Economics, 69*, 99–118.

Stohl, C. , & Putnam, L. (1994). Group communication in context: Implications for the study of bona fide groups. In L. Frey (Ed.), *Group communication in context: Studies of natural groups* (pp. 285–292). Hillsdale, NJ: Lawrence Erlbaum Associates.

Weick, K. E. (1993). The collapse of sensemaking in organizations: The Mann Gulch disaster. *Administrative Science Quarterly, 38*, 628–652.

Weick, K. E. (1995). *Sensemaking in organizations.* Thousand Oaks, CA: Sage.

Chapter 7

"We Ought to Have … Gumption …": A CRA Analysis of an Excerpt From the Videotape *Corporation: After Mr. Sam*

Robert D. McPhee
Steven R. Corman
Arizona State University

Joel Iverson
Texas A&M University

The recent chapter, "Discourse Analysis in Organizations," by Putnam and Fairhurst (2001), in the *New Handbook of Organizational Communication*, exemplifies the ways discourse analysis is relevant to, indeed a chief tool and intellectual inspiration of, organizational communication study. It also demonstrates that the label *discourse analysis* is itself polysemous to an uncomfortable if not torturous degree, in the range of phenomena, levels of organization, and assumptive bases that can inspire it. In this chapter, we depend on two complementary approaches to discourse analysis that were suggested by our specific reading of and interest in the meeting recorded in the *Corporation: After Mr. Sam* videotape. We came to this tape with a history of work in structuration theory, organizational knowledge and structure, and varied methods of discourse study. Watching the focal section of the tape (284–521) led us to note, in particular, the process of self-structuring enacted in the discourse, and the consequent implications of the meeting for organizational constitution and reproduction. These initial interests and interpretations, together with the methods choices they suggested and our assumptions about the taped interaction session, led to our chain of reasoning about the discourse itself.

SITUATIONAL BACKDROP OF THE ANALYSIS

The videotape and transcript we are treating is part of several longer discussion sessions, themselves part of a longer process of controversy in Steinberg Limited, a retail company with 180 stores in eastern Canada. President Sam Steinberg built the company from humble beginnings, virtually totally owned it, and until recently almost single-handedly managed it. He was retiring. In addition, the company had grown beyond the capacity of any one individual to manage. The discussion, which aimed to generate decisions about organizational goals and structure, as well as to determine procedures and criteria for choosing Sam's successor, is captured in a transcript generated under the following constraints.

First, the tape and transcript are edited and possibly reorganized from a much more extensive discussion among participants who are aware of the whole process (see the discussion by Wieder, Mau, & Nicholas, chap. 12, this volume). We have chosen to analyze these materials at face value, but we urge caution in regarding them as a basis for inference or generalization.

Second, the materials omit important sections of the discussion, which are summarized by a narrator. Among the narrator's statements of background information are these: In the section of the videotape we are concentrating on, the group has been assigned the task of "determining the senior management structure" of the company. This follows discussion in an earlier meeting, shown very briefly in the first part of the videotape, where participants argued whether to focus on goals or structure first, and Sam ended the argument unilaterally by deciding to start with goals and promulgating a statement of company philosophy, never explicitly referred to in the taped discussion. In a later segment, participants were assigned to discuss "barriers to professional management," and explicitly dealt with the impact of family relationships.

Third, Sam had virtually all the power, and would make his own decisions outside the meeting, so everyone knew that the meeting could have only advisory significance. Yet participants often argued and acted as though they were making a group decision.

Fourth, the issue of structure was especially controversial, according to the narrator, because up to then power had been concentrated in Sam's hands, and structural change could decrease the power of the presidency, for instance, by creating group executive jobs (often called executive vice presidents), who would have more power than other managers and act as countervailing powers to the new president. Of course, because Sam was the overriding power center, complaints about problems and calls for structural change could be interpreted as criticisms of him.

Fifth, the group had some consensus that structure and process changes were needed in the company, and that high-level executive decision making itself was flawed, including processes at the kind of meeting videotaped—but respect and nostalgia for Sam combined with awareness of his power to moderate descriptions of the current situation and structure.

Sixth, we noted a pattern before beginning formal analysis, and tried to adapt our analysis to explore it. The pattern was: Discussion would begin on a topic, describing "structural change" or "professional management" in implicit contrast to Sam's personal and family-oriented approach to management. After some discussion, a participant would point out that the group could not make any binding decision because Sam alone had the power to decide. Sam would follow this up with what we will technically call a "killer statement," indicating that he could and potentially would ignore the group's conclusions. Deprived of its sense of import, discussion would then shift to some other topic. For examples of Sam's killer statements in other parts of the tape, see (992–996), and of course the off-camera decision about goals reported by the narrator (202–205).

THEORETICAL BACKDROP FOR THE ANALYSIS

There are several questions about this decision-making session that spring automatically to the minds of organizational communication scholars: How does the organizational context affect the interaction? How will the interaction affect later organizational processes? We neglect those, more or less, in favor of a question that has been brought into prominence by the work of Smith (1993), along with some contributors to this volume. It is: How did or does the meeting recorded on the tape, the communication process objectified in the transcript, help constitute the organization Steinberg Limited?

This question has one advantage, of conceptual ambiguity: Our field does not yet have, to our knowledge, agreed schemata displaying the qualities, the shape, of a valid answer to the question of constitution. Our analysis shows how this decision-making group focuses on limited questions about organizational structure, while avoiding more basic challenges and thereby maintaining the facticity and legitimacy of power arrangements in the organization. In pursuing this line, our analysis rests on some theoretic assumptions.

First, we assume the main tenets of the theory of structuration. We assume that the interaction constitutes the organization by producing and reproducing it as an ensemble of rules and resources drawn on by its members in this, and other, interaction. Equally importantly, interaction depends on a variety of taken-for-granted routines, each able to be altered or challenged, but only within the broader reiterated background; on the basis of such routines any organization members can position themselves, claim knowledgeability, and rationalize their arguments and stands.

Second, we follow McPhee and Zaug (2000) in arguing that there are four key communicative processes or flows of organizational constitution. McPhee and Zaug label them as *membership negotiation, activity coordination, institutional positioning,* and the fourth, most directly relevant process, *organizational self-structuring.* This process is explicitly reflexive and system-focused, as they note:

> ... organizations are the objects not merely of reflexive attention but of reflexive control and design—of self-structuring. We would claim that this reflexive self-structuring distinguishes organizations from groupings such as lynch mobs or mere neighborhoods; it is essential to the explanation of the power of formal organizations in history, especially but certainly not only Western economic history (McPhee, 1985). It is important to emphasize that self-structuring is a communication process among organizational role-holders and groups; it is analytically distinct from, though often part of the same messages as, communication that helps coordinate the activities of members. It is unique in that it does not directly concern work, but rather the internal relations, norms, and social entities that are the skeleton for connection, flexing, and shaping of work processes. (Organizational Self-Structuring section, para. 1)

As in McPhee (1985) and elsewhere, we constantly face the problem of the polysemy of the word *structure*, which has a broad technical meaning in structuration theory that includes the narrower one in organizational theory. When we now use the term, we intend (except where explicitly noted) the organizational sense of system pattern and strictures, especially as formally stipulated, rather than Giddens' sense of all the rules and resources drawn on in acting in any way. In the videotaped meeting, the group is engaged in explicit discussion of, and has the power to make decisions about, the organization's structure and leadership. Thus, it falls into a category that McPhee (1985) called *conflict over structural design.* Clearly, conflict is present; in addition, as is obvious even to the narrator (212–213, 279–283), "rational" decision procedures are not followed. Most importantly, though, this group, with the power to determine structure, is not limited by the structure of the past—but of course that is a grievous overstatement, ignoring the ways current structure "enables and constrains" the ongoing decision making, most basically by determining who is present in this meeting and what issues they are most conscious of.

Our theoretical backdrop, then, contains a general commitment to the principles of structuration. It also adopts the four constitutive processes of membership negotiation, activity coordination, institutional positioning and organizational self-structuring as an orienting framework for our analysis. In the next section we describe quantitative and qualitative methods we used to identify evidence of these processes in the Steinberg, Limited discourse.

METHOD

To analyze the structurational process of constitution in this discourse, we resorted to analysis of the way repeated connections among concepts or themes relate, develop, and create coherence, and the way arguments develop, clash, and win hegemony or subside into irrelevance. We use two relatively formal methods of discourse analysis that would be described, in Putnam and Fairhurst's (2001) scheme, as modes of cognitive linguistics and rhetorical analysis. The first mode of analysis follows a tradition of concept mapping that is most notably exemplified in the work of Weick and of numerous cognitive and education scholars (reviewed in McPhee et al., 2000). Concept mapping that specifically represents discourse has been used in our field primarily by Danowski (1993). A powerful method for constructing such networks is Centering Resonance Analysis (CRA), developed by Corman and his associates (Corman, Kuhn, McPhee, & Dooley, 2002). This method is both powerful in its reliance on a fine network structure algorithm, and theoretically driven because it is based on *centering theory*, a respected theory telling how conceptual relations achieve text or discourse coherence. This method generates from sections of discourse a network of relations among the most influential concepts, where *influence* measures the *betweenness* or connective and coherence-creating force of the concept. We use such networks to analyze the varied production and reproduction of concepts along theoretical lines similar to Bastien, McPhee, and Bolton (1995).

Two modifications of the text were undertaken to prepare it for analysis. First, the method requires cleaning the transcript to eliminate fragments and irregularities, leaving grammatical text. Second, because we expected the group itself to be an important object of discussion, we manually disambiguated cases of the pronoun *we* (see Corman et al., 2002, for an explanation of conditions when this is advisable). When members of the group used the term *we* to refer to the group as a whole, the term *Topteam* was substituted. This substitution was made only in cases where the context clearly indicated that the speaker was referring to the management committee as a formal group, and not, for instance, to the set of individuals at the meeting considered severally, or to the whole group of employees of the company.

CRA is probably the method most unlike those used in this book's other chapters. At the 2001 ICA Preconference that gave rise to this book, it was a focus of some controversy. We want to emphasize several points: It is one method among many and, like the others, has its strengths and weaknesses. Among its strengths are uniform, definite treatment of the whole corpus being studied and clear quantitative/ graphical description of repeated patterns of word association that can be compared for different portions of the discussion. A weakness is that it abstracts words from their original context. However, it is not correct to say the method does this completely or even extremely. CRA encodes intentional acts of the author/speaker to generate a coherent message by arranging subjects, objects, and descriptors in particular ways. Thus the CRA network (unlike earlier automated text analysis methods) preserves a great deal of information about the semantic context in which the words were used. Of course it filters out other aspects of context. Yet all descriptions of communicative acts, including transcripts or other qualitative summaries, are abstractions of the actual phenomena being described. We show below that CRA is a useful abstraction, and rely on a concurrent analysis of arguments to help recover higher order context abstracted in the CRA analyses.

The analysis of argument development depends on the insight, perhaps originating in Simon's work but well articulated by Tompkins, Tompkins, and Cheney (1989), that arguments—the consequences traced from premises—are the ligaments not just of coordinated decision and activity, but of membership and relationships as well. We adapt a form of argument analysis described by Poole, Seibold, and McPhee (1985) for the study of group decision making, and modeled by Seibold, McPhee, Poole, Tanita, and Canary (1981). This method involves coding discourse to produce an array of argument premises or claims, plus warrants (reasons) and other supporting material where present in the discourse.

After seeing the videotape, and taking these background conditions into account, we noted two kinds of distinctions among the arguments. First, some were prescriptive, focusing on what the company *ought* to do, whereas other arguments were descriptive, dealing with what the company *is*. Second, some arguments focused on the company, whereas others focused on the meeting. This leads to four categories of arguments: *Oughts About the Company* (OC), *Oughts About the Meeting Process* (OM), *Descriptive or "Is" Claims About the Company* (IC), and *"Is" Claims About the Meeting* (IM). All four of these categories were controversial at some point in the discussion—members argued about whether the company should restructure before choosing a successor (OC), about whether nepotism currently existed (IC), about whether specific problem cases should be discussed (OM), and about whether the meeting was helpful or confusing to Sam (IM). In discussing the company, participants naturally mentioned and alluded to the corporate structure, but we should be equally aware that decision procedures in the management committee are equally a feature of the company's structure, and members exhibited awareness of their own group's procedural deficiencies.

ANALYSIS

We start with the CRA graphs; Fig. 7.1 is the graph for official transcript lines (1–521), and Fig. 7.2 is the graph for the discussion in (284–521)— our focal segment. In the graphs the darker the box surrounding a word, the more important it is in terms of tying together other words in the text, based on its structural position in the network. In the graph of the focal segment, the most influential terms are *president* and *vice president*, followed by the common terms *people* and *job*, then by an artificial expression, *Topteam* (standing for the use of "we" and similar expressions by members, as already explained). The graph, interpreted with knowledge of the transcript contents, has several important sections. One is at the left side of the graph, where the highly influential terms *president, job,* and *people* are strongly linked. Close to these terms are *vice president* and *Ontario*, a link that reflects early discussion about communication problems. The second important part of the graph is at the top, where three very influential terms, *recommendation, Topteam,* and *individual*, are linked to chains of other terms including *Palomino* (the meeting site), *discussion, meeting,* and *heated*. Clearly, this subnet represents reflective discussion about the tone of the meeting itself, as well as its goal of generating recommendations. Finally, toward the bottom of the graph is a net including the terms *good, organization, structured, position* (and from there, *vice president*), *grouping,* and *company*. As we see, this net represents one focus of argument later in the discussion. For more exploration of the segment's content, we turn to the analysis of the flow of arguments.

Company Level "Ought" Arguments

We must start by noting that this set includes, we believe, the most consequential and focal lines of argument for the participants. In our segment, they are working on the task of deciding on a senior management structure—a decision about how the company ought to change. We believe that almost every statement in our segment has implications for some facet of this decision. So this section of the analysis will be the most elaborated, and will bear on the other sections of the analysis.

A reconstructed array of major argument-serving statements about what the company ought to do is listed in Table 7.1, which includes statements from the first few pages of transcript as well, partly because

140

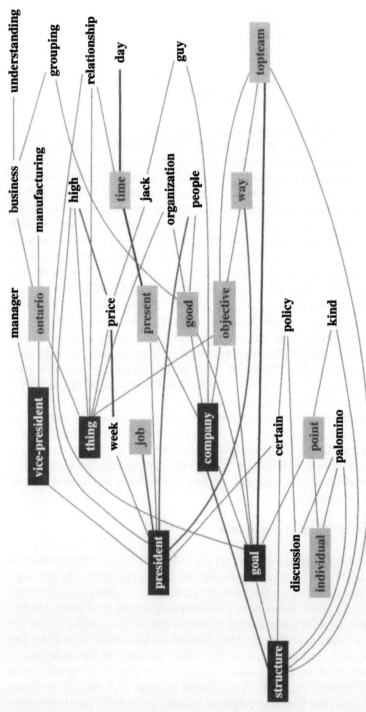

FIG. 7.1. Overall CRA graph of first part of meeting (41–207, 290–528).

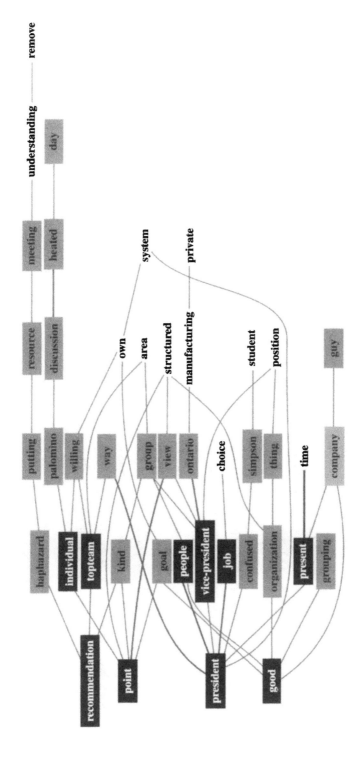

FIG. 7.2.   Overall CRA graph of focal segment of meeting (290–528).

141

TABLE 7.1
Company-Level "Ought" Arguments

[In many cases, the claims identified here recur, with different warrants or data; we have listed claims in order of their first introduction, and under them noted the claim's location in conjunction with the statement it was part of. In some cases it was thus necessary to list warrants or data that were not themselves company-level ought statements—alternative types are indicated by the initials in parentheses following the speaker and act identification.]

Goals/objectives should drive successor choice

Warrant: A person who can best achieve goals should be chosen (Sam, official transcript, 40–47).

Goals/objectives should be decided before structure.

Warrant: The purpose of structure is to help achieve goals (John, 58–60).

The company should make specific structural choices.

Warrant: Significant problems facing the company are structural (Jack, 87–88, 122–124) (IC).

Data: The pricing problem, and lack of uniformity (Jack, 87–124) (IC).

Structural choices must be made before goal decisions.

Warrant 1:   Structural choices define the basic nature of the company (Jack, 87–124).

Warrant 2:   Goal changes are either too complex or too easy, while structural improvement is just right (Jack, 42).

Warrant 3:   Specific goals require knowledge of specific structure (Jack, 87–124; Mel, 42).

Data: Current confusions about nature of the president's job, about "One company or two" (Jack, 87–124; Mel, 42) (IC).

Structural changes should remove barriers and be efficient and unambiguous (Sam, 308–315; James, 323–325).

Structural changes should reflect "natural groupings."

Warrant: Efficiency (Jack, 317–322).

The structure should be changed to include executive vice presidents (Implicit).

Warrant: Efficiency, lower span of control for the President (Sam, 369–377), and natural groupings" (Jack, 317–322).

We should not impose a structural change on the next President (Oscar, 351–354).

Warrant: The next President doesn't even exist yet (Arnold, 386–387) (IC).

Warrant: A structural change could be a waste of time if opposed by the Chairman and the next President (Arnold, 418–425).

Warrant: The President should determine the structure s/he has to operate in (Sam, 428–433; Arnold, 441–450).

Warrant: Traditionally, a chief executive can choose his/her own structure. (Arnold, 441–450)

Warrant: The "natural groupings" are the prerogative of the next President, and will depend on his/her appraisal of business and personnel (Irving, 500–516).

Warrant: The best interests of the company (Irving, 500–516).

The management committee has a duty to recommend needed structural changes.

Warrant: We should, and were changed to, make objective recommendations (James, 391–403) (OM).

Warrant: It resists doing so due to delicacy or a lack of courage in targeting changes needed in the President's role (James, 391–403; Jack, 405–406, 408–415, 434–439) (IM).

Warrant: It needs to be done to correct stultifying weaknesses (Jack, 408–415).

Warrant: We should act now rather than leave a haphazard situation that we will have to correct anyway later (Jack, 434–439).

Managers should be courageous and loyal enough to accept the decisions of the next President.

Warrant: The best interests of the company (Guy, 468–474; Jack, 477–493) their relevance carries over. The first four arguments in the list are from the early discussion; although the controversy there was about whether to decide first on goals or structural changes, several implications from that section are interesting. First, several members are arguing, even then, that decisions about structure must come before the succession decision. Second, arguments begin to build there about the importance of structural decisions. Third, a side note—after Sam decides in favor of deciding on goals, and lays out the company philosophy, that philosophy plays no part in later stages of the meeting when members suggest criteria for the successor president (outside our focal segment).

Our focal segment begins as several speakers, ending with Jack Levine, present their suggestions for structural realignment. The transcript begins as Jack finishes his presentation, and Sam raises a question about an ambiguity in Jack's proposal. Jack seems to have vice presidents in charge of other vice presidents. As Sam finally suggests, Jack's proposal tacitly assumes that some vice presidents will be elevated to be executive vice presidents (EVP) (369–370). The fifth through seventh arguments in Table 7.1 are introduced in this part of the transcript (214–385). The argument for "natural groupings" is a recognized justification for creating EVPs, but Jack tries to retain strategic ambiguity (Eisenberg, 1984) for his proposal, rather than raise the issue of EVPs. The issue gets raised anyway, by Sam, who seems to argue in favor of its greater efficiency (369–370, 372–373, 377). It seems plausible to us that Sam is not arguing sincerely for a restructuring around EVPs; instead, he is raising the issue in this very pointed way to stimulate the opponents of this change to speak.

We should note how the CRA graph (Fig. 7.3) shows the focus of argument here. The argument begins with the ambiguity of the VP position, then shifts to the issue of whether the group VP structure would be a change from the current system. Thus, vice president is by far the most influential term, the center of coherence in this part of the discussion.

In (351–354), Oscar begins an argumentative shift by stating his concern about EVPs, but muddies the discussion by claiming that creating EVPs would not alter the status quo. His relevant argument, that an EVP structure should not be "imposed" on the next president, gets resurrected by Arnold (386–387), then (418–425) and (441–450). After (386–387), however, James and Jack argue forcefully (391–403, 405–406, 408–415, 434–439) that the management committee has a duty to solve the kinds of problems discussed earlier, and specifically to be courageous (show "gumption" [408] rather than "delica[cy]" [403] and be "chicken" (406)) about correcting problems with the president's role responsibilities.

These arguments are opposed by Arnold, tentatively, but then by Sam, to whom Jack replies (428–433, and 434–439). Here are their statements:

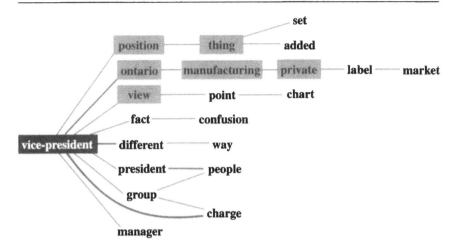

FIG. 7.3.   CRA graph of segment containing early company-level "Ought" arguments (290–384).

428	SAM S:	Listen. When a man is made the Chief (1.0) Executive Officer,
429		and I'm just using the President by way of example (0.5) >then
430		he::'s going to determine the kind of a structure that he can
431		operate with effectively in order to achieve the desired ↑goals.<
432		You say to him "We'll make you the President, but this is the
433		way you're gonna have to operate" uh
434	JACK L:	But we have we have we ↑h:ave (0.5) a I think a responsibility
435		as a group (.) to put this kind of recommendations on the board
436		the same way we did other recommendations, rather than leave
437		it again (.) for a haphazard uh uh putting together without the
438		resources to put together or call another meeting for that
439		purpose.

Sam's statement is not merely imperative: It fulminates facts. The chief executive officer (CEO) is going to determine the structure. Period. Jack does reply, but the "gumption" has diminished: "But we have we have we ↑h:ave (0.5) a I think a responsibility ..." (434). We see Sam's statement as a "killer statement," effectively closing off debate.

After a joke told by Harry, the discussion gets transfigured. Guy notes the conflict, but says that a time can come when a decision is made "in the best interest of the company" (471–472) and at that time Guy will accept it loyally even if it means his own demotion (472–473). This stance reconfigures "gumption" to be accepting a decision that goes against one's own interests for the company's good, and Jack cannot resist signing on, pledging loyalty even at the expense of his own personal goals (477–493). Irving (500–516) ends the discussion by claiming even more terms for the side opposing structural change: He argues that even the "natural groupings" (506) used to justify Jack's restructuring proposal must be determined by the new president, so decisions about structure are premature.

Several things about this segment of argument are of interest. First, there is a clear polarity between what we call the proponents of personalism and the proponents of professionalism. (By *personalism*, we mean the thesis that the CEO should be given the responsibility to decide on the structure he—in this case inevitably a "he"—prefers; *professionalism* is the thesis that the board should choose a structure itself on reasoned grounds, rather than delay solving current structural problems.) Yes, these are loaded words. But they foreshadow later discussion, where *professional management* is the term at issue.

Second, the personalists turn several concepts against the professionalists. It is unclear whether Guy favors personalism, or considers Sam to have made his decision, or is simply concerned that conflict is too intense. But his words do seem to turn the concept of courage or gumption in favor of the personalists—and, by the way, he also attaches the good of the company to the personalist side by saying that the "best interests of the company" (471–472) demand loyalty to the president's announced decision (which has favored the personalist side). Similarly, Irving turns the concept of *natural groupings* (506) to personalist uses. These turns in the argument are displayed in Table 7.2. Bastien et al. (1995) called this discursive move an "inversion." Its rhetorical effectiveness is hard to determine, because Sam's statement may have effectively settled the argument before these inversions were articulated.

Third, it is interesting to compare the main statements of the professionalists and the personalists, arrayed in Table 7.3 and Table 7.4; CRA graphs of these statement sets are Fig. 7.4 and Fig. 7.5. The CRA graphs are almost completely autonomous, and are somewhat separate parts of the overall graph of this section of the discussion (Fig. 7.6). This indicates that the two groups structured their discourse around completely different anchor points. For the professionalists, the most influential concept is *Topteam*, linked to *recommendation, haphazard,* and *nerve,* as well as to *individual* (in an appeal for objectivity). For the personalists, the most influential term is *president*, linked to *chairman* and then to *prerogative,* also to *job* and *judgment.* Interestingly, in Fig. 7.6, a subnet of terms, company, Guy, gumption, along with good and people, reflects the way the good of the company argument was turned in a personalist direction by Guy. Similarly, the arguments in Table 7.2 show no clash or refutation, except for the inversions late in the exchange. The personalists do not consider the argument that there are structural problems that require correction no matter who the president is, and the

TABLE 7.2

Flow of Arguments About Structural Change

Prochange (Professionalism):	Antichange (Personalism):
The structure should be changed to include executive vice presidents. (Implicit). Warrant: Efficiency (Sam, 308–315, 369–377), lower span of control for the President, and "natural groupings." (Jack, 316–322).	We should not impose a structural change on the next President (Oscar, 351–354). Warrant: The next President doesn't even exist yet (Arnold, 386–387).
The management committee has a duty to urge needed structural changes. Warrant: It's our task. (James, 391–403). Warrant: Objectivity (Ditto). Warrant: **The best interests of the company** (Ditto). Warrant: We resist doing so due to delicacy or a lack of **courage** (Ditto, Jack, 408–415).	We should not impose … Warrant: A structural change could be a waste of time if opposed by the Chairman and the next President (Arnold, 418–425). Warrant: The President should determine the structure s/he has to operate in (Sam, 428–433; Arnold, 441–450).
We have a **responsibility** [not to be] **haphazard** … (Jack, 434–439).	We should not impose … Warrant: Tradition—A chief executive chooses his/her own structure (Arnold, 441–450).
	Managers should be **courageous** and loyal enough to accept the decisions of the next President. Warrant: **The best interests of the company** (Guy, 468–474).
	I will subject my own **personal goals** to the **good** of the **organization** (Jack, 488–493).
	We should not impose … Warrant: The "natural groupings" are the prerogative of the next President, and will depend on his/her appraisal of the business, personnel (Irving, 500–516). Warrant: **The best interests of the company** (Ditto).

147

professionalists do not consider the argument that a President must mold structure to fit his or her approach to management. There are, of course, intellectually valid ways to approach this contrast, but they are deferred by this committee.

TABLE 7.3
Main Statements Arguing for Professionalism

[These statements are edited slightly from the transcript. They include only the statements made after the suggestion to let the next President decide on his/her own structure was made.]

(James, 391–403) In all our previous discussions, and we had before we came up here to Palomino, we thought, and many individuals raised the point, that we should be trying, difficult as it is for all of us, to be objective about what we say in these reports. We should think of the organization not in terms of the incumbency of any one position, but as to how the organization itself should be best structured from the point of view. And we are dodging the issue because we are saying this. It may possibly point the finger to any one of us, and that is too delicate an area for us to discuss.

(Jack, 408–415) Topteam ought to have enough nerve, or gumption, to look at the company and say to our present President in writing, this. Look, Mr. President, you have to be organized because we have certain weaknesses, and if we do not do this, the company is not going to move. Topteam was willing to do it, but when it comes to individuals, you want to chicken out, because you may have to give and you may have to take losses.

(Jack, 434–439) But Topteam has a responsibility as a group to put this kind of recommendation on the board the same way as Topteam did other recommendations, rather than leave it again for a haphazard putting together without the resources to put together or call another meeting for that purpose.

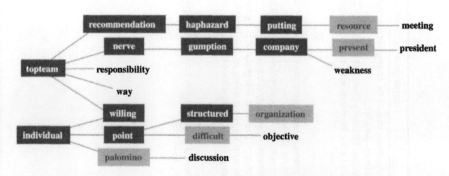

FIG. 7.4.   CRA graph of professionalist arguments (quoted in Table 7.3).

TABLE 7.4
Main Statements Arguing for Personalism

[These statements are edited slightly from the transcript.]

(Arnold, 418–425) It seems to me that while there may be some benefit from the exercise I really see that we will go through the exercise for several hours, maybe several days, and we will have a very heated discussion. It is inconceivable to me that it could be resolved without a heated discussion. Then the whole thing can be a complete waste of time because of the relationships between the chairman and the President and how they see the job.

(Sam, 428–433) When a man is made the chief executive officer, and I'm just using the President by way of example, then he is going to determine the kind of a structure he is going to operate in effectively in order to achieve the desired goals. You're saying to him, we'll make you the President but this is the way you're going to have to operate.

(Arnold, 441–450) Traditionally the President of the United States or the Prime Minister under the parliamentary system alone chooses his own cabinet and for the most part the choice of cabinet depends on the skills of that particular individual. I think it was obvious that Kennedy chose a very weak secretary of state because he himself wanted to do the secretary of state's job. I think that for a President to come unto the job without this choice being made by him puts him at a very serious disadvantage.

(Irving, 500–516) I think that the groupings that are made are really the prerogative of the chairman and whoever he nominates to be the President. And those groupings must be made on two bases, and I do not know if we can go much deeper with it over here. Number one is what is a natural grouping business wise, and number two is the competence of the people available, in the judgment of the chairman and his President. That will obviously have to determine to some degree the groupings fundamentally based upon the natural groupings that are available to us. But I think that beyond that, you have to take people into account and into consideration and Topteam should leave here ready to say that whatever these people deem to be in the best interest of the corporation, this is what we will have to go along with. I do not think we can go beyond that point.

What are the implications for production and reproduction in this argumentative exchange? As is evident later in this transcript, disagreement remains. Members remain aware of the contrast between professional and personalistic (later called *1-on-1*) management. Both have a claim to validity, professionalism in the consensual recognition that it is needed to solve problems in a large company, and personalism in past success, and in loyalty and respect for Sam, as well as recognition of his power. So the structure of this company, as reproduced here, is not merely formal or

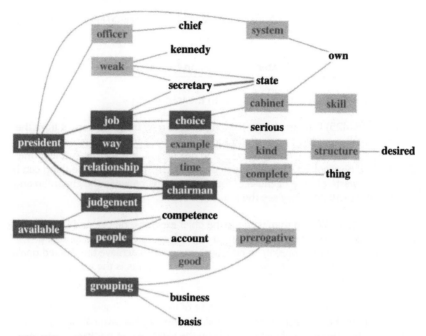

FIG. 7.5. CRA graph of personalist arguments (quoted in Table 7.4).

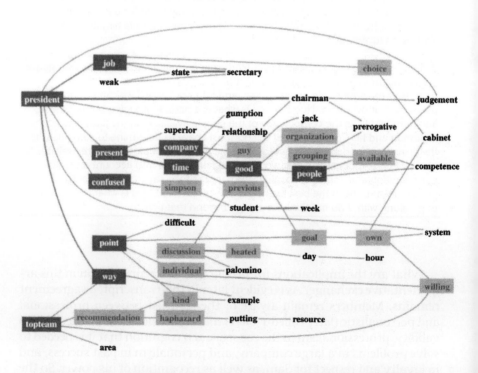

FIG. 7.6. CRA graph of segment containing both sets of arguments (389–528).

150

merely flawed: It is a mix of formal imperative and personal style that is, no doubt, contested in many other forums and at many other levels.

Company-Level "Is" Arguments

These are arrayed in Table 7.5. The CRA graph of the relevant portions of the transcript are shown in Fig. 7.7. Here the graph is divided between the two most influential words *Topteam* and *President*, with few interconnections between the parts of the graph connected to these words. *Topteam* is connected to high influence words like *structure* (which is connected to *company*) *objective*, and *incompetent*. This pattern is due to the fact that *Topteam* was conceived in the discourse as making judgments about the structure of the company and its objectives. The word *incompetent* indicates concern about the quality of these assessments. *President* is sparsely linked to this cluster of words, connected only through the word *certain*. Primarily, the discussion was about his connection to *manager* and *executive vice president*, that is, about how *President* relates to these lower levels of management.

In the light of argument analysis, there seems to be general acceptance of several descriptive propositions: (a) that the company has op-

TABLE 7.5
"Is" Arguments About the Company

We always talk about goals, never about a structure to operate to meet the goals, so we have no structure to monitor progress toward goals (Jack, 48–56).
  Used as Data to advocate structure change proposals.

We have not established our objectives (John, 58–63).
  Used as Data to support establishing goals first.

We have had 72 price increases recently, undermining policies/objectives about price consistency—report of the St. Lawrence/Cremazie manager (Sam, 64–67, 72–81).

Current policies are inadequate. [Used as Data to advocate structure change proposals.]

  Data: As in the St. Lawrence/Cremazie case, communication and oversight are so fragmentary and inadequate that Sam does not know events in a major company division—his role is badly defined (Jack/Sam, 87–128).

  Data: There is consensus that the sum total of everything that has been done has not been satisfactory, we have certain weaknesses, and we do not have systems that could allow the President to oversee the thousands of relevant events (Mel, 167–200, Jack, 408–415).

There are now 11 people reporting to the President, and that's too many (Oscar/Sam, 344–375).
  Used as Data to argue against Jack's change proposal.

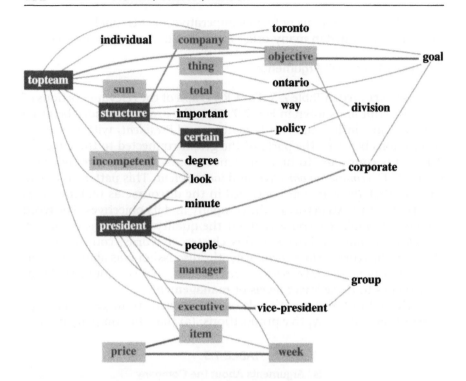

FIG. 7.7.   Company level "is" arguments (lined cited in Table 7.5).

erating problems, (b) that there are inconsistent and inadequate procedures for gaining information and coping with these problems, and (c) that the problems are centered in what will later be called "1-on-1 management" by Sam. Considering the respect universally shown toward Sam, the fact that these claims are made without quibbling is surprising, and implies that Sam has agreed with them, although he clings to the personal style of management. This depiction of the current situation is the background for the whole early discussion; the CRA and argument analysis both show no systematic or in-depth exploration or diagnosis of the current state of the company, and no further pinpointing of specific parts or processes in the company which require redress. So, as far as we can tell, this part of the meeting reproduces the inadequate state of information about the company, plaguing decision making here as much as it does general management of the company.

Let us now turn to the meeting-level arguments. These are comments that comprise the explicit metacommunication about the meeting that occurred during it. The two categories for the meeting level are "ought" and "is." The "ought" communication for the meeting focuses on what should be accomplished during the meeting. The "is" communication reflects what is presently occurring in the meeting.

Meeting-Level "Ought" Arguments

The OM claims, the way committee members communicate their expectations of the meeting during the meeting, are listed in Table 7.6. The CRA graph for the relevant sections of discourse cited in Table 7.6 is shown in Fig. 7.8. Here again the overwhelmingly most influential word is *Topteam* (influence = .63), whereas the second most influential word, *President*, is only one third as influential (influence = .21). This is perhaps not surprising given that this section deals with oughts about the meeting, and the meeting essentially constitutes Topteam. Patterns in the graph suggest four themes in the discussion about Topteam:

1. The word *point* is interesting in that it is connected to *view* as in "point of view" but also the argumentative term *contention*. This suggests a theme of framing of the meeting as an airing of points of view, with a norm of open, goal-directed argument.
2. The word *good* is also highly influential and is not directly connected to *Topteam* or *Point*. Its connection to words like *people* and *company* suggests a second theme framing the decision in terms of collective good.
3. Words like *objective* and *discussion* connected directly to *Topteam* indicate their concern with interpretation of and metacommunication about their task.
4. *President*, once again, is connected to a separate cluster of interconnected words. These have to do with his job in the *present* form of the *company*. There is also a concern with *Grouping*. As used in context in the original text, this refers to lower level structures below the president in the presumptive new organizational structure.

Several OM arguments support the claim that the structure of the meeting should be based upon what is good for the company (OC). When participants are determining what the company ought to do, that also determines what the members ought to talk about. As a result, the structural choices for the company determine the content of the meeting and thus the structure of the meeting itself. Also, because the meeting is occurring within the existing structure of the company, it reflects the current structure of the organization. In this way, the discussion

TABLE 7.6
Meeting-Level "Ought" Arguments

OM claims that directly support OC arguments are:

Goals/objectives should drive successor choice.

> Warrant: Objectives should be the first decision priority for the meeting. (Sam, 40–47).

Structural choices must be made before goal decisions.

> OM Claims: We should talk of structure first (Jack 87–88, 122–124). Leave objectives until the structural choices are settled (Mel 171–200).

> Warrant: Objectives can be solved in ten or fifteen minutes (Mel 171–200).

Structural changes should remove barriers and be efficient and unambiguous.

> OM Claim: The purpose of the meeting is to remove barriers (Sam, 310–313).

The management committee has a duty to recommend needed structural changes.

> OM Claim: This meeting requires our objectivity (James, 391–403).

Managers should be courageous and loyal enough to accept the decisions of the next President.

> OM Claim: The meeting is about what is best for the company, not each individual.

> Warrant: I am not looking at positions, just what is best for the company (Jack, 477–493).

Other OM claims:

Jack's example of one company or two is not the problem.

> Warrant: Jack's issue is not the best use of time for this meeting (Harry, 139–143).

Members of the committee ought to have the nerve to talk about corporate weakness (Jack 408–415).

> Warrant: If we cannot be honest, this meeting may be a waste of our time (Arnold 418–425).

> Warrant: We have a responsibility to come up with a recommendation (Jack, 434–439).

We must leave the meeting prepared to support any decision made (Irving, 500–516).

about what ought to happen in the meeting produces and reproduces the structure of the organization.

Most of the OC claims regarding the structure-versus-goals debate are interspliced with OM claims—this fact is supported by the similar CRA results as well. Starting with Sam (40–47), the structure of the meeting is developed by the expectation of an OC outcome. Jack indi-

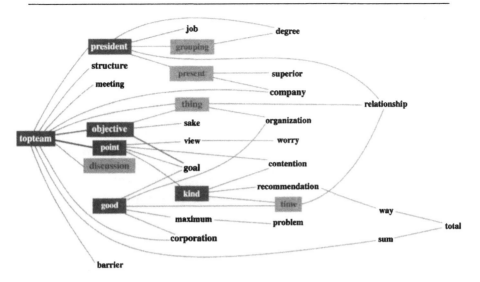

FIG. 7.8.   Meeting level "ought" arguments (lines cited in Table 7.6).

cates that because structure is the primary issue (which the goals discussion relies on), it should be talked about first (48–56). Mel uses time
allocation to support the notion of talking structure first when he
states, "we can resolve in ten or fifteen minutes, so I say we leave objective until the other thing is settled" (199–200).

The meeting level "ought" arguments are also used as a mechanism to
refute claims in the meeting. The most obvious example is Harry's
(139–143) dismissal of Jack's statement. Harry contends that the group
ought to bring the discussion "back on course" (139) and that they
should make "best use of [their] time" (141–142). Harry is seemingly attempting to avoid directly refuting Jack's claim (which is more of an attack on Sam) by labeling Jack's statement as a sidetrack, which is
outside of the scope of what ought to be covered during the meeting.

The final recommendation of the meeting is also an important topic
for the meeting-level "ought" discussion. The members of the committee
are talking about how they envision the meeting coming to an end. The
discussion is characterized by Jack's statement, "We ought to have
enough nerve, gumption, look at the company and say to our present
president ..." (408–409). Additionally, Arnold follows by pointing out
that heated discussion is going to be needed, but it may be a complete
waste of time because the president and chair may simply draw their
own conclusions (418–425). This point is seized on by Sam who uses the
OC answer that the president cannot be tied into a particular way of op-

erating (428–433). Sam's comment seems to reinforce Arnold's fears. Sam apparently believes that just as he would not want to be constrained as the president, the next president should not be constrained by structure. Jack follows up Sam by reasserting the need for this meeting to result in a recommendation anyway (434–439). This sequence develops the expectations for the meeting: A recommendation is needed, but it carries little weight.

On a similar note, Irving (500–516) indicates that the members ought to support whatever decision is made. This discussion parallels the earlier OC discussion of goals and structure in that it concentrates on the final product of the meeting itself and how that final outcome is used. One key difference is that Irving has accepted the limited role of the recommendation and the resulting conditions placed on the meeting outcome. "I don't know if we can go much deeper with it over here" (Irving, 505) indicates that the natural groupings depend on who the president and chair pick as successor. This statement, which concludes that the meeting will only result in a vague ordering of the structure, undercuts Jack's desire for specificity and reproduces the tensions of the meeting. Additionally, by contending that the structure depends on the person, it continues the organizational problem of personalism.

Meeting Level "Is" Arguments

These statements, reflecting how members interpret and enact the meeting in progress, are listed in Table 7.7. The CRA graph for these arguments is shown in Fig. 7.9. As in the case of oughts about the company, the graph shows a concern with *points of view* about how the *organization* should be *structured*, and about the *objective* of *Topteam*. The string of high-influence words on the left (truncated here for printability) indicates a separate thread about this being the *time* for a *decision* that is for the *good* of the *company*.

The IM comments are brief and mostly are either a part of a larger statement or are given as a point of support for OM, OC, or IC issues.

TABLE 7.7

Meeting-Level "Is" Arguments

"Is" Claims About the Meeting:

Goals are continually spoken about instead of how to meet those goals (Jack, 48–56).

We are dodging the issue (James, 391–403; Jack, 405–406).

We are making progress (Sam, 465–466, 518–521).

We are disagreeing now (Guy, 468–474)

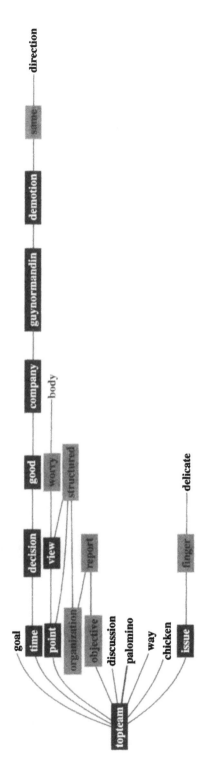

FIG. 7.9. Meeting level "Is" arguments (lines cited in Table 7.7).

These statements serve to either indicate that the meeting is not progressing as it should or to show support for maintaining the meeting as it is progressing. As a result, such comments serve as attempts to rationalize the current situation in support either of stability or change in the meeting structure.

The IM statements serve as points of comparison in order to produce change. In an attempt to induce change, Jack (54–56) uses the current history of meetings in order to stress the point that talking about goals gets nowhere. Jack instead advocates talk about structure. In another example, "I think we're getting chicken" (405–406), Jack supports James' (391–403) IM claim that they are dodging the issue. The IM claim comes immediately after James makes the OM claim that they need to stay objective and put the organizational needs ahead of their own. The IM claims by James and Jack are followed up with Jack's OM claim (408–415) that they need to have enough nerve to make a recommendation. The IM statements in this case serve as a point of comparison to show that the meeting is not going where it ought to go.

Guy (468–474) uses the IM as a point of comparison as well. He indicates that although they may be disagreeing now (which he believes is needed), after the meeting they all need to support the decision that is made (OC). Guy offers himself as an example of how they ought to act: "Guy Normandin won't resent (.) being (.) demoted if this is called demotion (.) and he will be prepared to pull 'n the same direction as other people" (472–474). Guy is supporting the disagreement for the meeting, but differentiates meeting behavior for corporate behavior outside.

Sam makes two IM claims (465–466, 518–521). Both provide support to the group by evaluating their progress: "Let me tell you I'm very pleased (0.8) the way we're progressing with this" (465–466). Sam is offering encouragement to continue the meeting as it is progressing. With his statements of support, Sam is encouraging the committee to reproduce the meeting structure as it has been so far.

Clearly, there is conflict over the status of the meeting that mirrors the difference in positions about change.

CONCLUSION

We have attempted here an analysis of the discourse of this meeting guided by organizational communication theory, specifically by an analysis, rooted in structuration theory, of how organizations are constituted. We have focused on the recurring concepts, claims, and other parts of arguments presented in discourse because these express the interpretive schemes and decision premises that organization members act on that comprise an important part of the stock of structural resources sustaining the organization. Of course, the concepts and arguments presented in this discourse are a paltry subset of the bases of knowledgeability of organization members, but they do have special importance in bearing on some vital organizational decisions.

One main conclusion is that this meeting, especially the excerpt we focused on, doesn't change very much. The tensions, urges toward both professionalism and personalism, past problems, past structural arrangements, and transformative ideas are expressed or re-expressed, but no transformations occur. All of these are part of the company's structural resources (in a structurational sense), of course, but they also can be properly regarded as part of the organizational structure per se; they are central features of the decision-making system and the enacted centralization of the company. The problem is that Sam, who apparently accepts the need for more professional management, cannot break away from a personalistic definition of the role of the next president, and has the power and persuasive ability to shoot down any attempt to convince him or the committee to do so. His power and decided stance seem to mirror his role in the company generally. Real change will probably come only after the choice of a successor (and in the end, we know from history, no successful new pattern was found).

We feel that the CRA and argument analyses were helpful in elucidating the dynamics of structural reproduction. Three results are of special note. First, the specific pattern of argument by the personalist side and by Sam is marshaled in subverting opposition. Second, the conceptual and argumentative focus of the meeting drifts, so that the concerns of the professionalists are not critically analyzed, refuted, or even clashed with.

Third, group-level self-reflection was an important focus of Topteam's discourse. The group regularly reproduced conceptions of itself as rational deliberative body, open to diverse points of view, acting for the collective good of the company, and focused on determining the current and future relationship of the president to the company. That these themes were so regularly reproduced across the discussion indicates that Topteam feels insecure about its mission and mandate, and regularly tries to anchor the disagreeing parties to a common ground of purpose. Apparently, the dynamics and fitfully attempted reflexive regulation of the meeting itself resembled the similar problem of management at the company level.

Whereas we offered some local and closely-grounded interpretations/imputations of actor strategy in the course of the analysis, we mainly see ourselves as providing a description of the recurrent discursive resources and patterns. Our methods are not oriented to identify and develop large-scale narrative grammars or high-level interpretations. For instance, suppose this specific argument-stream is one that has been played out over and over, so that all parties know the progression and outcome. Because that fact is not mentioned or explicitly revealed in the interaction, our methods would remain blind to it. Again, suppose all parties are consciously "making up" an argument as they go along, for the sake of the cameras. Our common sense might detect that; our methods do not. But contrariwise, if the parties are drawing on sincere views and rationales in reiterating or making up their debate, then our methods have captured and portrayed the resources they are using—resources that in fact ground the constitution of the organization.

Access to the discourse and other materials of the whole meeting would have strengthened our analysis, but even within pretty narrow limits, we feel that the analysis revealed significant ways in which the overall structure of the organization and the committee were produced and reproduced. "Self-structuring" is not simply a matter of drawing an organization chart; it includes the creation of relational postures and power arrangements enacted in this discourse, and the reproduction of the argumentative resources, and their relations, during the discussion. Those resources and relations are what we claim to describe through our analysis.

REFERENCES

Bastien, D. T., McPhee, R. D., & Bolton, K. A. (1995). A study and extended theory of the structuration of climate. *Communication Monographs, 62*, 87–109.

Corman, S. R., Kuhn, T. R., McPhee, R., & Dooley, K. J. (2002). Studying complex discursive systems: Centering resonance analysis of communication. *Human Communication Research, 28*, 157–206.

Danowski, J. A. (1993). Network analysis of message content. In W. D. Richards & G. A. Barnett (Eds.), *Progress in communication sciences* (Vol. 12, pp. 197–221). Norwood, NJ: Ablex.

Eisenberg, E. M. (1984). Ambiguity as strategy in organizational communication. *Communication Monographs, 51*, 227–242.

McPhee, R. D. (1985). Formal structure and organizational communication. In R. D. McPhee & P. Tompkins (Eds.), *Organizational communication: Traditional themes and new directions* (pp. 149–177). Beverly Hills, CA: Sage.

McPhee, R. D., Corman, S. R., Dooley, K. J., Kuhn, T. R., Zaug, P. J., & Iverson, J. O. (2000, November). *Discourse analysis of organizational knowing: A survey of assumptions and problems.* Paper presented at the meeting of the National Communication Association, Seattle, WA.

McPhee, R. D., & Zaug, P. J. (2000). The communicative constitution of organizations: A framework for explanation. *Electronic Journal of Communication, 10*(1-2). Retrieved from http://www.cios.org/getfile/McPhee_V10n1200

Poole, M. S., Seibold, D. R., & McPhee, R. D. (1985). Group decision-making as a structurational process. *Quarterly Journal of Speech, 71*, 74–102.

Putnam, L. L., & Fairhurst, G. T. (2001). Discourse analysis in organizations: Issues and concerns. In F. M. Jablin & L. L. Putnam (Eds.), *The new handbook of organizational communication* (pp. 78–136). Thousand Oaks, CA: Sage.

Seibold, D. R., McPhee, R. D., Poole, M. S., Tanita, N. E., & Canary, D. J. (1981). Argument, group influence, and decision outcomes. In G. Ziegelmueller & J.

Rhodes (Eds.), *Dimensions of argument: Proceedings of the second summer conference on argument* (pp. 663–692). Arrandale, VA: Speech Communication Association.

Smith, R. (1993, May). *Images of organizational communication: Root-metaphors of the organization-communication relation.* Paper presented at the 43rd International Communication Association Conference, Washington, DC.

Tompkins, E. V. B., Tompkins, P. K., & Cheney, G. (1989). Organizations as arguments: Discovering, expressing, and analyzing the premises for decisions. *Journal of Management Systems, 1,* 35–48.

Chapter 8

The Effect
of Interactional Competence
on Group Problem Solving

Robert E. Sanders
University at Albany, SUNY

In the analysis I present here of excerpts from the documentary *Corporation: After Mr. Sam*, I focus on the way the protagonists debate and settle one of the central issues among senior management depicted in the film—whether they should devise a new organizational structure prior to the advent of a new company president, or to wait for the new company president who would then decide whether, and how, to re-engineer the organization. Before going ahead with the analysis itself, there are two preliminary issues I want to address, one substantive and one methodological.

TWO PRELIMINARY ISSUES

The Substantive Issue of Competence
in Decision-Making Interactions

The substantive issue I want to address is one that emerged from a discussion with Robert McPhee about our respective chapters in this volume, when it became apparent that I start with a quite different concern from his in analyzing how people engage in debating and resolving disagreements. Rather than a concern with whether the participants succeed in debating the issues on the merits, my concern is how the participants interactively end up resolving the issue(s) before them as they do. Specifically, in the case of the film *Corporation: After Mr. Sam*, my analysis of the segment that I examine indicates that it ended up being resolved in a way favorable to the interests of some participants and contrary to the interests of others, and that it turned against the inter-

163

ests of certain participants because of a misjudgment by one of them about what should come next at a particular point in the interaction.

This is not to dismiss as unimportant the traditional concern in studies of decision making and problem solving with rational decision making, or real problem solving, that is, whether the participants decide the issues before them on the merits, based on talking about the matters at hand in such a way as will increase the chance of their adopting a solution that maximizes benefits and minimizes risks or costs. But if participants in a decision-making interaction do not end up engaging in a debate on the merits of opposing positions, we should not simply assume that they lacked the competence to engage in such talk, and discount their interaction as defective. We should instead assume that an interaction takes the course it does for a reason, not accidentally—that the participants had concerns or interests regarding the matter at hand that led them to participate in and influence the course of the interaction as they did.

My thinking about this issue echoes a point Aristotle made in his *Rhetoric:* that the "truth" of the matter can only come out when advocates on either side of the question are equally competent. When it comes to advocacy through the give and take of interaction, rather than through extended discourse in a public forum, the competence of advocates to engage in a debate on the merits of the question (based on their expertise and analytic and argumentative proficiency) is not a sufficient basis for participating effectively. Navigating the interaction itself is an additional, separate problem. It is thus worthwhile to consider what competence in interaction must advocates have, or what mistakes can advocates make, that strengthen or weaken their ability to get a hearing for their side.

The analysis here starts from the premise that what also matters for advocacy through the give and take of interaction, and arguably is primary, is the competence of advocates to produce and manage constraints in their successive turns at talk on what can meaningfully be said in the remaining interaction, and on how what gets said will be interpreted and thus judged. The force of these constraints is that what participants say (often with reference to details of content, phrasing, and sequential organization) can open up or shut down the relevance of what might remain to be said on the merits, or how future statements that might yet be made on the merits would be interpretable. From this perspective, when disputants address a disagreement, the advantage goes to persons more proficient (or the disadvantage to persons who make errors) in managing their turns to promote a course of the unfolding interaction that, independent of the merits of their position, is favorable to producing talk that advocates for their position on the question.

To come at this another way, this time borrowing loosely from the rhetorical theorist and critic, I. A. Richards, the two perspectives I just sketched on how to examine a group's engagement in discussion and debate correspond to the difference between a concern with what Richards terms the *scientific aspect of discourse* (Ogden & Richards, 1923/1956) versus a concern with the *rhetorical aspect of discourse* (Richards, 1936/1965, 1938/1973, 1955). What drives the content (and perhaps also the style and organization) of scientific discourse is ensuring its fidelity to what is (believed to be) existentially, scientifically true. But Richards noted that much discourse is not purely scientific (nor is it the converse, purely emotive). Rather, what drives the content and style of much discourse is its purpose, or end, and this involves what Richards considers its rhetorical aspect. A concern with the rhetorical aspect of discourse centers on "misunderstanding and its remedies" (Richards, 1936/1965, p. 3) and on "adapting discourse to its ends" (Richards, 1938/1973, p. 12)—or on language as "an instrument for controlling our becoming" (Richards, 1955, p. 9)—all of which I consider to shift the focus of an examination of discourse from a concern with its adequacy for expressing what is (believed to be) true, to a concern with its adequacy for achieving desired social-symbolic and interactional consequences (by virtue of what is expressed, how it is expressed, and especially where it is expressed sequentially in the unfolding interaction).

In terms of those distinctions, I follow Richards in having theorized, and observed, that people generally speak and participate in social life "rhetorically"—that they select the content and style of what they say for the sake of its effect (Sanders, 1984, 1987), and not (primarily) because it expresses (completely, accurately) what they believe is true. This contrasts with perspectives that privilege rational problem solving, which require of persons who engage in efforts to resolve disagreements that, in order to debate the merits of competing positions on an issue, they produce discourse on a scientific and not rhetorical basis. This makes it an empirical and theoretical question, apart from the normative one, of whether, and if so, when, and how, people do produce meaningful discourse that is scientific—shaped by beliefs about what is true—and is thus congruent with an emphasis on rational problem solving.

If the dominant or primary shaping influence on talk is a rhetorical one, then to say what one considers to be right or true would for practical reasons be a futile gesture in any instance where doing so would have unwanted social-symbolic or interactional consequences, that is, if it risked being misunderstood, or seeming incoherent or irrelevant, and perhaps as a result, of compromising one's role-identity. At the same time, this does not lead us to the absurd claim that people are unconcerned with saying what is true. Rather it predicts that their willingness to say what is (believed to be) true (the likelihood that they will do so) is reduced to the extent that doing so will have unwanted social-symbolic or interactional consequences.

Theoretically, persons do not have to be passive about these consequences, they co-construct them with others in the interaction. Accordingly, participants in interactions can be proactive in the way they formulate their turns at speaking so as to improve the chances that what they want to say can be said relevantly, without unwanted consequences. Hence, if it seems in some instance that saying what one believes is true will risk undesirable social and interactional consequences, the skilled communicator may be able to find a way to alter the wording or sequential placement of statements so as to end up being able to produce them without unwanted consequences. Failing that, the choices are to say what one believes to be true despite the risk of unwanted consequences, or to refrain from saying what one believes to be right or true, or actually to abandon a concern with saying what one believes and instead to cultivate wanted consequences by saying what one does not believe.

From this perspective, effective participation in group decision making depends on being able to manage one's discourse so as to lay the groundwork for being able to say what one believes without unwanted consequences. I propose that it was a mistake in this regard that led to the decision that the management group made in their deliberations.

The Methodological Issue of Using a Documentary as Data

The other preliminary consideration I want to address is the methodological one of whether the documentary film being used for data in this volume, *Corporation: After Mr. Sam*, is bad data because it is not a complete, unedited record of the meetings that were filmed of senior managers' deliberations in anticipation of the retirement of the company's founder and president, "Mr. Sam" (Sam Steinberg). Whether the film provides usable data despite the editing, and despite the filmmaker's having supplied background information about the issues and the participants, is an important issue both for the soundness of my own and others' analyses, and the value of this volume itself. It is also important because we have far too little naturally occurring, raw data, comprising the actual talk of organizational members in making decisions and solving problems. Given the rarity of such data, it would be a loss to conclude that we cannot use this or other such materials just because they are edited. My view in brief is that, although there is no substitute for an unedited record, the fact that the film provides us with an edited (incomplete) record does not in itself make it bad data, it depends on the question the data are being used to answer.

To consider more specifically what kinds of questions the film can and cannot be used to answer, it will help to give a summary characterization of the film. Over the course of these meetings, the main topics were: (a) ways of re-engineering the organization in anticipation of a future CEO who would not be founder and owner and thus whose personal traits and preferences would not be as binding; and (b) how the search for a new CEO would be conducted. The filmmaker has not only edited down many hours of meeting time to a film of less than 2 hours in length, but the filmmaker has an evident focal interest (as indicated by the narrative portions delivered by a voiceover)—an interest in the interpersonal dynamics surrounding the potential for a transition, in this case from a family-run company to a managed corporation. Accordingly, the film foregrounds the interplay between Mr. Sam, members of his family within senior management, and nonfamily members of senior management. Beyond the editing, the filmmaker supplements what we see with background information about the meeting participants and their interest in the specific issue of Mr. Sam's successor. The film thus amounts to visual anthropology. Based on the filmmaker's observations (the filmed meetings) and presumably interviews the filmmaker had with the company's principals, the film presents a record of members' practices and a minimal account of their meaning from the members' point of view. The question here, then, becomes whether an ethnographic report comprising such materials can be used reasonably as data.

The answer depends first on whether there is any reason to doubt the ethnographic report itself, and second whether the analyst's question can be answered with the data that the ethnographic report provides. As to the issue of whether there is reason to doubt this ethnographic report, the fact that the filmmaker had the participants' permission to make the film, and almost certainly got their consent to release the finished product, means that the principals themselves saw nothing in the film that was wrong. This does not rule out the possibility that unflattering or complicating events and perspectives were edited out, but it gives us reasonable assurance that what we do see and are told is accurate from those members' points of view. Hence, the film is good data insofar as an analyst relies on what is in the film, and does not stand to be contradicted by what might have been left out (or at least can identify those claims susceptible to being contradicted by what the film may have omitted).

Second, can the question at hand be answered with these data? In my case, the answer is yes. The focus of my analysis is on how the formulation of turns at talk can be consequential for the future course of the interaction, and that is something one can see in any recorded, naturally occurring data that gives an unaltered record of the way successive turns at talk build on each other. For that, the data need to accurately capture the sequential progression of turns and responses, and this film seems to present whole sequences within the fragments it displays (although admittedly, I have to rely on my intuitions as a native speaker that sequential order has been preserved, and not any certain knowledge about the editing). At the same time, the kind of analysis I do also requires attention to how the interests of the respective participants would be affected by what course the interaction follows. What the participants' respective interests are is something that always involves a degree of conjecture, and so it has to be introduced as a hypothetical (for members and analysts alike). It is something that at minimum generally can be inferred from the patterns of participants' responses across a sequence of turns when one lacks any additional, background information about the participants. In the case of the film, *Corporation: After Mr. Sam*, it is an additional benefit to have the background information that the filmmaker provided about who the unofficial contenders were among senior management to succeed Mr. Sam, and to know that aspect of their interests in the matters on which they were shown disagreeing.

More generally, I can think of several other reasons to be interested in the data this film provides. It would be fine data for Cooren's (2000; Cooren & Fairhurst, 2004) study of discourse and related practices that reify the abstract reality of the organization itself. It would also be good data for examining how transitions from "social talk" to "task talk" and back again are accomplished in naturally occurring (and contentious) meetings, what occasions them, and perhaps what their functions are. It would also be good data for examining what occasions humor, or how authority, or status symmetry or asymmetry, is expressed, presupposed, enforced, deferred to, and so forth. On the other hand, there are questions one could ask about this episode in this particular company's history for which this film would not be good data (or at least could not support unqualified claims). For example, if one were interested in examining how the "power" relations among the participants, or the organization's culture, affected what participants said, how they responded, whether they took an active part, what the issues raised were, and so forth, the film provides too little, and leaves out too much, to be of much help. Similarly, if one wanted to examine the adequacy of the group's decision(s) with reference to the evidence and reasoning both sides put forward for and against it, the omissions of an edited film make that unknowable, especially if edited as this one was to foreground the interpersonal factors that were at work.

EMPIRICAL AND THEORETICAL GROUNDS FOR THE ANALYSIS

The analysis here draws from two principal sources. One is Goffman's early work on the "presentation of self" (1959) and "face-work" (1967), and the vast empirical and theoretical literature that builds on Goffman, including Brown and Levinson's (1987) politeness theory. The other is my own empirical and theoretical work (Sanders, 1987, 1995a, 1995b, 1997; Sanders & Fitch, 2001; Sanders & Freeman, 1997) on the way participants in interactions constrain each other, and are constrained, by how their respective turns interconnect to form a coherent discourse whole (whether that ends up being a conversation or a quarrel, a committee meeting, a political debate, etc.). Rather than summarize the thinking in each of those streams, I will simply note their upshot, and some corollaries.

The upshot of both streams is to problematize the production of turns in an interaction; speakers are not free to say just anything in a specific instance, not even what is foremost in their thoughts or feelings just then. Speaking in an interaction can affect what ensues in ways that either favor the speaker's interests or work against them, and in both streams that consideration is regarded as a primary motivation for and constraint on what is said. From Goffman's (1959) perspective, one's interests are bound up with upholding one's own and the other participants' definition of the situation, and each participant's "face" (one's own and the other participants' respective role-identities as constituted by the situation). From my perspective, one's interests are bound up with how what one says will be interpretable, and with what is made relevant (or made irrelevant) in the ensuing interaction by what one says.

When one or more parties to an interaction have specific interests at stake that depend on what is included in the interaction or on how it concludes, then fashioning turns is problematic in the same way that making moves in a chess game is problematic; they need to be responsive, also to be anticipatory of what they make relevant in the ensuing portions of the interaction, and in addition (more so in social life than in chess) to present to others the self that the person claims to be and a commitment to the way the situation has been defined.

From that general perspective, one can posit that there exists, and can examine interactions in terms of, a certain artfulness in the way speakers sequentially place and phrase what they say for the sake of being responsive to what has gone before, and at the same time anticipatory of fostering desired consequences for the ensuing interaction and for their presentation of self—which I refer to as "neo-rhetorical" participation in interactions (Sanders, 1995a, 1997; Sanders & Freeman, 1997). I distinguish the interactional consequences of what one says that are the focus of neo-rhetorical participation in interactions from its psychological, sociological, or cultural consequences. *Interactional consequences* involve what future course the interaction can relevantly, coherently take (what it includes, how it concludes) following from the interpretation of one's current turn as warranted by how it is deemed relevant to what preceded it (Sanders, 1987).

It follows from this that the issue of how one's talk will be interpreted on the basis of constraints in the unfolding interaction on what participants can relevantly say (and on its sequential placement and phrasing) is a separate influence on what gets said from psychological, sociological, or cultural influences (e.g., Sanders, 1987; Sanders & Fitch, 2001). As a result, constraints on what can relevantly follow apply not only to the current speaker, but to all others in the interaction, so that all participants are constrained progressively in the ensuing interaction by what each says "now." Persons may thus find themselves unexpectedly constrained for the sake of being coherent and interpreted in a desired way so as to subjectively feel there are certain things they now "have to" say, or not say, contrary to their wants (as I think happened in the instance I analyze here). This is something that participants in interaction can strategically exploit as a means of directing the ensuing course of the interaction: They can formulate their current turns at speaking so as to have a desired effect on what can relevantly follow and how that might be interpreted, and thus, participate in interactions neo-rhetorically (Sanders, 1987, 1995a).

In examining the interactional fragments we see from several successive meetings in *Corporation: After Mr. Sam*, I was concentrating on what interactional problems the participants were coping with, that is, what consequences for the course of the interaction and its impact on their interests they faced as they took a turn. From there I considered how they either solved the problem by the way they fashioned their interactional turns or lost out. In this instance, I have not given as close attention as I could to fine details of phrasing, self-correction, and the like that are also relevant and revealing, but instead have concentrated on more gross considerations of content and sequential positioning.

What I discuss raises an issue for research in Language and Social Interaction (LSI) and a different one for research in Organizational Communication. For LSI, the issue involves the methodological premise that we should restrict our analysis to interactional details the participants themselves are evidently orienting to. The question is, how restrictive or open can we be in applying that premise. I will be pushing the limit here. For organizational communication, the issue is this. There is some basis for saying that in this instance, the substantive results of this discussion were based on who "won" and "lost" the interactional chess game that I think was being played. As noted in my preliminary comments, this is a basis for decision making that gives even less assurance than Simon's (1955) notion of satisficing that something enduring and right will come out of such discussions, except by accident. The question is, how then, do quality decisions get made (if in fact they do), and what if anything can be done to promote them?

DATA AND ANALYSIS

The Interactional Situation

The analysis here focuses on one meeting, the second one that the film shows us, where much of the discussion was about Jack Levine's proposal for how to re-engineer the organization. As noted, I am relying largely on the narrative provided by the film's voice-over to represent the situation along with the interactional fragments the filmmaker provides. There are four persons present at the meeting who, we are told by the voice-over, were considered the main contenders to succeed Mr. Sam as president: Steinberg family members Arnold Steinberg (nephew) and Mel Dobrin (son-in-law), and non-family members James Doyle and Jack Levine. It is overtly discussed in a later segment than the one I examine (over dinner at the company's country retreat, Palomino) that there was a perception among many organizational members that family members had an inside track with Mr. Sam. It is therefore possible, and consistent with what I find in the interaction, that as a result there was an expectation among the four whom we are told are contenders for succession (as well as the others present) that they were not equal contenders, but that Mr. Sam would choose as his successor someone from the family (either his nephew or his son-in-law). Indeed, he did end up naming his son-in-law, Mel Dobrin.

In the second meeting shown in the film (the first of the Palomino meetings), on the question of how to prepare for a new president, the debate is focused on a proposal advanced by Jack Levine to restructure the company (or management) so as to consolidate operations under a small core of vice presidents, giving that core considerably more power than any current vice president had, and the future president (and other executives in the room) correspondingly less. Assuming that having power and autonomy in the company is desirable (to anyone with ambition at least), then it is conceivable that if any of those four contenders thought of himself as having a chance of becoming president, he would resist such restructuring because it would limit the president's discretion and increase the power and autonomy of a few vice presidents. Conversely, if any of those four did not expect to be named president but might be named one of the new more powerful vice presidents, he would promote those restructuring proposals. As we will see, the restructuring proposal Jack Levine makes is supported by him and by James Doyle, the two non-family members named by the filmmaker as contenders for succession. It is opposed by one of the two contenders from the family, Arnold Steinberg. The other family member named as a contender, Mel Dobrin, who eventually was named president, is not shown in the film as taking a speaking turn at all during this discussion; it seems odd that he would not do so under the circumstances, but it is unknowable whether the filmmaker for some reason excised the remarks he made, or in fact he did not speak to this question during this meeting. In a previous meeting on this topic that was filmed, he did speak in favor of creating greater structure in the organization, but that was not in response to any specific proposal, especially one (like Jack Levine's) that might have run against his self-interest as the possible successor to Mr. Sam.

Based on this reasoning about where the self-interest might lie of each of the four main contenders to succeed Mr. Sam, an examination of their remarks indicates all three contenders who did speak to Jack Levine's restructuring plan argued from self-interest. For the two non-family members, if they assumed that they would not be named president, it would be in their self-interest to favor such major restructuring because it would give them an opportunity for increased power and a diminishment of the president's power, and they did argue for the restructuring. For the two family members, if they assumed that they were the likely successor, it would be in their self-interest to oppose restructuring, because any restructuring in advance of their becoming president would interfere with their power or discretion. Arnold S. argued accordingly. As noted, Mel D. was silent (or edited out), and it is an imponderable whether that supports or counters my analysis, or is irrelevant.

Of the three contenders who did speak to the issue of restructuring, if they were speaking from self-interest—more precisely, if they could be perceived by the others present to be speaking from self-interest—it is potentially of social-symbolic and, most importantly here, interactional consequence that they were doing so, and an imperative that they conceal or deny it. It is interactionally consequential for how others will respond to them if they seem to be motivated by their own interests ahead of the company's interests. It is also consequential for the kind of deliberations the group can engage in. If a position is taken that is visibly motivated by self-interest, there is little to be gained from deliberating on its merits because that would not be likely to sway its advocate(s). The problem they each had, then, was how to state their position and/or sequentially place their turns in such a way as to cancel the implicated self-interest, to offset the potential for their arguments (and position) to be discounted as merely self-interested. What these three advocated, what reasons they gave, and how they deflected (or did not deflect) potential inferences about their motives, is thus my focus in the following analysis.

The Interaction

What we learn from the film about Jack Levine's proposal for restructuring is that it created a new layer of senior executives (whose title was left an open matter), who would oversee clusters of divisions of the company that were at the time each reporting separately to the president. As the voiceover points out, this would increase power for some, reduce it for others ("demote" them), and redistribute some of the president's current authority to these new executives.

Again, this proposal is supported by the two contenders who are not family members and opposed by one of the two who were. I will first excerpt their respective statements of support and opposition for Jack Levine's proposal. Then I will call attention to their sequential interrelationships, and the inferences that could be made about the speakers' motives because of the sequential relationship among their statements (cf. Sanders, 1995b). Note that in both statements of support for the proposal from the non-family members, the speakers emphasize being objective and making the needs of the company the first priority; the statement of opposition, from a family member, downplays the importance of the debate and treats the matter as being entirely the discretion of the company's chairman and the new president that will be named.

First, the author of the restructuring plan, Jack L., makes a statement that his concern had been to devise a way to restructure that will "get the best efficiency out of the organization" (320), and that he has not bothered at this stage with what the job titles would be of the senior managers who headed these units. Speaking of the names they would give to the new executives, he says:

(1) lines 316–322

```
316  JACK L:   I didn't care what name it was. It was General Manager, it was a
317            a Vice-President, I said "What are the natural (.) groupings?" I I
318            said "If I was starting up from scratch what would I do?" I give
319            names a later date, I said "These are the natural groupings in
320            order to get the best efficiency out of the organization" and th'
321            assets would go. Based on that efficiency I grouped them
322            together.
```

Second, the other contender for the presidency who supports the plan, James D., makes a statement a short time later that puts a premium on being objective, and being concerned with "h:ow the organization itself (.) should be (.) best structured" (397–398) without being concerned about what job titles would be created or deleted and how current incumbents would be affected:

(2) lines 391–403

```
391  JAMES D:  All our previous discussions, and we had some before we
392            came up here to Palomino, we thought (.) uh it was impressed
393            on us and many individuals raised the point that we should be
394            try:ing (0.2) > difficult as it is for all of us< to be objective
```

395   about what we said in these reports (.) and to th:ink of the
396   organization (.) <u>not</u> in terms of the incumbency in any one
397   position but as to h:ow the organization itself (.) should be (.)
398   <u>best</u> structured from the point of view, and w:orry about the
399   b:odies to fill the positions afterwards. And that is what, if
400   we're going to be objective, we should be doing here (0.2) and
401   we're d:odging the issue because we're saying "Ah (0.5) it might
402   possibly point the finger at any one of us, and that's a- too
403   delicate area for us to discuss" =

In contrast, the contender for the presidency who opposes the plan
(and such planning altogether), Arnold S., spoke shortly after James D.
made his statement in Example (2), with a characterization of their current debate as an "exercise" that could end up being a waste of time because of the "relationship between the [future] chairman [Mr. Sam] and
the [future] president and how they see the job."

(3) lines 418–425
418 ARNOLD S: It just seems to me th't, th't while there may be some benefits
419   (.) from the exercise (0.2) I really see that (.) for the <u>most</u> part
420   we will go through the exerc', it will take several hours (0.5)
421   maybe several days (.) we will have a very heated discussion,
422   it's inconceivable to me that it can be resolved without a heated
423   discussion, and <u>then</u> (.) the <u>wh:ole</u> thing could be a complete
424   waste of time because (.) of the of the the relationship between
425   the Chairman and the President and how they see the job.

Assuming it would be as easy for the participants as for analysts to
infer that each of these three men might be speaking from self-interest,
then we can expect that the issue of speakers' motivation for their positions (and anyone else's position) was made relevant as a topic by these
statements, and along with it the potential to be charged with speaking
out of self-interest rather than company interest. And this is precisely
what happens: Motivation becomes a topic, in fact it becomes a topic
even before James D.'s statement in Example (2). This issue of motivation arises not only directly in what speakers say, however, but also indirectly, based on how their utterances are interpretable on the basis of
their sequential positioning.

The issue of motivation is voiced first, indirectly, as Arnold S. initially
speaks up in a statement that comes after Jack L.'s explanation of his
proposal (including Example (1)) and before James D. speaks in Example
(2). Arnold S. speaks negatively about Jack L.'s proposal, but then an
unidentified speaker interjects a charge of speaking from self-interest. It
is unclear whether the charge is initially directed at Arnold S. or Jack L.,
but Arnold S. hears it as being aimed at Jack L., or replies to it as if it
were not addressed to him.

(4) lines 382–389
382 ARNOLD S: All the areas now report to all the people in this ↑room, =
383 IRVING L: =Look=
384 (HARRY S): =Irving=
385 IRVING L: =Look, let me let me just add this =
386 ARNOLD S: =How can you. How can you talk about the President, a man a
387   man who doesn't exist at the present time..=
388 (   ):   =Talking about yourself.
389 ARNOLD S: Uh … but now you're gonna start talking about yourself =

Consider now that James D.'s statement on behalf of restructuring (Example (2)), including his call for being objective and not self-interested, comes just after this introduction of the issue of motive by Arnold S. James D.'s statement is thus interactionally positioned as being responsive to *that* issue—motivation, specifically self-interested motives—and because of its sequential position as a response, it is interpretable as being an accusation that prior speakers (Arnold S.?) had failed to do what James D. then calls for: "to th:ink of the organization (.) not in terms of the incumbency in any one position but as to h:ow the organization itself (.) should be (.) best structured from the point of view, and w:orry about the b:odies to fill the positions afterwards" (395-399).

Jack L. makes a follow-up statement immediately after James D.'s in Example (2). Its content and sequential placement bring closer to the surface the accusation implicated by James D. that "some" in the meeting were motivated by self-interest, adding to it an explicit accusation of cowardice:

(5) lines 405–416
405 JACK L: You know what I think? I think- I think we're getting
406   chicken!
407 JAMES D: Yeah!=
408 JACK L: =We all ought to have enough nerve, gumption, look at the
409   company hh and say to our present President (.) in writing
410   "Look Mr President, you have to reorganize (0.2) because we
411   have certain weaknesses that if we don't do this, the company is
412   not gonna move." (0.2) Along with somebody else, everybody
413   in this room was willing to do it. When it comes to
414   individually, you wanna chicken out because you may have
415   [to give, you may have to take.
416 JAMES D: [Exactly.

When Arnold S. states, in Example (3), that this discussion is an empty exercise, his comment comes after these veiled and overt accusations respectively by James D. and Jack L. When one takes into account the sequential positioning of this statement—specifically the claim that the discussion is a "complete waste of time because (.) of the of the the relationship between the Chairman and the [new] President and how they see the job"—the statement is susceptible to a possible interpretation that would not otherwise be visible. Positioned as a response to the accusations of not being objective, not having the company interest at heart, being chicken, being unable to rise above self-interest, Arnold S.'s statement about this being an empty exercise is functionally a defensive one, and he begins it with a defensive phrasing ("It just seems to me ..." [418]). Moreover, it does not counter the accusation of self-interest that has been indirectly leveled at him, but rather seems to justify it. With reference to social-symbolic and interactional consequences, when Arnold S. finishes speaking, we seem to have two champions of the virtue of putting the organizational need ahead of personal needs (James D. and Jack L.) against the self-interested posture that they had indirectly accused their principal rival (Arnold S.) of having. In the sequential position in which it occurs, for Arnold S. to have said that what is decided should depend on the relationship between the chairman and the president—a phrasing that underscores that there is already a relationship between the chairman and himself, the family relationship of uncle and nephew—implicates that he was indeed talking about himself and his personal desires in the matter.

This issue of who is being selfless and who is being self-interested is not just about *face*—about the type and qualities of "self" each speaker is presenting. The issue as noted is that positions taken on the basis of the company's interest are debatable—one can argue about what the company's needs are and evaluate proposals accordingly. Positions taken on the basis of the speaker's self-interest are not debatable. One either has to acquiesce or to confront. To assert (or be interpreted as asserting) self-interest is therefore either a discussion stopper or a preface to acrimony.

In the sequence that follows, coming just when we have Arnold positioned as self-interested (and thus potentially shutting off discussion or inviting confrontation), and his antagonists as selfless, honest, and objective, Mr. Sam intervenes to reframe Arnold's position. He does this in such a way as to make it now a principled matter to delay restructuring rather than self-interested, and thus amenable to debate. Jack L. counters the principle Mr. Sam presents with a competing principle, but is met by Arnold S., now in a position to rise above self-interest and reassert the principle his uncle introduced:

1. Lines (428–433): Mr. Sam takes Arnold's side, and elaborates his point that company structure should depend on who is president —but makes it a matter of principle. Where Arnold had said company structure will depend on the relationship between chairman and president, Mr. Sam says it will depend on what kind of structure the future president needs to operate effectively:

```
428  SAM S:    Listen. When a man is made the Chief (1.0) Executive Officer,
429            and I'm just using the President by way of example (0.5) >then
430            he::'s going to determine the kind of a structure that he can
431            operate with effectively in order to achieve the desired ↑goals.<
432            You say to him "We'll make you the President, but this is the
433            way you're gonna have to operate" uh
```

2. Lines (434–439): Jack L counters that something needs to be done about structure now, instead of leaving it for a "haphazard" (437) action later—but presents this as an outgrowth of the *group's* responsibility rather than his own agenda. He thereby counters Mr. Sam by claiming that it would implicate irresponsibility on everyone's part (if not self-interest by some) to sidestep the issue of structure now.

```
434  JACK L:    But we have we have we ↑h:ave (0.5) a I think a responsibility
435             as a group (.) to put this kind of recommendations on the board
436             the same way we did other recommendations, rather than leave
437             it again (.) for a haphazard uh uh putting together without the
438             resources to put together or call another meeting for that
439             purpose.
```

3. Lines (441–450): Arnold S. speaks next, but instead of being responsive to Jack L.'s tacit accusation, he builds on the principle Mr. Sam introduced for not making any commitment to structure yet, citing the privilege of executives at the highest levels (the U.S. President, the Prime Minister) to organize their staffs in a way that suits their personal strengths.

```
441  ARNOLD S: I think uh (.) traditionally the President of the United States or
442             the Prime Minister under the parliamentary system (.) alone
443             chooses his own Cabinet and for the most part (.) the choice of
444             Cabinet depends on the skills of that particular individual. I
445             think it was obvious that under Kennedy (0.2) uh he chose a
446             very weak Secretary of State because he himself wanted to be
447             the Secretary of State. (0.2) Uh uh I think that to for a a
448             President to come out into the job uh (0.2) without this choice
449             (0.5) d'uh being made by him, I think puts him at uh a very
450             serious disadvantage.
```

To sum up the interaction so far, it is conceivable that each of the protagonists in this meeting were speaking from self-interest, but two of them (James D. and Jack L.) frame their positions as selfless and in the company interest by what they say and where they sequentially position it. In so doing, they make relevant the group's discussion of the value of Jack L.'s restructuring plan for the organization. Juxtaposed with that framing, Arnold S.'s initial objection seemed so tainted by self-interest (in the objection's having its basis in the "private" matter of relationships between the chairman and the president, perhaps Arnold S. himself, rather than the public matter of the company's operational needs) that tabling the issue in response would have been interpretable as catering to his interests rather than the organization's needs. It is possible that this is what motivated Mr. Sam to intervene and reframe opposition to a restructuring plan as a principled concern with executive flexibility and prerogatives, in the process making it relevant and thus discussible to consider whether executive privilege should supersede restructuring, as opposed to discussing the merits of any restructuring plan in particular.

Conceivably, Mr. Sam's alignment with Arnold S., and his expression of a principled reason for not making a commitment to structure before a president is named, may have deflected the charge against Arnold S. that self-interest was at work (and dampened the enthusiasm with which Jack L. and James D. promoted restructuring), and in the process set aside the issue of motivation and opened up the relevance of a consideration of their choices on the merits.

However, the issue of motive is promptly reintroduced by Guy N. (after a tension-relieving side-sequence by the meeting chair, Harry S.). Guy N.'s declaration seems disconnected from what has preceded it, unless one goes back—prior to Arnold S.'s and Mr. Sam's statements—to Jack L.'s and James D.'s initial accusations that some people were being "chicken" about making a serious effort at restructuring because they were afraid of what they might personally lose:

(6) lines 468–475

```
468  GUY N:    Yah. (1.0) As far as I'm concern I must say (0.5) that (.) there is
469            a time to disagree (0.5) and this is what we're doing (.) the
470            present time .hh but I must say though that (0.2) as s:oon as a
471            decision is made .hh which is considered to be in the best
472            interest of the company hh Guy Normandin won't resent (.)
473            being (.) demoted if this is called demotion (.) and he will be
474            prepared to pull 'n the same direction as other people.
475            ((Some applause))
```

In producing talk at this juncture relevant to the talk about restructuring that preceded Mr. Sam's and Arnold S.'s introduction of a principled reason to not pursue the matter, Guy N. makes it relevant to now go ahead to debate the merits of restructuring plans, and not the issue Mr. Sam and Arnold S. introduced about the importance of preserving a CEO's flexibility.

It is here that Jack L. made an error or misjudgment in what he then said. He takes the floor after Guy N. spoke, and instead of reintroducing the topic of his restructuring plan, which Guy N.'s statement made interactionally relevant, he continues to address the topic of motivation, which was also made relevant by Guy N.'s statement, and professes his commitment and loyalty to the company's interests:

(7) lines 477–481

```
477  JACK L:    I (.) kn:ew we would get at some point (.) of this kind of
478             contention (0.5) and uh uh (.) I was willing, myself, to take that
479             risk and stand ab't to the job that I will be allocated to, to my
480             ability, based on the evaluation of my present superior, which
481             happens to be Sam Steinberg.
```

(8) lines 488–498

```
488  JACK L:    When I put these things out I feel deeply about the organization
489             and where it's going and where it should go. An' I'm willing to
490             (.) subject my own personal goals at this point- though I 'ave
491             personal goals- to the good or welfare of the organization. So
492             I'm not looking at j:obs or job descriptions or job titles hh what
493             will be best for the company I'm prepared to do.
494             (1.5)
495  SAM S:     That was always understood.
496  (    ):    Very good ((knocking on the table.))
497             (1.5)
498  SAM S:     And nobody [knows that better than me.
```

At this point, the substantive issue of restructuring that had been made relevant seems to have been set aside in favor of equally relevant professions of selfless loyalty. In the wake of these professions, instead of the prior relevance of going on to debate restructuring plans, it had now become just as interactionally relevant to debate the overriding importance of executive flexibility, especially in light of Jack L.'s having said, "I was willing, myself, to take that risk and stand ab't to the job that I will be allocated to, to my ability, based on the evaluation of my present superior" (478–480). In addition, because two opposing camps on these matters had emerged, with Mr. Sam in one camp, Jack L.'s profession made it just as relevant at that point to end discussion on both topics, and table the matter. And in the closing statement of this segment of the film, which comes immediately after Jack L. professes selflessness and loyalty, this is precisely what another senior manager proposes they do:

(9) lines 500–516

```
500  IRVING L:   I think that's the groupings that are made (0.2) .hh are really the
501              prerogative of the Chairman and whoever he nominates to be
502              the President .hh and those groupings, I only want to submit,
```

```
503                must be made on two bases =
504  (    ):       ((Someone coughing.))
505  IRVING L:     = and I don't know if we can go much deeper with it (.) over
506                here. And that is this: number one is what is a natural grouping
507                business wise? and the number two (.) is the competence, and of
508                the of the people available (.) in the judgement of the Chairman
509                (.) and his President .hh and that will obviously have to
510                determine to some degree the groupings uh fundamentally
511                based upon the uh natural groupings that are available to us. But
512                I think that pr-beyond that you have to take people into account
513                and into consideration .h and we we should leave here ready to
514                say that whatever these people deem to be in the best interest of
515                the corporation that this is what we will have to go along with
516                (.) and that's it, I don't think we can go beyond that point.
```

Irving L.'s statement could not easily be objected to by any of the three contenders who had spoken on the issue of restructuring. It was in Arnold S's interest to let this statement stand, considering that it dovetails with his own position. But from Jack L.'s and James D.'s perspective, whose position was opposed by this statement, it would reintroduce the appearance of being self-interested to dispute it. Note first that the statement incorporates the premises that Jack L. and James D. advanced, that there *should* be restructuring based on "natural groupings business wise" (506–507). However, it merges that idea with the opposite stance that the details should be left to those in charge later (i.e., the new president and Mr. Sam). It would be hard for either James D. and especially Jack L. (who pledged himself to accepting whatever the boss decided) to dispute this contention without seeming to be intent not just on bettering the company's structure, but on settling the matter "now" (before the new president could weigh in). Why "now"?—unless one attributes to them a greater concern with how they personally might benefit than with what would be best for the company, because to settle it "now" would assure them of having more influence over the decision than if it were settled "later" by the new president.

Of course, Jack L. or James D. could have tried to show that it nonetheless was in the company's interest and not theirs (or not just theirs) to settle the matter without further delay. However, sequentially placing a contention that restructuring is needed "now" after a proposal has been made to table the matter until a new president is named would ensure the attribution of selfish motives to its advocates. The time to have addressed the issue of the urgency of restructuring was when Jack L.'s plan was first presented—urgent either on the grounds, for example, that current operational problems made it imperative apart from issues of arranging for Mr. Sam's successor, or urgent to do it while they still had the experience and expertise of the current management team to draw on.

In sum, the protagonists of restructuring, particularly Jack L., were functionally blocked from deliberating the wisdom, and making a decision on the merits, of re-engineering the organization by interactional constraints largely of Jack L.'s own making.

CONCLUSION

In closing, I want to address the two issues I mentioned, one for researchers in LSI, the other for researchers in Organizational Communication. The issue for LSI is whether I have gone too far in attaching to utterances interactional meanings that the participants do not consistently orient to themselves. Although I think that there is some basis in the participant's talk for interpreting their utterances as I have (especially the progression from talk about restructuring to talk about motives), I grant that I have focused on what their utterances *could* mean (based on their interconnections and sequencing, and a formulation of where each speaker's interests lay), and not what we can say with certainty that they *did* mean (for either speaker or hearers). However, I think we sell our work short if we are overly rigid about shying away from meanings that utterances could have in the given interactional environment, even if participants do not orient to them as having that meaning. First, it would make it difficult to examine speakers' and hearers' indirectness (e.g., Drew, 1984; Pomerantz, 1980, 1986). Second, I contend that part of what participants often have to cope with in interaction is precisely indeterminacy about a speaker's meaning—knowing what an utterance could mean, without any certainty that the speaker means that by it. And speakers may or may not respond to those possible meanings, or that equivocality, in an overt way. Third, it is sometimes the mark of artfulness and success if one fashions one's turns to avoid a need or option for anyone to directly register their significance and effect, and we stand to render ourselves unable to capture those instances if our work centers on just those matters to which participants visibly attend. In short, to restrict ourselves to what meanings participants visibly orient to is to overlook some of the most difficult problematics of interaction (when speaker's meanings are only possible, not certain, but consequential, and possibly strategically effective). This leaves us with a methodological issue of course—how to tell fantasies about interactions apart from serious analyses—but I think it is important to attack this problem, and that we can solve it.

The issue for Organizational Communication is to consider how it is that, for example, quality decisions get made—and fail to get made—through group deliberation because of the problematics of interaction itself. Assuring that quality decisions get made, as did not happen here (at least if a good decision was made, it does not seem to have been made for good reasons), depends on more than the attitudes, the expertise and proficiencies, and the personalities and other personal qualities of the participants. It lies also in the interactional competencies (or perhaps better, proficiencies; see Sanders, 2003) of the participants. I have made a case here that in working to deflect inferences of being motivated by self-interest, the advocates of significant restructuring made themselves unable to rebut Irving L.'s contention that they could not reasonably settle the matter "here" but would have to wait until a new president was named. James D. and Jack L., abetted by Mr. Sam, established that the prime social imperative and interactional warrant for deliberating the issue of restructuring lay in the moral virtue of placing the company's needs ahead of individual interests. This opened the door (made it relevant) for Irving L. to put an end to deliberations by establishing it as not being in the company interest to settle anything "here." Once that had been said, it could not have been contested by Jack L. or James D. without their risking being interpretable as speaking from self interest. In that way, the social-symbolic and interactional consequences for Jack L. and James D. of continuing to argue their case made it untenable for them to do so.

It may be that Jack L. and James D. were taken in by their own professions when they spoke about their motives (were speaking scientifically and not rhetorically). But it may also be the case that they were not sufficiently adept interactionally to see that they had opened the door to the countermove made by Mr. Sam and then by Irving L. This countermove might have been deflected in advance without the social-symbolic and interactional consequences of trying to counter it afterward (by making a case for business reasons why attending to the matter "now" would avert damage to the company that would result if they waited any longer, and perhaps in addition that a way could be worked out to do this without tying the hands of the incoming president). Accordingly, we can say regardless of the merits of their position, that the main advocates for deliberating what may have been critically needed organizational changes made strategic interactional mistakes that derailed them.

What seems evident from this case study is that in group problem-solving, as in social interaction generally, the communication process itself is consequential for what ensues. What is communicated, how it is expressed, and what its sequential placement is, changes the interpretation and thus the desirability and likelihood of the talk and conduct that could ensue, regardless of what participants want to say or believe to be true. And it is precisely because of the consequentiality of the communication process itself that the interests of LSI researchers and organizational communication researchers intersect.

REFERENCES

Brown, P., & Levinson, S. C. (1987). *Politeness: Some universals in language usage.* Cambridge, England: Cambridge University Press.

Cooren, F. (2000). *The organizing property of communication.* Philadelphia: John Benjamins.

Cooren, F., & Fairhurst, G. T. (2004). Speech timing and spacing: The phenomenon of organizational closure. *Organization, 11,* 793–824.

Drew, P. (1984). Speakers' reportings in invitation sequences. In J. M. Atkinson & J. Heritage (Eds.), *Structures of social action* (pp. 129–151). Cambridge: Cambridge University Press.

Goffman, E. (1959). *The presentation of self in everyday life.* Garden City, NY: Doubleday.

Goffman, E. (1967). *Interaction ritual: Essays on face-to-face behavior.* New York: Anchor Books.

Ogden, C. K., & Richards, I. A. (1956). *The meaning of meaning: A study of the influence of language upon thought and of the science of symbolism* (8th ed.). New York: Harcourt, Brace. (Original work published 1923)

Pomerantz, A. (1980). Telling my side: "Limited access" as a fishing device. *Sociological Inquiry, 50,* 186–198.

Pomerantz, A. (1986). Extreme case formulations: A way of legitimizing claims. *Human Studies, 9,* 219–229.

Richards, I. A. (1965). *The philosophy of rhetoric.* New York: Oxford University Press. (Original work published 1936)

Richards, I. A. (1973). *Interpretation in teaching.* New York: Humanities Press. (Original work published 1938)

Richards, I. A. (1955). *Speculative instruments.* London: Routledge & Paul.

Sanders, R. E. (1984). Style, meaning and message effects. *Communication Monographs, 51,* 154–167.

Sanders, R. E. (1987). *Cognitive foundations of calculated speech: Controlling understandings in conversation and persuasion.* Albany: State University of New York Press.

Sanders, R. E. (1995a). A neo-rhetorical perspective: The enactment of role-identities as interactive and strategic. In S. J. Sigman (Ed.), *The consequentiality of communication* (pp. 67–120). Hillsdale, NJ: Lawrence Erlbaum Associates.

Sanders, R. E. (1995b). The sequential inferential theories of Sanders and Gottman. In D. P. Cushman & B. Kovacic (Eds.), *Watershed research traditions in human communication theory* (pp. 101–136). Albany: State University of New York Press.

Sanders, R. E. (1997). The production of symbolic objects as components of larger wholes. In J. O. Greene (Ed.), *Message production: Advances in communication theory* (pp. 245–277). Mahwah, NJ: Lawrence Erlbaum Associates.

Sanders, R. E. (2003). Applying the skills concept to discourse and conversation: The remediation of performance defects in talk-in-interaction. In J. O. Greene & B. R. Burleson (Eds.), *Handbook of communication and social interaction skills* (pp. 221–256). Mahwah, NJ: Lawrence Erlbaum Associates.

Sanders, R. E., & Fitch, K. L. (2001). The actual practice of compliance-seeking. *Communication Theory, 11,* 263–289.

Sanders, R. E., & Freeman, K. E. (1997). Children's neo-rhetorical participation in peer interactions. In I. Hutchby & J. Moran-Ellis (Eds.), *Children and social competence: Arenas of action* (pp. 87–114). London: Falmer.

Simon, H. A. (1955). A behavioral model of rational choice. *Quarterly Journal of Economics, 69,* 99–118.

Chapter 9

Bringing the Outside in: A Contextual Analysis

Cynthia Stohl
University of California at Santa Barbara

I wish I had as integrative and clever a way for starting this chapter as the legendary American speaker who was giving a speech in Tokyo to an audience of Japanese business executives. As the story goes, she began, "In the United States speeches typically begin with a joke. In Japan speeches are expected to begin with an apology. So I will start by apologizing for not telling a joke." The audience laughed, appreciating her cultural awareness and sensitivity, and immediately became more receptive to her message.

Here I face a similar issue. The field of organizational communication is typically interested in large-scale structuring and the interdependence among macro- and microprocesses. Commonplace assumptions in contemporary organizational theory include the unbounded nature of organizations across time and space, the interpenetration of the global and the local, the permeability of contexts, and the embeddedness of decision making in emergent matrices of relationships and practices. Moreover, new approaches to group communication including the one I am most identified with, the bona fide group perspective (Putnam & Stohl, 1990; Stohl & Putnam, 2003), emphasize "the emotional intensity, temporal fluctuations, and historical influences of group processes" as well as the need to view any particular group phenomenon as "a process that shapes and is shaped by dynamic group boundaries and multiple contexts" (Putnam & Stohl, 1996, p. 148). My academic culture is embedded in permeable boundaries, interdependence with context, and fragmented borders.

Yet, the two analyses to which I have been asked to respond adhere to many of the tenets of discourse analysis, which, according to Putnam and Fairhurst (2001), include "analyzing excerpts of discourse out of context" (p. 119). The analyses isolate textual material as "objects" for analysis and reify the "boundaries" of group interaction insofar as it is based solely on the ongoing interaction without resorting to contextual information. What counts is what is there, directly in the text. This approach differs fundamentally from my perspective. McPhee, Corman, and Iverson (chap. 7), for example, stress that they are specifically trying to answer the question "how did or does the meeting recorded on the tape, the communication process objectified in the transcript, help constitute the organization?" (p. 135). Accordingly, they suggest, their method may not "completely or ... extremely" "abstract words from their original context" but "of course it filters out other aspects of context" (p. 138). Sanders (chap. 8) is concerned with "constraints in their successive turns at talk on what can meaningfully be said in the remaining interaction, and on how what gets said will be interpreted and thus judged" (p. 164) and argues "that is something one can see in any recorded, naturally occurring data that gives an unaltered record of the way successive turns at talk build on each other" (p. 167).

Thus it would seem that my outsider perspective, as an organizational communication researcher interested in embeddedness, overlapping context, networks of interdependence, and bona fide groups is antithetical to discourse analysis. Someone who assumes the centrality of the interface between external processes, relationships, history, and culture and internal processes is not the person to be commenting on these chapters

However, after carefully reading these analyses it seems that there are points of intersection and complementarity that when considered together can enhance and make for a more comprehensive analysis that does not violate the integrity of discourse analytic approaches. For "what is there" in the text is influenced and framed by "what is not there"; "what is not said" is oftentimes as important as "what is said," implicit and underlying constraints and resources in one context are often significant and apparent in overlapping contexts. It is not merely that as an analyst I am bringing the outside in, but that the participants themselves bring the outside in, framing and reframing internal group processes through their multiple group memberships, multifaceted identifications, external norms, and cultural affiliations. Sanders (chap. 8), for example, distinguishes between rhetorical and scientific discourse.

> If the dominant or primary shaping influence on talk is a rhetorical one, then to say what one considers to be right or true would for practical reasons be a futile gesture in any instance where doing so would have unwanted social-symbolic or interactional consequences ... perhaps as a result, of compromising one's role identity. (p. 165)

As a discourse analyst, however, he is concerned that he may have "gone too far" in his "attaching to utterances interactional meanings that the participants do not consistently orient to themselves?" (p. 181). But he answers his own misgivings, "I think we sell our work short if we are overly rigid about shying away from meanings that utterances could have in the given interactional environment, even if participants do not orient to them as having that meaning" (p. 181).

I agree. How one gauges the potential yet uncertain effect of a message is always rooted in one's own cultural and contextual experiences as well as a perception of the networks in which the other is embedded. Thus, consideration of the larger context, the knowledge and intergroup relations which the participants bring to bear in their interactions and interpretations, can enrich the analysis, because they are part of the production and interpretation of the discourse itself. A bona fide group perspective posits that a tension that runs through virtually all groups is the struggle to manage dependence on and isolation from their social context. When a group depends too much on their external constraints and resources, it tends to fragment and the synergistic possibilities rooted in group decision making are minimized. When a group closes itself off from the outside environment, the extreme isolation leads to insularity, flawed information flow, illusions of invulnerability, reliance on shared stereotypes, all indications of ineffective decision making. Group deliberations, such as what we observe here

> require some sort of balance and linkage between internal and external units, especially when both boundaries and interdependence are negotiated.... Proposal arguments, decision premises, and even modus operandi for making decisions hinge on external norms, cultural changes, and directives from authority. (Putnam & Stohl, 1996, p. 165)

Internal and external dynamics work together to put checks and balances on and construct what group members can and will say.

By situating their analyses within a structurational perspective, McPhee, Corman, and Iverson's (chap. 7) work also can be enhanced by further attention to the group's interdependence with context and permeability of boundaries. They assume that "the interaction constitutes the organization by producing and reproducing it as an ensemble of rules and resources drawn on by its members in this, and other, interaction" (p. 135). Giddens' (1979) theory clearly illustrates the ways in which the political/sociohistorical cultural context of interaction is pivotal for understanding the productive and reproductive nature of social interaction. Communication constitutes organizations and decisions insofar as it is through communication that (a) the form and context of decisions are negotiated, and (b) social realities are created and maintained. Social realities, of course, are not merely rooted in the here and now of one particular communication situation. Stereotypes, cognitive schema, past experiences, cultural premises, shared emotional triggers are all part of constructing social reality. Context is nested in group interaction as each message references and negotiates individual identity, historical circumstance, and intergroup interdependence.

Indeed, just as there is no such thing as a culture-free organization (Sorge, 1983) there is certainly no such thing as a culture-free interpretation or a culture-free conversation. It is important to emphasize that I am not arguing here for some sort of cultural determinism nor suggesting that representative identities are fixed and inviolate, determining group interaction. In a practical sense, as already suggested, we know that just as extreme isolation of groups can lead to symptoms of groupthink (Janis, 1983); overly strong dependence on the external context restricts internal communication, lessens group identity, and often leads to ineffective decision making. Rather, in contrast to the argument that, according to Sanders (chap. 8), "how one's talk will be interpreted on the basis of constraints in the unfolding interaction on what participants can relevantly say (and on its sequential placement and phrasing) is a separate influence on what gets said from psychological, sociological, or cultural influences (e.g., Sanders & Fitch, 2001)" (p. 170), I am suggesting that these are not separate factors but interdependent and coterminous, each shaping and being shaped by each other and the group processes. Which contextual and cultural features become relevant and impinge upon particular interactions depend of course on the saliency afforded these features through the reflexive processing of participants. In other words, in the actual practice of group interaction, individual's cultural backgrounds, multiple memberships, past experience and knowledge as well as perceptions of role, position, and context often frame and become part of the interactions that take place. Sensitivity to these individual, shared and/or overlapping premises is crucial for understanding and assessing group discourse.

In this chapter, I hope to demonstrate how linking and embedding the actual discourse in the shared cultural context may develop a richer and more nuanced understanding of the impact and salience of particular interactive sequences. The interpretations and frames that members use to make sense of intergroup relations are the very frames that members use to help decide on the interactive import of their utterances. By considering the discourse as interdependent with this larger context, we will learn more about group dynamics and group deliberations. Boundaries and intergroup connectedness are salient exogenous characteristics that are socially constructed inside the group. Gender, race, political affiliations, friendships, and past relationships are just some of the possible influences on the nature of group discourse and role identities.

Group members shape their environments as they are influenced by them (Putnam & Stohl, 1996).

Finally, I suggest that incorporating a macrocontextual lens into the analysis of discourse is consistent with what the authors already have done. In chapters 7 and 8, the authors explicitly acknowledge that their interpretations are relying, in part, on the contextual information provided by the filmmaker (in the form of a narrative overlay) regarding who are the unofficial contenders/noncontenders for the next president and the larger-than-life portrayal of Sam Steinberg and his family ties. Throughout Sanders' (chap. 8) analysis of the segment, for example, he bifurcates the group in terms of family and nonfamily members, contenders and noncontenders. These factors are not fully present in the focal interaction but they serve as organizing features of the interaction. In a review of the literature on group decision making, Poole and Hirokawa (1996) noted:

> Studies of communication as a constitutive force necessarily have an interpretive component, because they are concerned with social reality as experienced by the participants. However this does not rule out causal components in explanation: some studies also attempt to trace the effects of exogenous factor on interpretive and constitutive process. (p. 8)

It is these exogenous factors that I concentrate upon, although not in the strict causal sense suggested by Poole and Hirokawa. Rather I am focusing on the interface between the interaction that is constructing the context and the context that impinges on the interaction. Exogenous variables include individual attributes, relations at previous time points, and relations outside the focal group that influence the interaction within the group (see Monge & Contractor, 2003, p. 55, for a discussion of the ways in which exogenous variables may help explain structural tendencies). Thus, my goal in this chapter is to analyze *Corporation: After Mr. Sam* with a lens sensitive to the discourse's permeable boundaries and interdependence with context. This work is not intended to substitute for the analyses done but to supplement them.

CONSTITUTING CONTEXT

The narrator of the film sets up the action by highlighting critical features of the context. The audience is told of the meteoric rise of Steinberg Limited from a small Montreal grocery store started by Sam Steinberg's mother to an international retailing, manufacturing, and real estate company with assets valued at over $224 million (Canadian) and more than 19,000 employees. Further we are told that Sam Steinberg is ready to retire and the issue of presidential succession has not been settled.

Possible replacements are identified and the status of participants (in terms of family membership, personal affiliations, and relational history) are described. All these exogenous variables are known by all the participants prior to the focal interaction. However, a significant feature of the larger context is not mentioned by the narrator; the Steinberg family is Jewish. Yet their religious/ethnic identity embodies a set of practices, experiences, stories, stereotypes, rituals, interactive sequences, and expectations that everyone is aware of and these factors are implicated in their discourse. It is not, of course, Jewish heritage per se that makes a difference, it is the saliency of "Jewishness" that is found in the talk and the social construction of this situation that makes a significant difference in the group's interaction and in my analysis.

Indeed, there is no question that the ethnicity of the family was well known at the time the film was made. Just as the story of Sam Walton has become an often silent but salient part of WalMart mythology and sense making (see, e.g., Greenhouse, 2004), in the early 1970s, Sam Steinberg, epitomized a Canadian success story. There are several case studies of the Steinberg family business and each makes reference to their well-known prominence and emphasizes the strength of the Jewish family ties and traditions at that time:

> Steinberg's primary motivation, apparently was to create a means of support for his large family. Steinberg continued to make place for every male member of the family in his business. He sidestepped the problem of competence by shoring up the family people with outside managers. ... But Sam Steinberg, born in Hungary, Jewish, and very old fashioned about the place of women in business, isolated his own children—four daughters, no sons, both from the day-to-day realities of running a large and complex business, and from the need to earn a living ... When the time came to pick a successor, he considered only his sons-in law. (Horowitz, 2004)

> Fils d'immigrants juifs hongrois très pauvres, Sam Steinberg hérite de sa mère Ida la détermination et le sens des affaires qui le pousseront à transformer une simple épicerie de quartier en colosse du commerce agro-alimentaire de détail [The child of very poor Hungarian Jewish immigrants, Sam Steinberg inherits from his mother Ida the determination and the direction of the businesses which will push it to transform from a simple local grocer to a colossus grocery chain]. (Bélanger, 2004, italics added)

Why is this Jewish heritage important? How does it permeate group interaction and discourse? There are many possibilities. Analyses could examine, for example, the ways in which stereotypes about Jewish immigration, family loyalty, the closeness and support for all members of the clan or fellow countrymen (what in Jewish culture is called being a *lantsman*), business shrewdness, the domineering mother, penetrate the arguments, affect the responses made, influence sense making, and so forth. A study of the ways in which ingroup (Jewish) and outgroup (non-Jewish) boundaries are discursively drawn could also provide insight into alliance development and the shape and shaping of discursive strategies including what is and what is not discussable. In this response, I focus specifically on one conclusion drawn from both sets of analysis, *the pivotal role of Irving Ludmer*, to illustrate how taking into account the fact that the Steinberg's and Irving share the cultural/religious identification of being Jewish helps make sense of events in ways that are not otherwise apparent.

THE PIVOTAL ROLE OF IRVING LUDMER

McPhee, Corman, and Iverson (chap. 7) conclude that the discourse did not result in any transformations of key issues or resolve any tensions. The bifurcation between professionalism and personalism exists throughout the interaction, and although transformative ideas are expressed and re-expressed, CRA identifies a dynamic of "structural reproduction."

Using more traditional content analyses the authors categorize statements in terms of two foci: (a) company and meeting oughts, and (b) claims about the company and the meetings. They identify Sam's "killer" statements, statements that indicate that Sam could and potentially would ignore the group's conclusions. Related to and embodying the dynamic tensions embedded in Sam's killer statements, they distinguish between and highlight the importance of personalist versus professionalist arguments, noting that the CRA graphs are consistent and autonomous, that is, the personalist statements and the professionalist statements are clustered separately and do not overlap. Irving Ludmer's statements are categorized as *personalist*, his discourse falls within that CRA cluster. Looking closely at their analysis, we see that Irving is discursively and argumentatively aligned with Sam and other family members, although he is not a member of the family.

The central importance of Irving's discourse is highlighted by McPhee, Corman, and Iverson (chap. 7). They explicate the ways in which Irving's statement regarding members' need to support whatever decision Sam makes undercuts Jack's desire for specificity and reproduces the tensions of the meeting. They further note how personalists turn several concepts against the professionals, reproducing the social system. But at the same time that Irving supports Sam's right to make his own decision, his utterances embody the other sides of a central tension—Irving is the one person in the group who has the gumption to raise issues related to the family and Friday night dinners—questioning the very personalist approach with which he is discursively linked. Using their analyses, we can see how Irving is a significant actor insofar as he is the only nonfamily member that is able to occupy two semantic spaces simultaneously—both within the family cluster (personalists) and outside the family cluster (questioning the personalist/family orientation of decision making). His discursive position personifies the tensions between tradition and change that are the essence of the group's constitution and reconstitution. His words embody the structural reproduction McPhee, Corman, and Iverson identify through their analyses. Why is that the case? I suggest that the duality of Irving's position, as insider/outsider co-opts his challenge to the status quo and helps explain the lack of transformation and the structural reproduction that takes place. However, the constraints and resources that enable Irving's dual positioning cannot be found directly in the discourse as it is uttered, but rather can be found in the outside context that permeates and transcends group boundaries through member identification, memory traces, and social norms, all part of the structuration process.

Sanders (chap. 8), too, highlights the significance of Irving's discourse. He focuses on the inability of group members to answer Irving's argument about self-interest as pivotal to why the contrary points cannot be voiced and shows how what McPhee, Corman, and Iverson call the personalist argument carries the day. These are the very arguments that reinforce the past ways of doing things and thus prevent innovative approaches. Irving puts an end to deliberations by establishing that it is not in the company interest to settle anything "here" and any response would seem like self-interest. It is significant that in this segment, Irving clearly separates himself from Sam and the family, "We should leave here ready to say that *whatever these people deem* to be in the best interest of the corporation that this is what we will have to go along with (.) and that's it, I don't think we can go beyond that point" (513–516, italics added) at the same time that he aligns with them. This is the same person who later on in the segment is the first person to confront Sam about the outsiders' concerns regarding organizational decision making and the Steinberg family's Friday night dinners. Sanders argues that for an interactant to say what is "right" or "true" at the cost of being incoherent, or having one's speech act misinterpreted, or having one's role-identity compromised, would for practical reasons be a futile gesture. Yet, Irving is able to and does say things that others can't or won't and his utterances are not futile gestures. His statements are critical to the structural reproduction of the group's dialectical dynamics. Why is he the one who has the rhetorical warrant to bring up issues that no one else is comfortable in doing? Why aren't his messages misinterpreted and cause for discursive ostracism in the group? How is it that

Irving's statements do not result in a compromise of his role identity and challenge the foundations of the deliberations? I suggest that by restricting the analysis to the discourse as it is reported, we only see part of the picture, and it is not the complete one the participants see nor the picture to which they react. Thus we miss a powerful significance of his utterances and the underlying dynamic of stability rather than change.

In summary, Irving Ludmer plays a pivotal role in the conclusions drawn in both sets of analyses. In McPhee, Corman, and Iverson's chapter 7, he represents group tensions and structural reproduction; in Sanders' chapter 8, it is lack of a coherent response to his argument that leaves the others compromised and maintains the status quo. In the next section, I demonstrate how Irving's discourse creates and is created through a nexus of internal and external processes that are hinged in part on the dynamic interplay of his multiple roles, status, and identifications. These interdependencies help construct an important framework for interpretative sense making by the group.

THE TEXT: BRINGING THE OUTSIDE IN

The first time Irving is mentioned, the narrator is providing the viewer with contextual information regarding who is and who is not considered a viable candidate for succession.

248	*Voiceover:*	*Others like*
249		*John Paré, Vice-President of Personnel, or Irving Ludmer, in*
250		*charge of expansion and development, were too recently with*
251		*the company or too specialized in their skills to be more than*
252		*remote contenders*

He tries to enter the conversation 100 lines later but, although acknowledged, others talk over him.

379 IRVING L: You know something (0.2) Can I say something (1.0)

385 IRVING L: =Look, let me let me just add this =

390 IRVING L: =You know, right now,=

Interestingly, if we consider traditional variables of group influence, talk time, number of turns, references to the speaker, Irving is discursively not very influential. It is not until (500) when he is once again recognized by Harry S. (506–516) that he voices his opinion that groupings are the prerogative of the Chairman, what McPhee et al. code as and use as an exemplar of a statement of personalism. There are five other places where Irving is actively engaged in the discourse for more than one line—(583–610, 824–858, 1136–1146, 1160–1179, 1201–1203).

It is important to note that in virtually every place Irving participates, he is playing a representative role that others refuse to play. He links the group to its external environment. He maintains a position separate and distinct from other group members. He is the sole boundary spanner between the "in" group (i.e., those at the meeting) and the "out" group (i.e., those organizational members and constituents who were not invited to attend). His outsider, "other" status is produced directly within the dialogue. In (583–610) when Irving uses the pronoun *we*, "I don't think that uh *we*'re leveling all that much" (583–584, italics added) it is immediately followed by others laughing and saying "speak for yourself," thus intentionally separating themselves from Irving.

We see this outsider status enacted in (813–823), after Sam gives an impassioned speech about competence trumping blood relations but then asserting that anyone who says that "if a member of the family who's in the firm who has the competence an' he can't be considered because he is a member of the family is wrong." (819–822). Virtually everyone (with the exception of Irving) deny that they implied any such thing (823). They distance themselves from Irving's "we" and align themselves as part of the "in" group. Directly following this assertion (824–829), Irving carefully reinforces his outsider status, "You know I'm a little younger and only joined the company .hh uh some eleven years ago" (826–827), enabling him to speak for those people *inside* the company but *outside* this context, that is, those who see the informal organization of the Steinberg organization as being linked to family.

Between (829 to 858), Irving says what no one else has had the gumption to bring up, the perception that Friday dinners are where the business really takes place and that people think if a man "goes to Friday night supper as opposed to the other party" (848–849), he will have his voice heard. The rhetorical danger of stating the obvious is clear, but Sam's reaction is much more complex than what we might have expected given the previous dialogue, for example, a simple rejection of Irving and the idea. Sam voices his disagreement with Irving but rather than becoming defensive (as he does so many times other times), he jokes in a sarcastic manner that keeps Irving a part of the group—"I just wanna ask you one question=Is it your charm or ability got you where you are now?" (860–861). This comment not only allows Irving, the boundary spanner who has brought in the outside, to remain part of the group by reminding people of the important role Irving plays; the statement functions as a boundary marker that draws the larger context into the perceived domain in which the group is operating. Sam discursively permeates and expands the group's boundaries, hence keeping Irving inside of the group.

Sam's comment is also inclusive insofar as the joke maintains a discursive style that is consistent with perceptions of Jewish discourse, something that Irving, as part of that designated group, would be comfortable with, taking it in the spirit it was intended and reacting accordingly. Mel D.'s (Sam's son-in-law) quick repartee—"No, he attended the Friday night dinner" (866)—further captures the underlying dynamic of simultaneous insider–outsider that we first see in the segment regarding who gets to decide the structure. Mel's banter is humorous to the group for two reasons: First, it is a play on the content of Irving's point and the tension embedded within it—those attending Friday night dinner are in a privileged position and Irving is clearly such a person. Irving said what others were fearful to say and Irving survived. Second, the comment is humorous because it is a play on the context of the tension. In other words, the statement is funny because everyone knows that Irving is not part of the family, hence not invited to Friday night dinners, but indeed he could attend Friday night dinner (the Sabbath dinner, an important tradition in Jewish families). Irving knows the rituals, what goes on at Friday night dinners, the lighting of the Sabbath candles, the focus on the children, the prohibitions about doing work on the Sabbath. Hence unlike others who are also concerned about the dinner, that is, James D. (who eventually speaks up in support of Irving's point), Irving COULD attend Friday night Sabbath dinner and not be out of place.

I suggest that by taking into account the larger context in which the statements are uttered, we can see how the discussion of the Friday night dinner moves the meaning of the interaction outside the literal—not who is family and who is not, but who could be family and be treated as such. Irving is Jewish and would fit in, whereas James D. who is not Jewish would be an outsider at the dinner and wouldn't belong. Irving is therefore more closely aligned with Mel D., whom we are told only attended Friday night dinner once but as a son-in-law (and a Jewish one). Therefore we see that it is not attendance at Friday night dinner per se that made a difference and made one part of the in-group, it is whether or not one could go to Friday night dinner. This insider status gives Irving the ability to challenge Sam and provides coherence to the discourse. It simultaneously reconstitutes and draws new boundaries in the discussion, bringing Irving into the fold and hence minimizing the discursive challenges he makes. In other words, by taking note of the larger context, we better understand Irving's ability to be a simultaneous insider and outsider, which in turn allows him to play the pivotal role that both McPhee, Corman, and Iversons's (chap. 7) as well as Sanders' (chap. 8) analyses suggest. Irving Ludmer reproduces the system while challenging it at the same time. By taking the larger context into account, the discourse takes on a far greater significance and Irving's critical role and dual positioning as personalist/professionalist is more clearly understood.

Overall, we see that Irving Ludmer is explicitly a boundary spanner. He evokes his outsider status—"people uh come to me and talk to me about this bec- may be because:e you know I'm a little younger and only joined the company .hh uh some eleven years ago" (825–827)—but the reason that Irving is able to say certain things that others cannot (particularly those outside the family) is because he is simultaneously part of the in-group and everyone knows it, although no one comments on it. It is this position as both an insider and an outsider that gives Irving a special place in the discursive field that cannot be seen without consideration of the larger context. His position in the external context, his Jewish identity, legitimates and strengthens the import of his comments yet paradoxically minimizes their effect.

CONCLUSION

Corporation: After Mr. Sam has provided a fascinating entry point into organizational communication and discourse processes. The interpenetration of local concerns with global identifications and the intertwining of multiple group memberships were just two of the factors influencing discourse processes. The organizational dynamics that were played out during the meetings illustrate the importance of boundary considerations.

The saga of the Steinberg succession has become an object lesson for many types of organizational analysts. Besides the fascinating analyses found in this book, the company and the decisions before, during, and after succession are the focus of several Harvard Business School case studies (Irwin, 1999; Roberts, 1992), several magazine and Web articles (e.g., The UMass Family Business Center; see Horowitz, 2004) and is highlighted in at least two books. For example, the Steinberg's dense familial/business network is profiled in *Controlling Interest: Who Owns Canada* (Francis, 1986).

In virtually all the analyses, the failure to develop a viable succession mechanism is highlighted. The lost opportunities for organizational transformation that were inherent at these meetings were never recovered and the result was disastrous. In fact, the embedded relationships and multiple group memberships, which were so influential in fragmenting and unifying the group's boundaries and discourse, proved to be an insurmountable problem. As recently as September 12, 2003, an article in *The Edmonton Journal* (Anthony, 2003) titled, "Dividing an Estate Can Rip Even a Close Family Apart," used the Steinberg case as a classic example of what happens when there isn't proper planning for succession or serious consideration of group identity and boundary specification:

> A classic case is the Steinberg grocery-store chain based in Montreal, a $4.5-billion empire with 37,000 employees when owner and company patriarch Sam Steinberg died in 1978 without designating a successor.
>
> His three daughters fought bitterly over how the company should be run, for a time speaking only through lawyers, says Gordon Pitts, author of *In The Blood: Battles to Succeed in Canada's Family Businesses.*
>
> "In the end it tore the company apart, and they eventually sold it," says Pitts. "There was no other resolution."
>
> The sale turned out to be a disaster. Steinberg's went bankrupt under its new owner and the stores were sold off among a number of competitors.
>
> "Sam Steinberg couldn't pull the trigger," says Pitts. "He couldn't resolve the estate-planning issues."

In summary, a consideration of the larger context augmented the discourse analyses by letting us see that the inability of the group to discursively manage and negotiate a balance between dependence on and isolation from its social context contributed to the reproduction of past practices and structures. Without acknowledgment and consideration of what the members brought to the table from the larger context, the description and interpretation of the discourse was incomplete. Clearly, however, an analysis of the context without close attention to the discourse as presented throughout this book would be rather meaningless.

Just as cognitive social network structures may have greater explanatory power than behavioral communication network structures (see Monge & Contractor, 2003), I suggest that shared assessments related to boundary identification and multiple group membership often have a more significant effect upon the discursive constraints created during group process and deliberations than the constraints of actual group boundaries. Our study of organizational communication and discourse will be enriched by consideration of both the internal and external dynamics in which the discourse is embedded. As in the speech referenced at the beginning of this chapter, the integration of two cultures produces new perspectives and greater understanding of communication processes.

REFERENCES

Anthony, L. (2003, September 12). The family fight: Planning to avoid it. *The Edmonton Journal*, p. A7.

Bélanger, J. M. (2004). *Biography: Sam Steinberg*. Retrieved September 7, 2005, from www.geocities.com/jeanmarc457plus/Steinberg.html

Francis, D. (1986). *Controlling interest: Who owns Canada?* Toronto, ON: Macmillan of Canada.

Giddens, A. (1979). *Central problems in social theory: Action, structure, and contradiction in social analysis.* Berkeley: University of California Press.

Greenhouse, S. (2004, April 18). Wal-Mart, a nation unto itself. *New York Times*, p. B7.

Horowitz, S. (2004). Sam Steinberg's non-lasting legacy. Retrieved September 7, 2005, from http://www.umass.edu/fambiz/steinberg_non_legacy.htm

Irwin, R. (1999). *New business ventures and the entrepreneur* (5th ed.). Boston: Harvard Business School Press.

Janis, I. (1983). *Groupthink: Psychological studies of policy decisions and fiascoes.* Boston: Houghton Mifflin.

Monge, P., & Contractor, N. (2003). *Theories of communication networks.* Oxford: Oxford University Press.

Poole, M. S., & Hirokawa, R. (1996). Introduction: Communication and group decision making. In R. Hirokawa & M. Poole (Eds.), *Communication and group decision making* (pp. 3–18). Thousand Oaks, CA: Sage.

Putnam, L. L., & Fairhurst, G. T. (2001). Discourse analysis in organization: Issues and concerns. In F. Jablin & L. L. Putnam (Eds.), *The new handbook of organizational communication: Advances in theory, research, and methods* (pp. 235–268). Newbury Park, CA: Sage.

Putnam, L., & Stohl, C. (1990). Bona fide groups: A reconceptualization of groups in context. *Communication Studies, 41,* 248–265.

Putnam, L., & Stohl, C. (1996). Bona fide groups: An alternative perspective for communication and small group decision making. In R. Hirokawa & M. Poole (Eds.), *Communication and group decision making* (pp. 147–178). Thousand Oaks, CA: Sage.

Roberts, M. (1992). *The Sam Steinberg Ltd. Case.* Boston: Harvard Business School.

Sanders, R. E., & Fitch, K. L. (2001). The actual practice of compliance-seeking. *Communication Theory, 11,* 263–289.

Stohl, C., & Putnam, L. L. (2003). Communication in bona fide groups: A retrospective and prospective account. In L. R. Frey (Ed.), *Group communication in context: Studies of bona fide groups* (2nd ed., pp. 399–414). Mahwah, NJ: Lawrence Erlbaum Associates.

Sorge, A. (1983). Cultured organization. *International Studies of Management and Organization, 13,* 106–138.

IV

Can We Study Interactions in Documentaries? Ways of Talking, Closure, and Data

In many respects, this last part offers a nice conclusion to the book by regrouping some metareflections on the possibility of studying interactions in documentaries. As mentioned in the main Introduction, the mere idea of envisaging documentaries as relevant sources of data can appear quite hubristic to many scholars. After all, documentaries suffer from at least three flaws that many would consider fatal to any serious scientific enterprise: (a) They tend to be highly edited, which means that the analysts have access to only a partial version of the reality the documentary is supposed to represent; (b) they normally represent the vision of reality that the director wants to project to the audience, which means that the documentary tends to be biased, whether for political or technical reasons; and (c) the context in which these documentaries have been shot is, most of the time, unknown to viewers, which means that the interpretation will, by definition, be limited to what is shown in the documentary and what can be reconstructed by the analysts.

At the same time, we all know that several insights into the functioning of interaction and communication have been gained over the last 30 or more years, thanks to scholars—especially conversation analysts—who dared study audio and video-recordings without necessarily paying much attention to the context of their production. In this regard, we should certainly give Sacks (1992) credit for being one of the first to believe in the possibility of analyzing the logic of interactions for their own sake. How people fish for information (Pomerantz, 1980), display or mark understanding (Heritage, 1984a; Schegloff, 1991), or perform invitations and rejections (Davidson, 1984) are interactional phenomena that have been identified and studied simply by listening to audiotapes and with very few clues about the context of their production.

This does not mean, of course, that there is nothing to be gained from having access to contextual cues. For instance, the following interaction, quoted by Heritage (1984b, p. 237), is a good illustration:

(Sacks 1968, 17 April)
    A: I have a fourteen-year-old-son
    B: Well that's alright
    A: I also have a dog
    B: Oh I'm sorry

As Heritage notices, had this example been invented, it could have been used to illustrate what an incoherent interaction looks like. However, when we learn that this interaction takes place between the potential tenant of an apartment (A) and a landlord (B), then we understand that A is actually describing her situation to the landlord in order to see if this situation disqualifies her from renting the apartment. In other words, context can sometimes add information that can be quite consequential vis-à-vis our understanding of what the interactants might actually be doing (Cooren, 2005).

However, even without access to this context, we could still understand that A is telling B two pieces of information about her personal situation (having a 14-year-old son and a dog), an action to which B reacts by acknowledging the first piece of personal information as acceptable ("Well that's alright"), while marking the change in his state of knowledge ("Oh") and apologizing for the second ("I'm sorry"). What is missing is indeed why A is telling B this kind of personal information and why B reacts the way he does, which might make this interaction seem incoherent or at least puzzling. What this example illustrates, though, is that it is possible to describe what is happening, even if this description is partial because of a lack of access to interactional circumstances.

Furthermore, were we to have access to a longer sequence in which we would have heard a doorbell ringing before the interactions starts as well as B explaining why he could not accept the dog, we could have easily guessed that this interaction was indeed taking place between a would-be tenant and a landlord. As Heritage (1984b) noticed, context is, in many respects, "something *endogenously* generated within the talk of the participants and, indeed, … something created in and through that talk" (p. 283, italics in original). Anyone who has already participated in data sessions could confirm this point, as he or she could also confirm that certain dimensions of what happens in the interaction always remain mysterious or ambiguous because of a lack of contextual information.

Incidentally, this parallels a point made by Derrida (1988) in his well-known critique of Searle (1977). As he wrote:

> Either the contextual difference changes everything, because it determines what it determines from within: in this case, it can hardly be bracketed even provisionally. Or it leaves certain aspects intact, and this signifies that these aspects can always separate themselves from the allegedly "original" context in order to export or to graft themselves elsewhere while continuing to function in one way or another. (p. 78)

It is, of course, the second option that Derrida favors. As he wrote elsewhere in the same book:

> Every sign, linguistic or non-linguistic, spoken or written (in the current sense of this opposition), in a small or large unit can ... *break with* every given context, *engendering* an infinity of new contexts in a manner which is absolutely illimitable. This does not imply that the mark is valid outside of a context, but on the contrary that there are only contexts without any center or absolute anchoring. (p. 78, italics added)

In other words, it is possible that any text (oral or written) can function outside its context of production, otherwise not only writing but conversation would be impossible. This does not mean that a given context cannot inform the text we are analyzing (as we just saw was the case with the tenant–landlord interaction), but that such analysis can be fruitful, not only because of this engendering effect, remarked upon by Derrida and Heritage, but because no context will ever completely determine a textual interpretation (Cooren, 2000).

This is, in a way, what Gerry Philipsen and James Leighter (chap. 10) demonstrate in their chapter devoted to the interactive function of the verb "tell," used by Sam Steinberg during successive management meetings. As they point out, there is, in principle, a real value in doing a close analysis of the words pronounced by the meeting participants, because these words are used as resources not only to talk about the world but to shape this world. Like many LSI scholars (but perhaps not all), Philipsen and Leighter implicitly claim that it is therefore possible to analyze how interactants use language as a resource without necessarily paying too much attention to contextual information that might be lost forever anyway.

As Philipsen and Leighter (chap. 10) show in their detailed analysis, the way Sam Steinberg recurrently uses the linguistic action verb "tell" in his turns of talk enables him, in many respects, to strengthen the force of his statements while making sure that they are given their proper due in the discussion. In other words, his rhetorical use of "tell" illustrates how he manages to frame and act on the discussion. Addressing parts of the analyses offered in the subsequent chapter by Stanley Deetz, Renee Heath, and Jessica MacDonald (chap. 11), Philipsen and Leighter (chap. 10) also reaffirm the value of these close studies of words by showing how they allow them to really focus on the participants' actions throughout the management meetings.

Even though Deetz, Heath, and MacDonald (chap. 11) appear quite skeptical about the whole project of analyzing the Steinberg management meetings through a documentary, it could arguably be said that their critical analysis confirms, in many respects, insights proposed in some of the previous chapters. First, they problematize most of the analyses appearing in this book by arguing that the "data" presented in the film are far from being neutral and that we should not consider these discussions to be "naturally occurring." As they point out, had they been free to choose the data from which to work, they would not likely have selected the data presented in the documentary and they would have wanted to know much more about the context.

In many ways, the assignment of completing a discourse analysis from this documentary went against most of their theoretical conceptions, because only ethnographically informed studies of discourse can, for them, say anything relevant about organizations. Deetz, Heath, and MacDonald (chap. 11) then reaffirm the social-historical character of any discourse as well as its normative conditions, and conceptualize why all research should be considered a political act. Having presented these limitations and theoretical positions, they finally focus on what they identify as the effects of discursive closure in the Steinberg management meetings, especially on instances where Sam Steinberg appears to stop the discussion each time it could have led the group to seriously engage issues, that is, make decisions. As do other authors in this book, Deetz, Heath, and MacDonald thus point out how these meetings could, for the most part, be considered as activities in not making decisions (see, especially, McPhee, Corman, and Iverson, chap. 7, as well of Sanders, chap. 8).

Finally, D. Lawrence Wieder, Heidi Mau, and Cheryl Nicholas (chap. 12) end this section by arguing that "documentaries are not data," that is, documentaries, as good as they are, will never constitute reliable and faithful sources of data. As they insightfully show in their chapter, even if the viewers can have the impression of watching "naturally occurring interaction-in-meetings," these impressions are actually skillfully and artfully produced by the way the film was assembled out of often discontinuous episodes. Instead of focusing, as do the other authors in this book, on how the meeting got done, Wieder, Mau, and Nicholas thus focus on how the film got done and highlight the different techniques and principles used by the filmmaker—Arthur Hammond—to make his documentary.

Drawing from two interviews with Hammond (see the transcript of these interviews at the end of this section) and the general values and principles of *direct cinema* (a filmmaking movement of which Hammond was an important representative), Wieder, Mau, and Nicholas (chap. 12) unveil all the techniques and practices that led to the making of the *Corporation: After Mr. Sam* documentary, whether in terms of preproduction, production, or postproduction. By showing how the film got done, they highlight the very limits of this book project, while pointing out the conditions under which the documentary can be used, especially for illustrative and pedagogic purposes.

REFERENCES

Cooren, F. (2000). *The organizing property of communication.* Amsterdam/Philadelphia: John Benjamins.

Cooren, F. (2005). *Pour un approche décentrée de l'énonciation: Le fonctionnement de l'énoncé de croyance en situation d'interaction* [For a decentered approach to language use: The functioning of belief utterances in interactional situation]. *Psychologie de l'interaction, 19–20,* 189–222.

Davidson, J. (1984). Subsequent versions of invitations, offers, requests and proposals dealing with potential or actual rejection. In J. M. Atkinson & J. Heritage (Eds.), *Structures of social action: Studies in conversation analysis* (pp. 102–128). Cambridge, England: Cambridge University Press.

Derrida, J. (1988). *Limited inc.* Evanston, IL: Northwestern University Press.

Heritage, J. (1984a). A change of state token and aspects of its sequential placement. In J. M. Atkinson & J. Heritage (Eds.), *Structures of social action: Studies in conversation analysis* (pp. 299–345). Cambridge, England: Cambridge University Press.

Heritage, J. (1984b). *Garfinkel and ethnomethodology.* Cambridge, England: Polity Press.

Pomerantz, A. (1980). Telling my side: 'Limited access' as a 'fishing' device. *Sociological Inquiry, 50,* 186–198.

Sacks, H. (1992). *Lectures on conversation.* Oxford, England: Blackwell.

Schegloff, E. A. (1991). Conversation analysis and socially shared cognition. In L. B. Resnick, J. L. Levine, & S. D. Teasley (Eds.), *Perspectives on socially shared cognition* (pp. 150–171). Washington, DC: American Psychological Association.

Searle, J. R. (1977). Reiterating the differences: A reply to Derrida. *Glyph, 1,* 198–208.

Chapter 10

Sam Steinberg's Use of "Tell" in *Corporation: After Mr. Sam*

Gerry Philipsen
James Leighter
University of Washington

Sam Steinberg (hereafter Sam) is the central figure in *Corporation: After Mr. Sam* (hereafter *AMS*), a documentary film that presents discussions in a top management team pertaining to how to choose a successor to Sam as president of the company, Steinberg Limited. Much of the discussion in *AMS* concerns Sam—his life, his authority in the company, and his role and intentions in choosing a successor.

We examine here how Sam, as not only the central subject of the discussions, but as a central participant in them, participates in those discussions in and through his use of language. Specifically, we examine how he uses one particular linguistic phenomenon, forms of the word "tell," in accomplishing what he accomplishes discursively.

In *AMS*, Sam uses a form of the word "tell" eight times. We examine each of these uses, with an eye (and an ear) to how he uses "tell," what other words accompany it on occasions of its use, how it is inserted into the flow of the discussion, and what it seems to be saying and doing in the course of the discussion. We build on our analysis and interpretation of Sam's uses of "tell" to show that, and how, linguistic action verbs, the class of words and expressions of which "tell" is a member, can be used not only to represent a speaker's thoughts but also to perform, through their use, interactive functions.

Our purpose for examining Sam's use of "tell" in *AMS* derives from a twofold interest. The first is in how participants do things with words in discussions, with particular reference to how people use linguistic action verbs, such as "tell." The second is in contributing to the colloquy about *AMS* that constitutes the present volume.

With regard to the first aspect of our interest, we suggest that when participants in a discussion speak, they use language not only to designate or represent reality but also to shape it (see, e.g., Austin, 1965, and Hymes, 1962). From this perspective, language is a resource not only for talking about the world but also for acting in and on it. Here we explore how a particular linguistic resource, verbs of saying, or linguistic action verbs, can be used to do such acting in and on the world. In doing this, we build on a strong tradition in language studies that provides detailed accounts of the semantics, or meaning, of linguistic action verbs (Verschueren, 1987). We show here how the work of that tradition can be extended to the pragmatics, or rhetoric, of linguistic action verbs, that is, to how they are used to serve particular purposes in social interaction.

Second, we are concerned here with the linguistic action of *AMS* and with the present volume's collection of papers, of which ours is one, about *AMS*. Taken together, the chapters in this volume examine a varied array of communicative phenomena in *AMS* and take diverse approaches to the examination of these materials. In this regard, we show that by focusing on one particular linguistic resource as a rhetorical resource in *AMS*, we provide an empirical point of discussion about what is being done through the linguistic action that comprises the text or conversation that *AMS* displays.

OVERVIEW OF THE CHAPTER

We proceed in three steps. First, we describe linguistic action verbs in general, and describe in particular how we use the linguistic action verb "tell" as an investigative and interpretive resource. Second, we examine the eight situated instances in which Sam uses a form of the word "tell" in *AMS* discussions. Finally, we comment on the contributions that our examination makes to the study of the use of language in social interaction in general and in particular to the present volume's efforts in interpreting the discourse of *AMS*.

"TELL" AS A LINGUISTIC ACTION VERB

A *linguistic action* verb is a word that refers to what a speaker or writer is doing in a particular linguistic action (Verschueren, 1987). As a preliminary move, we say a few words about linguistic action verbs in general and about the linguistic action verb "tell" in particular. Hereafter we refer to "linguistic action verb" as LAV and to its plural form as LAVs. LAVs are members of a larger class, linguistic action verbials, that includes not only single-word LAVs but also such expressions as "to lay claim to" and "to lay down the law." Here we focus exclusively on a single-word LAV, specifically forms of the LAV "to tell."

Linguistic Action Verbs

Our use of LAVs draws from, and adapts to the present purposes, the scenes-and-frames semantics of Fillmore (1977, 1982, 1985), the general treatment of LAVs by Verschueren (1987, 1999), and the specific treatment by Dirven, Goossens, Putseys, and Vorlat (1982), with particular reference to those authors' treatment of the semantics of "tell."

In his scenes-and-frames semantics, Fillmore (1977, 1982, 1985) showed how a particular word perspectivizes, or frames, a scene in a particular way. Fillmore uses the example of the words "shore" and "coast," words that presumably have the same objective referent, the strip of contact between sea and land, but that evoke different perspectives on the scene, with shore evoking water and coast evoking land. That is, "shore" frames the strip of land in such a way as to draw attention to water, and "coast" frames it in such a way as to draw attention to land. Each of these words brings something, or some set of things, into the picture, or more prominently into the picture, than does the other, and each of these words signals the hearer to think more prominently about something, or some set of things, than does the other.

Verschueren (1987) applied the idea of a scenes-and-frames semantics to one particular class of words and expressions, LAVs. He provides a model for examining any particular LAV for the purpose of ascertaining how it perspectivizes distinctively the scene of linguistic action. That is, he proposes that a speaker or writer's use of some particular LAV suggests that the speaker is focusing on some particular linguistic action, or some particular aspect of linguistic action. To say, for example, that someone is speaking, as opposed to complaining, is in each instance to use a LAV, but in each instance to use a particular LAV that frames the speaker's depiction of the scene of linguistic action in some particular way. If a speaker characterizes his or her own or another person's linguistic action as "complaining," he or she frames or perspectivizes the linguistic action differently from how she would have framed it with "speaking."

Through their detailed analysis of a large corpus of English speech, Dirven et al. (1982) examined the English LAVs "speak," "talk," "say," and "tell." They show that each of these words perspectivizes the linguistic action scene in a distinctive way. For example, "speak" and "talk" differ from "say" and "tell" in that the former two are more likely to perspectivize the linguistic action itself, that is, to emphasize speaking or talking in its own right, whereas the latter two are more likely to focus on the topic or substance of the message. Furthermore, within the "speak"/"talk" pair, "speak" differs from "talk" in that the former is more likely to perspectivize linguistic action as a more unidirectional act from a speaker to a receptor ("I am speaking to you"), whereas "talk" is more likely to perspectivize the addressee as a potential interactor ("Can we talk?"). Within the "say"/"tell" pair, "say" differs from "tell" in that the former does not necessarily involve an addressee ("This is what I say"), whereas the latter typically involves an act of a single speaker informing an explicitly designated addressee ("I tell you"). Thus, each of these LAVs refers to linguistic action, but perspectivizes the scene of linguistic action in different and significant ways.

Based on the semantic analysis that Dirven et al. (1982) have done for the four LAVs "speak," "talk," "say," and "tell," we interpret some of Sam's speech in *AMS*. If a purpose of an analysis of organizational speech is to interpret what the participants in an organizational discussion are saying and doing with the words they use with each other, the extant semantic analysis of four LAVs provides a backdrop against which to make such interpretations. Juxtaposing how the speakers in question frame their own and others' linguistic actions to the extant analysis of the meaning potential of the frames those speakers use helps us to interpret what it is a speaker is doing and what his interlocutors might take him to be doing, in a given utterance. Given that we illustrate this idea through a detailed examination of the use in *AMS* of one LAV, "tell," we turn now to an exposition of "tell" as an LAV.

"Tell"

Based on their examination of the 2355 uses of "tell" in their corpus of English speech, Dirven et al. (1982) showed that the principal senses of "tell" are INFORM-tell ("she told the court she had been sleeping badly of late") and NARRATE-tell ("I'm just going to tell you a little story"). More specifically, they report that:

> 97.68% of the examples of the use of the linguistic action verb tell in the corpus represent the INFORM-reading, and within this frame tell occurs in 96.45% of the cases in the structure 'Speaker tells Addressee Message,' which stands out clearly as the prototypical frame par excellence of the linguistic action scene with *tell*. (p. 160)

From this reading, "tell" occurs overwhelmingly in sentences in which a speaker is perspectivized as acting directly on an addressee or addressees ("you") as direct object of the speaker's linguistic action. Furthermore, they conclude that in its predominant sense (INFORM-tell), "tell does not imply interaction; the subject is as a rule a source/transmitter, not a sender/interactor, and the receiver a mere receptor, not a receptor/ interactor" (p. 169).

The first use of "tell" in *AMS*, for example, is in Sam's utterance "Now listen to what I'm telling, each and every one of you" (64–65). In this utterance, Sam characterizes his message ("I'm telling") as addressed directly to a designated hearer ("you"). This utterance, as is typical of a large class of "tell" utterances, involves the intentional action of a single speaking subject, directly drawing in the hearer. By contrast, an utterance by one of the other participants in *AMS*, "Now, I am saying, this is my assumption ..." (284), likewise involves the reflexive characterization of the speaker's own message ("I am saying"), but does not characterize it as addressed directly to a designated hearer (the complement, "to you," is not present in the latter utterance, nor in general is it necessarily present with "saying" to the degree that it is with "telling"). Given the understanding of LAVs suggested by Dirven et al. (1982), we are potentially able to unpack the framing of the scene depicted by these speakers in a way that might otherwise escape us, that in the first utterance, the speaker explicitly characterizes himself as drawing in the listener as the object of his (the speaker's) linguistic action, whereas in the second utterance, the speaker's characterization of his linguistic action is as an action that is, one might say, less directly imposing on the hearer. Thus, Dirven et al.'s treatment of the semantics of these LAVs provides a resource to use in interpreting their strategic and rhetorical uses. That is, it provides a way to make hunches about what speakers are saying when they invoke a particular LAV to describe their own or someone else's action, and a way to interpret what they might be trying to do through their situated use of "tell" in particular instances.

SAM STEINBERG'S USE OF "TELL" IN *AMS*

For each of Sam's eight uses of "tell," we examine (a) the focus of the linguistic action, for example, whether it is genuine speech reporting or reflexive speech reporting; (b) the variant of "tell," whether it is the prototypical use of "tell" or some other use; (c) particular words with which an occurrence of "tell" collocates; (d) where and how Sam inserts "tell" into the flow of discourse, and (e) how, where apparent, other speakers respond to Sam's use of "tell."

Segment 1: Items 1 and 2

The first two uses appear in a segment that we demarcate as five turns at talk, beginning with Sam speaking at (64). Prior to Sam's turn, there is a discussion within the group about whether to talk about organizational structure and goals prior to discussing presidential succession. At (64), with "this is exactly how I feel," Sam apparently expresses agreement with the suggestion to discuss organizational goals and structure before discussing what to look for in a new president. Then, with the utterance that begins "Now listen," at (64), Sam introduces a very concrete topic into what had been a more abstract discussion.

64	SAM S:	This is exactly how I feel (0.5). Now listen to what I'm telling,
65		each and every one of you. (0.5) Evidently over the past four o'
66		five weeks, (0.5) a hundred or two hundred items (0.5) have to
67		be increased in price
68	JACK L:	<Seventy-two items> =
69	SAM S:	= Alright, well, I'm telling you what I heard. [so- .
70	JACK L:	[(accumulated) on
71		four weeks, seventy-two items =
72	SAM S:	= Okay. Let's (0.2) let's say it's seventy-two items.

For the first instance of a "tell" form in Segment 1 (64–65), Sam says "Now listen to what I'm telling, each and every one of you." This is a reflexive use of "telling," that is, Sam uses the word to describe his own present conduct. It is the prototypical use of a "tell" form in that it takes the form Speaker Tells Addressee Message, with Sam directly drawing the listeners in as the objects of his linguistic action. Such words as "what," "I," and "you" appear with "telling," as would be anticipated in the prototypical form, according to Dirven et al. (1982). We also note the occurrence of "listen," apparently spoken here as part of a verbal command that prefaces the act of telling. Sam inserts this "telling" into the flow of discourse in his first turn at talk in this segment just after the prefatory "now listen," and prior to a concrete statement of fact, the apparent "what" that is being told.

For the second instance of a "tell" form in Segment 1, at (69), Sam says "=Alright, well, I'm telling you what I heard." This is a reflexive use of "telling"; a prototypical use of a "tell" form; and it appears with "I," "you," and "heard." We also note the occurrence of "=Alright, well," spoken here as a preface to the "tell" utterance. This utterance appears immediately after a preceding utterance by another speaker in which the other speaker corrects Sam's statement of fact at (65–67), and is followed (70–71) by the other speaker's further correction of Sam's earlier statement of fact.

To complete the description of the occurrences of "tell" forms in Segment 1, we also note a place in Segment 1 where, in Sam's third and final turn, we might expect "tell" to appear again (72), but it does not appear there. There, Sam says, "let's say it's seventy-two items." Here Sam brings up again the items that he previously characterized himself as "telling" about to each and every one of the people in earshot. But here, in talking about these items, Sam uses the LAV "say" as a hypothetical linguistic act, "let's say," jointly performed by himself and another (or others). Some words that appear in this utterance are "okay," "let's," and "it's." Here Sam replaces the content of his earlier message, that is, changes in the prices of 100 or 200 items in the past 4 or 5 weeks becomes, now, 72 items, the latter number agreeing with the number stated twice previously, by Jack. Sam also changes the LAV he uses to describe an action in which he agrees to participate, that is, to "say" that the number of items is 72. Thus, in his third turn in Segment 1, Sam acquiesces to Jack's correction as to the facts that Sam has previously alleged.

Sam changes his language use across his three turns in Segment 1. The changes occur in whether and how he prefaces the turn, how he characterizes the ostensible content of the turn, his invocation (or not) of an addressee, his use of a LAV, and words with which he accompanies the LAV. In the first turn, Sam begins with the command, "Now listen" (64); refers to an indefinite time period and an indefinite number of items; draws in the addressees, "each and every one of you" (65) directly; frames the scene of linguistic action as "I'm telling" (64); and uses such words as "listen," "what," "I," and "you." Jack responds to Sam's first turn by correcting Sam's statement of the number of items. Then, Sam prefaces his second turn with "=Alright, well" (69); reduces the statement of content to "what I heard" (69); changes the addressee from the collective "each and every one of you" to "you"; repeats the LAV expression "I'm telling" (69); and uses such words as "what," "I," "heard," "telling," and "you." Jack then repeats and expands his earlier correction of Sam's statement of the facts—Jack corrects Sam's original statement of number of items and time period, substituting for Sam's imprecise and apparently inaccurate statement a precise and apparently accurate one. Then, in Sam's third turn, he uses the prefatory expression "Okay" plus the invitational "let's" plus LAV; shifts his statement of content to agree with that supplied by Jack, to "seventy-two items" (72); shifts from a form of "tell" to "say," as in "let's say it's seventy-two items" (72); and uses such words as "okay," "let's," and "it's."

Although Sam uses "telling" in each of his first two turns, his second use can be heard as a weaker statement, although not at as weak as his third statement. In the second turn, in contrast to the first, Sam mitigates his second "I'm telling you" (69) with the preface "alright, well" (69). He qualifies his assertion of fact by saying it is "what I heard" (69), thus separating the statement of fact from Sam's own judgment about things, and which we hear as even less confident than the earlier hedge "evidently." He reduces the breadth of the address by diminishing the explicitly plural audience to "you."

By the third turn, Sam's linguistic action is that of acquiescence. He expresses agreement with Jack's proposed specification of number, does not reassert or defend any earlier stance, and changes the LAV with which he proposes that the content be talked about, from "tell" to "say."

Having described some features of Sam's use of "tell" in segment one, we can ask what this says about the meanings and uses of "tell" in Sam's speech in this segment. First, that in his first two turns he uses a form of "tell" at all suggests that he is doing something more than merely telling someone something. For each of these instances, Sam could have merely told his interlocutors what he wanted to say, but by stating that he is telling, he uses the rhetorical device of redundancy, saying more than is necessary for a mere telling. Sam not only tells his addressees what he wants them to hear, but also tells them that he is telling them.

Second, the way Sam uses LAVs, particularly "tell," in this segment, suggests something about its interactional meaning in AMS speech. When Sam frames his actions in terms of command and direct address to plural addressees, he uses a form of "tell" to characterize his own linguistic action. When he frames his linguistic action with prefatory hesitation, distances himself from the facts that he reports, and narrows the scope of addressees, he continues to use "tell" to characterize his linguistic action. But when he actually concedes a substantive point, he shifts from the LAV "tell" to the LAV "say." In this regard, we hear the use of "tell" in this segment as framing the scene of linguistic action as an interpersonally strong or powerful act, and Sam's reflexive use of "tell" as a way of characterizing his own actions as strong and powerful.

Segment 2: Item 3

Sam's third use of "tell" appears after an extended discussion of whether to discuss goals now or to postpone such discussion until after a new president is named. Immediately preceding the following segment that we have demarcated, Harry, who is serving in these meetings as a process facilitator, told a joke about someone expressing that, after a long discussion, although they were still confused, they are confused "at a much higher level" (457–458). Our gloss of Harry's moves prior to what follows, and in what follows, is that he is trying to lighten the tone, while moving the group to a new topic. After telling the joke, Harry turns to Sam, and the following ensues.

```
460  HARRY S:  Are you confused Mr. Presi[dent at a much
461  SAM S:                              [No,
462  HARRY S:  (0.5) Good =
463  SAM S:    = No sir
464  HARRY S:  Alright
465  SAM S:    Let me tell you I'm very pleased (0.8) the way we're
466            progressing with this.
467  HARRY S:  Alright. Guy
```

The use of "tell" (465) is reflexive, that is, Sam uses it to characterize what he is doing in the present action, and "tell" here is the prototypical use, that is, Speaker Tells Addressee Message. We note that (460) Harry asks Sam whether he, Sam, is confused. Sam's "no" (461) overlaps Harry's question that implies the possibility of Sam's confusion. On (462), Harry's "good" is followed without an audible gap in speech by Sam's second statement of "no," with the expression "No sir" (463). When Harry follows (464) with the words "All right," Sam, again, makes a statement in which he evaluates what has proceeded in the segment. We hear Sam's statement (465, 466) as possibly serving to provide, by Sam, a substitute formulation for Harry's implicit suggestion that he, Sam, might have been confused by the earlier discussion. Here, at (465–466), Sam reformulates what his mental state should be taken to be. That Sam is responding rhetorically, rather than merely with information, can be attested to by the fact that he not only says that he is pleased, but adds the otherwise redundant preface, "Let me tell you" (465), to his statement that he is very pleased. With his statement that he is pleased, framed as it is by a "let me tell you" preface, Sam effectively takes himself out of the role of someone answering to Harry's characterization of his, Sam's, state of mind, and casts himself as someone who is telling Harry about his own state of mind. Thus, with the statement "let me tell you I'm very pleased" (465), Sam uses a strong LAV, "tell," to frame his answer, that answer being the assertion by Sam of a characterization of his mental state that is different from Harry's previous characterization of it.

Segment 3: Item 4

Sam's fourth use of a "tell" form in *AMS* is (796). This use of a "tell" form appears as a move in a topical discussion that was initiated earlier when, at (766), Arnold, who is Sam's nephew, and thus a member of the family, introduced what he referred to as a topic to which he is "particularly sensitive" (768), the role of the family in the Steinberg Limited Organization. From (766–790), Arnold makes a statement in which he very delicately professes to speak for himself and for other members of the family in saying that they believe nepotism in the appointment of family members is not ultimately satisfying to those members of the family who are appointed to positions of leadership on such grounds.

Following Arnold's long and nuanced speech against nepotism, Sam takes the floor, so to speak. At (792–794), Sam speaks haltingly, with noncontent expressions ("hh," "now," "uh"), repetition of "uh" after a pause of 0.8 seconds, and a restart of "this moment" (793). This is followed by several people acknowledging that they had read the report to which Sam refers (795), and then Sam takes the floor again for a relatively triumphal statement, "Alright! So it tells you that ..." (796).

792	SAM S:	.hh now uh (0.8) uh the only comment I would like to make at
793		this mom- this moment was that I read a Harvard report (0.5)
794		where it deals with families in organizations=
795	( ):	=We all read it. ((People interrupting and agreeing.))
796	SAM S:	Alright! So it tells you that after a period of twenty years there
797		is more family than ever before=and that hasn't affected the the
798		performances as I read it in these companies.

The use of "tells" (796) is an instance of what Dirven et al. (1982) described as MAKE KNOWN-tell. Here Sam refers to a "Harvard" report about the role of family owners in organizations. The Harvard report is the "it" to which Sam refers in (796) as telling about the effects of family owners' involvement in the management of organizations that they own. Sam is here describing what the Harvard report "tells," or MAKES KNOWN, about the effects of family member serving in management roles in their businesses. "Tells" appears in the utterance here with the exclamatory "Alright!," "So," "it," and "you."

We hear Sam's use of "tells" (796) as part of a complex argument that appears within a discussion of an important issue, whether family owners' involvement in the management of a business is a good or a bad thing. Although we classify "tells" here as MAKE KNOWN-tell, we also point out that Sam situates this "tells" within a highly rhetorical utterance. There is the prefatory and exclamatory "Alright!," which, followed by "So," suggests that Sam thinks here that he has in the report evidence that supports a claim, and that claim, as Sam then makes it, is more friendly to owner participation in management than Arnold's earlier disclaimer. And Sam draws in the listeners directly with "you," that is, he addresses the findings of the report to his immediate interlocutors. In this complex rhetorical construction, "tells" fits quite happily. We interpret Sam's use of "tells" here as a framing of how the listeners should interpret the report, as telling, that is making a strong claim, and not just as saying, that is making a more speculative claim.

Segment 4: Item 5

Sam's fifth use of "tell" is embedded in a statement that he makes in relation to a discussion of criteria to be used in the selection of the new chief officers of the company.

1079	SAM S:	°I want yous to listen me out for a minute.° (0.8) Right now,
1080		one of the (0.2) largest organizations in our field (0.5) have

1081	recently as you all know appointed a President (2.0) and from
1082	m<u>y</u> point of view (1.0) it's a sorry spectacle (1.0) in an
1083	organization so <u>vast</u> (2.0) with the years of experience and the
1084	(1.0) you know how (0.5) how <u>large</u> an organization that is (0.5)
1085	doing the business in the billions and the this is what they have
1086	to end up with (1.0). So uh (1.0) just tryin' to tell you that uh
1087	we got to give serious consideration (1.0) and u:hh just uh I'm
1088	just <u>exasperated</u> to to to think (1.0) how I:I would have felt if I
1089	was a: substantial shareholder in that organization (0.5) as to
1090	what they (1.5) had to resort to in terms of a President.

"Tell" in the utterance "just tryin' to tell you that ..." (1086) takes the prototypical form Speaker Tells Addressee Message. We note its appearance in a longer speech that has already been prefaced with "I want yous to listen me out for a minute" (1079). Then there is a series of statements that is interlaced with long pauses. Beginning at (1079), with an 0.8 second pause, there is approximately one pause every five words, with these pauses averaging over 1 second in duration. "Tell" appears at (1086), in the following utterance: "So uh (1.0) just tryin' to tell you that uh" (1086). Words and expressions accompanying "tell" in this utterance are "just tryin'," "to tell," and "you." The speech preceding the "tell" utterance appears to us to be disorganized and incoherent. It contains several pauses, more, we think, than is typical of Sam's speech, certainly more than appear in the segments of Sam's *AMS* speech that we have used in our present examination. There is an apparent incompletion following "the" at the end of (1083). At (1084), there is a repetition of "how" after a pause of 0.5 seconds. The expression "the this" (1085) is awkward. And the "So uh (1.0)", with its hesitation and filler and its pause of 1.0 seconds (1086), suggests uncertainty on the part of the speaker. Then, there is the way the "tell" utterance itself is formulated: Sam implies the incoherence of what precedes the "tell" statement with the preface "just tryin'" in "just tryin' to tell you" (1086). One further aspect of the insertion of the "tell" statement into the stream of Sam's speech in Segment 3 is that the expression "to tell you that" (1086) is then followed by 45 words and noncontent expressions. That is, "tell" here is used not only to refer back to what Sam has already said but also, apparently, to introduce what he then goes on to say.

Given our descriptive exposition of the "tell" statement in this segment, we hear "tell" in the statement, on (1086), as a rhetorical resource that Sam uses to accomplish purposes within the long segment in which he holds the floor. First, at (1086) Sam endeavors to retrospectively frame his preceding remarks. We have shown how it is plausible that Sam and others consider those remarks in need of some bolstering as remarks to be taken seriously. With his retrospective characterization of his remarks as "tryin' to tell" (1086), Sam himself treats his remarks as an unsuccessful realization (trying but not succeeding) of his ambitious aim to produce a strong speech act, that is, to "tell" his interlocutors something. The invocation here of "tell" appears to provide a rhetorical contrast between what has gone before and what Sam had intended to accomplish in that preceding speech.

Second, at (1086) Sam endeavors to frame the scene of his present and forthcoming linguistic action in such a way as to assure that he keeps the speaking floor. In this regard, we point out that "tell" is a LAV that minimizes the possibility that addressees will themselves speak and thus Sam's use of it serves an apparent interactional purpose.

Segment 5: Item 6

Sam's sixth use of "tell" appears immediately after a long discussion of the considerations to use in selecting a new president. Jack effectively shuts down the substantive aspect of this discussion.

```
1475 JACK L:    I don't think we can go much further (0.5) And personnel
1476            selection is a one alone (.) u:h responsibility (0.2) so this
1477            becomes (0.5) with all the information=
1478 SAM S:     =I can tell you, you've made it very easy for me.
1479 JACK L:    We made it very clear to you what kind of person we want.
```

This is a reflexive, prototypical use of "tell" that follows the structure Speaker Tells Addressee Message. It appears here with such other words as "I," "can," and "you." We note that it appears, by its precise insertion into the stream of speech, to preclude an expression of thought by Jack that apparently does not get completed (1477). Although we do not know what Jack would have said had he continued beyond the expression "all the information" (1477), it appears from the grammatical structure of Jack's utterances, the one ending at (1477) and the one beginning at (1479), that the "we made it clear to you" statement is a new point, at least a newly formulated one, and not a continuation of the previous statement.

What line of thought does Sam's "tell" apparently preclude? In (1475, 1476), Jack expresses the opinion that the group cannot "go much further," presumably with the discussion of considerations pertaining to a new president, and expresses the premise that personnel selection is the responsibility of one person alone. Then, Jack apparently prefaces a further statement with his words "so this becomes (0.5) with all the information=" (1477). We suggest the possibility that what Sam precludes, with his immediately following "tell" statement, is Jack's possible elaboration of what the discussion reveals about the wishes of the group and their implications for the substance of the decision-making process that is to ensue. Here "tell," in "I can tell you, you've made it very easy for me" (1478) seems to frame Sam's act as precluding further elaboration, given that "tell" does not necessary or easily invite further talk from the hearer of a "tell" message, and given that "you've made it very easy for me" suggests a certain transparency or simplicity to the views the group members have expressed, thus making unnecessary an elaboration by Jack of the consequences of those views.

Segment 6: Items 7 and 8

Sam's uses 7 and 8 of a "tell" form appear in what we have demarcated as a complex storytelling segment in which Sam is the master narrator. First Sam tells a story in which someone else's telling of a story is embedded; then he does this a second time. At the level of discourse structure, these two tellings appear to be topically and rhetorically related.

```
1205 SAM S:   Some ten years ago (1.2) met a chap who was in my class in
1206          public school (0.8) and he said to me:e? (1.0) that at one t:ime
1207          the kids got together (1.8) and the person that they singled out
1208          who was least likely to succeed was me.
1209          (1.0)
1210 SAM S:   This is what he told me
1211          ((Contained laughter.))
1212 SAM S:   It's a fact.(0.5) The other was I was telling some of the boys uh
1213          (1.0) oh some about uh (0.5) thirty years ago there was a
1214          Liberty magazine (1.0) and they had an article (0.5) the new
1215          sciences that were being introduced in terms of selecting (1.0)
1216          uh people for employment in the organization. And they had a
1217          point system (.) and they'd rate them on the years of education,
1218          years of experience and the various qualifications added up and
1219          he'd had to have a certain point rating in order to get a job.
1220          (1.0) So finally after uh three or four pages of this it comes to
1221          the end of the uh story, the editor was asked or the person was
1222          asked "Well, what about the fellow who doesn't qualify at a:ll?"
1223          He said "Well you don't have to worry about him, he'll end up
1224          being the boss." (0.5) So, evidently this happens to be the story
1225          of my life?
1226          (2.8)
1227 (    ):  Uh ... Harry [xxx
1228 SAM S:            [The point I'm trying to make is that it doesn't
1229          always follow (0.5) that (.) person must have all these
1230          qualification to uh to be able to perform.
```

At (1210), Sam's use of "told" reports someone else's linguistic act. It is a prototypical use in that the act reported has the structure Speaker Tells Addressee Message. In this case, Sam is the addressee of the "told" message, which is the only time in all of *AMS* that Sam is the addressee of a "tell" form. In his use here of "told," Sam refers to the telling of an anecdote. We classify Sam's "this is what he told me" (1210) as an instance of INFORM-tell rather than NARRATE-tell because of the statement Sam makes, "it's a fact," (1212) immediately after his "tell" statement. NARRATE-tell statements typically imply an imaginative telling. Sam's "it's a fact" apparently acknowledges a fictive sense (as in NARRATE-tell) as a possible auditor hearing and at the same time apparently asserts that it should be heard as INFORM-tell.

How is "told" (1210) inserted into the flow of speech? Sam begins (1205) by invoking a concrete time frame, "some ten years ago"; at (1205) he introduces a narrator within the narrated event, a "chap" who was in his class in public school; at (1206–1208), he reports what this man "said" to him, that the kids judged Sam least likely to succeed; there is then a 1.0 second pause, followed by Sam's statement (1210), "this is what he told me"; at (1211), there is "contained laughter"; and at (1212), Sam says "it's a fact."

Lines (1205–1212) take the form of the telling of an anecdote (here we follow Bauman's, 1986, explication of the nature of an anecdote). Typically, published reports of the telling of an anecdote end with a punch line. There is a punch line in the lines of the segment being considered here, Sam's statement, "and the person that they singled out who was least likely to succeed was me" (1207–1208). Thus "told" is inserted following a 1.0 second gap that appears after the apparent punch line. For this anecdote, unlike some, there is a record of what happens after the punch line is delivered, that is, there is a 1.0 second gap and then there is what the transcriber records as contained laughter (1211), without identification of the source of the laughter. Immediately following the contained laughter, Sam says, "It's a fact" (1212); 0.5 seconds later he begins to tell another story.

Given the immediately preceding description of how "told" is inserted into the sequencing of this segment, we suggest that Sam's "told" statement is not strictly necessary for the purpose of informing the listeners as to the representational content of his utterance. A complete anecdote has been told, the requirements of the form being fulfilled with the punch line (1212). Bauman (1986) suggested that the use of "told" in an anecdote frames a slightly more emphatic utterance than "said" (p. 66). The "told" statement here appears 1.0 seconds after "the person they singled out ... was me" utterance (1207-1208), which utterance was followed by Sam's "It's a fact" (1212). What follows the apparent punch line, then, suggests that Sam is using "told" here to emphasize what he was trying to do with "the person that they singled out who was least likely to succeed was me" (1208). When there is a 1.0 second gap after that utterance, perhaps implying the absence of the uptake of that utterance as a punch line, an uptake that Sam might have felt he had a right to anticipate, Sam follows with his "told" statement, which is followed by contained laughter, which is followed by Sam's "It's a fact." We think there is a case here for hearing Sam's use of "told" (1210) as rhetorical emphasis of his not quite successful punch line (1212).

The second use of a form of "tell" in this episode is at (1212), where Sam says "the other I was telling some of the boys uh." In this case, "telling" frames a much longer anecdote than that about the "kids" and here, unlike in the preceding anecdote, the "tell" framing comes at the beginning rather than at the end of the anecdote. And in this case the anecdote is much longer.

"Telling" in "The other was I was telling some of the boys" (1212) reports the speaker's own linguistic act. It is a prototypical use in that it has the structure Speaker Tells Addressee Message. It is an instance of INFORM-tell. Where "told" in the preceding anecdote retrospectively re-frames the message to which it refers, in the second use of a "tell" form in this segment, the speaker uses it to frame in advance what he is about to say, which, as in the preceding segment, is a telling of an anecdote.

DISCUSSION

In each of the instances in which Sam uses "tell" in *AMS*, he seems to add something to the bare facts that he reports in his utterance. Evidence of this is that in each of Sam's "tell" utterances, it would have been possible, semantically and, with some adjustment, grammatically, to use a construction with "say" as the LAV rather than "tell." In each instance, however, there seems to be some value added the linguistic act by Sam's use of "tell" rather than "say" or some other LAV.

Our claim is that that the value added by "tell" where "say" could have been used is that "tell" frames the linguistic action being described as more weighty or as stronger than "say" would do. Briefly we illustrate this through a return to some aspect of the use of "tell" in each of the six episodes we already displayed and examined.

Segment 1 provides a negative illustration of our thesis. In Segment 1, Sam twice characterizes his linguistic action with "tell," but then in a third characterization of a particular linguistic action of his he shifts from "tell" to "say." He shifts to "say" when he makes a concession to Jack about the number and duration of price increases. He frames statements that in many other regards are strong or assertive with "tell," and then frames with "say" his act of concession. Thus when he shifts from strong to weak presentations, he shifts LAVs.

In Segment 2, Sam asserts that his mental state is different from that which Harry had attributed to him, an assertion we take to be a strong interpersonal action. Sam uses "tell" as the characterization of what he is doing in making that strong interpersonal action, and this "telling" occurs as the third and final of Sam's responses to Harry's initial characterization of Sam, with each of Sam's three utterances successively making stronger responses to Harry, culminating in the final "tell" response. Thus as Sam's self-assertion becomes stronger, he eventually produces an utterance that he frames with the reflexive "tell."

In Segment 3, when Sam challenges the view of Arnold, the previous speaker, he supports his challenge by invoking the evidence of a report, framing that report in terms of what it "tells." Thus Sam bolsters the rhetorical force of the document's contents through framing it as "telling" something to those listening to his report of the report.

In Segment 4, when Sam retrospectively characterizes his immediately preceding remarks, remarks that by our reading and hearing are halting, disorganized, and inchoate, Sam frames them retrospectively as something he is "tryin'" to "tell" his interlocutors, thus bolstering retrospectively the strength of his preceding action by framing it as telling.

In Segment 5, when Sam interrupts Jack's imminent elaboration of what the group is saying to Sam, Sam frames his action as telling Jack (and others) something, an action that precludes Jack from speaking further about the implications for Sam of what the group has just said to him. Thus, when Sam interrupts the speech of another speaker, he frames his interrupting statement as telling.

Finally, in Segment 6, Sam retrospectively frames an anecdote in terms of how he wishes his interlocutor to have taken it, using "told" to frame it as a statement of something that really happened as opposed to a fictive story.

Thus, in each of these instances of the use of a form of "tell," Sam does some work that is not necessary referentially but that serves a rhetorical function. And in each of these instances, "tell" is used to strengthen the force of a statement, give a statement greater weight, or add coherence to a statement. These efforts to bolster the statements as framed function rhetorically, that is, to assure that a statement is heard as one thing or another or to assure that a statement is given its proper due.

The rhetorical uses to which Sam puts "tell" forms can certainly be linked to the standardized meanings of "tell" as these have been ascertained by the semantic analysis of "tell" by Dirven et al. (1982). Such corpus-based linguists point to the usage of "tell" in English speech as a LAV that frames utterances that (a) inform the hearer and that (b) are less likely than utterances framed otherwise to perspectivize the communicative situation as one in which the hearers are invited or expected to respond with words of their own. That is, semantically "tell" utterances are used to describe what is sometimes referred to as "one-way communication." Thus, Sam's rhetorical use of "tell" utterances, as indicated, exploits their standardized usage and semantic meaning for the rhetorical purposes to which he apparently puts them. We have shown here how the semantic meanings of "tell" can be exploited not only for semantic but for rhetorical purposes.

Our first goal in this chapter was to show how the analysis and interpretation of Sam's use of "tell" in *AMS* could reveal how LAVs are used, not only to talk about the world but also to act in and on the world. Our further goal was to use the aforementioned analysis and interpretation to contribute to the present discussion of the discourse of *AMS*. Now we turn to this further goal. For this purpose we turn to the chapter in this volume that is juxtaposed to ours as a sort of companion piece, and which is the only other chapter to which we have had access in writing our chapter, the chapter by Deetz, Heath, and MacDonald (chap. 11). These authors provide what they describe as a "critical" analysis of organizational talk in *AMS*. Much of their critique focuses on the speech of Sam Steinberg. Although their treatment is much broader than ours is, there are at least some points where we can enter into a discussion with them.

One of those points concerns a claim that Deetz, Heath, and MacDonald (chap. 11) make about *AMS* and make in a very general way. At several points in their critique of *AMS*, they propose that there is a great deal in *AMS* that counts as "discursive closure," "conversation stoppage," and "blocked" or "distorted conversation." Much of this critique centers on the words and person of Sam, although the authors are careful not to make this merely a critique of one individual but of a systemic set of practices. Nonetheless, at several points these authors accuse Sam of stopping discussions (see also McPhee, Corman, & Iverson, chap. 7, and what they call "killer statements"). They do not make these charges in relation to any of the particulars we have engaged here, and thus we cannot challenge empirically their claims with our present materials, nor would we necessarily want to do so. However, we find it useful to juxtapose their analysis to one of our six segments, Segment 1, which contains a stretch of discourse in which we would claim that one participant's knowledge claims, Jack's, prevail over the assertions by Sam. In Segment 1, Sam begins by "telling" the others something, Jack twice vocally corrects Sam's statement of fact, and eventually Sam concedes the point of fact. Our interpretation of this segment, which we attended to because of the appearance in it of two uses of a "tell" form, is that Jack effectively challenges Sam's factual assertion, such that eventually Sam abandons his linguistic action of telling and then proposes that he join with other voices in saying precisely what Jack had asserted contra to Sam's earlier pronouncements. Now this is perhaps a small matter, but it is often in such small matters that discourse gets stopped or opened up, and in this instance it is Sam who is stopped and who is apparently persuaded to back down, at least from his factual claim. It may be noted that Jack, who forced this backing down by Sam, was eventually appointed as a member of the new top management team, so his open challenging of Sam here (and he challenges him quite vociferously elsewhere in *AMS*) did not result in his being denied further appointment as a senior executive in Steinberg Limited.

We would mention one other point where our detailed examination of *AMS* speech provides a useful point of consideration in conversing with Deetz, Heath, and MacDonald (chap. 11). In their discussion of "Succession and Family," they examine the segment of *AMS* discourse that we demarcate and examine as Segment 3. Their treatment of this segment is much broader than ours and so the juxtaposition might be not quite apt, but it might nonetheless reveal something useful, if only as a move in an open discussion. They write about the segment that begins with (796) and concludes with (804), that Sam "tries to direct the discussion away from these concerns [whether the new president must be a member of the family, etc.] by changing the definition of family ..." (p. 239). Although we do not challenge that Sam did what these authors say he did here, our examination of (799–901) provides a different observation and interpretation, specifically, that Sam presents a data-based claim about the relationship between family members in management and company performance. This, we noted, is what the "Harvard report" (793) "tells you" (796), according to Sam. Here we see another side of Sam—Sam the debater, Sam the rhetor, pleading his case and supporting it with an appeal to evidence that he frames in a particularly rhetorical way (with his use of a MAKE KNOWN-tell to frame his characterization of the report). That he does other things in the larger segment cannot be denied, but neither should it be ignored that there is something that Sam does in this segment that Deetz, Heath, and MacDonald apparently do not report. We have shown that there is more there than they say. Whether there is also less there than they say is something that our analysis in its present form does not speak to.

We have juxtaposed our interpretations to those of another set of authors not to enter into a debate with those other authors. Rather our purpose has been to show the value of doing close analysis of the words of organizational interlocutors, as best we can apprehend them as they have been captured, albeit imperfectly, electronically and then transcribed onto the written page. Such a close analysis may, as we think has happened in the present instance, show that global characterizations of what is or is not in an organizational text might not always or easily be sustained when we examine that text for its particulars. Our small study of Sam's use of "tell" in *AMS* does not take us very far in the examination of such particulars, but we think we have shown that such work can potentially provide a useful way to enter into a discussion of broad assertions and to open up the discussion of what we think is going on in a particular instance of organizational discourse.

ACKNOWLEDGMENT

The authors acknowledge with gratitude the stylistic and substantive suggestions of Dr. Lisa Coutu of the University of Washington.

REFERENCES

Austin, J. L. (1965). *How to do things with words*. New York: Oxford University Press.

Bauman, R. (1986). *Story, performance, and event: Contextual studies of oral narrative*. New York: Cambridge University Press.

Dirven, R., Goossens, L., Putseys, Y., & Vorlat, E. (1982). *The scene of linguistic action and its perspectivization by speak, talk, say and tell*. Philadelphia: John Benjamins.

Fillmore, C. (1977). Scenes-and-frames semantics. In A. Zampolli (Ed.), *Linguistics structures processing* (pp. 55–81). New York: North Holland.

Fillmore, C. (1982). Frame semantics. In The Linguistic Society of Korea (Ed.), *Linguistics in the morning calm* (pp. 111–137). Seoul: Hanshin.

Fillmore, C. (1985). Frames and the semantics of understanding. *Quaderni di Semantica, 6*(2), 222–254.

Hymes, D. (1962). The ethnography of speaking. In T. Gladwin & W. C. Sturtevant (Eds.), *Anthropology and human behavior* (pp. 13–53). Washington, DC: Anthropological Society of Washington.

Verschueren, J. (1987). Metapragmatics and universals of linguistics. In J. Verschueren (Ed.), *Linguistic action: Some empirical-conceptual studies* (pp. 124–147). Norwood, NJ: Ablex.

Verschueren, J. (1999). *Understanding pragmatics*. New York: Arnold.

Chapter 11

On Talking to Not Make Decisions: A Critical Analysis of Organizational Talk

Stanley Deetz
Renee Heath
Jessica MacDonald
University of Colorado, Boulder

The study of discourse as it occurs in organizational settings has become a central feature of the study of organizations. The interest is of little surprise. As Mumby and Clair (1997) demonstrate, "organizations only exist in so far as their members create them through discourse. This is not to claim that organizations are 'nothing but' discourse, but rather that discourse is the principle means by which organizational members create a coherent social reality that frames their sense of who they are" (p. 181). This volume at best only displays a small portion of the rapidly growing body of literature on organizational discourse with a multitude of different methods and objectives (see. e.g., Grant, Hardy, Oswick, & Putnam, 2004). We approach this task from the general orientation of critical scholarship in organization studies focusing on talk, and the Mr. Sam text specifically, with regard to the normative communication practice and the political nature of texts in organizational life (see Alvesson & Deetz, 2000; Broadfoot, Deetz, & Anderson, 2004; Mumby, 2004).

To get there we must accomplish a lot of up front work. We begin by posing questions on the task of this volume itself, arguing that the scope and nature of the data as well as the implied neutrality of the text already predisposed analysis in a noncritical way. Second, we sketch a critical orientation to the analysis of discourse in organizations focusing specifically on processes of discursive closure and use normative communication concepts to show how certain discursive practices stop decision making. And, finally, we illustrate parts of this analytic approach using the Mr. Sam text.

Our attention will be to theory and context as much as to the provided text. Given the complex and theory-laden discussion proceeding the analysis, the reader may well feel by the analysis's end that we were merely playing tiddlywinks with manhole covers, (or as Horace would claim, "The mountains were in labor and the mouse was born"). In doing so we might be accused of both delaying the analytic game of others and not making the best use of the elaborate scheme being brought to bear. We hope to be instructive in the process even if the outcome is only illustrative. Our process begins with the problems of the textual artifact.

THE MR. SAM TEXT

No piece of discourse is simply "naturally occurring," neutral, lying out there waiting to be found. All discourse is a social production/construction. It occurs in relation to a mass of other discourses, institutions, power relations, and so forth. Texts have contexts, producers, and receivers. Vocabularies, strategies, and talk styles have specific social distributions. Not only do discourses themselves have a socially contrived place, but they are recorded, chosen, and separated from their context by analysts and reconnected to other discourses, institutions, and political arrangements (see Watson, 1997).

Some authors in this volume worked from a different understanding. The Mr. Sam text is treated as a neutral object, contained, simply there, an object waiting to be looked upon, prodded, and dissected by individuals with different interests and orientations. Such an assumption has considerable theoretical and political import. It certainly suits some authors in this volume much more than others. We are asked to accept a metatheory that contradicts much of our theory. If we were to do a critical analysis of discourse in Mr. Sam's organization, we would not likely have selected this text and we would have asked much more about the context. Even if we stick to the level of language texts in this organization, we would have asked many questions about how much and which texts to be selected and what other texts that these need to be seen in relation to. But even more than that, we would need to ask about the economic situation, and look at specific understanding and practices common in the 1970s; we would need to ask about succession practices of Jewish families in Canada and how other decisions had been discussed and made. We are left in a situation like the archeologist finding a mere fragment of a clay tablet and from that, trying to detail specific social and political arrangements at a historically different time and place. Our danger is less that we will theoretically overwhelm it than that we will merely substitute our understandings at this time and place to fill out the structure, organization, and/or meaning of this text—that it will be understood as if it were our text rather than another's.

But the complications do not end there. From what we do know of context, this fragment was from a unique, planned meeting for special purposes by special people, not from the ordinary talk of members of the organization as they engaged in work and made decisions. And, as they talked they knew that the talk was being recorded, to be heard by a larger interested public of citizens as well as academics. They mugged for the camera, often explicitly. This is not just talk of family members, organizational members; it is talk of organizational and family members knowing that other family and organizational members were listening, overhearing. We cannot know which text to follow. Is a particular statement to the party and/or parties being videotaped, to other family members, or for remembrance and posterity? Is this meeting like speeches at retirement parties to be heard as reflections or productions of memory? The tape and our task ask us to enter a strange fiction-watching theater with the presumption of no motives and no audience. The members may contest what the meeting is really for, what their speech acts are, but we don't have access to the multiple audiences nor their relations to them.

And, it gets harder. We have not discovered a random fragment of talk. The fragment is left for us by a documentary filmmaker. What is here and what is left out is chosen. We lose the conversations at breaks, lunches, and dinners; conversations that analysts of organizations, if not of conversations, are very interested in. We do not know the filmmaker, his or her motives, sponsorship, past or future work. How was what was interesting and important and the conclusion decided? The text we see is of a "cultural other." What did the filmmaker know of the organization or culture? What does the maker think about organizations and how they work? Was this to be a statement about people, even business celebrities, or communication and decisional practices? Are the embedded values discovered and/or presumed of the speakers, or selected and/or produced in the documentary? Would we, if we were making the documentary, have selected more or different texts, shot from different angles? Would we have done flashbacks to discussions before this meeting, would we have displayed interviews with different members? Would we have shot the negotiations for making the documentary? Who is finally the relevant analyst here, the filmmaker or us? Are we analyzing organizational discourse or a documentary film?

The videotape itself pretends to be a realistic presentation; it hopes to be better than an audiotape, a snapshot, or mere notes. And precisely in this pretense, the fact that it is constituted as an object that is fixed, stoppable, rewindable helps us overlook its constitution as a particular abstract objectification. If only it had explicitly presented itself as a cartoon or caricature, its constitution as a social object would have been clearer. As a proclaimed documentary, its author fades to authority, its particular point of view is disguised as anyone's point of view. Of course the tape is a caricature; it is a rendering of the interaction, highlighting and hiding aspects of the meeting process. It is different than the interaction. Interactions are irreversible, what is said passes away, become reframed, have no clear beginning point in the production of meaning, and never end with any certainty.

Here we are doing an analysis of a produced interaction with the constitutive conditions for it remaining transparent like the camera of a documentary. The "I" positions retained by the discourse, the perspectives, are not just from the meeting participants but the camera (Deetz, 2003b). But we should not be fooled by its pretense of reality. We are led to see this and not that. As we use this "data," we partly enact and privilege a science that runs counter to our own, see objects constituted by only partly known theories that are different from our own, and have no access to data that is critical to the analysis. Even in this exercise, comparative analyses are not different readings of the same data but are responding to very different data (and should be).

In this critical reading, the tape is a double problem. Rather than treating it as a transparent rendition of the interaction, this tape should be seen as an artifact or even a piece of literature of a people who have passed away into history. Because these people (both those producing the tape and those depicted in it) are silenced as people, they cannot easily speak for themselves. If we think of it in this way, we are as interested in the people who produced it as we are of those shown in it.

We will be bold here. Although analysis of discourse can productively stay at the level of text excerpts if the interest is in general social features and the analyst shares a cultural background with interactants, only ethnographically informed analyses of discourse are likely to usefully say anything about organizations (see Boden, 1994; Fitch, 1998; Jackell, 1988). Our task is greatly limited here because we have to move ahead without such information.

CRITICAL ANALYSES OF DISCOURSE

A critical research orientation to the analysis of organizational discourse approaches talk in this meeting as a site of struggle between diverse forms of discourse and focuses on the multiple and diverse ways in which people discursively construct, contest, and understand organizing phenomena and processes. The critical engagement and evaluation of organizing phenomena from this perspective provides insight into the messy, moment-to-moment manner in which people fashion what appear to be coherent, complete organizing worlds out of essentially hidden, partial, and fragmented pieces of discourse (Alvesson & Deetz, 2000; Broadfoot et al., 2004). Focusing on discursive and organizing phenomena as situated, dynamic, interrelated, heterogeneous, and contingent provides a picture of organizing life as richly textured, ambiguous, and indeterminant.

Critical analyses of discourse in general are characterized by three core assumptions (see Deetz, 1982; Fairclough, 2001; Fairclough & Wodak, 1997; Mumby, 2004):

1. Interaction routines/settings/structures, meanings/information/ knowledge, and personal identities/roles/rights and obligations are social-historical constructions.
2. Discourses differ in their degree of openness and ability to represent a full variety of interests and peoples. Hence, some more than others are characterized by distortions and practices of exclusion and closure. Normative considerations of communication practices thus are necessary to display these pathologies.
3. The research act is itself a political discourse and standards applied to discourses under study reciprocally apply to the research processes and reports.

Social-Historical Construction

Routines, meaning, language, identities, and all the various ways of expressing the elements of the communication process are constructions. They are social products that are institutionalized sedimentations of past politically laden discourses; they represent the choices of winners in past political struggles. Institutional practices are historically produced and as such are imbued with and reproduce power differences and advantages. Any analysis that leaves out this history "innocently" overlooks the political content of talk that is embedded in the talk of others with potentially very different interests, or have their interests formed in politically charged ways.

Experience in that sense is thoroughly political. As the feminists are fond of saying, the personal is political. The politics is not in the competition of experiences but already in the experience at hand, the person, and perception produced. Every practice, every piece of equipment, every cognitive scheme institutionalizes a point of view, a point of view sedimented out of the politics of the moment of production; each user reproduces the view of the "winner" of that earlier decision process (see Deetz, 1992, 2003b). It is not that the user must do so, although sanctions and rewards may encourage it. It is in the habit, the natural, the routine, and the thoughtlessness that it is reproduced. But this is not to say that it is neutral or innocent. The configuration of routines and other practices leave perception and person formation inevitably and necessarily partial (one-sided and favoring a side). A core interest in critical analyses is to reveal the political in experience and talk so that values and interests can be opened to a more open form of discussion and redecided. An example may help.

When Stan's children were younger he hoped to teach them something of the micropolitics in modern society. To do this he used to transfer their breakfast cereal to clear plastic containers where he could insert side panels which replaced the typical pictures and discourse on breakfast cereal boxes. On high-sugar cereals, he placed pictures of fat and moody kids and in place of nutritional data, he placed statistics on stock and subsidiary ownership of the owner of the cereal company and other information indicating the percent of the cereal price paid to food producers and pickers compared to other groups. The point was not primarily influencing their choice of cereal, but in indicating how we subtly learn lifestyles and preferences and expectations for certain types of information at the expense of potentially equally important types.

In other words, the goal was to reveal a politics already present and initiate a discussion that was overlooked in the routine and naturalness of cereal box presentations; the hope was to open a greater variety of choice issues rather than to simply change the choices they made. In disclosing this practice to his own classes, most often the first concern was with the appropriateness of using propaganda on his own children. Apparently it is assumed that he made the cereal box political and that cereal companies have more of a right than he to define lifestyles and informational preferences of his children. Discussing better and worse discourse is not more political; it discusses the politics already present.

The politics embedded in organizational talk, hidden in the thoughtlessness and routine are actively protected from examination and alternatives. Such processes sustain misrecognition of interests and desires and obscure both advantages and alternatives. In doing so, they provide efficiency toward meeting certain goals but at the expense of determining the value of these goals and their comparison to others. Understanding how this works requires an understanding of power and how power both advantages and hides advantage. Meetings enact a complex set of institutional sedimentations. These include information strategies, decision-making premises and routines, preferences for particular ways of talking, and professional identities and privileges. To the extent that they are enacted and reproduced in any present interaction they unwittingly (as neutral and natural) instantiate political advantage. Wodak's (1996) analysis of power and discourse in school committee meetings illustrates this point:

> Important decisions were made, though the parents were not given precise information nor explicitly invited to participate. Criticism, debate and the open questioning of issues were pre-empted and thereby effectively prevented. Selection and manipulation of information thus provide good examples of how hierarchy and power relations in institutions are reinforced; democratic rules and means are neglected, often without those involved even noticing the infractions. (p. 91)

On the basis of this, we can suggest five initial moments or questions for a political analysis: (a) What are the assumed forms of knowledge, identity, meaning, and so forth that are present? (b) What are the constitutive conditions for each of these to be present (why these and not those)? (c) What are the power conditions within the constitutive processes (whose meanings are these, who is advantaged and in what ways by these forms)? (d) Because a dialectic of control is always present, in what ways do actors reproduce constitutive processes that are to their advantage and disadvantage (how does complicity in domination happen, e.g., Giddens, 1984)? (e) What are the specific acts of discursive closure or conversation stoppage that suppress conflict and contestation of constituted values, identities, social relations, and knowledge (Deetz, 1992; Thackaberry, 2004)? Because much of the constitutive activities are unavailable for our examination, we focus on the fifth question.

Normative Conditions for Discourse

To suggest that some discourses enable a more open formation of meaning with greater understanding of choices presumes the possibility of a normative ideal to guide analysis to places of closure and distortion. Frequently the quality of communication is judged as if it were primarily a reproductive informational problem. Did the interactants get what they wanted? Was information transferred? Such positions assume that the person, meaning, desires, and information exist outside of the communication process rather than being themselves products of it. When such views are assumed, effectiveness emerges as the primary criteria for evaluation. A critical reading by necessity is interested in communicational issues as a backdrop for the narrower consideration of information transfer. If the production, rather than reproduction, of identity, information, meaning, or knowledge is of concern, the standard of evaluation must be different. Because it is the production of people and their common future that is of concern and because outside of any particular historically situated discourse we cannot unilaterally establish grounds for the privilege of any person over others, judgments of communication quality ultimately arise from either power or some standard grounded in some type of reciprocal participation. To practice science at all requires holding out some hope for the latter (see Apel, 1979). The hermeneutic–critical theory tradition exemplified by Gadamer and Habermas provides one of the most straightforward description of ideals, if controversial. Because much has been written on this in other places, we will be very brief here (see Deetz, 1992).

Open communication can occur in two modes, genuine conversation and dispute in an ideal speech situation. *Genuine conversation* is the ongoing process of creating mutual understanding through the open formation of experience guided by the subject matter rather than the subjectivity of the interaction participants (Deetz, 1978; Gadamer, 1975). The communicative act should be responsive to the subject matter of the conversation and at the same time help establish the conditions for future unrestrained formation of experience (Deetz, 1990). Such normatively based interaction is not willed or chosen by the individual, nor does it conform to some predefined or routine social practice. Rather, in its natural state, the will is produced out of the demand of the subject matter in interaction. But, the "conversation" can be blocked or distorted in a variety of fashions. The maintenance of a blockage provides an arbitrary restraint on the interaction and prohibits the undistorted development and expression of human interests and the formation of an emergent consensus on the subject matter. Understanding how blockages are accomplished can be used to evaluate a variety of communication events.

Although it is possible to participate in genuine conversations, such opportunities are relatively rare especially in organizational meetings because of the limitations daily life imposes both on ourselves and others. Rarely is an experience so powerful that the disciplines, routines of life, and ordinary ways of seeing are spontaneously overcome. Our shared history carries unexamined beliefs and attitudes that maintain preference for the expression of certain views of reality and of certain social groups. Under such conditions, genuine conversation cannot take place because there is no proper "other"; there is no means or forum for "otherness" to be expressed (Deetz & Simpson, 2004).

Habermas (1979, 1984, 1987) took head on the issues Gadamer left aside. Systems of domination usually preclude the genuine conversation. What is the nature of interaction where a new consensus does not arise organically out of the interaction? What is the nature of the interaction by which competing claims can be resolved? How can one distinguish consensus reached regarding the subject matter from those knowingly or unknowingly produced by authority or relations of power?

Basically, Habermas argued that every speech act can function in communication by virtue of common presumptions made by speaker and listener. Even when these presumptions are not fulfilled in an actual situation, they serve as a base of appeal as failed conversation turns to argumentation regarding the disputed validity claims. The basic presumptions and validity claims arise out of four shared domains of reality and their relation to discourse: the external world, human relations, the individual's internal world, and language. The claims raised in each are truth, correctness, sincerity, and intelligibility, respectively. Thus we can claim that each competent, communicative act represents facts, including an opportunity for examination of the processes by which they were constructed, establishes legitimate social relations, discloses the speaker's point of view, and gives opportunities for different perspectives to be expressed. Systematically distorted communication arises when one of more of these conditions is not maintained, hence something that might be of dispute is left without contestation. The ideal speech situation must be recovered to avoid or overcome such distortions. It should be clear that this conception applies not only to the everyday and ordinary acts of communication but also models the ideal processes by which collective decisions can be made. They can be used in this sense as a guide to defining institutions and practices that advance participation and democracy. Participation modeled in this way is central to our moral responsibility to decide what our society will be and what kind of people we will become. In a less grand fashion, such ideals might be used to direct communication in meetings and the social production of shared knowledge; and can be used as a part of a critical analysis to demonstrate places of distortion and conversational closure in organizational discourse (Thackaberry, 2004).

Discursive closure and *systematically distorted communication* are terms used to describe the invisible constraints to open interaction. Here strategy and manipulation are disguised and control is exercised through manipulations of the natural, neutral, and self-evident. Both discursive closure and systematically distorted communication are common in human communication. Human thoughts, feelings, actions, and expressions are often skewed by historically arbitrary power relations. Certain dominant forms of reasoning and articulations stand in the stead of other valuational schemes. Such expressions can and should be examined for possible suppressions of alternative voices, not to implement alternative values, but as part of ongoing community development.

Processes of systematically distorted communication can be said to be pathological or morally inappropriate (a) to the extent that the communication system precludes responsiveness to an exterior, adaptation is limited; (b) to the extent that the ideal speech situation is denied, freely shared normative standards are violated; (c) to the extent that the self and experience are reproduced, concept formation cannot occur in regard to an exterior.

We already know a fair amount about pathological interpersonal systems. Interaction process analysts (Pearce & Cronen, 1980; Watzlawick, Beavin, & Jackson, 1967) initiated careful research into the way family systems can develop internal logics and rules that structure frozen identities for the participants, that preclude the meeting of critical needs in their production of other needs, and finally strip participants of responsibility and responsiveness. Such systems through closure and fixed meanings preclude moments of escape to see the system as it works. Yet they grow; they become supported by external structures, institutionalized, and engulf others in their peculiar logics. Although the theoretical base of these studies, particularly in regard to the social structure of identity and reality, is too weak to show their political character, their descriptions are often useful in showing what a political analysis would examine.

Good decisions require appropriately distributed information, openness to alternative perspectives, and reasoning based on personal insights and data rather than on authority relations. Perhaps everyone working within organizational meetings would accept this. Many analyses (and analysts), however, accept or presume as given assumed priorities, goals, and authority relations that are not necessarily warranted or freely selected. Critical analyses, in contrast, display the specific mechanism by which domination in the form of violation of these ideals occur. For example, Mehan (2001) described the case of Shane, a fourth-grade student who showed low academic performance and was recommended by his teacher for a special education class. Mehan wanted to discover how committee members including parents faced with deciding whether or not a child needed special education "lost their voices while routinely coming to agreement with the school's recommendation" (p. 351). He found that the modes of representing a child differed between psychologists, parents, and teachers and the psychologist's representation prevailed. This was so because the psychologist spoke ambiguously, used technical terms that no one asked for clarification on, and because the speech was difficult to understand. When difficulties arise, then, the appeal is rarely to discourse along the model of the ideal speech situation. In most decisional effectiveness analyses, problems in the process are often conceptualized as individual or technical, thus requiring technical structural adjustments or personnel training (Deetz, 2003a; Holmer-Nadesan, 1996). In cases of conflict, rather than reinvolving the community, higher order privilege is evoked backed by symbolic control and expertise. The problem is "solved" rather than addressed. Miscommunication and distortions may be inevitable in interactions but discursive closures and systematic distortions are distinct problems that maintain unwarranted advantages for some groups and their knowledge at the expense of others and general human development.

Some distortions are inevitable in interaction and some degree of random distortion in decision making always occurs (Forester, 1989). Time and information are limited, rationality bounded, and not all issues are worthy of reconsideration. Such limitations, being relatively random and unmotivated, balance each other out and/or are remedied over time in question asking, providing warrants, and conflicting interpretations. In these processes, meaningful changes are made and the decisional process claims a renewed legitimacy as openly derived asymmetries are reassessed, reaffirmed, or denied. The closures and systematically distorted communication of interest here, however, are different. In these cases, there is either a known or unknown strategic quality of the interaction that drives the interaction, thus providing a systematic distortion that is protected from assessment. For example, forgetting is a natural, relatively random human limitation, able to be overcome in part by social interaction. Received histories, on the other hand, are constructed selective memories, thus a produced condition that works against the social attempt to recall alternative understandings. Correction is difficult because the strategic interaction creates both false conflicts and/or false lack of conflict. Hence, the decisions are distorted, but neither the distortion nor conditions for it are known. Further, the interactant is less willing to be corrected because strategic gain is an issue. And perhaps even more importantly, the strategy can remain invisible as an embedded politics or disguised as a natural limitation. Systematic distortions thus can be blamed on individuals and inevitable system weakness rather than a hidden strategic interaction.

The distortions of greatest interest are produced by the structural configurations institutionalized in the system. To the extent that these institutional arrangements are taken as natural and self-evident, their political derivation is forgotten and their existence noncontestable. For example, arbitrary authority relations may be disguised as legitimate divisions of labor, thus producing a strategic skewing of decisions, but contestation can only take place within the structural confines, rather than to be about them. Pathological, rather than just bad, decisions are made. They are pathological, not because they do not effectively meet presumably shared goals, but because of the monopoly of the opportunities to define the system and its goals as well as the strategic processes of reaching them. Such ideals can be used both for critique and the development of moral practices (Forester, 1999; Haas & Deetz, 2000). We see this in the analysis of the text later.

Research as a Political Act

When examining the politics of discourse, it is clear that research is a discursive act itself. Because it represents a communicative relationship at least within a "subject" community, a research community, and a professional user community, issues in the production of knowledge, subjects, and routines are as applicable to it as to the communication process under study. The research process itself is not neutral, it is not outside of the social historical process of which the dialogue itself is a part and the general conditions of distortion and privilege present within the society. Research asserts its own arbitrary privilege and takes a point of view that is different from that of the participants but in no easy way better. Looking at the openness of the dialogue under study must be applied to the research process itself.

In many respects, the research here is quite inappropriate and systematically distorted. We are examining the behavior of people in a natural setting, yet only letting them engage us in a limited fashion. They cannot interrogate our concepts as we do theirs, our purposes as we do theirs. Although they enact forms of domination, at least they do so for serious purposes, we use them to illustrate, to play with in public. And neither they nor we can grow in the interaction. They learn none of our concepts to penetrate the systems of domination of which they are a part and they cannot object as real others to lead us to engage in concept formation. This practice of display in this sense violates the very communicative practice we would wish to accomplish. Because we accepted doing this book chapter, we are uncertain where to go with this at this point, but it certainly must be noted.

THE PRESENCE OF DISTORTION AND CLOSURE

Even with the limited materials available to us here, there are many different things to which a critical analysis might attend. These include implied conceptions of masculinity and femininity, particular systems for warranting hierarchical management and control and/or reporting systems, practices of inclusion and exclusion in decision making, and the absence of key stakeholder interests—employee well-being, environmental consequences, product development. We will be more restrictive here focusing on the discursive moves within the stated purposes of the meeting and their contribution to the opening and closing of discourse. Of course, many discussions did not and/or could not happen, for example, sale of the company. These potential discussions are of interest too, as well as how they were precluded, but we keep our treatment here much narrower than this. What is of greatest interest to us, here, is the specific ways discussion and decision regarding these issues were constantly cut off at the very moment that they might have approached an open determination.

Stated Purposes of the Meeting

The narrator suggests two but we see three quite different stated purposes of this meeting. First was the obvious issue of succession. Sam

Steinberg was stepping down and/or out from the presidency and someone else would take this role. Second was the issue of structure. Potentially, independent of who was president, issues of other offices, reporting structure, and divisional structure might also be discussed and determined. Third was the question of goals and objectives. The direction of the company including what the "business" was and how it should develop might potentially be a question worthy of answering before the other two.

Quite possibly unexpressed purposes also existed along with these or the stated ones may have only been a cover for more central ones. Given our understanding of common organizational processes, the specific cultural context and practices of the Steinberg family, and the information about what others in the company thought, the succession question at least may have already been answered. The meeting reads very differently if it was the case that some or all shared this secret but could not talk about it directly. Even the narrator hints in a coy way twice that the decision may have been made already. Given that the documentary would be of far less interest and value if the decision preceded the meeting, the filmmaker was clearly motivated to keep the issue in doubt. If the succession question had already been answered, it would be easier to explain the relative absence of talk (and what was accomplished when he did talk) by Mel Dobrin, the son-in-law who was eventually appointed president. And, it would give an account of the ways Sam Steinberg stopped discussion on each of the three stated purposes of the meeting. The meeting would appear to be more strategic and in virtually no way an open discussion of these important organizational issues. Our interest here, however, is not in trying to historically reclaim these motives but to see how Sam and Mel's talk functioned in the meeting.

Discussion Stoppage and Sam Steinberg

Of first interest is the way Sam Steinberg maintained total control of decision making throughout the meeting. On one hand, this might seem unremarkable given the family ownership and largely unquestioned nature of ownership and/or managerial prerogative and hierarchical organization of businesses. But, recall that this meeting was explicitly about succession, restructuring, and goals and objectives. The explicit point was not to preserve hierarchy but to determine it in the best interest of the preservation and success of the company. But individual roles and authority never became part of the discussion. Much of the talk came from positions/identities, and the narrator made these the most significant information about each participant, but little talk was about the individual identities and the structure of the meeting itself. The identities were largely uncontestable. Sam Steinberg explicitly claimed the decision right, and all seemed to accept that the meeting was at best consultative. Consistently, Sam's authority was accepted as natural and oddly neutral in the presumed open discussion that was occurring.

But of course his discursive moves in even a more specific sense were anything but neutral. Discussion occurred on each of the three stated potential agenda items. But a pronouncement by Sam successfully stopped the discussion at each moment that the discussion appeared to open up differences and offer potential to the group to begin to seriously engage the issue. Let's look at each in turn.

Goals and Objectives.   Jack L. was early on the most forceful in trying to open a discussion about the goals and objectives. He and Harry S. were at this point, and throughout the most concerned that the entire meeting was going to be pointless. The discussion would become a "fish market" (721), Harry S. later directly says. Or a "<u>mental</u> exercise" (737) as expressed by Jack L. Each attempted to claim a place for a rational discussion where authority/role/power was set aside for a serious assessment and determination of the direction of the company. This was met first by Mel D.'s most sustained and forceful statement of the meeting (173–200) reclaiming the place of leadership and prerogative in any determination of the direction of the company. When this did not apparently end the discussion, we learn from the narrator that Sam stepped in.

202	Voiceover:	((The argument over objectives versus structure was resolved at
203		last by the President reading a statement of company
204		philosophy. With that, objectives disappeared from the
205		Palomino agenda

Especially, if the issue of succession had already been determined, a discussion of company objectives had the greatest opportunity to involve all in a form of open discussion and self-determination. It was the one discussion that might limit Sam's and subsequently Mel's authority-based leadership, or at least show it for what it was.

Structure.   As the objectives discussion disappeared, the question of structure took center stage. As this discussion developed, the number of participants expands and statements are made by James D., Oscar P. and Irving L. Finally, Jack L. once more takes the strongest position and again the discussion becomes animated with differences being expressed, until Sam stops the discussion of structure.

428	SAM S:	Listen. When a man is made the Chief (1.0) Executive Officer,
429		and I'm just using the President by way of example (0.5) >then

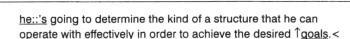

430   <u>he::'s</u> going to determine the kind of a structure that he can
431   operate with effectively in order to achieve the desired ↑<u>goals</u>.<

Voices are gradually lost. James D. and Oscar P. will basically withdraw from the rest of the discussion. Irving L. will again try to argue against structure based in authority relations in his plea for a "professional managerial style" (601). But again the appeal to modern rather than traditional organization is taken out of discussion, and with it any attempt to engage in open discussion in Habermasian terms.

Succession and Family.   The final issue concerns succession. And, within this cultural context, succession and family issues cannot be separated. Several concerns are raised as to whether the new president must be a family member, whether a family member would be best for the position, feelings and rumors, and so forth in the company. Again, the group begins the discussion airing feelings and being rather diverse in their concerns and positions. Initially Sam (as displayed in the first except to come) tries to direct the discussion away from these concerns by changing the definition of family to be inclusive in ways that would presumably not exclude anyone in the room. As the group gradually reopens the discussion trying to put their concerns back on the table, Sam (in the second excerpt) tries to reframe the discussion from the unfairness that individuals would be excluded because they were not family members to the unfairness of excluding someone because "he" was a family member. Finally, as the group works one more time to make this a discussible issue, Sam (in the third excerpt) ends the discussion by use of power and authority to end the issue and remove the possibility of further discussion.

796 SAM S: Alright! So it tells you that after a period of twenty years there
797   is more family than ever before=and that hasn't affected the the
798   performances as I read it in these companies. (1.0) On the >
799   other hand < (0.5) I think that when we look around the table
800   over here, we talk about family, (1.0) well (.) I looked upon
801   Jack as a member of the family=I look up:on (.) Oscar as a
802   member of the family (.) I've looked upon Jack Ginser always
803   as a member of the family (.) and I think that they look upon
804   ↑themselves as a member of family.

And:

926 SAM S: =Now if the man can't be considered for the <u>job</u> because he's a
927   member of the family we better know the ground rules right at
928   the beginning.

And finally:

```
992  SAM S:    One man (1.0) my own person have a hundred percent control of
993             this company. I don't have to ask anybody so it's no use even
994             talkin' about a discussion the the there's no need for a discussion.
995             (1.0) Uh (1.0) I don't need anybody's approval=
```

Mel D.'s role is interesting in this part of the discussion, partly because it is one of the few places where he joins in the discussion and as he tries to clarify for the group that little of significance happens in the Friday night family meeting. The irony, of course, is that he is apparently the only member besides Sam who attends and can dismiss the importance of the Friday nights, and he will become president, thus confirming the importance of them. This discussion, like Mel's absence of talk, might well be seen as strategically preparing the way for his succession. He does not have to push or win any argument. In fact, the more that the others appear to have had an open opportunity to have a say, the easier his succession. In many ways he approaches, or is enabled to approach, the discussion more strategically than Sam, who runs the risk of discussion closures reducing the legitimacy of the decisions to be, or already made. Mel has the option of being participatory, precisely because Sam has established the boundaries and the consequences of talking.

CONCLUDING WITH NATIVE MODELS OF COMMUNICATION

A critical read of the meeting shows a continued violation of even the most basic moral conditions for open communication. The meeting invited the open discussion of issues mutually affecting the lives of all in the room and others. The conduct of the meeting, however, stopped every attempt to discuss these core issues. Not only can such conduct be critiqued on moral grounds of inclusion and responsibility, but it also has the consequence of leaving the organization less able to respond to the environment and to make decisions to the benefit of stakeholder groups. This does not mean that the organization will fail on economic grounds, for success as is clear in this case is based on many external conditions of business and numerous other decision practices.

Still, this meeting can tell us much about how meetings that are established to make decisions can often be described as orchestrated activities in not making decisions. The trick seems to be to appear to engage in a decision practice but to forestall any attempt to genuinely deal with the issues or finally reach decisions. This would be one type of what Argyris (1986) called *skilled incompetence*.

Partly, this is able to occur because the models of communication brought into the meeting context lack themselves much critical import.

In the Palomino meeting, two models of communication were openly expressed. The first in its extreme version was denounced as the "fish market." But despite its deprecation in the extreme it was positively practiced throughout. In the positive version, this is the communication model derived from North American versions of liberal democracy. The talk that was prized was what could easily be called "expressionist." Everyone was invited to have their say, getting their feelings on the table. In most respects, the more the better. The meeting itself announced itself as all the effected parties have an opportunity to effect the outcome. The process was considered limited only in two ways: one when it lost its civility, someone's feelings were dismissed, or too many talked at once and were thus criticized as a "fish market"; and, the other when the group started to dig into real issues and might have reached consensus. At these places, Sam stopped the discussion.

But the real limitation and potentially why such a model is widely used in such contexts rests in the ways that expressionist approaches to meetings rarely allow people to critically understand and develop their own interests, where knowledge is routinely reduced to opinions, and creative win–win decisions cannot emerge (see Deetz & Brown, 2004). The control mechanisms in such an approach are great. For example, the pressure to reveal personal feelings in public allows one a kind of say but also allows a surveillance of one's interior and a sanitizing of what one might feel and/or say in private (Deetz, 2003a). The positive evaluation of the form of talk allows meetings to be deprecated as difficult places to decide things, rather than to see the form of talk itself as problematic and meetings as having positive potential. We have a lesson here in how to encourage talk but reduce voice and capacity of mutual decision making.

Finally, the narrator tips his hand at the end. The real model of communication is bridge filled with codes, deception and driven by winning. Contextually, the trick of the group is to have an apparent productive discussion among themselves, while they are trying to convince the chief executive officer who is textually produced as having the decision making capacity and who may well have already decided. This becomes focused in the discussion of the difference between commitment to disciplined talk and a decision process versus a spirited fish market. The sustained fish market worked to display command but precluded group decisions. We have not been listening to a discussion about the future of the company, but a game to fill time. The conversation was never intended to be genuine. We conspire with them to play and not make decisions.

1044 Voiceover:	*((In bridge a player may have two objectives, to win by making*
1045	*his contract or to prevent the opposition from winning, which is*
1046	*another kind of victory. The game has rules, which the players*
1047	*must observe if they want to play at all but it also has*

1048	*conventions outside the rules, mainly the elaborate system of*
1049	*bidding by which the players signal the strengths and*
1050	*weaknesses of their hands. Through bidding a way has been*
1051	*found for players to say indirectly what the rules won't allow*
1052	*them to say openly. In the succession discussion, which ended*
1053	*the Palomino Conference, there were some who hoped to win*
1054	*and others who merely hoped to prevent someone else from*
1055	*winning. No participant could propose himself or criticize*
1056	*another candidate directly. So more indirect ways had to be*
1057	*found of saying things, which could not be said out loud.))*
1058	*((People sitting on the sofas discussing what happened at the*
1059	*meeting quietly.))*
1060 Voiceover:	*((To make matters worse, the exercise had to take place under*
1061	*the eyes of Sam Steinberg, a man who none of them could afford*
1062	*to offend and whose choice might already have been made.))*

In the end, the narrator beats us to the punch line. Has our analysis merely elaborated his story? Was he playing bridge too?

REFERENCES

Alvesson, M., & Deetz, S. (2000). *Doing critical management research*. London: Sage.

Apel, K. O. (1979). *Toward a transformation of philosophy* (G. Adey & D. Frisby, Trans.). London: Routledge & Kegan Paul.

Argyris, C. (1986). Skilled incompetence. *Harvard Business Review, 64*(5), 74–79.

Boden, D. (1994). *The business of talk*. Cambridge: Polity Press.

Broadfoot, K., Deetz, S., & Anderson, D. (2004). Multi-leveled, multi-method approaches to organizational discourse. In D. Grant, C. Hardy, C. N. Oswick, & L. Putnam (Eds.), *The handbook of organizational discourse* (pp. 193–211). London: Sage.

Deetz, S. (1978). Conceptualizing human understanding: Gadamer's hermeneutics and American communication research. *Communication Quarterly, 26*, 12–23.

Deetz, S. (1982). Critical-interpretive research in organizational communication. *Western Journal of Speech Communication, 46*, 131–149.

Deetz, S. (1990). Reclaiming the subject matter as a guide to mutual understanding: Effectiveness and ethics in interpersonal interaction. *Communication Quarterly, 38*, 226–243.

Deetz, S. (1992). *Democracy in the age of corporate colonization: Developments in communication and the politics of everyday life*. Albany: State University of New York Press.

Deetz, S. (2003a). Disciplinary power, conflict suppression and human resource management. In M. Alvesson & H. Willmott (Eds.), *Studying management critically* (pp. 23–45). London: Sage.

Deetz, S. (2003b). Taking the "linguistic turn" seriously. *Organization: The Interdisciplinary Journal of Organization, Theory, and Society, 10*, 421–429.

Deetz, S., & Brown, D. (2004). Conceptualizing involvement, participation and workplace decision processes: A communication theory perspective. In D.

Tourish & O. Hargie (Eds.), *Key issues in organizational communication* (pp. 172–187). London: Routledge.

Deetz, S., & Simpson. J. (2004). Critical organizational dialogue: Open formation and the demand of "otherness." In R. Anderson, L. Baxter, & K. Cissna (Eds.), *Dialogue: Theorizing difference in communication studies* (pp. 141–158). Mahwah, NJ: Lawrence Erlbaum Associates.

Fairclough, N. (2001). Critical discourse analysis as a method in social scientific research. In R. Wodak & M. Mayer (Eds.), *Methods of critical discourse analysis*. London: Sage.

Fairclough, N., & Wodak, R. (1997). Critical discourse analysis. In T. van Dijk (Ed.), *Discourse studies: A multidisciplinary introduction: Vol. 2. Discourse as structure and process* (pp. 258–284). London: Sage.

Fitch, K. L. (1998). Text and context: A problematic distinction for ethnography. *Research On Language and Social Interaction, 31,* 91–107.

Forester, J. (1989). *Planning in the face of power.* Berkeley: University of California Press.

Forester. J. (1999). *The deliberative practitioner.* Cambridge, MA: MIT Press.

Gadamer, H. G. (1975). *Truth and method.* New York: Seabury Press.

Giddens, A. (1984). *The constitution of society: Outline of the theory of structuration.* Berkeley: University of California Press.

Grant, D., Hardy, C., Oswick, C., & Putnam, L. (Eds.). (2004). *The Sage handbook of organizational discourse.* London: Sage.

Haas, T., & Deetz, S. (2000). Between the generalized and the concrete other: Approaching organizational ethics from feminist perspectives. In P. Buzzanell (Ed.), *Rethinking organizational and managerial communication from feminist perspectives* (pp. 24–46). Thousand Oaks, CA: Sage.

Habermas, J. (1979). *Communication and the evolution of society* (T. McCarthy, Trans.). Boston: Beacon Press.

Habermas, J. (1984). *The theory of communicative action: Vol. 1. Reason and the rationalization of society* (T. McCarthy, Trans.). Boston: Beacon Press.

Habermas, J. (1987). *The theory of communicative action: Vol. 2. Lifeworld and System* (T. McCarthy, Trans.). Boston: Beacon Press.

Holmer-Nadesan, M. (1996). Organizational identity and space of action. *Organization Studies, 17,* 49–81.

Jackell, R. (1988). *Moral mazes: The world of corporate managers.* Oxford, England: Oxford University Press.

Mehan, H. (2001). The construction of an LD student: A case study in the politics of representation. In M. Wethrell, S. Taylor, & S. J. Yates (Eds.), *Discourse theory and practice* (pp. 345–363). London: Sage.

Mumby, D. (2004). Discourse, power and ideology: Unpacking the critical approach. In D. Grant, C. Hardy, C. Oswick, & L. L. Putnam (Eds.), *The Sage handbook of organizational discourse* (pp. 237–258). London: Sage.

Mumby, D., & Clair, R. P. (1997). Organizational discourse. In T. A. van Dijk (Ed.), *Discourse studies: A multidisciplinary introduction: Vol. 2. Discourse as structure and process* (pp. 181–205). London: Sage.

Pearce, W. B., & Cronen, V. E. (1980). *Communication, action and meaning: The creation of social realities.* New York: Praeger.

Thackaberry, J. A. (2004). Discursive opening and closing in organizational self study: Culture as the culprit for safety problems in wildland firefighting. *Management Communication Quarterly, 17,* 319–359.

Watson, T. J. (1997). Languages within languages: A social constructionist perspective on multiple managerial discourses. In F. Bargiela-Chiappinin & S.

Harris (Eds.), *The language of business: An international perspective* (pp. 211–227). Edinburgh, Scotland: Edinburgh University Press.

Watzlawick, P., Beavin, J., & Jackson, D. (1967). *The pragmatics of human communication: A study of interactional patterns, pathologies and paradoxes.* New York: Norton.

Wodak, R. (1996). Critical discourse analysis and the study of doctor–patient interaction. In B. Gunnarsson, P. Linell, & B. Nordberg (Eds.), *The construction of professional discourse* (pp. 173–200). London: Longman.

Chapter 12

Documentaries Are Not Data

D. Lawrence Wieder
University of Oklahoma

Heidi Mau
University of Oklahoma

Cheryl Nicholas
Southern Illinois University

Like many of the other authors in this volume, Deetz, Heath, and Mac-Donald (chap. 11) and Philipsen and Leighter (chap. 10) treat *Corporation: After Mr. Sam* (hereafter *AMS*) as unproblematic data for their analyses. It is true that Deetz, Heath, and MacDonald do list a series of problems with the initial collection of the film-data that might trouble their analysis, but they then go on as if these problems did not exist. Both sets of authors assume that what is seen on the screen unproblematically presents what went on in the meetings in just the fashion that an ideal data tape of interaction does. Although we recognize that one can make problematic the way that the ideal data tape represents the sphere of interaction and cannot be said to directly present it, for our purposes, it is the difference between a well-made documentary and an ideal data tape that is of interest. We show what that difference consists of, how it is produced, and what consequences it has for the argument of any analysis of interaction that does not take it into account. We also briefly discuss the appropriate use of documentary films by social scientists.

THE PROBLEM

On the surface, *AMS* appears to be a filmed record of the meetings of a managerial group for a large Canadian company. The film conveys a vivid impression of naturally occurring interaction-in-meetings. It is even more vivid than the usual interaction data tapes of meetings produced by social scientists. The film is persuasively effective in appearing to place us at the table with the officers of Steinberg Limited, and it appears to be a truly faithful display of naturally occurring interaction-in-meetings.

But there is the rub: The vivid impression of the naturally occurring interaction-in-meetings dissolves when attention is shifted from what the film depicts to how the film was assembled out of often discontinuous sound bites. Our account of how documentary films are made relies on the filmmaking skills and knowledge of one of the authors, Heidi Mau,[1] two interviews with Arthur Hammond, the director of *AMS* (see Appendix 12.1, p. 268, and Appendix 12.2, p. 278), and writings indigenous to the documentary filmmakers' community such as Nichols (1991, 2001), Rosenthal (2002), Vaughan (1992), Barnouw (1993), and Issari (1991).

The vivid impression of naturally occurring events is particularly cultivated in that genre of documentary films called *observational, direct cinema, fly-on-the-wall,* and *cinema vérité.* In the well-known and widely adopted genre categories developed by Nichols (1991, 2001), the observational genre contrasts with poetic, expository, participatory, and reflexive forms. The effort to give the audience the vivid impression of

> observing lived experience spontaneously [honoring] this spirit of observation in post-production editing as well as during shooting resulted in films with no voice-over commentary, no supplementary music or sound effects, no intertitles, no historical reenactments, no behavior repeated for the camera, and not even any interviews. What we saw was what there was, or so it seemed in *Primary* (1960), *High School* (1968), ... *Gimme Shelter* (1970) ... [and] *Monterey Pop* (1968) ... We look in on life as it is lived. Social actors engage with one another, ignoring the filmmakers.... We make inferences and come to conclusions on the basis of behavior we observe or overhear. The filmmaker's retirement to the position of observer calls on the viewer to take a more active role in determining the significance of what is said and done. (Nichols, 2001, pp. 110–111)

AMS has some voice-over commentary and several intertitles, but in all other respects it fits the specifications of observational films. Hammond's films are regarded as exemplars of observational films (Evans, 1991).

Taking our leads from ethnomethodology and several forms of phenomenology,[2] our question is "How did the film get done?" instead of the question that occupies most of the authors in this volume, "How did the meeting get done?" If we directly inspect the finished film, the very construction of the film itself resists our efforts to learn definitely how it was actually done in its particulars, although it does enable us to see, in a general way, at what points the film may have been edited and in other ways "worked over." This is no accident; the standards of filmmaking craft that are followed and respected by observational documentary filmmakers guide the filmmaker to specifically cover over the work that goes into making a film. One of our tasks in this chapter is to describe those standards and to show their consequences for the completed film, particularly their consequences for any effort to treat the observational filmmaker's product as *factual data* in the sense of *fact* and *data* meant by social scientists and particularly communication scholars studying interaction.

As a documentary filmmaker in good standing, Hammond's visions of truth, fairness, and what counts as an honest professional product are standards that he generally shares with the community of observational or direct cinema documentary filmmakers. A description of these standards permits us to form judgments about the data qualities of observational or direct cinema documentary films at large, as well as about this film in particular.

AMS, like virtually all other documentaries, is a highly and specially edited rendition—a collection of selections made into a representation (an account) of the meetings it depicts. This does not mean that its rendition misrepresents the sense, point, or gist of the goings-on at the management meetings of Steinberg Corporation. It is not likely to be a biased account or a misrepresentation in its own terms, but its terms are not our social scientific (communicational) terms and its object is almost surely not a direct representation of interaction-in-meetings as organizational communication or language and social interaction scholars would understand interaction-in-meetings. Whatever the film's claims actually are and whatever object they actually concern, analysts relying on the film as an adequate empirical record of interactions-in-meetings run a number of risks: They risk drawing the sorts of unwarranted inferences that one would run in taking a written ethnographic report and culling its details to answer questions that the original ethnographer never had in mind;[3] they run the risks that accompany the fact that determining exactly what the claims and objects of an observational or direct cinema documentary are is hopeless—hopeless because the claims are, for the most part, not propositionally stated but are insinuated, awaiting an active audience to find them as the nonformal implications of an assembly of sound bites: In such a case, no one can say definitely what the claims are; and they run the risk that what they encounter as analysts (like the rest of the untutored-in-filmmaking audience) is, as Vaughan (1992) so brilliantly developed it, "a form of crypto-fiction: a mode in which, though the relation of the material to a prior world is intellectually acknowledged, such relationship remains marginal or irrelevant to the meaning that we-as-viewers attribute to the whole" (p. 110).[4]

To deepen these claims, our grasp of the invisibility of the film's production, and the certainty that some parts of the actual full meetings are absent in the completed film, we turn to an examination of the observational or direct cinema community's shared understandings, standards, and practices in conjunction with an examination of the film itself and Hammond's own remarks to formulate *how the film was produced* and what the film might and might not tell us about our object, *this meeting* and *interaction-in-this-meeting.*

THE COMMUNITY OF DIRECT CINEMA FILMMAKERS

Within the larger overarching community of documentary filmmakers, there is a community of observational filmmakers. Calling its work *direct cinema*, the community of observational filmmakers affiliated with The National Film Board of Canada was recognized for its filmmakers' inventive use of the new lightweight 16mm cameras and sound equipment (Evans, 1991; Appendix 12.2). Hammond was drawn to, and became a member of, one of the internationally recognized centers of this form of filmmaking, The National Film Board of Canada, especially Unit B and Unit C. He served there as a writer, directed his own films, and ultimately produced films directed by others (Appendix 12.2; Evans, 1991).[5] In keeping with the fact that the observational film genre is called *direct cinema* in Canada, we will use that term hereafter.

The Aims and Values of Direct Cinema

The direct cinema community feels an obligation to give a fair rendering of the gist of filmed events. Like other public performers and exhibitors, direct cinema filmmakers recognize that the documentary film should be an attention-holding, pleasing, followable, entertaining product that exhibitors will show and that audiences will seek out and will attend to. To make the film interesting and watchable requires starting with good shots and with good sound. Direct cinema documentary filmmakers share the understanding that they should film and edit in such a way as to make the filming and many aspects of editing invisible, so as to avoid turning the audience away from giving exclusive attention to the content of the film. Including the filmmakers' activities within the frame alters the perceptual object for the audience, for example, from interaction-within-a-meeting to interaction-within-a-filmed-meeting-in-the-presence-of-filmmakers. In fiction films, showing the filmmaker and filmmaking activities characteristically is not just a distraction but it destroys the perceptual object.[6]

A competent direct cinema documentary filmmaker selects sound bites that she or he believes to be the most pertinent to the gist or flavor of what the event was for the actual participants, and does not misrepresent persons or events that appear in the finished film. The commitment to representing an event as closely as possible is tied to an understanding that the representation is not the actual event.[7] Direct cinema filmmakers also hold each other to ethical editing. Ethical editing does not require that the film show the fullness of the event (e.g., the step-by-step progress of a conversation) but it does require that the filmmaker attempt to convey the feel, the impression, and the general ideas and concepts that were at stake within the event. In *AMS*, the filmmakers represent 12 minutes of conversation-in-a-meeting in less than 1 minute.

Hammond's (1973) views on objectivity are informed by his adoption of some features of sociological–anthropological ethnography. In the 1973 interview (Appendix 12.1), he says "[In the corporation series films] I was interested in exploring a world ... It's like going up the Amazon to see what's there and how the people live up there ... I compare the films more to the Netsilk Eskimo films than to anything else. They're an observation."

Hammond aims at showing the way things work from the inside to an audience who has never directly experienced this particular scene, organization, or society for themselves. Like his objectivist counterparts in the social sciences, he takes a position of value neutrality. He says:

> I don't observe a thing absolutely purely. It goes through a certain amount of filtering as it goes through me. I have certain views or preferences about life and the world which are bound to show up at certain times. [But] ... I try not to mistake those for reflections of objective truth. I think life [and society] is very complicated.... If the films ... are successful ... they would make people realize ... that the issues are complicated.... There's certainly a big argument about objectivity. There are filmmakers who would say not only do you have no right to make an objective film, but that it's impossible. I obviously don't agree with that. But they'd also go further and say, because you cannot be completely objective, you shouldn't try. You should go all the way and make films which clearly take a point of view, and identify it. I think that's one way of making films, but I think there are many ways. It doesn't appear to be the way I make them. (Appendix 12.1)

The Aims and Values of Direct Cinema Filmmakers and Observational Social Scientists

Although the general aims of direct cinema filmmakers and observational social scientists are similar on most issues, they are poles apart on the critical felt need to be entertaining.

1. Direct cinema filmmakers hold themselves to the ideal of giving a fair rendering of the gist of filmed events through the selected sound bites that convey the gist or flavor of the events for the actual partici-

pants. The concerns of social scientists regarding fair renderings and adequate coverage are satisfied by filming from an angle and distance that includes the activities of all the parties to the event and that includes the "whole event" from beginning to end (DuFon, 2002; Erickson, 1992; see also Goodwin's, 1993, treatment of what to include within the frame). These are often imperfectly realized ideals. Such a filmed record is thought to show what an observer would see if he or she were present.

2. Direct cinema filmmakers are committed to treating the participants fairly and to an objectivity that has as much to do with a journalist's sense of fairness (through presenting both sides of issues recognized by participants) as it has to do with a Weberian notion of value neutrality. The social scientist's data tape is collected for analysis, not public presentation. Fairness and objectivity are warranted by the adequacy of the data tape as a record of the event and by the typicality of the event as an instance of "events of this sort" (Bottorff, 1994; DuFon, 2002; Erickson, 1992; Feld & Williams, 1975; Grimshaw, 1982).

3. Direct cinema filmmakers give high priority to producing a film that is attention-holding, pleasing, followable, and entertaining. These are low priority concerns for social scientists producing interaction data tapes. What they exhibit at scholarly meetings as part of a talk, however, often shows signs that a data segment is selected for its entertainment value as well as its cogency in supporting an argument.

4. In the interest of making their films more interesting and watchable, direct cinema filmmakers attempt to obtain good shots, good sound, make their filming and editing evidently skillful and invisible, and avoid including the filmmakers' activities within the frame. Social scientists producing ideal interaction data tapes also aim for all these qualities, though they are of less importance. Good shots and good sound are aimed for because they make the materials more accessible to analysis (Bottorff, 1994; Goodwin, 1993).

THE FILMMAKERS' WORK I: PREPRODUCTION— THE CINEMATIC FIELD WORK OF MAKING THE ARRANGEMENTS AND PREPARING THE SITE

Preproduction Agreement With the Participants

In direct cinema, the filmmaker typically establishes a set of ground rules in a contract with the subjects of the film, which does much of the work of an informed consent form for contemporary social scientists (see Rosenthal, 2002, pp. 271–273).[8] In the case of *AMS* and the other films in the corporation series, Hammond says that, "the arrangement we made with them didn't give them any right to veto. The agreement was that we wouldn't use anything in the films which was confidential in the sense that it could be useful to their competitors—financial information and things of that kind (see Appendix 12.1; Appendix 12.2, Question 19).

Preproduction Research: Letting Natural Events Occur Naturally

Another understanding among direct cinema filmmakers is that the director and cameraperson do "no prompting, directing, or interviewing [of] ... the subject" (Rosenthal, 2002, p. 266).[9] Hammond attempted to assure himself that he was getting footage of naturally occurring events which were little influenced by the presence of his film crew. Needing to determine how interesting the corporation would be and how accessible it would be to the filming he had in mind, he spent several months scouting out the locations and activities within the Steinberg Corporation, looking for sites and activities that

> would render well on film, and which also would typify the Corporation in an interesting way. I also wanted to know the place sufficiently well that [I could recognize] ... the normal operations ... Then suddenly one Thursday afternoon I simply announced that I was going to do some shooting the next morning [when] ... they held their top management meeting. [This is the first meeting we see in *AMS*]. My assumption was that if any area was going to be sensitive that was the area. But when I went in Friday morning with a crew the meeting proceeded just like all the meetings I'd attended. So I knew that the prospects were very good that I was going to get the real genuine article on film. (Appendix 12.1)

While scouting out locations, the filmmaker also spends time with the participants to build their belief that the filmmaker is interested in them, concerned for them, and is unlikely to want to harm them (cf. Rosenthal, 2002, p. 189). That is, he or she builds rapport.

Preproduction: Arranging the Sets

Direct cinema filmmakers film participants engaged in actions and conversation in the places where these activities occur naturally. In the boardroom in Montreal, the camera is "seated" at the table. At Palomino, it is on a rolling tripod and the soundman carries his sound recorder on a shoulder strap, which permits him to move around the room, placing his microphone where it is needed at the moment. The filmmaker's crew and equipment require space in those surroundings that is often occupied by something else requiring that a space be "constructed." In *AMS*, the construction is minimal involving some rearrangement of furniture to accommodate the camera with tripod and sound equipment and to make paths through which the soundman and camera on a rolling tripod could move. Also out of our view are small overhead lights that Hammond's crew brought in and set up (Appendix 12.2). These arrangements are all but invisible within the film.

Preproduction for Filmmakers and Social Scientists

In a number of respects, the early stages of filmmaking and of preparing to make a data tape are similar. The filmmaker's contract with the subjects of the film parallels a social scientist's informed consent form. Typically, the participants do not have veto rights over the final film and its contents, and this is also the typical case for the social scientists' interaction data tapes. While scouting out the scenes, the filmmaker builds rapport with the participants. In the analysis of interaction that relies on data tapes, the relationship between participant and investigator is often unreported. However, Corsaro (1982) noted that the background information gathered as well as relationships formed while in the field not only influences research objectives but also the choice of audiovisual recordings generated in later phases of the research. Bottorff (1994) and DuFon (2002) noted the risks that are run in using video recordings as data in the "absence of contextual data beyond what is recorded" (Bottorff, 1994, p. 247). On the other hand, some conversation analysts argue that ethnographic knowledge of context can be a troublesome resource when invoked in the analysis of interaction data tapes (Schegloff, 1991, 1992).

Both social scientists collecting interaction data tapes and direct cinema filmmakers do not prompt or direct their subjects and do film them in the naturally occurring conversations and actions in which these activities occur naturally. Both make minimal changes to these sites in order to provide space for their work, and in both cases these arrangements are made invisible within the film. Because social scientists often employ smaller crews, smaller cameras, and do not use mikes on booms, they are somewhat less intrusive than filmmakers, but both filmmakers and social scientists share the aim of being nonintrusive.

THE FILMMAKERS' WORK II: PRODUCTION— DOING THE FILMING AND THE SOUND RECORDING

With only a loose notion of what topics and characters the finished film will include, the director instructs the cameraperson before and during the filming to obtain shots of selected matters and particular characters. He or she also gives standing orders to film such matters as conflicts, emotional displays, and other outbursts whenever they occur. In the case of *AMS*, this would have included discussions of the family, the issue of nepotism, succession, the characters of Mr. Sam and several other executives, and contextual matters that could be used to frame a "chapter" within the film, for example, an evening dinner and the bridge game (*see* Appendix 12.2; Rosenthal, 2002, pp. 193–196 and pp. 268–270). The director and cameraperson must anticipate where the storyable action within a setting will happen: Which day, which hour, which room or small space (and within a specific meeting, which minutes, which part of the room, and which speakers) will, in the-story-discovered-in-the-editing, turn out to be the object of shots that were needed. In this search for shots that will give them good coverage, they shoot from 10 to 60 minutes of film for every minute that will be shown in the final film.[10]

Filming in direct cinema, like other documentary forms, aims at producing high-quality, well-framed, well-lighted, smooth shots whenever possible, with clear sound at every point. As mentioned before, filmmakers regard these as important features in making the film watchable over its course; they are important in making a film with the capacity to sustain the audience's interest and attention. In seeking good smooth shots, camerapersons avoid including distracting microphones within the frame and avoid including any other thing that would obstruct the audience's view of the subject.

At the meeting at corporate headquarters (1–206) the single cameraman (see Appendix 12.2, Question 14) is, in effect, sitting at the table and can get a clear shot of almost everyone at the meeting. At Palomino, the single cameraman scoots around behind the speakers with the camera on a wheeled tripod. The full crew consisted of Hammond as director, the camerman, his assistant, and the soundman. They aimed for minimal interference in keeping with the style of direct cinema filmmaking (see Appendix 12.2, Question 14).

In the ideal case, all the activities of the crewmembers, including the cameraman and soundman, are invisible. Furthermore, the editing, which will be discussed in the next section, is also invisible. Hammond and his editor use very little footage that shows the crew moving around, although filming (not necessarily using) some footage showing the crew is unavoidable. Furthermore, the editor and director may decide that including a filmed moment that shows a crew person is a better choice than missing that moment altogether.[11] In *AMS*, there are occasions in which the soundperson is caught on camera, usually out of focus, for example, in the background (965).[12]

There are additional production concerns that are managed by the crew on location. The cameraman has to stop filming to reload the camera or quickly change the film magazine, typically every 10 to 15 minutes if filming with a continuously running camera. Hammond says that for *AMS*, the interval was 10 minutes—which is the exact amount of a 400´ film magazine—and that the camera was running continuously (see Appendix 12.2). Changing the film magazine produces unavoidable gaps in the film record of 10 to 15 seconds if a magazine is being used and 60 seconds or more if film has to be threaded. In direct cinema, the filmmaker does not typically ask the participants to stop their activity while a new magazine is loaded, and, therefore, part of the action is missed.

The audio recorder for the film is separate from the camera and is typically capable of longer recording times than is a standard film magazine load. With only one camera, continuity of the event for the filmmaker is provided by a continuous audio recording. Consider that with only one camera, the cameraman must get cutaways (shots other than the speaking subject, e.g., an apparent listening response) while the speaking is going on and being audio recorded. The cameraman will have the standing task of obtaining the cutaways. He or she is supposed to make the judgment that the current speaker is not being quite as interesting as the others so that he or she can take this moment to turn toward getting 5 to 10 seconds of, for example, Mr. Sam listening, 5 to 10 seconds of another speaker listening, of still another lighting his pipe, and 5 to 10 seconds of an ashtray filling. Turning away to obtain these shots means that shots of the current speaker, while he or she is speaking, are briefly missed. Furthermore, in single camera filming, whenever the edited footage does not show panning of the surroundings between the current speaker and the listener, some transitional moments have been removed in the shooting or editing, that is, there is an unavoidable gap in the visual record. Without the transitional pan, the viewer cannot know if the shots of listening are shots of a person listening to what the viewer hears.

In *AMS*, there are occasions in which an apparently important topic is voiced off camera and then the cameraman rushes to catch the new speaker. Because the camera is moving, and the cameraman is trying to locate the speaker in the viewfinder, the picture loses focus and then comes back into focus. Prior to the development of direct cinema, scenes that were out of focus because of a fast pan to catch a new speaker were deleted from the final cut of the film in order to make the film appear seamless. But within direct cinema style of documentary filmmaking, an occasional out-of-focus shot is thought to emphasize the film's appearance of reality.[13] Direct cinema filmmakers try to avoid including in the finished film shots with a rapid zoom or pan with the camera out of focus, but if the content of the shot is what they are looking for, they do not feel it is bad craftsmanship or bad art to leave it in.[14]

In *AMS*, the camera is rarely unsteady or out of focus, and fast zoom or pan shots are not shown. With many hours of film available,

Hammond and his editor had an abundance of material that permitted much cutting and the use of mostly high-quality images. Good shots are also well composed with standard framing and standard composition, and this shows clearly in *AMS*. In well-made direct cinema films, the composition is always active—the cameraperson continuously seeks to achieve a well-framed and composed shot in which the eyes of the principal subject are at the lower margin of the upper third of the frame and the subject's head or head and torso occupy the right or left two thirds of the frame. A conventionally composed and framed shot is meant to be easy to watch. The audience is accustomed to watching shots in fiction and nonfiction films framed and composed in this way: The audience finds it easy to locate the focal point of the shot (where the filmmakers intend for them to be looking) through this practiced way of viewing. In a film like *AMS*, which portrays conversations that are sometimes hard to follow, the good, usable, well-framed images and sound that Hammond was able to get are even more important than usual because they help sustain the audience's interest.

Production Work for Documentaries and Interaction Data Tapes

Direct cinema filmmakers typically shoot selected parts of an event. In doing so, they shoot from 10 to 60 minutes of film for every minute that will be shown in the final film. Aiming at producing high-quality, well-composed, smooth shots that render all the activities of the crew invisible, their techniques produce unavoidable gaps in the filmed record—a filmed record that is selective at several different levels.

Social scientists studying interaction almost always employ video camcorders with much less costly videotape that can record for an hour or more and can be reloaded quickly so recording the full extent of an event is done with few or no short gaps. Whatever appears on the tape is subject to analysis (if it can be recognized), not just those parts that are of broadcast quality. Shots that include all the participants are much preferred to close-ups of a speaker or listener, and cutaways, if done at all, are accomplished by panning to a listener or next speaker while retaining the transitional content (Goodwin, 1993).

THE FILMMAKERS' WORK III: POSTPRODUCTION— EDITING AND NARRATIVE STRUCTURE

Some General Understandings and Rules About Fair and Appropriate Editing

Despite all their efforts to obtain the footage that they need while filming, direct cinema filmmakers depend on finding the story in the editing:

Sometimes in documentaries and in feature fiction films, no coherent film can be found and the project is abandoned. Hammond says, "The shape of the material is found in the cutting room. 'Writing' this kind of film is not one stage of the process, but the whole process, from choosing what to shoot, through editing the footage, to actually writing the narration—if there is one" (Appendix 12.2, Question 6; see also Rosenthal, 2002, pp. 202–203 & 270–271).

In documentary films, the director and editor work closely together to pull sound bites (make selections of segments) from the raw footage or rushes. Hammond says he "hardly left the editor's side" (Appendix 12.2, Question 24). While the director and editor try to find a place for the most compelling interactions and compelling aspects of interactions that fit into the developing story, less compelling interactions are left out, especially if they are within shots that lack good footage or good audio and are included only if they increase the coherence of the story.

Although direct cinema filmmakers generally leave pieces of the raw footage (sound bites) in the sequence that occurred naturally, it is not uncommon to move things around when that is deemed necessary. Hammond says that for *AMS*, he can't be sure about the editing of sequences more than 30 years after the work was done, but as he recalls it, the pieces of *AMS* are presented in their natural historical sequence. However, he says "I certainly wouldn't hesitate to edit out of sequence, if it told a better and clearer story, and didn't falsify, but I don't think that happened here" (Appendix 12.2, Question 27). Direct cinema filmmakers and other documentarians regard it as proper to join any piece of footage to any next piece as long as it fits and does not grossly misrepresent the views of the speakers.

Increasing the coherence and enhancing the pace of a set of sound bites is one very likely ground for moving sound bites out of sequence. For the filmmaker, *the gist* of an issue, for example, of nepotism and *the gist* of what was said about it (*as the filmmaker understood the gist of the issue*) is presented as faithfully in the film as the coherently arranged sound bites permit. The direct cinema documentary filmmaker, and most other documentary filmmakers, see presenting the gist of an event or conversation as they understand it as meeting their obligation to the truth (Nichols, 1991, 2001; Plantinga, 1997; Vaughan, 1992; Winston, 1993).

Because the soundtrack is independent from the visual image, a scene can be constructed with one continuous intact segment of soundtrack with the visual image alternating between the face of the speaker speaking and the faces of apparent listeners. Whenever the visual image is not that of the speaker, the editor has the opportunity to make cuts in the soundtrack. There are several ways to accomplish such a cut so that it sounds like continuous talk to the audience, when it really isn't. For example, in *AMS*, there are many opportunities provided by the audible shuffling of paper (e.g., 242). The editor or sound mixer can mix the sound of shuffling paper right over a pause (sometimes a pause created by the editor) occurring after the apparent completion of an utterance. At that point, the editor can introduce any statement that coherently fits in and sounds like a beginning. It is common practice to lay down a whole track consisting exclusively of ambient sound, for example, people sitting at a table, shuffling paper, or other background noise. This track of ambient sound can be brought up in volume to mask the hearability of a hard cut of a segment of a conversation being removed and another inserted.[15]

AMS contains many cutaways to someone listening, to someone smoking, to someone looking, to someone writing. The initial meeting at corporate headquarters (1–200) was allocated 8 minutes and 45 seconds of screen time. This segment contains five cutaways and eight other cuts.[16] The first cutaway occurs 38 seconds into the first meeting at (8). Arnold S. is speaking and there is a cutaway to other executives in the room, apparently listening. In 2 seconds, there is a cutaway to other executives in the room and then a cutback to the face of Arnold S., still speaking. Each of the 13 cutaways and other cuts offer the editor the opportunity to edit the soundtrack without drawing attention to the cut. A cut made in the soundtrack when a continuous uninterrupted shot shows the face of the speaker who is speaking would be obvious to the audience and would degrade the film. The aim is *invisible editing* and doing invisible editing well is a mark of the editor's skills and artistry. This kind of editing enables the viewers to have the impression that they are watching a continuous live event. Even though the viewers know that it is edited (because they are seeing, in the case of *AMS*, several full days of meeting presented in just over 1 hour), they do experience the continuity of a live event.

We should consider the ambiguity of any particular sequence within the film as a record of what happened at the meetings in light of the art of invisible editing. Dai Vaughan, a direct cinema style documentary filmmaker, examines the difficulties posed for close interpretation by the juxtaposition of two shots that are formally identical to those found in *AMS*. In *AMS*, there are scores of juxtaposed shots where the first shot shows a corporate officer speaking and then there is a cut to the face of an apparent listener while we still hear the speaker off camera (e.g., 267). Vaughan (1992) says of such juxtapositions that:

This simple cut opens up a range of possibilities.

1. The sound continuity is genuine and the second shot is also genuinely synchronous, i.e., [if it is synchronous, it must be] taken with another camera.

2. The sound continuity is genuine, but the second shot is a 'cut-away' taken from a similar context elsewhere in the rushes [or un-cut footage].
3. Both shots are synchronous, but taken with one camera; and there is a concealed cut [in the sound track] (perhaps not *exactly* match-ing the picture cut).
4. The second shot is a cutaway designed to conceal the fact that the sound is discontinuous.
5. The cutaway is taken from a *dissimilar* context elsewhere in the rushes [raw, unedited footage]. (p. 106)

Only the first alternative can be considered a faithful record of the filmed event, but this requires two cameras, and *AMS* was filmed with only one camera. The second alternative is troublesome for any analyst who wants to make something of the nonverbal response of listeners as true responses. For any analyst who makes something of the internal sequence of utterances within a turn at talk (as in conversation analy-sis), the third and fourth alternatives are so troublesome as to destroy the analyst's grasp of the object if he or she sees the possibilities of miss-ing, rearranged, or exchanged constituents within the sequence. The fifth alternative (along with the second, third, and fourth) disorders any analysis that depends on relating the immediate nonverbal response of others to the action that is underway, for example, an analysis like that of Birdwhistell (1970). In a well-edited film like *AMS*, the five possibili-ties are exceedingly difficult to identify, and, even when a cut in the sound track is identified, it is not possible to distinguish among the third alternative (both shots are synchronous, but taken with one camera; and there is a relatively short concealed cut in the sound track), the fourth (the second shot is a cutaway designed to conceal the fact that the sound track has been cut and spliced, removing a substantial segment of the soundtrack), and the fifth (the cutaway is taken from a *dissimilar* context elsewhere in the raw, unedited footage); and note here that the fifth alternative can also hide cuts in the sound track of various sorts.

Every cutaway loses the visual image that is filmed simultaneously with the audio track and every cutaway can mask cuts (as removals) and hidden crypto-fictional rejoinings in sound, visual image, or both.[17] The prospect is that what is then seen and heard on the film is crypto-fictional in this way: Utterance A occurs, followed by Utterance B and then Utterance C. Utterance C is analyzable as a comment on and an analysis of Utterance B. If Utterance B is removed from the sequence, Utterance C then may become a comment on Utterance A, thereby alter-ing the in-vivo sense of both Utterance A and Utterance C. As will be ex-plained in the following summary section, Utterance A and Utterance B function as constituents of a gestalt contexture.

Postproduction in Documentaries and Interaction Data Tapes

Direct cinema filmmakers count on finding the story in the editing. The aim of increasing the coherence and enhancing the pace of a set of sound bites sometimes requires moving sound bites out of sequence. As mentioned previously, the direct cinema documentary filmmaker and most other documentary filmmakers see presenting the gist of an event or conversation as they understand it as meeting their obligation to the truth, and, in doing this, it is proper to join any piece of footage to any next piece as long as it fits and does not grossly misrepresent the views of the speakers.

Cutaways cover cuts in the sound track. Whenever the visual image is not that of the speaker, the editor has the opportunity to make cuts in the soundtrack. A cut in the soundtrack that is not audibly recognizable may be made underneath the visual images of the cutaway. *Invisible editing* enables the viewers to have the impression that they are watching a continuous event when they only see moments of it. The achievements of editing pose severe difficulties for the rigorous analysis of talk or action. Whenever two or more visually discontinuous shots are presented, the techniques of invisible editing prevent the viewer from recognizing that audio or visual materials have been omitted or that two phases of apparently the same action are in actuality the initial phase of one concrete action and the terminal phase of another, and so forth. Every cutaway loses the visual image that is filmed simultaneously with the audio track and every cutaway can mask cuts (as removals) and cryptofictional rejoinings in sound, visual image, or both.

The phases of action or conversation that are pictured in a sequence of sound bites have the continuity, pace, sequence, and motivation (in the sense of one thing leading to another) that they do because the sense of each pictured phase is reciprocally determined by its relationship to the other phases within the sequence in which they are presented. A change in or omission of any phase can potentially change the sense of every other phase and the meaning of the whole. Garfinkel (2003) referred to these features of gestalt contextures as Gurwitschian for Gurwitsch's (1964) pioneering respecification of the findings of gestalt psychology. Only loosely referred to by speaking of context and holism, gestalt contextures have been a recurrent interest in ethnomethodological work (Garfinkel, 2003; Garfinkel & Wieder, 1993; Lynch, 1993). By omitting and rearranging the segments of film and sound, the editor makes the picturing crypto-fictional.

An ideal interaction data tape is filmed for the analysis that can be done on it (Grimshaw, 1982; for specific concerns about retaining natural temporal sequences for data tapes, see Bottorff, 1994; Corsaro, 1982; and DuFon, 2002). The adequacy of an analysis of interaction does not depend on the data tape's having an interesting story, or that its images, sounds, and pace prompt the attention of an audience. For the purposes of analysis, an interaction data tape should not be edited (Bottorff, 1994; Corsaro, 1982; DuFon, 2002; Grimshaw, 1982).[18]

As a prelude to editing, direct cinema filmmakers typically take some initial systematic steps in organizing their work.

Developing a Narrative Structure or Storyline: Step 1, Logging. It is very common to have an assistant log all footage, shot by shot, or scene by scene, and for the director or editor to construct on paper an editing script or editing plan with a storyline or narrative structure before editing begins.[19] After these steps, the editor begins to pull particular sound bites, that is, select segments from the raw footage—the rushes.

Developing a Narrative Structure or Storyline: Step 2. In searching for the best sound bites, the editor and director look for a developable dramatic structure in the raw footage, and then they look for smooth transitions between all the pieces they selected. Documentary filmmakers understand that there are two things that create interest: characters and conflict (cf. Rosenthal, 2002, p. 203).

Hammond expresses this as an interest in character and story:

> I was always equally interested in both story and character, with maybe a slight edge to story. The research period in documentary is like the casting process in fiction film: you are looking for people who are going to be interesting on screen, so that you can tell an interesting story through them. Sam Steinberg cast himself as soon as I met him, and the Steinberg's Little Theatre Company wasn't far behind. One thinks about both story and character from the beginning. (Appendix 12.2, Question 26)

Filmmakers attempt to develop a narrative structure with a rise and fall of tension that typically happens multiple times (cf. Rosenthal, 2002, p. 203; Nelms, 1969, pp. 234–251). Hammond says, "I knew the central issues were succession and nepotism [and they were] ... also most likely to be accessible to the audience" (Appendix 12.2, Question 10). There is evident conflict over both these issues.

Developing a narrative structure with a rise and fall of tension several times requires a story line that can be segmented. Hammond says:

> I needed material to break the film up into three parts, to give the viewer some relief, so I shot anything that might serve the purpose. Dinner made parts one and two more digestible, and to allow me to bridge parts two and three, the good Lord provided me with a game of ... It wasn't set up. It was obvious what the bridging narration needed [to] say, but to get it right, I must have read a bridge book, because I don't play the game (I'm telling you secrets.). (Appendix 12.2, Question 23)

Making–Finding Structure and Making Transitions.   Mr. Sam's rather decisive remarks that can be heard as ending the discussion of a particular topic are employed as they are in order to construct the dramatic structure, and this would undermine an analysis that depended on their placement. Hammond notes that

> discussions didn't necessarily close when they do in the film, but when in editing we felt the subject had been covered and we had a good closing point [we found a way to end the discussion there]. Mind you, if Sam indicated that a discussion was over, it was over. Just as, when he decided, at the screening of the films for the Exec Cttee, that the films were good, it was agreed that the films were good. (Appendix 12.2, Question 23)

Mr. Sam, as a character in the film, is exceedingly useful for constructing a dramatic or narrative structure because, no matter what he says or how he conducts himself, the audience already knows he has the most power in these meetings and owns the lion's share of the company and, as its founder, owns its traditions as well.

A film constructed in this way gives the audience a narratively structured experience that they may not be quite conscious of while watching the film—namely that the film has "chapters" within it, each one of which has parts that lead to a conclusion doing so at a planned-for tempo and pace (cf. Rosenthal, 2002, pp. 114–117 & pp. 209–211). Such an organization makes the film followable and, retrospectively, understandable as consisting of one thing leading to another. The way that Mr. Sam's remarks are used in the construction of the film is an important constituent of this structure.[20]

The filmmaker understands that what keeps the viewer watching is the drama of the event. Dramatic structure is built though many devices, for example, in *AMS*, these include the voice-over narrative mentioning titles, relationships, and the anticipation of Mr. Sam's retirement.[21]

The filmmaker is faced with a multitude of narrative themes, and these must be balanced with the need to be sparse in the allotment of screen time to any particular topic or event—the latter in order to maintain the audience's attention. A passage from Vaughan (1992) displays these challenges and is particularly instructive for us because it so precisely analyzes the situation of the editor of *AMS* and any other direct cinema documentary containing long and dense segments of interaction:

> Consider another example of what occurs in the editing process: ... The event is an argument between two people in a small office. The argument lasts for an hour and a half, out of which the camera is running for approximately fifty minutes, panning between the two people and occasionally

shifting position to favour one or the other. The attitude of the characters emerges only slowly, with much repetition of key points ... The relevance of this sequence to the theme of the film does not justify allowing it more than about twelve minutes of screen time ... [In *AMS* it would be likely to be allotted even less screen time.] The problems confronted by the editor therefore present themselves in the form of such questions [questions nearly identical to those inevitably faced by the editor and director of *AMS*] as: 'Does this sequence, whilst avoiding undue repetition, repro- duce the spiral nature of the interaction? Does it do justice to both posi- tions ... Does it respect the integrity of each participant, in the sense of not allowing a change of emotional state to appear unmotivated ... or even more rational—than that which it took in the actual debate?' And beneath these, of course, lie more fundamental questions. Are we trying to be fair to the people as individuals or to their strategies, or to the insti- tution of whose ethos they are the temporary embodiment? Are we seek- ing to demonstrate the arguments used or to clarify the actual intellectual positions that these partly express but partly mask? Is the tedium of the event's repetitiousness—a quality it may possess only for the observer uncommitted to either viewpoint—something which should be retained or avoided? Such things need to be asked not just in a liberal spirit of impartiality, but in an attempt to ground the film's putative meanings— even, where appropriate, its polemic—in a correct apprehension of the world. (pp. 107–108)

Not all of these concerns can be simultaneously respected: In any par- ticular case, it may not be possible to do justice to both positions, respect the integrity of each participant, show changes in the emotional states, and cut the 50 minutes of footage that displays all of this to 12 minutes of screen time. Irremediable troubles are posed for the analysis of inter- action-in-films, because the analyst may never know whether or not the filmmaker cut exactly that footage needed to adequately display the analyst's phenomenon or the footage that was needed to substantiate or to falsify the analyst's argument, and all this can happen without the analyst's awareness.

Dramatic Structure and the Ideal Interaction Data Tape

The editor and director look for a developable dramatic structure in the raw footage. They attempt to develop a narrative structure with a rise and fall of tension that typically happens multiple times and this re- quires a story line that can be segmented into "chapters" that lead to a conclusion. Some features of the characters, their views, and their speech and action are sacrificed in assembling sound bites drawn from an hour of footage to make a 10-minute segment of screen time. An analysis of interaction based on such films is problematic because the analyst may never know whether or not the episodes of interaction are *crypto-fictional* (being created out of discontinuous fragments from multiple events) and whether or not the filmmaker cut exactly that footage needed for the analyst's argument.

An ideal, pure data tape is filmed for the analysis that can be done on it. No story structure is assembled from selected segments of the tape or film. The adequacy of interactional analysis does not depend on the data tape's having an interesting story with a dramatic structure having rises and falls in tension. For the purposes of analysis, an edited tape may obscure the phenomena under study and, therefore, should not be used for analysis (Bottorff, 1994; Corsaro, 1982; DuFon, 2002; Grimshaw, 1982).

CONCLUSION

Our concern has been with how a well-made documentary film differs from an ideal data tape, how it is produced, and what consequences the difference has for the argument of any analyst who does not take these issues into account. One of our tasks has been to describe the standards and practices of the direct cinema film community and to show the consequences of these standards and practices for completed films, particularly their consequences for any effort to treat the observational filmmaker's product as *factual data* in the sense of *fact* and *data* meant by social scientists and particularly communication scholars studying interaction.

We understand the ideal interaction data tape in terms of the methodological standards that govern its production. We must ask what the parallel standards are for the production of observational or direct cinema films. Only in that way can we say how the direct cinema film is and is not comparable to the ideal interaction data tape.

For communities of filmmakers, what counts as a factual film and what about a film is factual? Consider that this question is comparable to asking what do communities of newspaper reporters count as a factual story. Fishman (1980) extended Wieder's (1965) formulation of what counts as fact from the standpoint of newspaper reporters. "Reporters are held accountable by editors, fellow reporters, and newspaper readers that what they write is ... factually correct" (Fishman, 1980, p. 85). "The fundamental principle of news fact ... [is that] *something is so because somebody says it* [but] ... it must be somebody in a position to know what they say, somebody entitled to know what they say ... [In short, the factual is a quotation from a] competent knower or observer" (pp. 92–93) and typically this is somebody who holds a position within a government, governmental agency, or some other recognized organization. In their concern for the facticity of a news story, editors and other reporters ask what is being quoted or paraphrased and who it is that is being quoted. If the reporter has truly quoted the proper source, the story is, within the newspaper community, factual. The transcendent claims that are attributed to sources is not at issue in this judgment, although they may provide the grounds for further inquiry, a matter also developed by Fishman.

What do direct cinema filmmakers promise? They promise that their films consist of sound bites that were filmed of the real people portrayed in them doing real things in the real setting in which they do them. These participants were not prompted, instructed, or directed. The sound bites fairly represent the gist of what they were doing and saying. The filmmaker's obligation to truth and fairness has been honored as long as the filmmaker is faithful to his or her understanding of the gist of the event or interaction depicted. Within that limitation, splicing any segment of film or soundtrack to any other segment of film or soundtrack is proper. The direct cinema documentary filmmaker artfully employs a patchwork of footage (discontinuous "samplings") of fragments of the sounds and images of a real event to represent that event.

The direct cinema or observational filmmaker makes no promise that his or her film is a literal record of these doings and sayings. The film was not assembled with an eye to sustaining social scientific claims that might be formulated about it. Indeed, when we asked Hammond about the suitability of using the film *Corporation: After Mr. Sam* for conversation analysis and other microanalysis of the interactions represented in the film, he said, "I think it would be useless, scientifically, for that. Too much cutting and trimming and shifting has gone on" (Appendix 12.2, Question 29). Direct cinema or observational films including *AMS* do not warrant claims about what goes on in the interactions they picture.

If the analyst has done independent research on the phenomena pictured in a direct cinema or observational film and finds that what the analyst already knows is pictured there, then it is appropriate to employ the film illustratively as a vivid, dramatic, but indefinite approximation of the analyst's phenomena. Obviously this would satisfy the needs and standards of many pedagogic uses. The rushes or raw footage of a trustable filmmaker would be usable as an interaction data tape as long as the analyst knew enough about the circumstances of the filming. Individual sound bites are also potentially useable if they were physically extracted from the context in which they are presented in a film. They would need to be extracted because we cannot know just how fictional the final sequence of sound bites really is: Leaving them within the film and attempting to disattend the sequential context requires a feat of consciousness comparable to grasping simultaneously both alternatives of a gestaltist ambiguous figure, such as the faces or vase in Rubin's vase.

ENDNOTES

1. Professor Mau is an independent media artist who works in film, video, and digital media and teaches courses in filmmaking, documentary production, and cinema theory and criticism in the School of Art at the University of Oklahoma.
2. Ethnomethodology and various forms of phenomenology often begin an investigation by asking what kind of data, phenomena, or experience is this—what are the data as objects in their own right and not as appearance of transcendent things in themselves. What does it consist of, what are its aspects, how was it gathered (if gathering was done), did the gathering and bringing it to our attention require alteration or processing (for removal, for preservation, for transporting it here)? Procedurally, what did the chain of custody (as in the treatment of legal evidence) consist of? Did it have to be "worked on" to display its features? There is likely more to the list than this. This is the kind of question we ask when we say, regarding the film *AMS*, "How did the film get done and what kind of data is this?"
3. These risks include those engendered by differences in focus. For example, the original ethnographer may have focused on a ritual performed at the beginning of a gathering, whereas the secondary analyst is concerned with the status of the persons who attended. The described gathering might have been a perfect example of ritual in such gatherings, but a poor example of attendance at such gatherings. Or the ethnographer may have deliberately obscured the status of those in attendance in the interest of preserving the anonymity of their identities in a way that was somewhat misleading when we ask questions about their status. It is a commonplace of ethnographic reportage that ethnographers deliberately mask, cover over, misdirect, and fictionalize their accounts to protect themselves and their subjects. Attributing a remark to "a staff member" rather than to "the director" is only one device among many that, at the very least, limits the utility of the account for purposes beyond and different from the author's. There is more to these standard reporting practices. A striking collection of them are analyzed by Ken Stoddard (1987).
4. This last risk is more intense, obscure, and obscuring when the filmmaker and audience are competent members of one culture and the film's subjects enact the competencies of another cultu re.
5. Hammond says that it was some of the films and filmmakers of the NFB's Unit B that attracted him to it. (For specifics, see Appendix 12.2.)
6. In contrast to observational or direct cinema documentary filmmaking, *reflexive documentary filmmaking* deliberately places the filmmakers and their interactions with the native participants within the frame, thereby "attemp[ting] to invert the familiar system of looking" (Pinney, 1992, p. 38). For reflexive filmmaking, also see Nichols (1991, pp. 56–75). Nichols (2001) called that form of filmmaking that focuses on the encounter between participant and filmmaker the participatory mode (pp. 115–124).
7. Even Fredrick Wiseman, one of the best known and most naturalistic of the direct cinema filmmakers, insisted that there is no way to provide the audience with the literal experience of the person who was actually in the filmed scene. See Vaughan (1992), Nichols (1991), Plantinga (1997), and Winston (1993) for discussions of Wiseman's views on this.
8. The contract is likely to define when shooting may occur, whether or not the filmmaker may do prelighting, that is, may set up lights that will remain in

place for the duration of the shooting, and the contract is likely to define where filming may take place and topics and places that are off limits. When the film will be released is also articulated in the contract. Although subjects would not be likely to have veto rights, the direct cinema filmmaker of the late 1960s attempted to avoid conflict with the subjects over what had been included in the film, unlike some contemporary documentary filmmakers such as Michael Moore. Nonetheless, any filmmaker is likely to risk offending his subjects as displays of emotion and interpersonal conflict are likely to be included in a film because they tend to add interest. Exposing the subjects' emotions and interpersonal conflicts are also likely to make the subjects feel vulnerable. One of the Steinberg executives took sharp exception to some of the content of the corporation series films (see Appendix 12.1).

9. Although the filmmaker would not instruct the subjects concerning their actions, he or she might offer suggestions or instructions about disregarding the camera, the soundman, and other crew members. When subjects look steadily at the camera, they create a relationship with the camera or audience that looks like an interview, breaking the direct cinema mode.

10. The attempt to obtain coverage parallels the plight of ethnographers taking field notes. Ethnographers can, however, do interviews after the fact. Ethnographers, too, collect many pages of field notes that play no part in their final reports.

11. In a fiction film, showing an obvious crew member rearranges the perceptual object witnessed on the screen and undercuts its sense because it destroys the audience's suspension of disbelief. See Schutz's (1967) essay, "On Multiple Realities." Some lesser anomalies are permitted when the footage is crucial and unique (see IMDB.com "trivia" and "goofs" for John Frankenheimer's The Manchurian Candidate, 1962).

12. Most of our observations are based on very specific parts of the film. The reader who wishes to see for him- or herself just what we are describing should turn to the film itself, using the transcript furnished in this volume as a guide to locating the relevant parts of the film. The film is available from the National Film Board of Canada (1-800-267-7710; http://www.nfb.ca).

13. It becomes a sign of the real, in Plantinga's sense (1997, p. 16), an index of the real and a conventional characteristic of documentary films that cues the audience to see that this is a real, live event.

14. In the 1960s, cinema vérité (an evolving form of direct cinema) had a lot of roving camera, and some out-of-focus moving shots were seen by the filmmakers as adding to the film's credibility, a sign that this was a film of a live event. The audience saw that the shot was not set up in advance because the camera was not focused. The rapid pan and out-of-focus shot did give the audience a certain feeling of chaos. Like the cameraman, the audience did not know what was happening, just as they would experience it had they been there.

15. Because the audience hears this ambient sound that is actually recorded on a separate track, it will not notice the sharp cutoff of a squeaking sound when someone made their chair squeak right in the middle of a cut, and the squeaking sound is not carried over into the next part.

16. The 5 cutaways occur at (8, 9–10, 19, 76, 185). The 2 cutbacks occur at (11) and (78), while there is a cutwide, cut to a wide shot in (185) after the cutaway in the same line, and there is a cut-in to a closeup at (197). There are 4 very smooth hard cuts between (42 and 43), at (47), (59), and in the middle of (67).

17. In fiction films, cutaways offer many opportunities for magic and mischief, for example, swapping out an actor for a stuntman or manikin in dangerous action scenes. Directors sometimes attempt to reassure viewers who take notice of cutaways throughout a scene by employing long continuous shots with no internal editing in order to overcome the possibilities offered by cutaways that are "obvious upon reflection" (see director's commentary in John Herzfeld's, 2001, feature film, *Fifteen Minutes*).

18. There are occasions in which the soundtrack may be electronically enhanced but that is understood as bringing out the sounds that would have been heard by those actually present.

19. The director may be directly involved in every stage of the editing and may even do all the editing himself or herself. All the footage would be logged by the camera crew as the film was shot, by the editor after shooting, or both (Rosenthal, 2002, pp. 194–195 & 201–202). The location of each shot within the rolls of film, its length (e.g., 25 seconds), and its content would be briefly coded or described.

20. In editing the film, the editor and director have the power to leave clues for the audience and to do so in rather covert ways. When audience members look back over the film, they see the evidence of a historical–causal complex in which one thing leads to another. Even if they do not see it coming, they can look back and grasp the steps that led to the ending.

21. If the audience does not already know it, it learns that he is an important person and that prompts the audience to pay attention to him and to what happens to him. The drama is deepened by the revelation of Mr. Sam's impending retirement as president of the corporation. The narrator says that who is going to take his place is not known but it is likely to be one of a small set of identified candidates (252–260) which prompts the audience to watch these four people because the drama-narrative concerns who is going to become president. The voice-over narration also heightens the tension by stating that there are competing interests in the decision and in the related issue of structure (260–266, 274–283). The expositional voice-over part of the film (Nichols, 1991, pp. 34–38) foreshadows the structure of this drama.

APPENDIX 12.1: INTERVIEW WITH ARTHUR HAMMOND

Appendix 12.1 is an interview with Arthur Hammond that was published in the National Film Board of Canada's newsletter, Pot Pourri *(1973).* It is preceded by an introduction by Patricia Thorvaldson, the editor of the newsletter. The original interview was accompanied by responses to the film, both positive and negative. Ms. Thorvaldson mentions these responses in her introduction but we do not reproduce them here because of their limited relevance to our chapter.*

Corporation
A series in controversy

NFB's new film series CORPORATION has just been released. The films document Steinberg Ltd. of Montreal, major retailers, manufacturers, and real estate operators, well known in Quebec and Ontario largely through their chain of supermarkets, one of the four largest chains in Canada.

The series, consisting of six films, is described in the enclosed promotional brochure, part of a national campaign by NFB to make the public aware of the films, and to elicit response from as many sectors of the Canadian population as possible. So far reactions have covered the full spectrum from very good to very bad, and almost everything else in between.

Some of these reactions appear here, as well as an interview with series Director Arthur Hammond, who comments on the series, and reactions to it.

As Mr. Hammond points out, the series was not intended to reinforce any particular point of view, but to stand outside points of view as much as possible in order to grasp the significance of corporations in a much broader sense.

But if the range of opinion so far is any indication it appears that people tend to bring their already set attitudes and opinions to the films, and go away with the same attitudes and opinions. One man calls them PR for Steinbergs, another calls them part of a conspiracy to overthrow the capitalist system, another calls them the same old tired slam against big business.

But what we have here, in front of us for the same time are films which attempt to show the inner workings of a large corporation made by an outsider. They are not films made about the corporation by the

---

*From Corporation *by P. Thorvaldson and A. Hammond, December, 1973,* Pot Pourri, *pp. 2–7. Copyright © 1973 by NFB. Used with permission of the National Film Board of Canada.*

corporation. They are an attempt, whether successful or not, to show objectively what goes on inside a corporation.

Mr. Hammond calls himself a curious observer, likening his films to the Netsilik Eskimo series—a documentary in that tradition, but this time about corporate man. Looked at in that way we can wonder whether the films aren't giving us a look as well at our society and ourselves if we read between the lines. In short, there's a lot more in them than the inner workings of a corporation, and in fact the directions they can take you, and the questions that arise from them are quite endless. For example, why did Sam Steinberg allow the films to be made? Are they, or should they, or can they be objective? What does the fact of the corporation in society say about the people they serve? What does your shopping list consist of? Would you want Sam Steinberg's job? Why do you shop in a supermarket? Why don't you? What's the relationship between supermarkets and television? What comes first, the chicken or the egg?

There's confusion about corporations, but there's confusion about just about everything these days. The people in the Steinberg Corporation themselves are confused about the films. Reflecting the cross section of opinion so far, now they like the films, now they don't. The films appear to be for them, then against them. Judging from the overall reaction it might just be possible that Arthur Hammond has succeeded in making his film series an exploration by a curious observer. But whatever it is, if you've got your eyes and ears open, the possibilities are enormous.

Patricia Thorvaldson [Editor of *Pot Pourri*]

Arthur Hammond, Director

As far as the choice of Steinberg's is concerned, it was first a stroke of good luck.

A few years ago when I worked with Donald Brittain and John Spotton on *Never a Backward Step*, the film about Lord Thompson of Fleet, I realized that we had an incredible opportunity to do an inside look at the Corporation. But at that time we were primarily doing a personality study of Lord Thompson himself so I decided that afterwards I would try to find another Corporation and instead of doing the personality of the guy in charge, try to do the personality of the Corporation. I decided I was looking for a Canadian Company, although I wouldn't really have objected if I'd come up with an American subsidiary. Also I wanted a large corporation and if possible a fairly diversified one.

At first I started very generally thinking about it. Then it happened that I was looking through a book that Peter Newman did some years ago called *Flame of Power*, and there was a chapter in it about the Steinberg brothers. There wasn't very much in it but it drew my attention to the fact that there was a company called Steinbergs that I was aware of locally, which was very suitable from the point of view that many people were superficially familiar with the supermarket, without having any more of an idea than I had about what goes on behind it—the superstructure on which the supermarket stands.

It also seemed to be suitable because it was a family-owned business with Sam Steinberg clearly in charge, and there's an enormous advantage in trying to get permission to film if there's one guy who can say yes or no. I didn't think it was going to be as easy as it turned out to be. I didn't think I was going to be lucky the first time. I initially wrote to Sam Steinberg and told him what I was interested in and suggested that if he would like to see the Thompson film I could screen it for him. He came and saw the film and interestingly, reacted in a way which was parallel to my own thinking. He said he wasn't interested in a personality study, and was most interested in the parts of the Thompson film that had to do with the business. Well, I had already made the decision that this was the way I wanted to go, so that was an encouraging sign. Finally he agreed.

It's very difficult to disentangle why people agree to be filmed. When I went in at the beginning and spoke to Sam Steinberg about the whole project he obviously wanted to know what it was for. I said it was in a very general sense for educational purposes, that very few people had seen corporate operations from the inside, and that I thought it would be a very useful piece of public education.

I think Sam Steinberg is an interesting guy, and he has, I believe, a great sense of social responsibility. He's one of the few people for instance, who has served two terms on the Canada Council. I think he bought the idea because he felt the project would be really useful. But you can't discount the possibility that there might be a little ego involved too. He's built a really big business and he's proud of it, and it's only human that he shouldn't be unwilling to have some sort of record of that.

But anyway, for whatever reason he decided that he would let us film and as a result we've got some very interesting stuff of a kind which I imagine has not been filmed before—the inner workings of a Corporation.

Once I got permission to film, it became a question of my being able to investigate their Corporation further to see just how interesting it was, and how available it really would be for the kind of filming I wanted to do. So I spent several months working my way through the company, spending time not only with Sam Steinberg, but with virtually all aspects of the business, in order to pick out the ones I thought would render well on film, and which also would typify the Corporation in an interesting way. I also wanted to know the place sufficiently well that when I came to film I would know whether anything was changing and whether I was really getting the normal operations as I'd seen them.

Then suddenly one Thursday afternoon I simply announced that I was going to do some shooting the next morning, which was the morning they held their top management meeting. My assumption was that if any area was going to be sensitive that was the area. But when I went in Friday morning with a crew the meeting proceeded just like all the meetings I'd attended. So I knew that prospects were very good that I was going to get the real genuine article on film.

Originally the project was meant to be a 1 hour film for television. Then when I got into it, when I was doing the research and starting the shooting, I realized that there was more than one film there, though I wasn't sure how many or what they were all about. All the shooting was done in 1969 and the films are all done with the original material. I shot 123,600 feet, which is about 57 hours of film.

It all seems like a very long time, four years from the beginning of the project to the end. And it's not entirely over yet. Looking at it now with hindsight the main thing involved became stamina and somehow keeping one's morale up. It's a very demoralizing thing, being involved with one project for so long, but fortunately in this case the material was good enough and interesting enough to hold my interest up to the end.

The Steinbergs' people were very good actually, and very patient. I'm grateful to them for allowing us to do the films. I think it was enlightened of them.

The arrangement we made with them didn't give them any right to veto. The agreement was that we wouldn't use anything in the films which was confidential in the sense that it could be useful to their competitors—financial information and things of that kind. I'd explained also at that time the obvious fact that even if we were making one film it would be about a year before it came out and there would be very little that would still be confidential at the end of a year. There is nothing of that kind in the films anyway. But I said also that they would see the films before anyone else did and showed them the final cutting copy sometime last winter. Steinbergs were the first people to see them, as a matter of courtesy, and also because I wanted to check the accuracy of the commentary and the content. The films were also checked by a department of justice lawyer to be sure there was nothing libelous in them.

When the people at Steinbergs saw the films they seemed quite pleased. There was only one thing they totally objected to and that had already been removed from the original copy on the advice of the lawyer. However, they've subsequently become upset because of a letter from John Paré, a former vice-president of Personnel at Steinbergs, who appears in one of the films. When he heard that the films were finished he was anxious to see them so I arranged for him to screen them one day with a group of American teachers. He liked the films at first but afterwards we joined the group of teachers, got involved in discussion, and it emerged not surprisingly that several of them had different views. In one case, one woman, a Canadian, said she would never shop at Steinbergs again. But when I asked her why, she said it was because she didn't like their meat or cashiers, which indicated it was an opinion she already had quite apart from the films. Then there was a fair amount of discussion and criticism about the way the supermarket was affecting the culture of France (International Operations), and about the film which Paré was principally involved in (Motivation).

A few days after the screening I received a letter from Paré indicating that he had decided the films were biased, manipulated the material, and were the same old attack on big business.... I was frankly very surprised by the letter, so I wrote back and suggested we get together and talk about it, which we did. At that time he backed off in certain areas of his criticism but not in others. He still feels very strongly that the films are not a very fair representation of the Steinberg Company.

But the problem that arose from the letter was that a copy was sent to Steinbergs, and naturally the shit hit the fan. Sam Steinberg was not happy and wanted to discuss Paré's letter with their Board of Directors and wanted to re-screen the films. I've heard little more since then except one indirect indication that they are still a little cool.

There may be a process that people who are filmed go through. I think probably the initial reaction is fascination at seeing yourself on the screen and therefore acceptance of it, which may be followed by a period where you realize that some of your warts may be showing, or that some people may not like you, or whatever. So you have a reaction in which you feel uneasy about it. Then perhaps there's a third stage in which you come to accept it. I think they're going through the second stage right now, but I suspect with some more favorable reactions they will change their minds and the situation will right itself.

But there are going to be negative reactions—inevitably. One of the interesting things about the six films has been the enormous range of reaction. An American teacher of Business Administration criticized at least one of the films as a P. R. Job for big business. He said his students wouldn't sit still and watch it because they were already anti-business and wouldn't want to watch that sort of apology for what big business was doing. Then at the other end of the spectrum, I've had people say the films are revolutionary and will lead to the overthrow of the capitalist system. I think both views are absurd, and what it indicates to me is that people tend to see in the films what they bring to them, what's already in their heads, and the more objective the film the easier it is for them to do it.

I think the truth about the films lies somewhere in the middle—that they are a fairly objective account of the operations and social influence of large corporations. Now what you make of that fact is another matter, and obviously different people make different things of it. You see I wasn't interested in doing a pro or con thesis on the Corporation. I was interested in exploring a world and that's, I guess, the way that documentary interests me. For me it's a very lively and exploratory process. It's like going up the Amazon to see what's there and how the people live up there. That's why, in a way, I compare the films more to the Netsilik Eskimo films than to anything else. They're an observation.

I don't have a specialized background in business and economics, but what I seem to have and what compels me to make this kind of film, I think, is an attitude of curiosity and a wish to explore situations, which is very much related to what is said about sociological attitudes in one chapter of a book called *Invitation to Sociology* by Peter L. Berger. I don't claim to be a sociologist but I think some of the things Berger says about sociologists and their method of operation can be applied to my motives and method of operations as a documentary filmmaker. It's almost controlled voyeurism in a way, which is very allied to the motives of the sociologist, and if I have any equipment for doing this kind of film, it's a sort of sociological attitude towards the subject matter, which would account also for the fact that the films aren't political. Sociology isn't political either. What you do with Sociology is something else.

Now obviously I don't observe a thing absolutely purely. It goes through a certain amount of filtering as it goes through me. I have certain views or preferences about life and the world which are bound to show up at certain times, and I think in the International Operations film it's fairly clear where my sympathies lie as far as the kind of culture involved is concerned.

But that doesn't mean that I don't shop in a supermarket. I accept the technology even though I regret some of the implications of it. I have certain emotional sympathies about a certain way of life and I suppose that's true in the case of the Real Estate film too. It's very largely an objective observation of how they go about their real estate operations, and yet I have certain views and feelings about the kind of cities we live in which are largely formed by that kind of process, and that feeling is apparent in the film.

I really didn't come out of that research or out of that filming with the sense that this Corporation anyway, was screwing the consumer. What that consumer group is saying (The Market) is that it's up to the consumer to a large extent to decide what he or she buys or boycotts, that there still is a certain amount of decision left to people. I wouldn't want to generalize from that to the total market situation, but the interesting thing to me is that the new big flurry about high prices, the recent work of the parliamentary committee on food prices, and the Beryl Plumptree Commission, have come pretty well to the same conclusions—they cannot find a conspiracy. They keep on enraging people by saying there is no conspiracy. They say people can still decide what to buy and what not to buy. But people rise up in their wrath and say, where's the villain? It's very unsatisfactory to people not to have one.

The way I look at it is that the Corporations are part of a whole process of growth and technological development and that kind of process is going to go on. If it becomes very undesirable in certain ways it can be influenced, and if enough people object to farm land being built over, they can bring influence to bear on a government to do something about it. You can actually pass an act of parliament saying that farm land is frozen. It's happening in B.C. now. You have to deal with the total process. Certain overall social decisions have to be taken and only now in certain places are they beginning to be taken.

But the films are only a description of one part of a process. If people then want to go from there and say they don't like that part of the process, and have ideas about what should be done about the process, that's fine. Then the films themselves might be part of another process.

I have my own view about how much films can influence people or events. I believe it's a very limited influence. I think that occasionally a film might cause a specific change, but that's probably fairly rare. I think what may happen more is that films, like other creative work and other information, are part of a total process of information, which may lead to formation of opinion, which may lead to changes. But they're just little drops along the way. And if these films have that effect on some people—fine. But that wasn't my intention. I didn't set out to make films on social change, and if they do it I really can't claim credit for it.

Also, I believe that your view of the films would depend very much on how you reacted to the human beings in the films. I personally find it incredible for example that anyone looking at the film would think of Sam Steinberg as villainous. In fact I can't think of any character in any of the films that way. What is true is that the films do personalize the process of the Corporation. The Corporation in abstract you can have very bad thoughts about, but once you see it's a bunch of guys doing their various things like the rest of us, more or less struggling to make a living, a big one or a small one, that kind of thinking becomes much less easy I would say.

I suppose I have an attitude to the material. Maybe it's an attitude I have to life, and maybe that's a bad handicap, but the fact is that I think life is very complicated. I think society is very complicated. I don't think that the processes we're involved in or the solutions to them are simple.

I suppose if the films do anything, or are successful to my mind, it would be that they would make people realize, or convey to them that the issues are complicated. If the films don't provide clear answers, or point clearly to villains, it's because I don't know what the answers are and I can't identify the villains. So I guess in that sense they're a reflection of my own confusion.

I may have certain prejudices, or preferences which may show at times, but I try not to mistake those for reflections of objective truth. And besides I don't know whether that's a valuable thing for films to do or not. I'll just have to wait and see what use can be made of them by the people who use them, and what they do to the audiences that see them.

One of the interesting things is to discover what other people can see in the material, or get from the material, and one never totally knows or guesses what that will be. I guess it's true in all creative work. It's certainly true in writing poems or books. Sometimes you don't know what you've put into them until people tell you. The person that makes the thing doesn't necessarily know best what it's about. He may know what he intended it to be about, but what it might also be about is something else again.

But there's certainly a big argument about objectivity. There are filmmakers who would say not only do you have no right to make an objective film, but that it's impossible. I obviously don't agree with that. But they'd also go further and say, because you cannot be completely objective, you shouldn't try. You should go all the way and make films which clearly take a point of view, and identify it. I think that's one way of making films, but I think there are many ways. It doesn't appear to be the way I make them.

I suppose if you want to talk about my own prejudices and feelings, it reveals something of the same kind of attitude as appears in the Real Estate film. And I suppose there is a relationship between the film and one I did before about the B.C. Indians, called *This Land*. I have a kind of attitude which comes through in that film I guess, which is very sympathetic to the Indians and their aboriginal land claims because I have a feeling about the country as against the city, I suppose, or a more natural way of life as against the technological way of life. But I suppose if I were to be completely consistent I would say that any of these films in which my attitude or point of view does become clearer, are less success-ful because I shouldn't be influencing the way the audience is reacting to the material at all. But I don't try to be consistent so ...

I also don't feel that the passage of time since the films were made has been very important. You know you can film a subject at any point and within a week or a month or a year some aspects of it are going to be out of date in detail. But, since what the films are really about are general situations and general processes, that really doesn't matter. For example, the International Operations film. It's true that since the time of the shooting, Steinbergs decided that the French operation just wasn't worth the candle—that they couldn't achieve the kind of con-trol of the operation that they wanted at 3,000 miles distance, and they've pulled out.

But from the point of view of the film it doesn't matter at all because what the film is about is in fact the impact of technology on culture. It's about what kind of effect the supermarket has on the social scene. I think all the films generalize in that kind of way. They were intended to generalize. That's why I call it Corporation rather than Steinbergs. It's because I wasn't being particular. And I think that the generalizing character of the film works, and will continue to work.

There's another film about another aspect of the Corporation that I'm just completing now. It should be ready by the end of the fiscal year. It's ninety minutes long and covers a major conference of the Steinberg Corporation held in 1969.

They were going to be talking for three days about problems like pro-fessional management, decision-making, and top management struc-ture, but the focus of the whole thing was the problem of the succession. Sam Steinberg, who had been the dominant influence in the company for fifty years, was retiring and they had to make a decision about who was to succeed him. From a sociological point of view I would like to have shot the whole thing because it was such a unique opportunity to capture an event of enormous fascination. But I had a limited budget so the focus for me was very clearly the succession and the role of the fam-ily and that's what I concentrated on although I shot other material as well which I felt would be relevant to the succession aspect and help to put it all into context.

The film is different from the others in texture. What it consists of ba-sically is the top executives of the Corporation around a table discussing a complex of problems. People take time expressing their ideas so it's paced more slowly than the other films. It's ninety minutes of film in three parts representing the three days of the conference and, unlike the series, the parts are not independent and have to be viewed as one unit.

I think people who see this film will likely have seen at least some of the others, but for those who haven't we'll be introducing Sam and the company at the beginning. And the results of the conference will be mentioned at the end of the film. At the moment the working title is *After Mr. Sam*, though that might conceivably change.

I've been thinking it would be quite interesting to try to do a similar kind of study of a major multi-national Corporation if one could get inside. I've idly toyed with the idea of doing something like that but right now I think I need a change to some other sort of subject. But that is something I might come back to.

APPENDIX 12.2: E-MAIL INTERVIEW WITH ARTHUR HAMMOND, JUNE 15, 2004*

Conducted by Heidi Mau *(her questions are in italics)*

Dear Heidi Mau:

1. *I know that you worked on quite a few films before the Corporation series and "After Mr. Sam"—what was your background before directing films and how did you come into filmmaking with the National Film Board?*

Mostly I had worked in publishing, the major job being editing a series of children's mystery-adventure books for Little, Brown of Canada, of which I also wrote two; and as a freelance writer in radio, television and newspaper book reviewing. At a certain point, I decided to try for full-time work in either CBC television or the National Film Board, and was luck[y] enough to get a short-term contract as a writer with the latter, which lengthened into 22 years in a variety of jobs: directing, producing, studio head, director of English programming.

2. *As you were learning filmmaking or even later, as a director of your own works, was there a community of filmmakers that you interacted with, discussed your ideas with—who would you say were important peers to you at which stages of your career? Other influences?*

The NFB was itself a community of filmmakers of a wonderful and probably unique kind. What had attracted me to it first was some of the films of Unit B: Universe, Glen Gould—On and Off the Record, City of Gold, Paul Tomkowitz, Corral, etc., made by Roman Kroiter, Colin Low, Wolf Koenig, Terry McCartney-Filgate, John Spotton and others, under Tom Daly as producer. These were the first fruits of the new lightweight 16mm cameras and sound equipment, which led to the flowering of observational ("candid") film. Once at the NFB, I worked on a couple of films with Donald Brittain, as researcher on "Memorandum," and co-director on "Never A Backward Step" (which led me on to "Corporation," as the article in "Pot Pourri" explains). I also made "This Land" on the Nishga Indians of British Columbia and their land claim, which I suppose was also an earlier expression of the "sociological/anthropological" approach of "Corporation"—though "This Land" was much more parti pris than "Corporation."

3. *In the interview you refer to your style of filmmaking as a kind of "controlled voyeurism, in a way ... very allied to the motives of the sociologist. You also mention that you aim for objectivity ... not always achieving it but aiming at it nonetheless. Did you work with other filmmakers who also held*

---

*Reprinted with permission of Arthur Hammond.

these views—what were your thoughts or thoughts in the group (if there was one) about trying to get the gist of an event, or conversation or meeting?

A great part of the NFB's documentary work at that time was of this kind, I would say, though other parts, like the "Challenge for Change" programme were quite different, involved with social activism.

4. Do you recall how you came to read Peter Berger's "Invitation to Sociology"? The interview mentions that this was a book that you read that somewhat influenced how you saw yourself as a documentary maker.

Don't remember how I came across it, but I believe it was actually while I was making, or after making, "Corporation," and I had an "ah-ha" moment: "So that's what I'm doing." I think it was confirmation, rather than influence.

5. When spending time at Steinberg's before shooting for the Corporation, you mention in the interview that you were there to pick out the aspects of the business that you thought would render well on film, and which also would typify the corporation in an interesting way—can you talk about what kind of details that you would look for, or notice, as a filmmaker, that you feel are important for a film?

I suppose there are a mixture of factors in deciding what to shoot: is it a socially interesting aspect of the subject—something people, and I, haven't seen before; is it visually or verbally interesting (the toy buyers or grocery buyers in "The Market" film, for example); is the character interesting—Sam Steinberg himself, and some of those around him. Perhaps one could sum it up as: "I think this person, activity, is fascinating; I think other people will too." One can call it instinct, a feeling for "story"—or flying by the seat of one's pants—but after having spent a good deal of time looking over the possibilities (research).

6. Ethnographers often learn a great deal about their subject matter after they have collected all the material but while they are writing up the results. Is it like that in the style of documentary you used for "The Corporation" series and "After Mr. Sam"?

It's certainly true that in unscripted, observational documentary, the shape of the material is found in the cutting room. "Writing" this kind of film is not one stage of the process, but the whole process, from choosing what to shoot, through editing the footage, to actually writing the narration—if there is one. (Re: ethnography, see #34)

7. You mention in the interview that you performed several months of exploration of the corporation before shooting for "The Corporation." Do you recall approximately how long shooting took once you started actually shooting?

Not really. "Palamino" took three days; "International Operations" three or four days; the rest was spread out over three or four weeks, I would think, but not continuously.

8. The article mentions that when initially thinking through the Corporation, you originally thought you were going to shoot a one hour film for television—how did projects like this develop at that time at the NFB—was this something that you proposed as a director out of the production unit or did the NFB also have goals/areas they wished to have addressed? This would be around the time that you started proposing/researching and working on "The Corporation" and "After Mr. Sam."

Both things happened at the NFB, but films like this originated with the film-maker, who then had to hook up with a producer and make a submission to the Programme Committee (largely composed of other film-makers). As I said above, the NFB was a unique place, especially at that time. Some thought the inmates were running the asylum, and films often started out innocently as one thing, at one length, and finished up as something else entirely at some other length: though there was a wish on everyone's part to try to make them of usable length for audiences, whether educational or television. Hence "Corporation" is 6 half-hours and one 80-minute oddity (which is a length people are used to sitting through for films), rather than a single film of 4 hours and 20 minutes. The short ones have all been on educational television a number of times, and you are evidence that some people are still even watching "After Mr. Sam" (which I may say, delights me, because—having just looked at it again—I think it is a fascinating, and at moments quite funny document. Thanks: it was like meeting old friends).

I should add that the reason this project outgrew its britches also has a personal side, which only my analyst could explain, if I had one. Every project I undertake tends to grow and grow. "Imperfect Union," on organized labour and Canadian politics, which was the only thing I wrote and directed at the NFB after "Corporation," also started out to be an hour and finished up as four 1-hours, in the process curing me of the desire to make any more films. I am now researching a small piece of mid-19th century history for a book, which threatens to consume the rest of my life. Fortunately I enjoy research, because I doubt that I'll ever get the book written. (You see what I mean, from the length of this answer?)

9. Did the NFB, at the time of these films, have any guidelines that you needed to follow in your work—production guidelines or for lengths of completed work, style of work for documentary film, any related production guidelines? Were there NFB concerns that you needed to keep in mind while working on these films, other than meeting the mission statement (being in the national interest, etc.)?

See above. The official mandate was "Interpreting Canada to Canadians and other nations, and making films in the national interest," or something like that—generally educational, in a very broad sense. Many odd carts were driven through that gate.

10. In the interview, and referring to "After Mr. Sam," you mention that your budget did not permit shooting all of the three-day conference at Palomino but that you knew that you needed to get footage dealing with the family, nepotism, and the succession. Can you say anything about how you decided, over the course of the meeting, to not shoot a portion of the meeting or surrounding activities?

Had it been the age of video, I would have shot the whole thing, and would still be editing it. I knew the central issues were Succession and Nepotism (also most likely to be accessible and interesting to an audience), so [I] concentrated on those, with the necessary set-up material for the conference, and other framing material.

11. The Corporation series had about a 19:1 shooting ratio—which seemed a very common (if still surprising to outsiders) observational cinema shooting ratio at the time—do you remember at all about how much footage you shot for "After Mr. Sam"?

No. It should have been about the average, maybe a little below. Actually, ratios of 60:1 were not unknown in this kind of filming.

12. Did you already plan to shoot the meeting at Palomino before you got the footage for the meeting that led up to it?

Can't remember exactly. I suspect the meeting which led up to it was what made me decide it had to be filmed. As you can see from the footage, Palomino took place in the winter, before the main body of the film was shot. I must have been doing my test shooting of the Executive Committee, to see if I was going to get the real goods, when the subject came up.

13. Did you rearrange the furniture or make other adjustments in the corporate headquarters meeting room for filming the first meeting in "After Mr. Sam"? At the Palomino meetings?

No, except for moving in a couple of small lights, we made no changes.

14. Was this a one-camera shoot with one sound person? Were you also there as the director? How big was the crew present at filming? Any lighting aside from natural light and/or room fixtures?

One cameraman, his assistant, sound man and me. I don't even think we ever used an electrician: the cameraman and his assistant set up the couple of lights themselves. Observational, minimum interference.

15. *How often did you, or the crew, have to stop to change film magazines or sound reels—did the meeting continue as you did this? Was there any time that you stopped the meeting or asked them to restart their discussion or revisit a topic?*
Mags lasted 10 minutes, but there were always others loaded, and changing them was done quite quickly. No stopping or repeats.

16. *Do you recall if the walk through the Palamino gate and the President getting into his car was reenacted, or was this all captured "on-the-fly"?*
On-the-fly. One looks out for such opportunities to get framing material.

17. *Did you (your crew) shoot the shots of Mr. Sam being honored at the beginning of the film? Do you recall when Sam's honorary degree was awarded in relation to the times of the meetings?*
It was in the summer, so it followed the winter Palamino shoot.

18. *Why do you think Sam Steinberg agreed to the final film—or was this still part of the Corporation series agreement?*
It was actually shot before the rest of the films. When the subject came up, I told Sam that I wanted to shoot it. He checked what his Executive Committee thought (or said he did—maybe he checked with the "Friday night supper") and agreed. So, I guess one could say it was an add-on to the original agreement, made on the wing.

19. *Was there an agreement at all with Sam Steinberg as to when the film "After Mr. Sam" was to be released?*
Only to the extent that, like the other films, it would be long enough after the event that there would be no confidentiality problems. By that time, the new President would be in place.

20. *"After Mr. Sam" seems to have quite a bit of narration for a film that largely evokes the observational style—was this planned / part of your existing style—or did you feel this necessary to cover gaps and clarify material for the audience?*
I wasn't a pure observationalist, and if I were making films today I wouldn't be a Dogmatist. (I would, however, be using video like mad, and fatally.) I believe in doing what you need to do to tell a clear story and provide a clear image.

21. *The narration at one point also seems to set up a narrative or story in the film—that of, who is going to succeed Sam Steinberg. At this point in the film it seems then that one starts to watch the film with this outcome in*

mind as opposed to more general observational documentary, where a viewer is the "fly on the wall" at the meeting and left to his or her own devices on how to interpret the meeting. Was the narration that "sets up" the succession part of the film intended to have this shift?

See above, and answer to #5.

22. Did you write and perform the narration?—You are credited as the writer, but we could not find a narrator credit.

Yep, that's me.

23. Do you recall how you decided on, or the thinking surrounding the narration that was with the bridge game—that discussed the rules of bridge and related it to what was happening in the meetings?

Well, I needed material to break the film up into three parts, to give the viewer some relief, so I shot anything that might serve the purpose. Dinner made parts one and two more digestible, and to allow me to bridge parts two and three, the good Lord provided me with a game of ... It wasn't set up. It was obvious what the bridging narration needed [to] say, but to get it right, I must have read a bridge book, because I don't play the game. (I'm telling you secrets.)

24. What was your role in editing—how did you work with your editor in assembling the final cut of "After Mr. Sam"?

Hardly left his side. Documentary directors live in the cutting room (so do some feature directors, I hear). That is where the story is shaped. See # 6 above.

25. The editing is done very well—it is both seamless and also includes the energy of shots that "occur on the fly," trying to catch up with the action. For the viewer, it really feels as if one is at the meetings—yet in the end it is only 78 minutes worth of many days of meetings. What kinds of methods were used in editing to obtain this outcome?

Well, to begin with, we didn't shoot the whole three days. See #10. For the rest, it was the usual agonies and ecstasies of editing, unhealthy amounts of coffee and, in David Wilson's case, fatal numbers of cigarettes, bitter struggles between director and editor, danger of blood on the Steenbeck. Occasionally I would go away and let him make a splice on his own.

26. Did you use a paper edit at all—script the film in post in some way? When editing, did you think about story or character or other such elements that sometimes are used in documentary filmmaking?

I don't recall a paper edit in this case, though it is possible I did one. I think I was always equally interested in both story and character, with maybe a slight edge to story. The research period in documentary is like the casting process in fiction film: you are looking for people who are going to be interesting on screen, so that you can tell an interesting story through them. Sam Steinberg cast himself as soon as I met him, and the Steinberg's Little Theatre Company wasn't far behind. One thinks about both story and character from the beginning.

27. How is the final film different than the original raw footage—is the final film sequential in its presentation of topics of discussion—in each area of discussion is the material sequential or edited out of sequence to present itself more smoothly, while still obtaining the "gist" of the discussion—were there any decisions on how to transition from one area of the discussion to another through editing choices?

I can't be sure at this remove, but I'm pretty sure it is sequential, leading up to the climax of "Friday Night Supper." I certainly wouldn't hesitate to edit out of sequence, if it told a better and clearer story, and didn't falsify, but I don't think that happened here. For transitions, see #23.

28. Some viewers of the film feel that Sam Steinberg chooses when to close discussion on a topic—do you remember whether or not this was how this might have occurred at the meeting or whether this was an editing choice used to transition the subject matter in the film—or was this a director commentary at all, within the film?

Discussions didn't necessarily close when they do in the film, but when in editing we felt the subject had been covered and we had a good closing point. Mind you, if Sam indicated that a discussion was over, it was over. Just as, when he decided, at the screening of the films for the Exec Cttee [sic], that the films were good, it was agreed that the films were good.

29. This question might be too detailed—but I am going to try it out anyway: In your opinion, how well could the film "After Mr. Sam" be used for conversation analysis—where a researcher evaluates conversations between people—to the minutiae of pauses and mumbles in speech patterns—in this way would the edited film be an accurate portrayal of sequential conversation—are there parts of the film that are directly sequential, or where perhaps very minor, what I call "nip and tuck" edits were made (only to smooth out camera movements, etc.)?

I think it would be useless, scientifically, for that. Too much cutting and trimming and shifting has gone on.

30. Do you feel that the interactions at the meetings featured in "After Mr. Sam" have any inherent "Canadianness" to them—in the interactions between the members at the meeting? Has anyone ever commented on this?

Wouldn't have thought so; and no, no one has ever mentioned it.

31. Additionally, do you feel any inherent "Canadianness" as a participant in Canadian film culture (as a writer, filmmaker, producer, viewer of Canadian films)—in some way that you are part of a community that does things differently than a U.S. film culture, European film culture, or other film culture?—if so, can you put a finger on what that is or feels like?

Within the international band of brothers and sisters who make documentary films, the NFB has had its own special place. It's certainly a Canadian institution now, but it was started by a Scot, and heavily influenced in the beginning by the British documentary school of the 30's and 40's. But then there was a major French Canadian implant (whence Denis Arcand et al.) after the Board moved to Montreal from Ottawa. In my time, there were some brilliant American and Dutch animators, working there, and Alanis Oboomsawin made a native film-maker bridgehead. The current Film Commissioner, a director in my day, was born in Algeria. I'm sure now it's on the way to being as much of a cultural and ethnic mosaic as much of the country is. (50% of the population of Toronto was born elsewhere than in Canada.) Me personally? Born and educated in England, a year in Indiana, here since 1956—Montreal 15 years, Toronto the rest—feeling quite at home, but still totally uninterested in hockey, baseball, basketball and other local religions.

32. Obviously, the fact that "After Mr. Sam" was chosen for analysis for a book topic is somewhat a testament to how well the meeting was felt to be represented on film and that the meeting still has relevance for these researchers some 30 years later is a comment on the longevity of the material that you've captured on film. What do you think documentary film provides for an event analysis that other media cannot provide as well and what do you think are the shortcomings of documentary film, for event analysis?

I'm delighted that it's being useful in its middle age, but I don't have an answer to the event analysis question. Sorry.

33. Has your philosophy of documentary-making changed over the years? If you were to make or produce a contemporary version of the "Corporation" series would you approach it in the same way? (or some of the examples from how your later business-related documentaries [as producer] were affected by this experience?)

I'm no longer in the game, nor wish to be. I sometimes think that if I had it all to do again, I would, or should, make more political films, like Michael Moore, say, but I probably wouldn't be any good at it: not confrontational enough. I gather someone has just done a "Corporation" film of that kind, which I haven't got around to yet. And then again I think that I would want to go on exploring and giving people interesting inside looks at aspects of our society and the world which they might not otherwise see.

34. Do you view "After Mr. Sam" any differently as the years pass—or have you heard any other reactions to the film as the years have passed? Do you have any reaction to the ongoing or certainly the recent interest in the film?

I've looked at it today for the first time in years, and it was like meeting old friends, and quite funny at times. Yours is also the first interest in it I have heard of in years. I conclude that you are people of high intelligence and excellent taste. I think it will be of even greater interest, certainly to sociologists, in 100 years, if there are still sociologists, or anyone else, to see it.

Anthropologists, too, incidentally. My old friend Asen Balikci (now retired in his native Bulgaria), who worked as advisor on the wonderful Netsilik Eskimo series, and was a prof of anthropology at the University of Montreal, was an admirer of the Corporation films, and used them in some classes. He was instrumental in getting "After Mr Sam" screened at the Margaret Mead Film Festival in New York a year or so after it was made.

35. Was "After Mr. Sam" screened for Sam Steinberg before its release—do you recall his reaction? (The interview we have with you from 1973 was before the release of "After Mr. Sam.") What were other reactions that you recall?

He certainly saw it, but I don't remember his reaction to this one in particular. He liked the films at first, then got alarmed by reports of some negative reactions (vide "Pot Pourri"), then I think warmed to them again. I was certainly asked by the family to contribute a piece to a memorial volume after his death, so they obviously felt okay about them by then.

36. Do you have any stories or anecdotes related to the making of "After Mr. Sam" or the Corporation series that you would like to share?

No, I'm done.

37. Do you have any thoughts you would like to share on how documentary has evolved over the years or on contemporary documentary practices?

See # 36.

38. Have these questions brought forth any other moments, ideas, thoughts or questions that you would like considered?

"My God, I was brilliant then."

Otherwise, I'd emphasize that the whole series is a series and, I think, gains from being viewed in toto—though not at the same sitting, obviously. Viewing the other six films gives one a context for Palomino, and a greater insight into the various characters who perform there. They were never numbered as a series, but a natural sequence is: Growth, Real Estate (more growth—social/environmental impact), International Operations (yet more growth—cultural impact), Motivation (dealing with employees), The Market (dealing with customers), Bilingualism (dealing with politics).

I'm not clear what your book is about exactly. Does "Corporation" feature in one chapter? When is publication expected? Will you send me a copy?

Best wishes,
Arthur Hammond

REFERENCES

Barnouw, E. (1993). *Documentary: A history of the non-fiction film.* Oxford, England: Oxford University Press.

Birdwhistell, R. L. (1970). *Kinesics and context: Essays on body motion communication.* Philadelphia: University of Pennsylvania Press.

Bottorff, J. L. (1994). Using videotaped recording in qualitative research. In J. M. Morse (Ed.), *Critical issues in qualitative research methods* (pp. 244–261). Thousand Oaks, CA: Sage.

Corsaro, W. (1982). Something old and something new: The importance of prior ethnography in the collection and analysis of audiovisual data. *Sociological Methods and Research, 11,* 145–166.

DuFon, M. (2002). Video recording in ethnographic SLA research: Some issues of validity in data collection. *Language, Learning and Technology, 6,* 40–59.

Erickson, F. (1992). Ethnographic microanalysis of interaction. In M. D. LeCompte, W. L. Millroy, & J. Preissle (Eds.), *The handbook of qualitative research in education* (pp. 201–225). New York: Academic.

Evans, G. (1991). *In the national interest: A chronicle of the national film board of Canada from 1949 to 1989.* Toronto, ON: University of Toronto Press.

Feld, S., & Williams, C. (1975). Toward a researchable film language. *Studies in the Anthropology of Visual Communication, 2,* 25–32.

Fishman, M. (1980). *Manufacturing the news.* Austin: University of Texas Press.

Frankenheimer, J. (Director). (1962). *The Manchurian candidate* [Motion picture]. United States: Metro-Goldwyn-Mayer.

Garfinkel, H. (2003). *Ethnomethodology's program: Working out Durkheim's Aphorism.* Lanham, MD: Rowman and Littlefield.

Garfinkel, H., & Wieder, D. L. (1993). Two incommensurable, asymmetrically alternate technologies of social analysis. In G. Watson & R. M. Seiler (Eds.), *Text in context: Contributions to ethnomethodology* (pp. 175–206). Newbury Park, CA: Sage.

Goodwin, C. (1993). Recording human interaction in natural settings. *Pragmatics, 3*, 181–209.

Grimshaw, A. D. (1982). Sound-image data records for research on social interaction: Some questions and answers. *Sociological Methods and Research, 11*, 121–144.

Gurwitsch, A. (1964). *The field of consciousness*. Pittsburgh, PA: Duquesne University Press.

Hammond, A. (Producer/Director/Writer). (1974). *Corporation: After Mr. Sam* [Film]. Montreal: National Film Board of Canada.

Herzfeld, J. (Director/Writer). (2001). *Fifteen minutes* [Motion picture]. United States: Warner Home Video.

Issari, M. A. (1991). *Cinema vérité*. East Lansing: Michigan State University Press.

Lynch, M. (1993). *Scientific practice and ordinary action: Ethnomethodology and social studies of science*. Cambridge, England: Cambridge University Press.

Nelms, H. (1969). *Magic and showmanship*. New York: Dover.

Nichols, B. (1991). *Representing reality*. Bloomington: University of Indiana Press.

Nichols, B. (2001). *Introduction to documentary*. Bloomington: University of Indiana Press.

Pinney, C. (1992). The lexical spaces of eye-spy. In P. I. Crawford & D. Turton (Eds.), *Film as ethnography* (pp. 26–49). Manchester, England: Manchester University Press.

Plantinga, C. R. (1997). *Rhetoric and representation in non-fiction film*. Cambridge, England: Cambridge University Press.

Rosenthal, A. (2002). *Writing, directing, and producing documentary films and videos*. Carbondale: Southern Illinois University Press.

Schegloff, E. (1991). Reflections on talk and social structure. In D. Boden & D. H. Zimmerman (Eds.), *Talk and social structure: Studies in ethnomethodology and conversation analysis* (pp. 44–70). Berkeley: University of California Press.

Schegloff, E. (1992). On talk and its institutional occasions. In P. Drew & J. Heritage (Eds.), *Talk at work: Interaction in institutional settings* (pp. 101–134). Cambridge, England: Cambridge University Press.

Schutz, A. (1967). On multiple realities. In M. Natanson (Ed.), *Alfred Schutz: Collected papers I* (pp. 207–286). The Hague, Netherlands: Martinus Nijoff.

Stoddard, K. (1987). The presentation of everyday life: Some textual strategies for "adequate ethnography." *Urban Life (15)*, 103–121.

Thorvaldson, P., & Hammond, A. (1973, December). Corporation. *Pot Pourri*, 2–7.

Vaughan, D. (1992). The aesthetics of ambiguity. In P. I. Crawford & D. Turton (Eds.), *Film as ethnography* (pp. 99–115). Manchester, England: Manchester University Press.

Wieder, D. L. (1965). *An ethnography of a daily newspaper: Fieldnotes and reflections*. Unpublished manuscript.

Winston, B. (1993). The documentary film as scientific inscription. In M. Renov (Ed.), *Theorizing documentary* (pp. 37–57). Los Angeles, CA: The American Film Institute.

Chapter 13

Closing Words (and Opening Discussions?): An Afterword on *Corporation: After Mr. Sam*

Cliff Oswick
University of Leicester, UK

It is not my intention in this closing chapter to attempt to endorse or critique, either individually or as a whole, the chapters that constitute this edited collection. Rather, I wish to take this opportunity to encourage readers to avoid limiting themselves to reflecting on the issues covered in the rich array of contributions contained in this volume and instead to move toward formulating their own insights. In order to facilitate this process, I want to tentatively sketch out some possible directions that seek to locate the interactional episodes contained in *Corporation: After Mr. Sam* within a wider contextual framework. In adopting this approach, it is hoped that this will open up further discussion as opposed to offering the sense of closure more typically associated with afterwords.

The line of argument that is developed here foregrounds aspects of time, space, and relationships as core components in the process of making sense of interactional episodes. More specifically, this contribution considers the ways in which multiple constructions of temporality, locale, and relationships are intertwined and implicated in both the content and context of particular discursive events. In this regard, the issues of time and space addressed in relation to the *Corporation: After Mr. Sam* documentary extend beyond the notions of "landscape" (Schama, 1995) and "timescape" (Adam, 1998) to encompass what might be more aptly described as the "textscape" (Keenoy & Oswick, 2004) of a corporate management meeting. When approached in this way, the conjugation of aspects of visibility, materiality, and presence—which Adam associates with timescapes—can be treated as discursive phenomena with the

289

time dimension being complemented by the incorporation of space and agency as intrinsic features of the social construction of a textscape. Textscapes can be seen as encompassing the conversational and the intertextual, but they are more than this. They go beyond these issues to locate episodes of interaction and networks of social actors within a broader spaciotemporal discursive framework.

The textscape of the corporate meeting at Steinberg Limited can be explored at differing levels (i.e., from the macrocontextual to the micro-conversational) and from different stakeholder perspectives (e.g., corporate participants and nonparticipants, filmmakers, public audience). In the following three main sections, aspects of the temporal, spatial, and relational dynamics of the board meeting at Steinberg's are elaborated and brief illustrative vignettes of application are also provided to demonstrate how readers, as analysts themselves, might engage with these phenomena.

TIME-IN-INTERACTION

Although traditional conceptualizations of time typically hinge on the unproblematic delineation of the past, the present, and future, this distinction fails to capture the substance of interaction at the board meeting insofar as an instance of discourse is in reality informed by a retrospective context, a real-time context, and a projective context. As Keenoy and Oswick (2004) observed: "the past, the present and future are simultaneously embedded within a discursive event (i.e. the 'past-in-the-present,' the 'present-in-the-present' and the 'future-in-the-present')" (p.138).

For participants in the meeting, the past is evoked in the present via reminiscences about Steinberg Limited. This is, in effect, a kind of "retrospective context." It also has implicit intertextual connotations (i.e., past texts are evoked within interaction in the meeting). In particular, this form of "intertextuality" (Kristeva, 1980) is both "hypertextual" (Genette, 1997) and "metatextual" (Allen, 2000) in nature. It involves both an explicit and direct borrowing from previous texts (i.e., hypertextuality) and also on occasions takes up a position of implicit commentary on the past (i.e., metatextuality). For example, recollections of Sam Steinberg as an entrepreneurial leader tend to be overt and, hence, hypertextual, whereas the role of "the family" and how this has previously been seen by the workforce remain veiled and, as such, metatextual. We also find that a form of "recontextualization" (Bernstein, 1990) occurs as these past conversations from different domains and locales are reconstituted and reconfigured for consumption within the meeting at "the retreat." This is illustrated in the exposition of James

Doyle (vice president and general counsel) when he evokes previous discussions and re-presents them to support his view:

```
391  JAMES D:  =All our previous discussions, and we had some before we
392            came up here to Palomino, we thought (.) uh it was impressed
393            on us and many individuals raised the point that we should be
394            try:ing (0.2) > difficult as it is for all of us< to be objective
395            about what we said in these reports (.) and to th:ink of the
396            organization (.) not in terms of the incumbency in any one
397            position but as to h:ow the organization itself (.) should be (.)
398            best structured from the point of view, and w:orry about the
399            b:odies to fill the positions afterwards. And that is what, if
400            we're going to be objective, we should be doing here (0.2) and
401            we're d:odging the issue because we're saying "Ah (0.5) it might
402            possibly point the finger at any one of us, and that's a- too
403            delicate area for us to discuss" =
```

The real-time interaction (i.e., the present) that unfolds in the *Corporation: After Mr. Sam* documentary is not, however, exclusively informed by past interactions. There is also an element of spontaneity, unpredictability, and, to a certain extent, uncontrollability that impacts on the process of collective sense making (Weick, 1995) and de facto the ability to manage the meeting and the agenda. Therefore, we can think of the present as existing within the moment (Pearce & Cronen, 1979). To this end, readers might expect to find instances where the meeting wanders, meanders, or goes in unanticipated and unscripted directions. In fact, such episodes are notable by their absence within the documentary. This is perhaps not surprising given the documentary makers' desire to create a coherent narrative. Any occasion where the conversation significantly deviated from the main purpose of the meeting would have been perceived as irrelevant to the central theme of succession and therefore would have been susceptible to being "edited out" by the filmmakers (see, in this regard, Wieder, Mau, & Nicholas' insightful points in chap. 12, this volume). This does mean to say that they did not arise; it simply means they were removed in order to present a sanitized, albeit unrealistic, version of the interaction.

There is also a projective dimension to the meeting (i.e., the future-in-the-present). Most obviously, there is the inescapable question: Who will take over from Sam? It is somewhat inescapable that for some the desire to takeover from Sam in the future is going to have a significant effect on behavior in the meeting (i.e., in the present). A less obvious, but nevertheless important aspect of projection, is the way in which "discursive formalization" (Iedema, 1999) impacts on the present by evoking the future. Iedema (1999) drew attention to the importance of the modes of capturing and representing (i.e., formalizing) discourse in shaping and configuring the actual interaction. He shows how the formalization of meetings, via minute taking, mediates the actual dialogue insofar as the anticipation of how the minutes will represent the discussion and actually influence the discussion in real time. In effect, the minutes (which will appear in the future) are shaping, albeit partially, the discursive construction of the meeting (which is occurring in the present). This formalization process is arguably replicated in the board meeting at Steinberg Limited if we think of it as involving a substitution of minutes for videotape. In effect, the actual interaction in the meeting is mediated by the concerns of stakeholders about how they, and the company as a whole, will be judged by both employees and the subsequent TV viewers. We find a process of formalization occurring in the discussion about how to present the outcomes of the retreat to subordinates:

```
1518*JAMES D: There's another aspect I think we should discuss briefly (0.2)
1519          We have a very sad history (.) of leaking out (.) all kinds of (.)
1520          uh semi-official (scutterbug) (.) rumor through the organization,
1521          which (.) again I think does more harm than good.
1522(    ):   You mean (xxxx) the President?
1523*JAMES D: I beg your pardon?
1524(    ):   (xxxx) the President?
1525*JAMES D: No, I'm not concerned with that (0.5) ((people speaking at
1526          once)) But I do think that we we should have some consensus
1527          (.) as to what we want to say to our subordinates about what
1528          went [on here.
1529(    ):        [Issue a diplomatic communiqué.
1530          (1.5)
1531(    ):   A frank and open discussion ((laughing)) (xxxx)
1532*MEL D:   No, I think Jim raised a very good point, we ought to=
1533*JAMES D: =The rumor mill will be churning at a frantastic rate with all of
1534          us up here (.) [for three days.
1535*MEL D:                 [Well, everyone knows we're all up here. I mean
1536          do we go back and tell our people uh (0.5) what the topics we
1537          discussed and so on? It's a very vital issue.
1538          ((People talking at once.))
1539(    ):   There are only four items on the agenda. Why not list that there
1540          are the items xxx
1541*JAMES D: I would say uh communiqué worded something like this "That
1542          the President and the top executives of the company have met
1543          for the last uh two and half days (0.2) three days whatever (.) is
1544          at Palomino Lodge in uh (.) Laurentians and u::h uh and have
1545          conducted an extensive review of the (.) uh current situation of
1546          the company with particular reference to its future uh and and
1547          this discussion included, such subjects as professional
1548          management and and itemize the four topics and stop right
```

1549   there. Say nothing more.
1550 (   ):   That's right. Very good.

In this extract, the use of a communiqué is proposed as a means of formalizing the meeting for consumption by employees. In the discussion, both the structure and the content of the communiqué are simultaneously addressed (i.e., the general wording and then the listing agenda items).

SPACE-IN-INTERACTION

Just as differing constructions of the temporal context of the board meeting impact on the interaction, so too do issues of locale and space. On occasion, problematic boundaries are imposed on episodes of interaction. This can lead to the creation of a "contained space," where naturally occurring talk is uncoupled and investigated independently of the physical surroundings and the wider social context in which it occurs. In the case of *Corporation: After Mr. Sam*, the actual interaction is central to any analysis, but the immediate physical context of the meeting, the extended organizational arena, and the wider sociocultural context in which this particular discursive episode is located cannot be ignored. These contexts (i.e., other spaces) are not simply a backdrop to the text, they are an intrinsic part of it.

Within the board meeting interaction, subtle shifts of emphasis between different locales are apparent (e.g., the retreat itself, back at the company, and the unspoken, but ever-present public space created by the film as an artifact of the meeting). For example, references to "the workplace" when at "the retreat" are frequently used by board members as a means of simultaneously making negative comments (e.g. about "the family") while externalizing and maintaining a distance from the view expressed (e.g. by attributing it to employees). Equally, it is interesting that casual clothes are worn at the retreat, but the large table and chairs are laid out in classic boardroom style. This suggests that the choice of location (i.e., away from the workplace) promotes informality, but the arrangement of the immediate physical environment (i.e. the room) indicates that the meeting actually remains quite formal.

RELATIONSHIPS-IN-INTERACTION

The relational context of the board meeting can be considered at two levels (i.e., a local organizational level and a wider social level). First, it is perhaps useful to superimpose a social networks perspective on the *Corporation: After Mr. Sam* documentary protagonists. Embracing "social network analysis" (Scott, 1991) enables us to consider the enduring relationships that transcend a particular discursive episode. Moreover, it requires us, as analysts, to become sensitized to the alliances, antagonisms, and complex configurations of interest that underpin the surface-level interaction (e.g., without an appreciation of aspects of the ongoing informal relationship between two parties, veiled irony or sarcasm is likely to be missed by the observer). By superimposing a network perspective on discursive phenomena, we access the "local relational context" (i.e., the links between a set of stakeholders) of a piece of text or instance of discourse (Steward & Conway, 1998). This relational context is significantly different to the "social context" identified within "critical discourse analysis" (Fairclough, 1992; van Dijk, 1997) that privileges broader institutional factors and wider social practices. The analysis of the board meeting reveals the interplay between the maintenance of existing relationships and the identity work associated with the self-promotion of individuals and championing of others as suitable or unsuitable CEO successors. The individual posturing and positioning of particular social actors occurs against a backdrop of cliques around family versus nonfamily and traditionalists versus modernizers.

Second, and at a broader level of relationships, the corporate event can be seen as a form of theatre. This perspective draws up the concept of *triadic collusion* (Cole, 1975), where the "carrying off" of a theatrical event involves an elaborate interplay between three parties (i.e., the author, the actors, and the audience). When this collusive element is acknowledged, it becomes difficult to regard an audience as passive observers or recipients of a play; they are implicated in the performance as active co-constructors of the particular dramaturgical event. The complex nature of the interaction between the three parties gives rise to a number of possible scenarios to the extent that the same play may be well received by one audience on one night but badly received the next night by another audience.

In effect, the board meeting involves a tripartite relationship that is comparable to that found in the theater; the alignment of the respective parties being the executive board members as actors, the filmmakers as authors, and nonparticipating employees of the company and the documentary viewers as audience. Various aspects of triadic collusion resonate with the Steinberg meeting as a piece of drama. For example, instances where certain vice presidents (as social actors) "play to the camera" are discernible and the way in which Arthur Hammond (the director and co-producer of the film) and his colleagues chose to edit down a 3-day meeting into a short documentary (of 77 minutes duration) represents a highly significant aspect of authorship (see, e.g., how Irving Ludmer looks repeatedly at the camera with a smile, as to call the audience to witness the fact that he is unable to get a word in).

CONCLUDING REMARKS

As indicated earlier, the overriding intention of this afterword has been to present some possible avenues of further investigation for readers. The insights offered in relation to the three main strands of inquiry discussed (i.e., time, space, and relationships) are intended to be illustrative rather than exhaustive. In closing, I wish to re-emphasize the interconnectedness of time, space, and relationships as mutually implicated elements of the board meeting. For example, the nature and pattern of interaction in the documentary (the text) is informed by the social construction and social negotiation of how the event will subsequently be perceived by others (a temporal dynamic). This in turn relies on considering the public domain (the locale) constituted by employees and TV viewers (as stakeholders) and their perceived or actual reactions (an aspect of triadic collusion). There are undoubtedly many other permutations that readers may wish to explore.

Finally, the corporate meeting at Steinberg Limited is more than a coherent, linear, decision-making session (a univocal, positivist interpretation). Furthermore, although it is perfectly plausible to capture and characterize the event in terms of multiple readings (a plurivocal, postmodern interpretation) or competing readings (i.e., a critical interpretation based on a hegemonic struggle between privileged and marginalized voices), this does not sufficiently capture the subtleties and nuances of the situation. Rather than thinking of the discursive event at Steinberg's as constituted through different and distinctly separate readings, it can be thought of as an amalgam of overlapping and interpenetrating interactions that coalesce around the discursive construction of time, space, and agency to form a textscape.

REFERENCES

Adam, B. (1998). *Timescapes of modernity*. London: Routledge.

Allen, G. (2000.) *Intertextuality*. London: Routledge.

Bernstein, B. (1990). *The structuring of pedagogic discourse*. London: Routledge.

Cole, D. (1975). *The theatrical event: A mythos, a vocabulary, a perspective*. Middletown, CT: Wesleyan University Press.

Fairclough, N. (1992). *Discourses and social change*. Cambridge, England: Polity Press.

Genette, G. (1997). *Paratexts: Thresholds of interpretation* (J. Lewin, Trans.). Cambridge, England: Cambridge University Press: Cambridge.

Iedema, R. (1999). The formalization of meaning. *Discourse and Society, 10,* 49–65.

Keenoy, T., & Oswick, C. (2004). Organizing textscapes. *Organization Studies, 25,* 135–142.

Kristeva, J. (1980). *Desire in language: A semiotic approach to literature and art* (T. Gora, A. Jardine, & L. Roudiez, Trans.). New York: Columbia University Press.

Pearce, W., & Cronen, V. E. (1979). *Communication, action and meaning: The creation of social realities.* New York: Praeger.

Schama, S. (1995). *Landscape and memory.* London: HarperCollins.

Scott, J. (1991). *Social network analysis: A handbook.* London: Sage.

Steward, F., & Conway, S. (1998). Situating discourse in environmental innovation networks. *Organization, 5,* 483–506.

Van Dijk, T. A. (Ed.). (1997). *Discourse as structure and process.* London: Sage.

Weick, K. E. (1995). *Sensemaking in organizations.* London: Sage.

Transcript of the Management Meeting*

((Title: National Film Board of Canada))

((*Voice of person speaking in French*. Background image of a fountain. English sub-titles: Mr. Chancellor))

((Sub-titles: the Faculty of Management is proud to honour one of Quebec's business leaders-Mr. Sam Steinberg))

((Commencement Ceremony))

((Sub-titles: Starting with his mother's small store, which opened in 1917 on St. Lawrence Blvd ... he heads one of the largest chain of stores in Canada

((Camera focuses on the speaker at the commencement ceremony. Sub-titles: It has 180 supermarkets in Quebec and Ontario and a new store in Paris-its third in Europe))

Voiceover: ((*In the summer of 1969, Sam Steinberg, President of Steinberg's Limited of Montreal, received an honorary degree in Business Administration from Sherbrooke University in the province of Quebec. In the 50 years of one man rule he had built a small mainstream grocery store into an international retailing, manufacturing and real estate company with assets of 224 million dollars, sales of 553 million dollars and more than 18 thousand employees*))

((*Voice of speaker*. Subtitles: We therefore ask you to bestow on Mr. Steinberg an Honorary Doctorate of Business Administration))

---

*From *Corporation: After Mr. Sam* [Film], by A. Hammond (Producer/Director/Writer), 1974, Montreal: National Film Board of Canada. Copyright © 1974 by National Film Board of Canada. Reprinted with permission of the National Film Board of Canada.

Voiceover: ((*But such honors marked the closing stages of a man's career. By 1969, the business had grown too large for one man to control and Sam Steinberg was ready to retire as President. As a result the corporation was in trouble, worried about its future leadership and unclear about where it was going*))

((Scene of cars on a busy road and a close-up shot of an office block))

((Title: THE NATIONAL FILM BOARD OF CANADA PRESENTS))

((Title: CORPORATION—AFTER MR. SAM))

1	ARNOLD S:	Uh, this company has been uh directed u::h by, Sam Steinberg
2		for- for some fifty years now and the company has been built up
3		ar<u>ou</u>nd <u>his</u> leadership. And it's been built up uh on the
4		assumption that u:h (.) that nothing will happen to Mr. Sam
5		Steinberg in:n- for time in memoriam. If uh anything <u>did</u>
6		happen, that- we- we would be faced with a catastrophic
7		situation of- uh, in <u>my</u> opinion of a, of a most serious nature. I
8		put number one in- I put succession as number one because
9		(0.2) of this ↑catast<u>rophi</u>c situation that would result, I think that
10		everything else would pale by com<u>pari</u>son (0.2) in the event of
11		something happening to- to the President. [cut?] Again the-
12		there's a question of definition of su<u>ccess</u>ion. Succession, in
13		my o<u>pi</u>nion, is the <u>steps</u> that have to be taken ↑<u>n:ow</u>: so that in
14		the event of the President retiring or if uh God forbid,
15		something catastrophic happened, uh..th- th-t-there's a- a
16		natural order of things come into play (0.8) and uh and this is
17		the reason [I see it,
18	( ):	[This is the reason [you chose
19	ARNOLD S:	[this is the reason <u>I</u> see it as
20		number one.
21	JAMES D:	I think [what we're co- I think what we're coming to]=
22	SAM S:	[You listen, but that's not the (xxxx) I'm thinking]=
23	JAMES D:	= Mr. President, I think that what we're coming to is, uh (.) a a:
24		realization that there's a sufficient difference of opinion in the
25		group. [which is not likely to be resolved (xxxx)
26	*Voiceover:*	[(((*In early 1969, The President asked senior executives*
27		*for their views on the problems facing the company and in*
28		*February the management committee met to consider their*
29		*reports. Succession was the key issue but it was not the only*
30		*one. Many saw this as an opportunity to radically restructure*
31		*the company and shift a great deal of the power of the*
32		*presidency into the hands of senior executives. Others,*
33		*including the President, argued that neither succession nor*
34		*structure could be decided until the company's goals and*
35		*objectives were clarified. The outcome of this argument would*
36		*determine the agenda for a three-day top management*

37		*conference at Palomino, the company lodge.*))

37   *conference at Palomino, the company lodge.*))

38 JACK L: ... topsy turvy. ↑How can you start with all these objectives

39   before you know (.) that a (stop manager) [has taken !

40 SAM S: [The way I look at it

41   is this (.) that I think it's much e:asier determined (.) the kind of

42   succession you want (.) after y:ou look at (0.8) what you're

43   reaching ↑out for, and how you gonna go about attaining it. =

44 JACK L: = But Mr. Sam =

45 SAM S: = Then it follows you- (0.5) ((*facial expression, fingers tap on*

46   *table*)) then it follows (0.8) u:h what competence you require

47   now.

48 JACK L: But we always talk about pie in the sky, we always talk about

49   g:oals (.) but we never talk about (.) h:ow we're gonna operate

50   to meet those goals (.) and if we don't start with the the the the

51   ↑crux of the matter of talking about the succession and talk on

52   the structure and the- leadership, and THEN put in goals that

53   anybody here today can put goals (.) this far along, everybody

54   has a a a idea on goals. Then we again will leave Palomino with

55   (.) no structure (0.2) to monit' ourselves (.) against the goals

56   that we have set ourselves to go.

57   ((*Possible edit/cut in tape.*))

58 JOHN P: I think that the structure of the company has one single (0.5)

59   overwhelming purp- purpose and that is to facilitate the

60   achievement of company goals and objectives. (0.8) I'm been s-

61   eh. (1.0) I feel we have not esh-established our our objectives.

62   (0.5) And I think that's gotta come first. (0.2) Where we going,

63   what do we wanna be.

64 SAM S: This is exactly how I feel (0.5). Now listen to what I'm telling,

65   each and every one of you. (0.5) Evidently over the past four o'

66   five weeks, (0.5) a hundred or two hundred items (0.5) have to

67   be increased in price

68 JACK L: <Seventy-two items> =

69 SAM S: = Alright, well, I'm telling you what I heard. [so- .

70 JACK L: [(accumulated) on

71   four weeks, seventy-two items =

72 SAM S: = Okay. Let's (0.2) let's say it's seventy-two items. (1.0) So

73   here's what happens. I meet one of our managers having lunch

74   upstairs who's the manager of St-Lawrence and Cremazie. I

75   walked over an' say "Hello, how are you?" and everything else,

76   "How is it going?" He says "Very fine, sales are up thirteen or

77   (0.2) fourteen percent" but he says he's terribly disturbed. (0.5)

78   They got in a wh:ole list of items that they have to increase the

79   prices on (0.5) and he's disturbed because now they'll be going

80   back to what they did in the past, erasing prices an' (.) putting

81   on higher prices an 'everything else.

82 JACK L: Mr. President =

83 ( ):   = [hhuhh

84 ( ):   [Could I..Could I=

85	JACK L:	=No, [just a minute
86	( ):	[Could I..could I..could I get =
87	JACK L:	=Will you wait a minute? Mr. President look, this is what-
88		this's <u>why</u> I want to talk about structure first. (1.0) It happens
89		that I and you communicate. (0.5) > Twice a day three time a
90		day four times a day- no matter what time of day it is eh? <
91	SAM S:	Ri[ght.
92	JACK L:	[We communicate, I communicate to you, you com'nicate to
93		me. And I brought up to you (1.0) this perplex thing. 'Cause I
94		have to have somebody to speak to too (.) outside of my peers
95		who we speak to, eh? So I communicate with this. ((*Spoken*
96		*with intensity and pointing finger*)) Have you got the same
97		problem in Toronto?
98		(1.0)
99	JACK L:	Do you know what's happening at Toron[to?
100	SAM S:	[No, (I don't).
101	JACK L:	((*Spoken with intensity and pointing finger.*)) Are you running
102		one company or two companies? Is the <u>struc</u>ture that's wrong?
103		Is it professional management's wrong? Is it a (box) wrong?
104		<u>How</u> do you communicate? <u>They</u> communicate an' listen to this
105		an' an' I this is why I say structure (.) is so important an' how
106		we're gonna do it an' feedback an' control. .hh <u>Th:ey</u> been
107		raising prices from the first week. We kept prices back four
108		weeks, we did- though we got a co-co<u>st</u> increases, four (0.2)
109		three four weeks 'go three weeks 'go, so forth, we kept back
110		four weeks. They've been e- every week, putting in the price
111		changes though they come in- the same problem with- They
112		discuss it with you?
113		(.)
114	SAM S:	No =
115	JACK L:	= Have they communicated with you? =
116	SAM S:	= No.
117	JACK L:	((*Spoken with intensity and pointing finger.*)) = Have they
118		communicated with anybody here? (0.5) How many companies
119		are you running? (0.5) <u>What</u> philosophy do you want? That's
120		why my <u>first</u> thing on page <u>six</u> (0.2) page <u>six</u> and I want you to
121		go back and read it. This is exactly- I I am <u>very</u> glad you
122		brought it up. Because page six I say, for God sake, "the
123		<u>objec</u>tives and goals and corporate philosophy, the objectives
124		and goals must be spelled out." ↑<u>What</u> is your goals for Tor- ?
125		Are you running one business? Are you still running an- an
126		Ontario business? You wanna be the general manager here? Or
127		do you want to act as the President? Do you wanna act as a
128		corporate- as a corporate President for everybody or for one?
129		(1.0)
130	( ):	[Jack
131	JACK L:	[That's a very, exactly the same [as I'm bringing out.
132	( ):	[Jim (xxxx)

```
133  (    ):      [I just want to make sure we get, Mr. President
134  HARRY S:   [Um Uh ... uh ... C'd I- C'd I [bring this back (0.5)
135  (    ):                              [I just want to raise =
136  HARRY S:   = C'd I bring this back on course (1.0) th[at uh
137  SAM S:                                              [You're bringing it
138             back on course
139  HARRY S:   I'm bringing it [right back on course] and say let's get right=
140  SAM S:                    [ (We're on course)  ]
141  HARRY S:   =back to the problem of making maximum use (0.5) best use of
142             our time (0.8) and I don't think that this kind of interchange
143             (0.5) has contri[buted anything
144  ARNOLD S:                  [Well, I think Jack has raised a good
145             ex[ample ((several voices speaking at once.))
146  (    ):      [a ve[ry good example
147  ARNOLD S:        [a good [example
148  (    ):      ((Yelling.))      [The whole purpose of all our exercise is if
149             we're not going to run our business right.
150  ARNOLD S:  I think Jack has given an excellent ((voices speaking at once))
151             example of the shortcomings =
152  (    ):      =Yes.
153  ARNOLD S:  in the struc[ture
154  HARRY S:                [Alright. [Alright.
155  ARNOLD S:                        [toward (xxxx) control
156  JACK L:    That's right!
157  (    ):      It's all how you interpret it. I thought Jack gave an excellent
158             example=
159  (    ):      =Excellent=
160  (    ):      =of the shortcomings of not having clear un-
161             [clear understanding of the business.
162  (    ):      [Right. That's the way I interpreted it.
163  JACK L:    ((Yelling.)) Yeah! That's right. But you first have to have
164             struc[ture to, in order to do it.
165  HARRY S:        [Alright
166  HARRY S:   Alright, Mel Mel has the floor.
167  MEL D:     Obviously (.) gentlemen, inherent in each of our reports, (0.5)
168             although we don't state it (.) in negative terms hh we're a:ll
169             try:ing to look at what the deficiencies (.) have been, what they
170             a:re, and how we're goin' to correct them. This is (.) what
171             everyone really wants to do deep down. [Nobody is=
172  SAM S:                                           [Absolutely.
173  MEL D:     =saying "Look so and so is incompetent." We might think it
174             each of- whoever they think is incompetent or degrees of
175             competence and so on, but that is secondary at the moment 'cuz
176             we're not now evaluating individuals. All we are saying (.) is
177             that the sum total (.) of everything that has been done (1.0) in
178             one way or the other has not (.) been satisfactory. So we're
179             trying to change.=Now (0.5) if we had a structure that (.) certain
180             types of policies ((fist tap on table for emphasis)) must be
```

181		cleared and spelled out > to the nth degree prior to

181   cleared and spelled out > to the nth degree prior to
182   implementation, and a consistent follow up and discussion on
183   these policies (.) in all divisions, not only the Quebec Division,
184   the same applies to Ontario and everywhere else < then (.) these
185   things wouldn't happen. So they'd be prevented from
186   occurring. But it's no use telling Jack right now "Don't you
187   raise these prices" because (.) for two weeks the President was
188   away? and there's four thousand other items that are happening
189   simultaneously? and it's physically impossible for any one
190   individual to consistently follow up and check and get
191   clearance? Therefore I submit that from my understanding, and
192   maybe it's limited, that unless we clearly spell o:ut, which is a
193   f:ar (.) less arduous task, the organizational structure, and how
194   we make decisions and how the reporting relationships will
195   function, to permit these things to happen. Once that's cleared,
196   then we gonna spend (0.2) a ↑year, if need be, on spelling out
197   the objectives. Now (.) if you say objectives is just broadly that
198   we wanna maintain a profit, we wanna reverse a trend, who is
199   against that? That we can resolve in ten or fifteen minutes, so I
200   s:ay (0.2) that we leave objectives until the other thing is settled
201   ((*Talk covered over by voiceover*)).
202 *Voiceover:* ((*The argument over objectives versus structure was resolved at
203   last by the President reading a statement of company
204   philosophy. With that, objectives disappeared from the
205   Palomino agenda. (Cut away to a shot of Sam S., Mel D. and
206   another person walking along a snow-laden path towards the
207   gate of Palomino.) At Palomino itself, a new and critical stage
208   in the life of the company was to begin. Ultimate power would
209   remain in the hands of Sam Steinberg through his control of the
210   company's voting shares but his authority and operating
211   control were about to be redistributed. (Shot of Palomino.)
212   That was something, which, in one way or another, touched the
213   ambitions of almost everyone taking part in the conference.*))
214 HARRY S: The need to revise the present structure is perhaps the most
215   agreed upon problem identified by those submitting reports.
216   (0.2) A number of different assumptions are made about the
217   need to reorganize at the top level for example, (.) "No business
218   boasting annual sales of half a billion dollars can afford to be so
219   organized (0.2) that in the absence of a Chief Executive, no one
220   knows who is in control ..." ((*Talk covered over by the
221   voiceover*)).
222 *Voiceover:* ((*The conference was chaired by the corporation's Director of
223   Organizational Development, Harry Suffrin. The agenda
224   consisted of four items: decision-making, professional
225   management, succession, and structure.*))
226 HARRY S: ... structure should look like. The most important point (.) is that
227   everyone recognizes a need for a new look into this (.) structure.
228   (2.0) ((*Rustle of pages being turned.*)) Your task gentlemen

229		(0.8) based upon <u>your</u> reading of the organizational reports
230		submitted to the President, the pre-reading provided for you,
231		and the discussion outline, dete<u>r</u>mine the senior management
232		structure of Steinberg's Limited, taking into consideration the
233		decision-making process, the implementation of the decision,
234		the relationship of senior management to the rest of the
235		organization, the integration of divisional organizations, and the
236		functioning of the corporation. (3.0) ((*Rustle of pages being*
237		*turned.*)) Now how do you wish to proceed. A suggestion was
238		made to me during the ... ((*Talk covered over by the voiceover*)).
239	*Voiceover:*	((*These were the formal channels in which discussion would*
240		*flow. But what underlay the discussion and gave it impetus was*
241		*the fact that Sam Steinberg was stepping down as President to*
242		*become Chairman of the Board.*))
243	OSCAR P:	((*At writing board*)) I j's' wanted to go over what I put down.
244		Now (0.5) We have a Chairman of the Board and a President at
245		the present time ... ((*talk covered over by the voiceover*)).
246	*Voiceover:*	((*Not all the senior executives present could hope to replace*
247		*him. Some like Oscar Plotnik, Vice-President of the Ontario*
248		*Division, were approaching retirement themselves. Others like*
249		*John Paré, Vice-President of Personnel, or Irving Ludmer, in*
250		*charge of expansion and development, were too recently with the*
251		*company or too specialized in their skills to be more than*
252		*remote contenders. Attention focused on four people: Arnold*
253		*Steinberg, Sam Steinberg's nephew, a Harvard Business School*
254		*graduate and Vice-President Administration; James Doyle, the*
255		*corporation's widely respected Vice-President and General*
256		*Counsel; Mel Dobrin, the President's son-in-law and Executive*
257		*Vice-President Retailing, currently in charge of the*
258		*(Department Store) Division, and Jack Levine, Vice-President*
259		*of the Quebec Division, the corporation's largest, the most*
260		*profitable retail division. But for everyone in the room, as*
261		*important as the question of who was to be President, was the*
262		*question of how much power he should have and how much he*
263		*should share with other senior executives. This was the essence*
264		*of the debate over structure. Only one man could have the top*
265		*job but the right kind of structure before he was appointed*
266		*would guarantee others significant power.*))
267	JACK L:	((*At writing board.*)) Now one of the barriers (.) we have, in-
268		everybody in the committee has said consistently- is that the
269		<u>food</u> business, we're, we're not getting the mileage out of our
270		<u>food</u> business because we're running two different kind of food
271		businesses, and not together. And there's inefficiencies, so I put
272		the the the the uh all the retail, <u>food</u> business under one man.
273		((*Talk covered over by voiceover*)).
274	*Voiceover:*	((*Various structures were proposed. Most contentious was the*
275		*suggestion that the corporation's existing divisions be*
276		*regrouped under two or three executives or group vice-*

```
277              presidents. They would be powerful enough to have a
278              significant influence over any future President. But every
279              division already reported to someone in the room. Increased
280              authority for two or three people might seem like demotion for
281              the rest. At this point, the common interest in decentralizing
282              authority from the President might come into conflict with
283              individual ambitions.))
284  JACK L:     ((At writing board.)) Now, I am saying, this is my assumption,
285              maybe other people, and the regroupings may be done
286              differently, but definitely, this is the the thing I am subscribing
287              to, with these two added add'd functions.
288  SAM S:      No but I'm still confused
289              (0.2)
290  JACK L:     Sorry if I am not
291  HARRY S:    (xxxx) the President
292              (2.0)
293  SAM S:      I'm looking at your chart and uh, I felt that uh as I said, I started
294              out to say, the cobwebs have somewhat (1.0) lifted (1.0) and
295              when I look at this (.) chart so to speak and looking at it from
296              your point of view I see Vice-President Quebec, Ontario (0.2)
297              manufacturing, private label, market research. (0.5) Now are we
298              saying that the Vice-President (0.5) of my Quebec Division
299              (0.8) is the Vice-President over the Vice-President of Quebec
300              and Ontario Division?
301  JACK L:     Yes, I'm tellin' one Vice-President is respons' for all this so
302              they have a man- you'll have a man (.) res[ponsible
303  SAM S:                                                   [A Vice-President for
304              Quebec?
305  JACK L:     Yeah! If [he's (xxxx)
306  SAM S:               [A Vice-President 'n Ontario=
307  JACK L:     I don't care [names
308  SAM S:                   = [And we'll have another Vice-President (0.5) in
309              ch:arge of all of these three operations, beside you've added a
310              couple (.) uh of others. Now, we said the purpose of this
311              meeting i::s that we arrive at some understanding that removes
312              b:arriers that makes it more uh practical, and more efficient to
313              operate. Now you can't call yourselves all Vice-Presidents but
314              one Vice-President is different to the other Vice-Presidents (0.2)
315              without saying what that is?
316  JACK L:     I didn't care what name it was. It was General Manager, it was a
317              a Vice-President, I said "What are the natural (.) groupings?" I I
318              said "If I was starting up from scratch what would I do?" I give
319              names a later date, I said "These are the natural groupings in
320              order to get the best efficiency out of the organization" and th'
321              assets would go. Based on that efficiency I grouped them
322              together.
323  JAMES D:    There's nothing inherently wrong in one Vice-President
324              reporting to another (.) other than the fact that it
```

```
325            [might possibly put confusion in somebody's mind.=
326  SAM S:    [Alright but then but then ah J-Jim- =
327  JAMES D:  =But if we [want to overcome xxx
328  SAM S:                 [Jim then >listen to me Jim< (.) listen, stay there for
329            a minute. I'm not, I'm not saying no, I'm just uh I'm fully
330            aware of what's happening. But are we saying that th:e Vice-
331            President in charge of Quebec Division (.) is gonna act in a dual
332            capacity?
333  (    )    No
334  (    )    N:o
335  (    )    No
336  (    )    No
337            (0.5)
338  SAM S:    Well, it doesn't [show anything here-
339  JAMES D:                   [He's not been talking about whether there
340            was a Vice-President in charge of Quebec Division. He is
341            saying there's a Quebec Division there and there is an
342            [Ontario Division there and somebody is over the two of them.
343  (    ):   [Yeah, you've got one man in (xxxx).
344  OSCAR P:  U::h so what is really the (0.2) you know it's it's no difference
345            really =
346  SAM S:    =The difference- the main thing is [do you accept =
347  OSCAR P:                                      [Yeah
348  SAM S:    =[it whether you call it=
349  OSCAR P:   [Yeah but I, I=
350  SAM S:    =super Executive Vice-President.
351  OSCAR P:  =don't accept it because .(0.5) uh I think that the uh. (0.5) I
352            know we're imposing u:h you know these uh Executive Vice-
353            Presidents on the President maybe (.) uh uh the next President
354            may not want Executive Pr-Vice-Presidents I don't know but all
355            I know (.) hhh and what I feel right now is that (.) what we are
356            what is being suggested by A [and B
357  SAM S:                                [They're one and the same, they
358            shouldn't make [no difference
359  OSCAR P:                  [They're the same they're the same and two men
360            agree. I say that they'll be no different than the way we're
361            operating today.
362            (1.0)
363  SAM S:    The point is this. Are you goin' along with it? (0.8) Do you
364            think that would be helpful to us to =
365  OSCAR P:  = I'll say that there's that there's too many people (0.5) too
366            many people are going to be answering to the President and the
367            President (.) hh will not be able (0.2) under un-under this
368            [plan
369  SAM S:    [There will be fewer people, there will be fewer people if you
370            have group Vice-Presidents.
371  OSCAR P:  No we'll gonna have uh..[(xxxx)
372  SAM S:                            [Fewer people than he would now
```

373		↑ha:ve, then the man couldn't be in charge of a group of areas =
374	OSCAR P:	=I'm talking about the people answering to the President.
375	( ):	Eleven now.
376		(2.0)
377	SAM S:	There'd be fewer people.
378		((*Five or six people talking at the same time.*))
379	IRVING L:	You know something (0.2) Can I say something (1.0)
380	HARRY S:	Irving.
381	IRVING L:	Could I say something? (1.5) Could I say something?
382	ARNOLD S:	All the areas now report to all the people in this ↑room, =
383	IRVING L:	=Look=
384	(HARRY S):	=Irving=
385	IRVING L:	=Look, let me let me just add this =
386	ARNOLD S:	=How can you. How can you talk about the President, a man a
387		man who doesn't exist at the present time.. =
388	( ):	=Talking about yourself.
389	ARNOLD S:	Uh … but now you're gonna start talking about yourself =
390	IRVING L:	=You know, right now, =
391	JAMES D:	=All our previous discussions, and we had some before we
392		came up here to Palomino, we thought (.) uh it was impressed
393		on us and many individuals raised the point that we should be
394		try:ing (0.2) > difficult as it is for all of us< to be objective
395		about what we said in these reports (.) and to th:ink of the
396		organization (.) not in terms of the incumbency in any one
397		position but as to h:ow the organization itself (.) should be (.)
398		best structured from the point of view, and w:orry about the
399		b:odies to fill the positions afterwards. And that is what, if
400		we're going to be objective, we should be doing here (0.2) and
401		we're d:odging the issue because we're saying "Ah (0.5) it might
402		possibly point the finger at any one of us, and that's a- too
403		delicate area for us to discuss" =
404	( )	= (x[xx)
405	JACK L:	[You know what I think? I think- I think we're getting
406		chicken!
407	JAMES D:	Yeah!=
408	JACK L:	=We all ought to have enough nerve, gumption, look at the
409		company hh and say to our present President (.) in writing
410		"Look Mr President, you have to reorganize (0.2) because we
411		have certain weaknesses that if we don't do this, the company is
412		not gonna move." (0.2) Along with somebody else, everybody
413		in this room was willing to do it. When it comes to
414		individually, you wanna chicken out because you may have
415		[to give, you may have to take.
416	JAMES D:	[Exactly.
417		((*Two or three people talking at the same time.*))
418	ARNOLD S:	It just seems to me th't, th't while there may be some benefits
419		(.) from the exercise (0.2) I really see that (.) for the most part
420		we will go through the exerc', it will take several hours (0.5)

421		maybe several days (.) we will have a very heated discussion,
422		it's inconceivable to me that it can be resolved without a heated
423		discussion, and <u>then</u> (.) the <u>wh:ole</u> thing could be a complete
424		waste of time because (.) of the of the the relationship between
425		the Chairman and the President and how they see the job.
426	JACK L:	I disagree.
427		((*Two or three people talking at the same time.*))
428	SAM S:	Listen. When a man is made the Chief (1.0) Executive Officer,
429		and I'm just using the President by way of example (0.5) >then
430		he::'s going to determine the kind of a structure that he can
431		operate with effectively in order to achieve the desired ↑goals.<
432		You say to him "We'll make you the President, but this is the
433		way you're gonna have to operate" uh
434	JACK L:	But we have we have we ↑h:ave (0.5) a I think a responsibility
435		as a group (.) to <u>put</u> this kind of recommendations on the board
436		the same way we did other recommendations, rather than leave
437		it again (.) for a haphazard uh uh putting together without the
438		resources to put together or call another meeting for that
439		purpose.
440	HARRY S:	Arnold you're speaking. I recognize you.
441	ARNOLD S:	I think uh (.) traditionally the President of the United States or
442		the Prime Minister under the parliamentary system (.) <u>alone</u>
443		chooses his own Cabinet and for the most part (.) the choice of
444		Cabinet depends on the <u>skills</u> of that particular individual. I
445		think it was obvious that under Kennedy (0.2) uh he chose a
446		very weak Secretary of State because he himself wanted to be
447		the Secretary of State. (0.2) Uh uh I think that to for a a
448		President to come out into the job uh (0.2) without this choice
449		(0.5) d'uh being made by him, I think puts him at uh a very
450		serious disadvantage.
451		((*People talking at the same time.*))
452	HARRY S:	I'm (xxxx) for (xxxx) President, imagine the story told to me by
453		(Hoag) Simpson, most of you know him. He was now speaking
454		to a student who took a six weeks' a- advanced course. After
455		the six weeks are over he says "How do you feel now?" hhh and
456		the student replies "Mr. Simpson when I came here I was
457		confused (.) but now I'm still confused (.) but at a much higher
458		level."
459		((*Laughter from the audience.*))
460	HARRY S:	Are you confused Mr. Presi[dent at a much
461	SAM S:	[No,
462	HARRY S:	(0.5) Good =
463	SAM S:	= No sir
464	HARRY S:	Alright
465	SAM S:	Let me tell you I'm very pleased (0.8) the way we're
466		progressing with this.
467	HARRY S:	Alright. Guy
468	GUY N:	Yah. (1.0) As far as I'm concern I must say (0.5) that (.) there is

469		a time to disagree (0.5) and this is what we're doing (.) the

469   a time to disagree (0.5) and this is what we're doing (.) the
470   present time .hh but I must say though that (0.2) as s:oon as a
471   decision is made .hh which is considered to be in the best
472   interest of the company hh Guy Normandin won't resent (.)
473   being (.) demoted if this is called demotion (.) and he will be
474   prepared to pull 'n the same direction as other people.
475   ((*Two applause.*))
476 HARRY S: Alright. Jack, you have the legitimate floor.
477 JACK L: I (.) kn:ew we would get at some point (.) of this kind of
478   contention (0.5) and uh uh (.) I was willing, myself, to take that
479   risk and stand ab't to the job that I will be allocated to, to my
480   ability, based on the evaluation of my present superior, which
481   happens to be Sam Steinberg. (1.0) I think that if we don't look
482   at the barriers and put [ourselves
483 SAM S: [You'd be up in Siberia if it was up to
484   me.
485   ((*Laughter.*))
486 JACK L: Then I'll [go.
487 (   ):   [That's where you'll put 'em.
488 JACK L: When I put these things out I feel deeply about the organization
489   and where it's going and where it should go. An' I'm willing to
490   (.) subject my own personal goals at this point- though I 'ave
491   personal goals- to the good or welfare of the organization. So
492   I'm not looking at j:obs or job descriptions or job titles hh what
493   will be best for the company I'm prepared to do.
494   (1.5)
495 SAM S: That was always understood.
496 (   ): Very good ((*knocking on the table.*))
497   (1.5)
498 SAM S: And nobody [knows that better than me.
499 HARRY S: [Irving.
500 IRVING L: I think that's the groupings that are made (0.2) .hh are really the
501   prerogative of the Chairman and whoever he nominates to be
502   the President .hh and those groupings, I only want to submit,
503   must be made on two bases =
504 (   ): ((*Someone coughing.*))
505 IRVING L: = and I don't know if we can go much deeper with it (.) over
506   here. And that is this: number one is what is a natural grouping
507   business wise? and the number two (.) is the competence, and of
508   the of the people available (.) in the judgement of the Chairman
509   (.) and his President .hh and that will obviously have to
510   determine to some degree the groupings uh fundamentally
511   based upon the uh natural groupings that are available to us. But
512   I think that pr-beyond that you have to take people into account
513   and into consideration .h and we we should leave here ready to
514   say that whatever these people deem to be in the best interest of
515   the corporation that this is what we will have to go along with
516   (.) and that's it, I don't think we can go beyond that point.

517		(0.2)
518	SAM S:	I think that you just like Guy and just like Jack before you said
519		now whatever is finally decided (1.0) this is what the, you go
520		in- you're prepared to go along with. And I think that's very
521		nice.
522		((Cut away to the next scene. Everyone is seated for dinner and
523		conversing.))
524		((Title: Part Two-The Family.))
525	Voiceover:	((Dinner was a family affair with Mrs. Sam Steinberg
526		supervising the cooking and waiting on table. The business had
527		been a family affair from the beginning, built by Sam Steinberg
528		and his four brothers from the small grocery store their mother
529		had opened in 1917. But its growth had created needs the
530		family could no longer supply, both in numbers of senior
531		executives and in specialized professional skills. Outside
532		professionals like James Doyle, the corporation's Vice-
533		President and General Counsel, now sat on the management
534		committee alongside Morris and Nathan Steinberg, two of the
535		President's three surviving brothers. Sam Steinberg had no
536		sons but a nephew, Arnold Steinberg, was on the management
537		committee, as was one of the President's four sons-in-law, Mel
538		Dobrin, the Executive Vice President Retailing and at least one
539		grandson was already being given a glimpse of the action.
540		The continuing dominant role of the family and a feeling that
541		this would unduly influence the choice of a new President, were
542		matters of concern throughout the company, concern which
543		underlay the apparently contented family atmosphere at
544		dinner.))
545		((Cut way to close up shots of writing on newsprint.))
546	Voiceover:	((The family problem surfaced in the discussion of professional
547		management. The many barriers to professional management
548		were first listed on sheets of newsprint. They included such
549		problems as poor decision-making and bad inter-divisional
550		relations, as well as family organization.))
551	JAMES D:	… tremendous amount of success. (0.5) There <u>has</u> to have b:een
552		(0.2) a certain degree (.) of professional management (0.2) and
553		for its time (0.2) and the time in which we've been profes-we
554		have been successful, I think we have to recognize .hh a certain
555		pro<u>fess</u>ional (.) competency if you like. (0.2) Now (0.5) uh
556		>somebody mentioned intuition < (0.5) and I say that in any
557		company that's ever going anywhere and succeeding you must
558		have a h:<u>igh</u> degree in your top management .hh of (0.2)
559		intuitiveness or at least an understanding of (.) <u>w:hat</u> the
560		company can do best and can succeed best (.) at doing. And
561		this I think in the past we had. (0.5) <u>But</u> (0.5) <u>ve</u>ry <u>large</u>ly I
562		think this was based on the talent and judgement (.) of our
563		<u>Pres</u>ident (0.5) and partly because of his s-strong convictions
564		his personality and (.) the rest, (0.2) we have (.) tended perhaps

565		to be more foll:owers than <u>lead</u>ers.
566		*((Possible cut/edit in tape.))*
567	JAMES D:	Doesn't per se mean [that as individuals we lack the talents=
568	( ):	[Of course.
569	( ):	=That's right.
570	( ):	No.
571	JAMES D:	or the aptitude (.) to be professional managers=
572	( ):	=We're lacking an integrated approach this is [the-
573	SAM S:	[That's right.
574	( ):	An integrated approach.
575		*((Three or four people talking at the same time.))*
576	JAMES D:	The way the [way (xxxx)=
577	SAM S:	[We're lacking a team a team approach.
578	JAMES D:	=The way we operate is (.) unprofessional.
579	SAM S:	That's it (.) this is what he is saying.
580		[It doesn't mean we lack professional.
581	JAMES D:	[I just wanna make a <u>distinc</u>tion.
582	SAM S:	That's right. It doesn't follow that we lack professional skills=
583	IRVING L:	=Look, we've been passing a lot of platitudes uh up to now I
584		don't think that uh we're leveling all that much. And I think that
585		by ta[king these barriers
586	( ):	[Ha! Ha! Ha!
587	( ):	Speak for yourself=
588	IRVING L:	=Well, I <u>am</u> speaking for myself. And uh I think that uh in
589		[if we took these barriers
590	( ):	[See, you're not leveling (xxxx)
591	IRVING L:	Alright, let's say I'm not leveling=
592		*((Two or three people are talking at the same time.))*
593	IRVING L:	=*((With a wry smile.))* 'Cos I got a lot more that I have not even
594		come <u>close</u> to saying=
595		*((People speaking at the same time.))*
596	( ):	(xxxx)
597	IRVING L:	=and I will (.) Alright so I say, to start it off, why don't we give,
598		why don't we take the barriers .hh as Oscar just suggested and
599		say we have a whole bunch of stuff listed that-these are the
600		reasons <u>w:hy</u> we're not a professional (.) uh company eh? We
601		don't run a professional managerial style. hh so let's take these
602		things and let's put 'em on the table=I would like to suggest that
603		we do this .h and let's hear <u>w:hy</u> people have suggested them
604		and why they feel or what things they're referring to and I don't
605		think we should defend any of these things, > I don't think the
606		objective is to come and say "Well you know why we did this
607		was because we had that." I think we should just bring out and
608		let the people say <u>w:hy</u> they feel these things were suggested (.)
609		and I think we're gonna learn more (.) about what's wrong (.)
610		than we would in any other manner. <
611		*((Several people talking at once.))*
612	( ):	(I think that was) a good suggestion (.) actually?

613 (   ):   The that we look at barriers to [xxx
614 HARRY S: [How do you feel about barriers?
615   You wanta go into barriers?=
616 (   ):   =Yes I would=
617 (   ):   =I think it's a good suggestion.
618 (   ):   (xxxx)
619 (   ):   Absolutely.
620 HARRY S: (xxxx) We're on barriers now.
621   (0.2)
622 ARNOLD S: I think (.) there's been a number of very m:ajor decisions which
623   have been taken (.) uh (.) there seems to be an assumption (.)
624   that there's a-an eternal t:ap? that we turn on and the cash just
625   flows out. And frankly uh unfortunately we're at the stage
626   where just the reverse happens to be true where there is no more
627   cash. And unless we we follow these events very closely we
628   could find ourselves in serious trouble. Let me give you
629   another example: we at the present time (0.2) have four million
630   dollars invested in the restaurant business (.) four million
631   ↓dollars (.) There was never a decision made to invest anything
632   like that kind of money (0.5) by any one individual= I doubt
633   frankly that anyone in this room even ↑knew we have four
634   million dollars (.) invested in the restaurant business and that
635   doesn't include the buildings. This is I'm talking just about the
636   leasehold improvements and the equipment and the inventories,
637   four million dollars. Now that was no planned decision (0.5)
638   and yet it someh:ow with the loose kind of organization we
639   have, we find ourselves at the beginning of nineteen sixty-nine
640   with a four million dollars investment and we will lose this year
641   something like four hundred thousand dollars in that business.
642 JAMES D: Well Arnold, that particular type you've been
643   [giving an example
644 ARNOLD S: [I've been giving an example of the barriers.
645 JAMES D: You have given an example of what I was going to cite myself
646   as a combination of a) one-to-one decision-making and b) and f)
647   family organization. 'Cos if ever there was an example of the
648   family (0.5) and one-to-one decision-making (.) getting us in a
649   spot (.) that is it. (1.0) As every- uh certainly Bill knows this (.)
650   and I'm I'm sure uh Bill did it (.) and I did it (0.2) we were
651   against this whole thing. (1.0) We (.) vr'—I was most
652   vociferously against it (0.5) uh in principle > right from the
653   start=I said "If we're going to go into this kind of an outside
654   venture< (.) let us go out and get the best possible people we
655   can (0.8) and (1.0) let's not settle for any second best (.) let's not
656   go into the basis of (.) buying a company that is already (0.8)
657   not making money (0.2) but losing money." (0.8) That there's a
658   a specific (.) eviden- example of two barriers (.) where the one-
659   to-one decision-making is made (.) and at the same time (.) it's
660   the family organization=when I say organization (.) the family

661		(.) if you like (.) pulling rank (.) on the rest of the non-family
662		executives in the corporation an' saying "Well that's the way it's
663		goin' to be."
664		(2.0)
665	JAMES D:	An' an' an' in effect (.) the non-family part of the business had
666		absolutely nothing to say about that and what they did say (.)
667		was absolutely ignored.
668		(1.0)
669	JACK L:	I want to keep [on this (xxxx)=
670	JAMES D:	[Certainly.
671	JACK L:	=only because I think we're getting some feelings out. For
672		three, four, five years, Mel and I have been saying very clearly,
673		yearly, we used to do it yearly, that the organization being (.)
674		built at corporate was much too heavy for our retail k:ind of
675		operation that we're into. .hh and we just talked against the
676		wind. As we talked it grew bigger and as we talked it grew
677		bigger .hh and (.) it- this costs us time and money and
678		competitiveness because of this one kind of act=and we couldn't
679		make any change. We had no power=I had no power making
680		change, .hh M:el (.) didn't have the power because I know Mel
681		yelled as much I did, no power. Now where is there an
682		organization ↑responsibility? (0.5) and a function of a
683		management (.) in order to take this kind of v-view into fact and
684		see if we can afford what we're building. (0.5) Never was? Is
685		that, is that making manag- professional management as a
686		professional management exercising (.) decision-making? I
687		think we, we've failed=
688	ARNOLD S:	=I'm (not sure) about that Jack. Which what you're saying
689		impl:ies (.) that there was duplication (.) that was unnecessary
690		building. [Isn't that what you're implying?
691	JACK L:	[Mmh, yes, absolutely.
692	ARNOLD S:	But surely the corollary to that (.) is that the duplication existed
693		at the corp- at the divisional level. You're saying that the
694		divisional level had to have what the corporate didn't. Wo' but
695		surely (.) in in a discussion (0.2) which is now coming out in
696		the in in work that Bill's group is doing (.) they're discovering\
697		that the duplication is in fact taking place at the division (.) and
698		the real need is at ↑corporate? I mean all I'm saying Jack is that
699		in fact I agree that duplication exists.
700	JACK L:	But Arnold=
701	ARNOLD S:	=But you're assuming that duplication is at the corporate an' not
702		at the division
703	JACK L:	((Shouting.)) But (.) corporate started to build up (immaterial)
704		that was at the division. Now where should it be?=
705	ARNOLD S:	=Maybe [xxx corporate who say the division grew up not=
706	JACK L:	[xxx at corporate?
707	ARNOLD S:	=even though it was at the corporate. (xxxx) Jack, I am agreeing
708		that some[one should have sat down.

709 JACK L: [Okay (0.5) Right! That's all what I am saying.
710   ((Everybody talking at the same time.))
711 HARRY S: Would you please speak (.) one at a time and I think
712   professionalism can start right here the way we conduct the
713   meeting. Too many meetings in the past have been
714   unprofessional in that (.) problems in an unorganized manner
715   have been tossed on the table. Philosophies are spewed out.
716   (0.5) So professional at the meeting means (.) identifying the
717   problem? (0.5) moving from there to different means of solving
718   them (.) a:nd this is where we fall flat on our (.) backs again and
719   again (.) is not nailing down ((hand taps table)) who's to do
720   what and when ((hand taps table)) and how ((hand taps table)).
721   (0.5) If you want to turn this thing into (.) a >fish market
722   gentlemen<, it's your meeting but=
723   ((Harry's gaze during above comment was directed to the entire
724   table, moving from person to person))
725 JACK L: =Look Harry, uh I I wanna stop (.) and critique what you're
726   saying with your=
727 HARRY S: =Go ahead=
728 JACK L: =I am saying that at least if you don't get out feelings ((hand
729   tap)) on this ((tap)) table ((tap)) today ((tap)) and Monday
730   ((tap)) and Tuesday ((tap)), we'll all go ((tap)) back and say
731   "We're-we should have said and we didn't say" ((tap)) and it's
732   the feelings ((tap)) that count ((tap)). It's the commitment
733   ((tap)) one feels inside (.) that counts, it's not words (.) and it's
734   not it's the deeds and the feelings and the commitment we have
735   (.) to this organization to be better tomorrow and today. And I
736   for one am objecting to your system of method and monitoring
737   because I am not doing this for a mental exercises, I am doing
738   this much more, there's much more at stake than a mental
739   exercise (.) and I don't want that kind of monitoring from you=
740 HARRY S: =But m:y [my commitment
741 JACK L: =[I want some heat to come out (.) ((repeated finger-
742   pointing shake probably toward Harry)) I want some feeling to
743   come out and I want this thing to come out so that when you go
744   away we know we've done the job (.) thoroughly and we
745   understand our job to do so we all go back and do the job
746   together (.) not disjointedly (.) and not feeling that we haven't
747   been heard and seen and felt'n put the things we feel on the
748   table
749   ((People talking at once.))
750   ((Jack's gaze during the above comment was directed solely
751   toward Harry))
752 SAM S: When I started out the meeting I said each one of you in your
753   report there must be something that you feel and we recognize
754   that and this is one of the reasons we're here. So if there are in
755   tho:se those items that you (.) consider uppermost that you
756   reduce to writing and felt free to say so (.) what is uppermost in

757		your minds that you feel has some restraining influence I think
758		it should like Jack said (0.5) uh (0.7) <u>brought out</u>?
759	JACK L:	°Absolutely°
760	SAM S:	Fr:ee<u>ly</u> spoken.
761		(0.5)
762	( ):	[Well I I
763	SAM S:	[To the extent that we think it's pretty well <u>covered</u> by what's
764		already been said then we move ↓forward.
765		(1.0)
766	ARNOLD S:	Harry, I would like to deal with a barrier that has been talked
767		about and uh by many people. One which (.) I am, I guess
768		particularly sensitive to, that has to do with number f) family
769		organization.
770	( ):	(xxxx)
771	ARNOLD S:	Uh uh I think there's implied in many if not (0.5) most of the
772		submissions that deal with professional management leadership,
773		> I think all of them pretty much do < (.) the idea that <u>most</u> or
774		a:<u>ll</u> of the members of the family (.) would prefer working in an
775		organization (.) where professional management takes a
776		secondary role (.) to nepotism or or or fam- or family
777		preference. (0.5) An' in this area I I can obviously only speak
778		for myself (1.0) but I think I'm speaking for for most if not a:ll
779		of the second generation (.) family members when when I state
780		that that nep- that n-nepotism (0.2) generates sa-satisfaction to
781		any (.) particular individual for a very short period of time. (0.8)
782		And that in the long run uh career satisfaction of an individual
783		(0.2) uh let me put it differently (.) that that when (.) nep-
784		nepotism plays an important role (.) in the choice (0.2) of an
785		individual for management (.) the satisfaction that <u>comes</u> from
786		that is very short lived to any particular individual (.) who
787		thinks of himself (.) in a management capacity (.) and I think as
788		I said I speak well I know I only speak for for myself (.) in <u>fact</u> I
789		<u>suspect</u> that I'm voicing the opinion (.) of all if not most of the
790		members of the family.
791		(1.0)
792	SAM S:	hh now uh (0.8) uh the only comment I would like to make at
793		this mom- this moment was that I read a Harvard report (0.5)
794		where it deals with families in organizations=
795	( ):	=We all read it. ((People interrupting and agreeing.))
796	SAM S:	Alright! So it tells you that after a period of twenty years there
797		is more family than ever before=and that hasn't affected the the
798		performances as I read it in these companies. (1.0) On the >
799		other hand < (0.5) I think that when we look around the table
800		over here, we talk about family, (1.0) well (.) I looked upon
801		Jack as a member of the family=I look up:on (.) Oscar as a
802		member of the family (.) I've looked upon Jack Ginser always
803		as a member of the family (.) and I think that they look upon
804		↑themselves as a member of family.

805		*((Four or five people talking at the same time.))*
806	( ):	That's not a very good example.
807	( ):	Your definition of family and everyone else's xxx
808	SAM S:	I'm not will you please listen to me? I'm just giving you by way
809		of example because (.) he started right at the very beginning
810		with us.
811		(1.5)
812		*((People talking at once.))*
813	SAM S:	But (.) now let's go to the next step (.) let's take where people (.)
814		let's say (.) blood blood relations=
815	( ):	=That's better=
816	SAM S:	=No? We'll go the next step regardless the next step, blood
817		relations. (0.5) Wherever the m:an (1.0) could not measure up
818		or we had somebody more competent in job (0.2) the person
819		that was most competent got it but to s:ay (.) .hh that if a
820		member of the family who's in the firm who has the competence
821		an' he can't be considered because he is a member of the family
822		is wrong.
823		*((People denying they implied that.))*
824	IRVING L:	Well I tell you, I just wanna comment a little on this because uh
825		(0.2) I've had a lot of uh people uh come to me and talk to me
826		about this bec- may be because:e you know I'm a little younger
827		and only joined the company .hh uh some eleven years ago and
828		uh went through all this and in my case obviously it was no
829		great deterrent for me. .hh but uh let me just say this, that uh
830		there is an awareness (0.5) in the co- in many of the people in
831		the company that uh there is such a thing as an informal
832		organization at Steinberg's (0.8) which is directly linked to the
833		family (.) and there's an informal organization perhaps in every
834		company but this one happens to be directly linked to the family
835		.hh to the point wh:ere (.) there uh there (.) if you're sitting
836		among a group of peers (0.5) that the fact th', and I'm gonna
837		level here and tell you that the standard joke is (.) that the key
838		decisions are not made at the management committee (.) or with
839		the President (.) but at Friday night supper (1.0) and this in itself
840		is very indicative because I'm sure you've all heard the same e-
841		expressions used (0.2) and it's very indicative (.) as to how
842		people see the organization an' how they read it. They don't see
843		(.) equ:ality; if one fella happens to be Vice-President of this
844		and another fella Vice-President of that and they're both putting
845		forth their opinions, if one happens to be related (.) the feeling
846		is (.) that he's got an awful lot more to say (.) a) because he is
847		much closer, b) it's sort of his money involved and, c:) it's
848		because (.) he goes to the Friday night supper as opposed to the
849		other party (.) and I think that this (.) is the feeling among a lot
850		of the people (.) in the organization. They feel it definitively
851		has hampered in the past (.) and I might add (.) that uh perhaps
852		from my own point of view anyways is probably is less so now

853		than it has been (0.5) and it's been very severe in the past (.) in
854		my opinion.
855		(2.0)
856	IRVING L:	And I can tell you there's a lot of people they spend a lot of
857		time talking about this stuff (0.2) a lot of ↓time. And so I think
858		we have to recognize it and be aware of it.
859		(4.0)
860	SAM S:	I just wanna make (.) I just wanna ask you one question=Is it
861		your charm or ability got you where you are now? That's all I
862		want to know. *((laughing.))*=
863		*((People speaking at once.))*
864	( ):	=Good looks ...
865		*((Laughter.))*
866	MEL D:	No, he attended the Friday night dinner.
867		*((Everybody laughing.))*
868	JAMES D:	No yeah but to to support everything that Irving is saying uh
869		there is also and I think Irving could, might call in on this (.)
870		there's a sort of uh (0.5) another:r feeling around (0.5) that (0.5)
871		a a certain amount of this has (.) definitely been taken care of in
872		a much better way in recent years with the appointment of other
873		non-family people to very senior positions. But running along
874		with that wh-whether we like to admit it or not there's a there's
875		one school of thought going around which sort of looks as us a
876		little bit like the Negroes in a cabinet (0.5) you know (.) that
877		really we're we're there more for show *((starting to laugh))* than
878		for performance. And that the real decisions are still made as
879		Irving says in the in the Friday night eh meetings whether that's
880		(0.5) has validity or not, that's what they believe=
881	SAM S:	=(xxxx) I don't think I need to answer that but certain you were
882		never put on for show.
883		(1.2)
884	MORRIS S:	Nepotism can actually ex<u>ist</u> (.) not only in <u>family</u> but when a:
885		General Manager in his own division can have nepotism in his
886		*((one person speaking at the same time))* own family. So
887		nepotism does not only exist in a in a uh family.
888		(0.5)
889	ARNOLD S:	The whole question of nepotism (.) in my opinion is not really
890		(.) coming out on the table. (0.5) In this sense from what I
891		gather and and it's may be not right for me to to bring it up uh
892		(.) uh but (.) throughout the reports (0.8) throughout the reports
893		(0.2) there is (0.2) if not (0.2) written certainly between the
894		lines (1.0) there is the the the uh obvious statement (.) that this
895		company h:as been <u>ruled</u> (.) and is suffering (0.8) <u>badly</u> (.) as a
896		result of nepotism. And <u>frank</u>ly I have a feeling that if a vote
897		was taken (1.0) by the people here more people would vote in-
898		in to the correctness of that statement than to the wrongness of
899		that statement.
900		*((Several people talking at once.))*

901 JACK L: (xxxx) I think (xxxx) you're pushing, I guess y:ou're u:h you're
902   rightly so. I think what uh some of us said in our report was that
903   (.) u::h it's inconceivable that a decision of succession (.) u:h
904   would not been u:h 'cos size of our company, would not have
905   been made that decision before now if it wasn't for the di<u>lemma</u>
906   (0.5) of the family.
907 SAM S: You're talkin' about how would you say eh (3.0) I had the word
908   on the tip of my tongues when you say franchise but <u>this</u> (1.0)
909   u:h (.) I'll say is this=I'll put it simpler "Does this rule out (0.5)
910   ((pointing to Arnold)) Arnold because he's a member of the
911   [family?"
912 ( ):   [No ((several people speaking)) no, no.
913 SAM S: Well, of course I've got to make sure that I understand that
914   clearly, he's a member of the [family.
915 ( ):   [We're coming to that (xxxx)
916   We're coming to that.
917   ((People still talking at the same time.))
918 JACK L: <u>What</u> are you asking? Come <u>on</u>. What is he asking?
919 ( ):   I'm not sure.
920 JACK L: I don't know what he is asking?
921 ( ):   Are you are you doing something underhand?
922 ( ):   Our boss is doing something (xxxx)
923 ( ):   I don't know, I mean.
924 SAM S: Let me finish please (0.5) let me finish.
925 HARRY S: Satisfied?=
926 SAM S: =Now if the man can't be considered for the <u>job</u> because he's a
927   member of the family we better know the ground rules right at
928   the beginning.
929   ((People talking, some laughing.))
930 JOHN P: That the idea of a professional manager and the [idea of (xxxx)
931 ARNOLD S: [I don't think
932   one would define nep-nepotism as saying that <u>even</u> wh:<u>ere</u> a
933   member of the family (.) is su<u>p:erior</u> (1.0) uh uh or or the <u>lack</u>
934   of nepotism I should say where (.) I don't think the <u>lack</u> of
935   nepotism means or the non-existence of nepotism uh impl:ies
936   that even where a member of the family (.) is suitable (.) eh or is
937   the most suitable candidate for the job (.) that it's not available
938   to him=
939 JOHN P: =Well if I understood Mr. Sam right, he was saying that uh all
940   things being equal (.) the member of the family would get the
941   the job. (1.0) I don't see that's (0.5) ((someone speaking at the
942   same time)) I mean it's almost like uh seniority=
943 JACK L: =I think that the company in a position (0.2) uhh that (0.2)
944   cautiously (0.2) must make a decisions (0.2) that uh (0.2) >
945   everything being equal < the family member <u>won't</u> get it (.)
946   ((people talking at the same time)) for the nineteen (xxxx). I
947   think it would be better for (.) the company.
948 ( ):   That's reverse (prejudice)?

949 (   ):   That's right=
950 (   ):   =Um hum=
951 JACK L: =No (.) it isn't. *((People still talking at the same time.))*
952 SAM S: Listen (.) foremost in my mind there's al:ways <u>been</u> (0.5) the
953   person's ability to cope with his job (0.2) at the ↑point when he
954   was no longer able to measure up to that job (.) he was replaced
955   and that'll go all the years that we've been in business. Doesn't
956   matter wh:at that relationship (.) happened to ↑be. (0.2) Now,
957   <u>however</u> it's viewed (0.5) from the outside (1.0) as long as I am
958   in the job in any case (0.8) family will always be given
959   consideration but <u>always</u> (.) subject to the person's ability to
960   discharge that responsibility.
961 JOHN P: We (.) brushed over the Friday nights=
962   *((Several people laughing.))* Ha ha ha!
963 JOHN P: =I'd like to be in a position to say with con<u>vic</u>tion not (0.5)
964   the organ- (0.2) <u>Cer</u>tainly the family discusses business
965   when they get together (.) but the decisions are
966   [made in the management committee.
967 SAM S: [xxx We don't discuss business at Friday night.
968 JOHN P: Well you don't, I'm surpri[sed. *((Noise of people talking.))*
969 SAM S: [You couldn't hear yourself talk with
970   my grandchildren there.
971   *((Noise of some people laughing.))*
972 JAMES D: I think Friday night is a sort of uh (0.8) *((everyone speaking at*
973   *once))* =a family get-together. And I think that the=
974 SAM S: =The family hasn't met in years.
975 MEL D: I think first of all the President if he wants to but uh I think it's
976   up to him to say <u>who</u> meets on Friday night (1.2) because
977   there's a- [there's a- there's a feeling
978 JAMES D: [I think I think (xxxx)
979 MEL D: <u>No</u>, there's a <u>statement</u> that uh the *((he starts to smile))* mana-
980   management members here might think that fifteen members of
981   the family meet. (0.8) I've been the only one there=
982 JAMES D: =Twelve of which [are children.
983 MEL D: [Is that correct. I've I've never seen Arnold
984   there, I've never seen Nathan there, I've never seen Morris
985   there in the last five years (.) so
986   *((People responding.))*
987 MEL D: I don't know <u>what</u> they think (xxxx)
988   *((People still talking at the same time.))*
989 SAM S: I don't even need to have a family get-together.
990   (1.0)
991 (   ):   This is true.
992 SAM S: One <u>man</u> (1.0) my own person have a hundred percent control
993   of this company. I don't have to ask <u>anybody</u> so it's no use even
994   talkin' about a discussion the the there's no need for a
995   discussion. (1.0) Uh (1.0) I don't need anybody's approval=
996 (   ):   =No, right!

997	JAMES D:	No one is, no one is is denying to you the prerogative of saying
998		here I have two or three or four or five however many people
999		you have, might have in mind as an ultimate (0.5) successor (.)
1000		but you're gonna be the person who is is gonna make that
1001		decision. First if it weren't for any other reason is because on
1002		strictly legal grounds, as you just pointed out, you wouldn't
1003		have to ask anybody else (.) even on a straight legal ground you
1004		could say "To hell with ya," if you felt so inclined, "I'll make
1005		that decision personally" and everybody here knows that. .hh
1006		But you being the kind of <u>person</u> (.) you <u>a:re</u> (0.5) I think are
1007		unlikely to make that decision of, a decision of that magnitude
1008		<u>without</u> referring (.) to the family. (1.0) But the fact is, if you're
1009		willing to accord then (.) because of the (.) family ties, the
1010		matter of discussion on a rational basis (.) with the family (.) we
1011		think that it should be done (.) on a rational basis also with your
1012		senior executives.
1013		(0.2)
1014	SAM S:	That's why you're here tonight=
1015	HARRY S:	=Well eh Jim that's in view of the eh (0.5) we agree to adjourn
1016		at ↑nine > I don't think there's much sense in starting the next
1017		item on the agenda, which is succession < (.) With a your
1018		agreement, I suggest we adjourn (.) here and ↑now gives us a
1019		good night's ↑rest.
1020	( ):	(xxxx) finish it off in ten minutes.
1021		((Laughter and people talking.))
1022	HARRY S:	Huh?
1033	( ):	I think we'll all sleep on it.
1024	HARRY S:	Alright, we'll all sleep on it. (0.5) ((Somebody starts to speak.))
1025		(1.0)
1026	HARRY S:	Alright the (.) meeting is adjourned 'til tomorrow morning at (.)
1027		nine o'clock when we'll discuss succession.
1028		((Everyone starts to leave the table. Cut away to the next scene,
1029		the executives relaxing in the evening at the bar, sitting down to
1030		play bridge or talking to each other on the sofas.))
1031		((Title: Part three-Succession.))
1032	Voiceover:	((The Palomino sessions ran late but there was time before bed
1033		for a hand of bridge, an appropriate game for the last night of
1034		the conference.))
1035	( ):	((At the bridge table.)) Sam?
1036		(1.0)
1037	( ):	You deal.
1038		(1.5)
1039	JAMES D:	I think it's a great great shame to let a man (xxxx) play with his
1040		wife.
1041		(0.5)
1042	JAMES D:	They probably they [probably play a lot of bridge together.
1043	HELEN S:	[We fight we fight? ((laughing.))

1044	*Voiceover:*	*((In bridge a player may have two objectives, to win by making*
1045		*his contract or to prevent the opposition from winning, which is*
1046		*another kind of victory. The game has rules, which the players*
1047		*must observe if they want to play at all but it also has*
1048		*conventions outside the rules, mainly the elaborate system of*
1049		*bidding by which the players signal the strengths and*
1050		*weaknesses of their hands. Through bidding a way has been*
1051		*found for players to say indirectly what the rules won't allow*
1052		*them to say openly. In the succession discussion, which ended*
1053		*the Palomino Conference, there were some who hoped to win*
1054		*and others who merely hoped to prevent someone else from*
1055		*winning. No participant could propose himself or criticize*
1056		*another candidate directly. So more indirect ways had to be*
1057		*found of saying things, which could not be said out loud.))*
1058		*((People sitting on the sofas discussing what happened at the*
1059		*meeting quietly.))*
1060	*Voiceover:*	*((To make matters worse, the exercise had to take place under*
1061		*the eyes of Sam Steinberg, a man who none of them could afford*
1062		*to offend and whose choice might already have been made.))*
1063		*((Cut away to the scene of the continuation of the meeting the*
1064		*next morning.))*
1065	HARRY S:	The task then is (2.2) based on your reading (.) of the
1066		organization reports (.) submitted to the President (.) the pre-
1067		reading provided and the discussion outlined (.) determine (0.8)
1068		what procedures (.) and criteria (.) should be used (.) for the <
1069		selection of the chief officers. > (0.8) Now (.) on criterion and
1070		(1.0) procedures, I thought you would find helpful that you have
1071		this in your kits (1.0) the extract from the ... *((talk covered over by*
1072		*voiceover)).*
1073	*Voiceover:*	*((The method adopted was to describe an ideal candidate for*
1074		*the Presidency. By proposing specific criteria, each member*
1075		*hoped to point towards the candidate he favored or away from*
1076		*those he did not. On one point there was almost total*
1077		*agreement, the winner had to be someone in this room.))*
1078		*((Harry S. starts to write on the newsprint.))*
1079	SAM S:	°I want yous to listen me out for a minute.° (0.8) Right now,
1080		one of the (0.2) largest organizations in our field (0.5) have
1081		recently as you all know appointed a President (2.0) and from
1082		<u>my</u> point of view (1.0) it's a sorry spectacle (1.0) in an
1083		organization so <u>vast</u> (2.0) with the years of experience and the
1084		(1.0) you know how (0.5) how <u>large</u> an organization that is (0.5)
1085		doing the business in the billions and the this is what they have
1086		to end up with (1.0). So uh (1.0) just tryin' to tell you that uh
1087		we got to give serious consideration (1.0) and u:hh just uh I'm
1088		just <u>exasperated</u> to to to think (1.0) how I:I would have felt if I
1089		was a: substantial shareholder in that organization (0.5) as to
1090		what they (1.5) had to resort to in terms of a President.
1091	HARRY S:	Are you really sorry about that? [I think=

1092 SAM S:	[No but I am xxx
1093 HARRY S:	=I think of Churc[hill's=
1094 SAM S:	[This is for our own people.
1095 HARRY S:	=of Churchill's remarks (0.5) that the Israeli secret weapon (.)
1096	was the Arab ability to fight.
1097	*((Everybody laughing at length.))*
1098 HARRY S:	One of our competitive advantage may be exactly that kind of
1099	appointment that our competitor.
1100	*((Laughter continues.))*
1101 SAM S:	What you're saying is that we're betting on our competitor's
1102	ignorance and not on our own skills and abilities.
1103 HARRY S:	Not (xxxx) people of that ability.
1104	*((People's laughter still continues.))*
1105 SAM S:	You can see, you can see the talent we possess (2.0) by Harry's
1106	definition.
1107	*((Some laughter continues and some people talking.))*
1108 JOHN P:	Uhm (1.0) One I'd like to propose is that (.) we make ref- it's
1109	made reference to in the uh (0.8) material you've just read as
1110	well, the n:eed to maint:ain a dyn:amic (0.5) organization and to
1111	do so implies that (0.8) uh this <u>character</u> has to be established
1112	at the top, so the (0.5) certainly the kind of individual who
1113	would give leadership to this organization ought to have a
1114	dynamic, forceful, initiating an' (0.5) risk-taking (1.0) qualities
1115	(.) that are needed to <u>ensure</u> the dynamism (.) is maintained.
1116 HARRY S:	Alright uh you're saying uh the attributes, would they be
1117	dynamic *((writing on the newsprint.))* (2.5). Would you say
1118	"forceful," John? *((Still writing.))*
1119 JOHN P:	Forceful, initiating and risk-taking
1120 HARRY S:	Dynamic, forceful *((writing))* (2.5) initiating and risk-taking.
1121	(3.0)
1122 ( ):	°As contrasted with mechanical, repetitive, dull, aimless and
1123	backward looking.°
1124	(4.0)
1125 HARRY S:	The individual chosen should have proven (0.5) in the light of
1126	his past performance *((reading from the newsprint))* (2.5) uh
1127	evidence of dynamism, forcefulness (0.2) taking initiative (0.5)
1128	and risk-taking.
1129	(2.5)
1130 HARRY S:	Bill?
1131 BILL H:	He should have a <u>broad</u> gr:asp of (.) business (.) in general (1.0)
1132	and our business in particular.
1133	*((Harry S. writing on newsprint.))*
1134	(10.5)
1135 HARRY S:	Yes, Irving?
1136 IRVING L:	Harry, I think he should have (.) a very out<u>standing</u> record of
1137	his personal uh philosophy and personal mode of living and all
1138	the rest of it that goes with it.
1139	(1.2)

1140 HARRY S: You wanna qualify what kind of philosophy?
1141 IRVING L: Well … I'm just [saying …
1142 HARRY S: [You're not saying nine, nine=
1143 IRVING L: =He's got to be rather clean living, let's put it that way
1144   ((Some laughter.))
1145 HARRY S: Clean living?=
1146 IRVING L: =That's right.
1147 JAMES D: That's not the words I'd like to see going up on the paper
1148   ((Laughter and people talking.))
1149 (   ):   A pure blooded (.) Canadian boy.
1150   ((Laughter and people talking.))
1151 (   ):   A little Alger.
1152 JAMES D: You're trying to disqualify yourself for future
1153   ((Loud laughs.))
1154 (   ):   Just put down Horatio Alger
1155   (1.0)
1156 HARRY S: ((Laughing)) I am not going to ask which one of us matches xxx
1157   (0.5)
1158 IRVING L: A lot of integrity
1159 MEL D: Well, let let Irving make his point. May be the word [xxx
1160 IRVING L: [No, the
1161   point I'm trying to make is and I don't want to mention names
1162   'cos we're on film here and everything else .hh but there are ex-
1163   examples in the industry of leading industrialists (.) who uh (.)
1164   because of their own personal uh uh meanderings or difficulties
1165   or what have you are just not running their industries.
1166   (0.2)
1167 OSCAR P: They get into that position and then they start fooling around=
1168 JAMES D: =Maybe they don't start fooling around 'til they get (xxxx) ((he
1169   laughs.))
1170   (0.2)
1171 IRVING L: That's right Oscar.
1172 HARRY S: Irving, do you hear what you're saying?
1173   (1.0)
1174 IRVING L: What I said
1175   ((Some people talking at once.))
1176 HARRY S: High personal standards of ethics and mor:ality. Will, will
1177   that'll do it?
1178   ((Some laughter.))
1179 IRVING L: No problem
1180 JAMES D: I think I'd knock out "clean-living," it's it's-
1181   ((Some laughter.))
1182 BILL H: Accepted accepted as a leader (0.8) by his peers.
1183   (3.0)
1184 HARRY S: ((Writing.)) Accepted as a leader by his peers.
1185   (4.0)
1186 HARRY S: Does this man exist this side of heaven?
1187 (   ):   No

1188 (   ):   Sam Steinberg.
1189   (0.5)
1190 (   ):   Do you wanna a raise?
1191   *((Everybody laughing.))*
1192   *((Three or four persons talking at the same time.))*
1193 HARRY S: As of right now I'm the only guy that fits and one more
1194   statement and I'll be out of the (xxxx)
1195   *((Everybody laughing.))*
1196   (2.0)
1197 IRVING L: *((Raising his hand))* Harry, I think he's got to be uhm hungry in
1198   the sense that not foodwise (.) but in the sense that the man who
1199   must (.) <u>feel</u> (.) an urgency, a motivation and so on to n'uh to
1200   build the business, to improve the business and so on.
1201 HARRY S: Does this capture hungry, Irving?=
1202 IRVING L: =Yeh, it does, I guess.
1203 (   ):   Hungry for success.
1204   (2.5)
1205 SAM S: Some ten years ago (1.2) met a chap who was in my class in
1206   public school (0.8) and he said to me:e? (1.0) that at one t:ime
1207   the kids got together (1.8) and the person that they singled out
1208   who was least likely to succeed was me.
1209   (1.0)
1210 SAM S: This is what he told me
1211   *((Contained laughter.))*
1212 SAM S: It's a <u>fact</u>.(0.5) The other was I was telling some of the boys uh
1213   (1.0) oh some about uh (0.5) thirty years ago there was a
1214   Liberty magazine (1.0) and they had an article (0.5) the new
1215   sciences that were being introduced in terms of selecting (1.0)
1216   uh people for employment in the organization. And they had a
1217   point system (.) and they'd rate them on the years of education,
1218   years of experience and the various qualifications added up and
1219   he'd had to have a certain point rating in order to get a job.
1220   (1.0) So finally after uh three or four pages of this it comes to
1221   the end of the uh story, the editor was asked or the person was
1222   asked "Well, what about the fellow who doesn't qualify at a:ll?"
1223   He said "Well you don't have to worry about him, he'll end up
1224   being the boss." (0.5) So, evidently this happens to be the story
1225   of my life?
1226   (2.8)
1227 (   ):   Uh ... Harry [xxx
1228 SAM S: [The point I'm trying to make is that it doesn't
1229   always follow (0.5) that (.) person must have all these
1230   qualification to uh to be able to perform.
1231   (0.8)
1232 ARNOLD S: I think what we wanna do is to (.) in a sense direct our own\
1233   destiny and it goes back again to the (.) story that my father tells
1234   (.) of (.) picking only six footers (.) if you gonna train people to
1235   play basketball only start with six footers 'cos at least you know

1236	you're not gonna- you're you're- That doesn't mean you can't get
1237	a four foot uh basketball player who could be good. But why
1238	take, why take the chance, you might as well train the six
1239	footers to start with- Your chances of success
1240	*((Everyone talking at once.))*
1241 SAM S:	I'm just saying
1242 ( ):	I think what Arnold is trying to say
1243 SAM S:	You're making a good point.
1244 ( ):	You're making a very good point.
1245 SAM S:	That you can't go by the exception.
1246 ( ):	That's right.
1247 ( ):	I agree.
1248 HARRY S:	(I don't buy that.) The only message is (that the man xxx)
1249	whether it's Truman (1.5) ((coughing)) or whether it's Trudeau,
1250	how the man changes when he assumes office and changes in
1251	some direction [xxx.
1252 ARNOLD S:	[The reason why he was so good was 'cos he
1253	was a retailer you see and that's how [xxx
1254	[((loud laughs.))
1255 JAMES D:	No but the Harry, Harry (0.5) you've *((people talking at once))*
1256	you've, you've thrown, you thrown something on the on the
1257	table which I think has a disturbing effect (0.2) What you're
1258	really saying is (.) there's no sense in going through all this
1259	because the job changes the man (such that) it goes out of the
1260	window anyway and this we know.
1261	*((People talking at once.))*
1262 HARRY S:	I I am saying use every criterion you h:ave (.) and so on but
1263	bear in mind (xxxx) statement (.) that something happens when
1264	the man (.) assumes responsibility=
1265 ( )	=We know that
1266 JAMES D:	=Which is incalculable, so why bring it out?
1267	*((People talking at once.))*
1268 JOHN P:	We've already agreed that the candidates for any of these key
1269	assignment (.) are those who are best qualified (.) whether these
1270	individuals are (.) in the organization (.) or outside the
1271	organization=We shouldn't close our eyes to the possibility
1272	(0.5) that uh more qualified people (0.5) meeting these
1273	candidates (.) meeting these criteria better than (.) our internal
1274	resources.
1275	(0.8)
1276 HARRY S:	Are you saying look both inside and outside the organization?
1277 JOHN P:	I-I I'm saying we shouldn't exclude (0.5) looking outside the
1278	organization (0.5) if we (0.8) in trying to find the right
1279	candidate.
1280 JAMES D:	That's a kind of a negative, questionable procedure isn't it
1281	*((People talking at once.))*
1282 JAMES D:	We should look inside to see if there are people=
1283 JOHN P:	=No, I don't agree. I think that uh looking inside would be

1284	myopia. I think we oughta (.) look beyo:nd at the same time.
1285	(1.8)
1286 JOHN P:	Here's a statement that I think is worth considering
1287	"Promotional of internal personnel into key executive
1288	assignments without regard to the qualifications of those outside
1289	the organization who may be of superior superior caliber (0.2)
1290	can result in promoting mediocrity (.) The best qualified man
1291	for a key position may not be available in the firm and therefore
1292	a sounder approach would be to look [outside"
1293	[((Several people talking at once.))
1294 ( ):	May not be available=
1295 JOHN P:	="This may be a particular- particularly necessary when a
1296	decision is made to go in a new business and so forth
1297	>Furthermore, when promoting from within has been a long
1298	established practice the risk is increased that the vitality of the
1299	organization will become sapped and those promoted tend to
1300	imitate their bosses rather than to introduce new ideas"<
1301	[Now ((People talking at once.))
1302 SAM S:	[You said you spoke of when you're going to a new business
1303	(too) now how much qualification ((People talking.))=
1304 ( ):	=The word was "not available"
1305	((People talking.))
1306 JOHN P:	Can I finish?=
1307 IRVING L:	=I tell you why I don't agree. Because it sort of indicates to
1308	your people (.) that if this is your attitude, striving for
1309	excellence in this way, now what happ:ens every time you have
1310	a job through your organization. If you want better, you can
1311	always find better, nobody here is the best in his capacity in the
1312	world I guarantee you or even in North America (.) and that's
1313	from Sam Steinberg right through every job here. So then
1314	people say "What's the use of working and everything else 'cos I
1315	can't seem to better myself, they always find a guy in Alabama
1316	and then they come with a fella from Washington and so on and
1317	so forth" And you never really build a culture and sort of (.)
1318	family, quotation marks (.) into your organization
1319	[((People talking.))
1320 ARNOLD S:	[I think there's no question, John that we could find someone
1321	more capable (.) than anybody in this company. ((People talking
1322	at once.)) For any standing any position in the company=
1323 ( ):	=Right!
1324 ARNOLD S:	For any position that you've have have have put your own
1325	people into (0.2) if you went outside you would have gotten
1326	better people (0.2) for every job that's ever have been filled in
1327	this company we could have found better people if we went
1328	outside if we did it long enough, hard enough, (.) we would
1329	have found better people=
1330 JACK L:	=I dunno (0.5) I dunno (.) how many more people in this
1331	industry are better than we as a group.

1332 HARRY S: Well I think what Arnold is saying [here …
1333 SAM S: [Now he added the group,
1334   you see (xxxx)
1335   *((People talking.))*
1336 ARNOLD S: From an academic point of view, Jack, I <u>think</u> (.) if we searched
1337   the world we'd find someone [better … Okay?
1338 JACK L: [Okay, I agree=
1339 HARRY S: =I think what Arnold is [saying..
1340 ARNOLD S: [That doesn't mean that for every job
1341   we must search the world.
1342 (   ):   Okay
1343 ARNOLD S: It's impractical and I'm <u>not</u> sure it's the best possible
1344   [approach to running a company.
1345 JAMES D: [I think (0.5) the the Can I say something now?=
1346 HARRY S: =Yeah, well I wanna say something harking back to the role I
1347   play as professor and a rabbi and so on
1348   *((People laughing.))*
1349 (   ):   (xxxx)
1350 HARRY S: This is to give you part of my personal style of feedback,
1351   gentlemen, >here it is<
1352 (   ):   (xxxx)
1353 HARRY S: U::h well the point i:s (.) uh Levitt in his book on Managerial
1354   Psychology, if you hadn't read it I recommend it highly to you.
1355   He is now talking (.) he's saying where we go through
1356   problem-solving talking about the best solution he is now
1357   saying that this is a lot of crap (.) in economic words, he's
1358   saying in effect (.) he gives the example of a man looking for a
1359   used car (.) and he says the man (.) in Montreal is not going to
1360   reply and investigate every single used car (.) nor is he going to
1361   visit every single used car lot in Montreal, he says the guy will
1362   take a lifetime to do it (.) So he now says (.) that you take a
1363   "satisficing" solution that's how he calls it, that is one which
1364   meets the needs of the time (.) and the best one that you come
1365   up with in the circumstances (.) I now withdraw from my role of
1366   professor and rabbi and become chairman.
1367   *((People laughing.))*
1368 GUY N: Wouldn't the risks be a lot greater actually to (0.5) if this were
1369   to be the case to hire [somebody from outside.
1370 SAM S: [xxx observed in our industry (.) where
1371   they found it necessary (.) to seek in the outside, now we've had
1372   a series of <u>presidents</u> changing over like you'd churn butter.
1373 (   ):   That's right
1374 SAM S: [When they go outside.
1375 JACK L: [(xxxx), Colonial Colonial=
1376 SAM S: =I could name any number, when they went outside they were
1377   just like churning butter (.) The only time I see that happen (.)
1378   where the financial <u>interests</u> (.) [are such that=
1379 (   ):   [Forced forced

1380	SAM S:	=That's right forced! Otherwise uh they loose their shirt
1381		(1.0)
1382	SAM S:	Like Safeway with McGovern at that time (xxxx)=
1383		((People talking.))
1384	JOHN P:	=What we're really saying is that thought be given to the (.)
1385		possibility that there are superior qualifications outside the
1386		company.
1387		(1.5)
1388	JOHN P:	°So°
1389		(0.5)
1390	HARRY S:	I've written half a statement on the board. (2.0) "Seek out best
1391		man bearing criteria in mind, look" (.) and where you're divided
1392		(.) is it first outsi- first inside and then outside or are you
1393		looking at one shot (0.2) everywhere (.) I think this is a
1394		question, which you have to resolve=
1395	JAMES D:	=I think we all agree, except John, we look inside (.)
1396	( ):	Yeah, that's right.
1397		(2.8)
1398	HARRY S:	Any further suggestions or steps on (.) procedure?
1399		(1.0)
1400	JACK L:	My conviction is, that it's not onl:y (.) uh this group that is
1401		concerned (0.5) The group below us (.) are very very concerned
1402		about the leadership function (.) of the company and the po-xxx
1403		position we're talking about (0.8) They have certain
1404		assumptions of certain people that they would not (.) wanna be
1405		associated as a leader. (1.0) And we must take (.) their opinions
1406		(0.2) into consideration (.) when we deliberate.
1407		(0.5)
1408	ARNOLD S:	You don't think that the people in this roo:m reflect the opinions
1409		properly reflect in their discussions with the President the views
1410		of the people below them?
1411	JACK L:	I did (.) I did, I did in my document.
1412		((People talking at the same time.))
1413	SAM S:	You say now you do?!
1414	( ):	Yeah! I do
1415	JACK L:	I do.
1416	SAM S:	Okay.
1417	IRVING L:	I do too. I don't think (.) anything could be served by the
1418		President running around (.) and asking, soliciting opinions.
1419		((People talking at the same time.))
1420	SAM S:	I can't ((noise of a person tapping on a glass))=I would I would
1421		I would like ((noise of a person tapping on a glass.))
1422	JAMES D:	The significant thing is that each person in this room be free to
1423		advance his own feelings directly and privately to the President
1424		(.) so that the President gets a feedback of what [everyone here=
1425	( ):	[xxx
1426	JAMES D:	=FEELS ABOUT HIS PEERS without my having to say "I
1427		don't think Sam Gerstel should get the job, out on the table."

1428 ( ):	That's right.
1429	(1.5)
1430 ( ):	Sam?
1431	*((People speaking at once.))*
1432 IRVING L:	I would say that
1433 ( ):	He doesn't really mean that=
1434 JAMES D:	=I don't mean that.
1435 ( ):	Those were your exact words.
1436 JAMES D:	I didn't mean it I didn't mean it=
1437 IRVING L:	=Sam (0.5) Sammy, you've put in years (.) you put in and look
1438	what happen here.
1439	*((Extensive laughter.))*
1440 JAMES D:	A hypothetical example, Sam (.)
1441 SAM G:	A bad choice a bad choice.
1442	*((Extensive laughter and talk from a number of people.))*
1443	*((Harry S. is writing on the newsprint.))*
1444 ( ):	(xxxx) it would be helpful to your (xxxx)
1445 ( ):	It's not compulsory that you speak to (xxxx)
1446 HARRY S:	The statement is- statement we have up there is (.) "The
1447	President at his discretion (.) will consult with members of his
1448	management group." And I think in part the President already
1449	has conveyed this that anyone of you (0.5) should feel free to (.)
1450	see him on this matter=
1451 ( ):	That's right
1452 HARRY S:	°alright(°)…
1453	[*((Two people talking.))*
1454 JAMES D:	[The two are not compatible in my mind=this is why I raised the
1455	question .hh Obviously, if he consults (.) say with the first three
1456	people there (.) and he never consults with the next three (.) the
1457	next three, if they find out that he's consulted with the first three
1458	are not gonna feel very free to go in and voluntarily on their
1459	own offer any opinions.
1460	(0.5)
1461 JOHN P:	Funny, I wouldn't hesitate
1462	(2.0)
1463 JOHN P:	I think we got (.) the kind of (.) uh a relationship here uh whether
1464	it's up there or not [and I, though if I have something to say-
1465 SAM S:	[I'm satisfied in my mind that I don't know
1466	anybody here who wouldn't *((almost laughing))* be wouldn't feel
1467	free to come and talk to me when they think it's uh.
1468 ( ):	I never have yet
1469 SAM S:	What?
1470 ( ):	I never have yet.
1471	*((People laughing.))*
1472 JAMES D:	I think that's your answer.
1473 HARRY S:	Any further suggestions on (.) procedure?
1474	(5.0)
1475 JACK L:	I don't think we can go much further (0.5) And personnel

1476	selection is a one alone (.) u:h responsibility (0.2) so this
1477	becomes (0.5) with all the information=
1478 SAM S:	=I can tell you, you've made it very easy for me.
1479 JACK L:	We made it very clear to you what kind of person we want.
1480 JAMES D:	As as easy as we can.
1481 ( ):	That's right
1482 JACK L:	As hard as we can.
1483 MEL D:	We've made it very easy for you (.) We've narrowed the choice
1484	down to fifteen people? (.) What better can you expect than
1485	that? I mean all fifteen are candidates and here (.) we made it
1486	simple, it could have been a choice of a thousand.
1487	(1.5)
1488 ( ):	°Fifty?°
1489	(4.5)
1490 HARRY S:	Are we going to talk about time dimension here? (0.2) no?
1491 ( ):	Yeah I=
1492 ( ):	=I think we should=
1493 ( ):	=Absolutely.
1494	((A few people talking at once.))
1495 ( ):	Would you expand that, John?
1496 SAM S:	I think that this this decision will be taken (.) in a period, may
1497	be three to six months
1498	(0.5)
1499 SAM S:	Not sooner.
1500	(1.0)
1501 ( ):	Three to six months?=
1502 SAM S:	=That's right.
1503	(1.0)
1504 ARNOLD S:	You're saying it will be at the earliest three months at at the
1505	latest six months, or at at the earliest three to six months?
1506	(0.5)
1507 SAM S:	You put it well, at the earliest three months at the latest six.
1508	(4.5)
1509 JACK L:	In my opinion that's too long. But uh (.) I think that uh (0.5) the
1510	organization as a whole is waiting (0.5) And I think three to six
1511	months is uh a long time for uh after going through what we've
1512	done (.) now I was thinking about I would have had hoped (.)
1513	that the final decision will be with<u>in</u> three months, not three to
1514	six months.
1515 SAM S:	Well you don't happen to be the- (0.5) in my position, sitting in
1516	my seat, so
1517	(2.0)
1518 JAMES D:	There's another aspect I think we should discuss briefly (0.2)
1519	We have a <u>very sad</u> history (.) of leaking out (.) all kinds of (.)
1520	uh semi-official (scutterbug) (.) rumor through the organization,
1521	which (.) again I think does more harm than good.
1522 ( ):	You mean (xxxx) the President?
1523 JAMES D:	I beg your pardon?

1524 (   ):   (xxxx) the President?
1525 JAMES D: No, I'm not concerned with that (0.5) *((people speaking at*
1526   *once))* But I do think that we we should have some consensus
1527   (.) as to <u>what</u> we want to say to our subordinates about what
1528   went [on here.
1529 (   ):   [Issue a diplomatic communiqué.
1530   (1.5)
1531 (   ):   A frank and open discussion *((laughing))* (xxxx)
1532 MEL D: No, I think Jim raised a very good point, we ought to=
1533 JAMES D: =The rumor mill will be churning at a frantastic rate with all of
1534   us up here (.) [for three days.
1535 MEL D: [Well, everyone knows we're all up here. I mean
1536   do we go back and tell our people uh (0.5) what the topics we
1537   discussed and so on? It's a very vital issue.
1538   *((People talking at once.))*
1539 (   ):   There are only four items on the agenda. Why not list that there
1540   are the items xxx
1541 JAMES D: I would say uh communiqué worded something like this "That
1542   the President and the top executives of the company have met
1543   for the last uh two and half days (0.2) three days whatever (.) is
1544   at Palomino Lodge in uh (.) Laurentians and u::h uh and have
1545   conducted an extensive review of the (.) uh current situation of
1546   the company with particular reference to its future uh and and
1547   this discussion included, such subjects as professional
1548   management and" and itemize the four topics and <u>stop</u> right
1549   there. Say nothing more.
1550 (   ):   That's right. Very good.
1551   *((The meeting is adjourned.))*
1552 Voiceover: *((Four months after the Palomino Conference ended, Sam*
1553   *Steinberg announced the appointment of his son-in-law, Mel*
1554   *Dobrin, as President, and, in the months following his*
1555   *appointment, a major change took place in the top management*
1556   *structure of the company. Jack Levine was promoted to*
1557   *Executive Vice President of all the company's retail operations*
1558   *and Arnold Steinberg became Executive Vice President,*
1559   *Administration and Finance.*
1560   *The thirteen-man management committee, which had been the*
1561   *advisory body to Sam Steinberg and, which had taken part in*
1562   *the Palomino Conference, gave way to three smaller*
1563   *committees; a seven-man President's committee under Mel*
1564   *Dobrin, a retail committee under Jack Levine and an*
1565   *administration committee under Arnold Steinberg. It was a*
1566   *compromise; the case against a family appointment had been*
1567   *lost but the argument for strong Executive or Group Vice-*
1568   *Presidents and a decentralization of authority from the*
1569   *President had apparently been won.))*
1570   *((Shot of Sam Steinberg and his grandson getting into his*
1571   *chauffeured limousine to depart Palomino.))*

1572 ( ):   So long all, cherio.

1573 *Voiceover:* *((With Sam Steinberg's retirement from the Presidency and the*
1574   *new team in place, many of the problems, which had led to the*
1575   *calling of the Palomino Conference, seemed to be resolved. In*
1576   *the next four years, the corporation's sales doubled to over a*
1577   *billion dollars. It shares rose from a low of eleven dollars in*
1578   *1969 to around twenty dollars in 1974. But for all this, a*
1579   *fundamental aspect of the business had not changed, ((Shot of*
1580   *the car driving off)) Sam Steinberg was still Chairman of the*
1581   *Board. Long after the Palomino Conference ended, it was*
1582   *evident that ultimate power and the dominant influence on the*
1583   *business still lay where they had for over fifty years.))*

1584 SAM S: *((Speaking from the back seat of his car.))* I think it's (.)
1585   harmful to the business if you don't give it the drive and the
1586   energy (0.5) you've got to stay with it. It's not enough to have
1587   good ideas and everything else but you've got to bring them
1588   into being. You've got to give somebody else the opportunity
1589   to do that (0.5) I'll always be a driving force whether I'm (.)
1590   President of the company or not. (0.8) Always.
1591   END OF THE TAPE
1592

Transcribing Conventions[1]

• Brackets indicate that the encased portions of the utterances are produced simultaneously. Left-hand brackets designate the beginning of simultaneity, whereas right-hand brackets mark its end.

Bob: I wish [he was on time].

Kathy: [He is always] always late.

Bob and Kathy respectively say "He was on time" and "He is always late" at the same time.

• Underscoring indicates that the speaker is emphasizing this specific portion of the utterance.

Bob: I cannot <u>stand</u> him.

Bob emphasizes the word "stand."

• Equal signs indicate that there is no time elapsed between two utterances.

Bob: He's a very nice guy=

Kathy: =and so considerate toward them

When Bob finishes with "guy," Kathy starts right away her turn by saying "and." There is no interval between the two turns.

• Period in parentheses indicate a very short pause (less than one tenth of a second).

Kathy: So we could, (.) you know

The pause between "could" and "you know" is almost imperceptible.

• Number in parentheses indicate intervals in the stream of talk. These intervals (indicated in seconds and tenth of seconds) can be identified within an utterance or between utterances.

Bob: How do you change that?

(2.5)

Eric: How do you change what.

This indicates 2.5 seconds elapse between the completion of Bob's turn and the beginning of Eric's turn.

• Double parentheses indicate that what is encased is a description of what is happening during the interaction. What is enclosed is not a transcription.

Mark: Honestly.

((Harry's cell phone rings))

• Hyphens indicate the prior syllable was cut off short.

Bob: He is so biz- he is so strange.

Bob is about to say "bizarre" but stops and rephrases his assessment.

ENDNOTE

1. Based on Gail Jefferson's (1984) transcript techniques. For more details on these transcribing conventions, see van Dijk, 1997, as well as Atkinson and Heritage, 1984.

REFERENCES

Atkinson, J. M., & Heritage, J. (Eds.). (1984). *Structures of social action: Studies in conversation analysis*. Cambridge, England: Cambridge University Press.

Jefferson, G. (1984). On stepwise transition from talk about a trouble to inappropriately next-positioned matters. In J. M. Atkinson & J. Heritage (Eds.), *Structures of social action: Studies of conversation analysis* (pp. 191–222). Cambridge, England: Cambridge University Press.

Van Dijk, T. A. (Ed.). (1997). *Discourse as social interaction*. London: Sage.

A Brief History
of Steinberg Limited

Born in Hungary of Jewish descent, Sam Steinberg was only 6 years old when he arrived in Canada with his parents and five siblings in 1911. After some very difficult years, Ida Steinberg, his mother, opened a grocery store in 1917 on *rue Prince Arthur* with only $300. Wilmosh, Sam's father, who was a very religious man and spent most of his time at the synagogue, then left his wife and children to devote himself almost exclusively to religion. From the very beginning, Ida's store was a success, mostly because of her general approach to clients; her motto was "Always give them a little more than what they expect" (Gagnon, 1988; Gibbon & Hadekel, 1990). She quickly moved her store to 4419 *Boulevard Saint Laurent*, one of the popular main streets in Montreal, and successfully kept most of her clientele. Sam, who regularly helped out by delivering the orders, was only 12 years old when he left school to devote himself exclusively to the running of the store.

Early on, Ida gave him two important responsibilities: getting supplies from farmers and wholesalers at the *Marché Bonsecours* every morning (a task that he and his brother Nathan quickly mastered) and keeping the books after the store closed every night. Progressively, Sam became the acting manager and, in 1919, started to expand the store by renting and transforming an adjacent shoe store, which doubled the surface of the premises (a poignant moment in his life shows him destroying the separating walls with a sledgehammer). In 1926, at 21 years old, he opened his first branch, prophetically called "Store #1," on *rue Bernard*, a street located in the affluent Outremont neighborhood of Montreal. Despite the Depression that followed the 1929 Black Friday,

Steinberg's stores remained successful, perhaps especially because he refused to take advantage of the situation by raising prices to the detriment of his clients, a practice in which most of his competitors at that time did not hesitate to engage (Blandford, 1996).

By 1930, he already owned four stores under the name Steinberg's Service Store Limited, and in 1933 he opened the Wholesale Groceteria, the first self-service grocery store in Canada. This move allowed him to sell his goods at prices that were 15% to 20% lower than those of his competitors, which in turn led him to phenomenal success (Gagnon, 1988). Throughout the next 40 years, Mr. Sam, as everybody called him, continued to open more branches and to become famous for implementing several innovations in the grocery business: refrigerated display counters for meats, a grading technique for eggs, car delivery, conveyor belts at the counters, shopping carts, coupons, and so on. He was not necessarily an inventor, but everybody agrees that he was a master in copying and improving what he saw during his travels in North America, and later in Europe.

Steinberg expanded his business not only by opening more stores and buying up those of his competitors, but by becoming more self-sufficient. In 1945, he started to buy warehouses to store his supplies, formed a whole fleet of delivery trucks, created his own real-estate agency, Ivanhoe, in 1954, and even diversified his activities by opening, among other things, a chain of restaurants in 1962. Little by little, Steinberg became a veritable empire. By 1969, the company had 180 supermarkets in Canada, assets of $224 million, sales of $553 million, and more than 18,000 employees (Hammond, 1973). Despite this incredible growth, the company still remained, in many respects, a family organization. Most of the important decisions were made, not during management meetings, but in Sam Steinberg's house during the Sabbath suppers every Friday night. This did not happen without some resentment from top management, especially from people who were not related to Sam and who felt that the company suffered from nepotism.

Since the company's inception in 1917, it had always been clear to Sam Steinberg that the company had been built, first and foremost, for the family, and this was to remain its guiding principle until his death (Gibbon & Hadekel, 1990). However, the situation started to create some problems when it came time for Mr. Sam to retire as the CEO of the company. Having no sons and not imagining that one of his four daughters could take over the business, Sam had to find a successor outside his immediate family. In March 1969, Mr. Sam and his 15 top managers got together over 3 days of meetings at the Palomino Lodge, the company's chalet in the Laurentians, to discuss, among various topics, the question of succession. It is mainly excerpts from this series of meetings that constitute Arthur Hammond's documentary, *Corporation: After Mr. Sam*, on which this whole book is based.

As mentioned by Arthur Hammond (1974) in his film, only four executives could reasonably hope to replace Sam Steinberg at the top of the company: Arnold Steinberg, Sam Steinberg's nephew (Nathan Steinberg's son), a Harvard Business School graduate who was then vice-president administration; James Doyle, vice-president and general counsel, who started to work for the company in the 1950s; Jack Levine, vice-president of the Quebec division, a self-made man who entered the company as a simple clerk in the 1930s and went up the corporate ladder; and Mel Dobrin, executive vice-president retailing, Sam Steinberg's son-in-law, the husband of his eldest daughter, Mizi, and the man who appeared to be Sam Steinberg's favorite candidate. Commenting on this series of meetings, Gibbon and Hadekel (1990) mentioned Henry Mintzberg's hypothesis, according to which a consensus had tacitly been developed to prevent Mel Dobrin from acceding to the presidency or at least to make it clear to Sam that he had to give a chance to people other than the family members.

On August 1, 1969, 5 months after the Palomino meetings, Sam Steinberg unsurprisingly appointed Mel Dobrin, his son-in-law, CEO of the company, while he [Sam] became president of the board of directors, a position that had recently been created for him. Justifying his decision to the other top executives, Sam Steinberg did not hesitate to mention blood ties. Gibbon and Hadekel (1990) noted that by appointing Mel Dobrin as president, Sam was sending a clear message: The company was to remain a family business. Although Mel Dobrin was officially the head of the company, Mr. Sam was able to maintain relative control over Steinberg Limited until his death on May 24, 1978, at 72 years old. After Sam Steinberg's death, Mel Dobrin became president of the board of directors and it was Jack Levine who succeeded him as the head of the company until he retired in 1982.

At that time and for the first time in the history of Steinberg Limited, the subsequent CEO was chosen from outside the company: Peter McGoldrick, an American who came from Virginia, was appointed by Mizi and Mel Dobrin to replace Levine. However, his reign was not long-lasting, and he resigned in 1984, mostly because of marketing decisions that hurt the company's profitability (Gibbon & Hadekel, 1990). Following McGoldrick's departure, the board of directors appointed a former top executive of the organization as CEO—Irving Ludmer. After leaving the company in 1971, Ludmer had returned in 1983 as the vice-president in charge of Ivanhoe, Steinberg's real-estate agency, which was by far the most profitable branch of the company. Although he had initially left the organization because he did not see any future in a company where blood ties dictated decision making, for many people, he came to represent another Mr. Sam.

As many commentators have remarked, Ludmer was the son that Sam Steinberg never had (Blandford, 1996; Gibbon & Hadekel, 1990). Like Sam, he came from a very poor Jewish family, his father from the Ukraine and his mother from Poland. After graduating from McGill University, he was hired in 1957 as an engineer by Steinberg, and 6 years later, he was working for Ivanhoe, where he excelled. Noticing his performance, Mr. Sam started to develop a real affection for this young self-made man who rapidly climbed the corporate ladder, becoming the head of the real-estate division in 1968. Commenting on Ludmer's relationship with Sam Steinberg during this period, Gibbon and Hadekel (1990) were quick to say that he was at that time the most influential man in the company, not only for the real estate division, but also for retail. Ludmer had become, in many respects, Sam's confidant, a situation that had shown him how attached the CEO was to his family, and especially to Mel Dobrin, his son-in-law.

This made him realize that there was no future for his ambition to one day become the CEO of the company, a realization that led to his resignation in 1971. It was Arnold Steinberg, Mr. Sam's nephew, who convinced him to come back as the head of Ivanhoe 12 years later. On his arrival in the company, he was welcomed as a hero, symbolizing in many respects the former success of the organization. Although his presidency was successful in many regards, an open confrontation with Mizi Dobrin finally led to his resignation in 1989, at which time the company was sold to Marcel Gaucher, a Québécois millionaire. At that time, the company was the 21st-largest Canadian company, with sales of $4.5 billion and 37,000 employees in Canada and the United States. In 1992, the company filed for bankruptcy and its assets were sold to its competitors.

REFERENCES

Blandford, M. (1996). *Qu'est-ce qui a tué Steinberg?* [What killed Steinberg?] Montreal: Productions Sovimage, Inc.

Gagnon, F. (1988). Sam Steinberg: *Le concepteur du supermarché moderne* [The designer of the modern supermarket]. *Vidéo-presse, 18*(1), 24–27.

Gibbon, A., & Hadekel, P. (1990). *Steinberg: The break up of a family empire.* Toronto: Macmillan.

Hammond, A. (Producer/Director/Writer). (1974). *Corporation: After Mr. Sam* [Film]. Montreal: National Film Board of Canada.

Author Index

Subject Index

*For Product Safety Concerns and Information please contact
our EU representative GPSR@taylorandfrancis.com Taylor & Francis
Verlag GmbH, Kaufingerstraße 24, 80331 München, Germany*

T - #0054 - 230425 - C0 - 229/152/20 - PB - 9780805848564 - Gloss Lamination